HEROES <u>AND</u> VICTIMS

**Indiana-Michigan Series in Russian
and East European Studies**

Alexander Rabinowitch and
William G. Rosenberg, general editors

HEROES
AND
VICTIMS

Remembering War in
Twentieth-Century
Romania

Bloomingh, 28 March, 2016

MARIA BUCUR

For Pa dear,
Thank you
for all your
help with this
project!

Indiana University Press
Bloomington and Indianapolis

Publication of this book is made possible in part with the assistance of a Challenge Grant from the National Endowment for the Humanities, a federal agency that supports research, education, and public programming in the humanities.

This book is a publication of

Indiana University Press
601 North Morton Street
Bloomington, IN 47404-3797 USA

www.iupress.indiana.edu

Telephone orders	800-842-6796
Fax orders	812-855-7931
Orders by e-mail	iuporder@indiana.edu

Manufactured in the United States of America

Library of Congress Cataloging-in-Publication Data

Bucur, Maria, [date]
  Heroes and victims : remembering war in twentieth-century Romania / Maria Bucur.
    p. cm. — (Indiana-Michigan series in Russian and East European studies)
  Includes bibliographical references and index.
  ISBN 978-0-253-35378-8 (cloth : alk. paper) — ISBN 978-0-253-22134-6 (pbk. : alk. paper) 1. Memorialization—Romania—History—20th century. 2. Memory—Social aspects—Romania. 3. War and society—Romania. 4. World War, 1914–1918—Social aspects—Romania. 5. World War, 1939–1945—Social aspects—Romania. 6. War memorials—Social aspects—Romania. 7. Collective memory—Romania. 8. Romania—History, Military—20th century. I. Title.
  DR268.3.B83 2009
  303.6'6094980904—dc22

                          2009014577

1 2 3 4 5 15 14 13 12 11 10 09

TO ALL THE

Bucur Deckards in my life

Contents

Preface

The kernel of this book was planted in 1997. Visiting Romania for the first time since completing my dissertation on the history of eugenics, I looked forward to refocusing my attention on the publishing industry's initial flourishing in the first decade after Communism. As I scoured bookstores and vendors for new and interesting materials, I came to realize that a new phenomenon was taking place before my eyes. Everyone wanted to publish a memoir, and everyone else wanted to buy these memoirs, read them, talk about them, and critique them. The genre of the memoir was seeing such unprecedented growth, with some examples appearing in very small runs but still somehow making the rounds, that I began to collect these publications. Soon I realized that there were two periods favored by most readers: World War II and the Stalinist years of Communist persecution. Observing this literary phenomenon and also speaking to people who were more than a generation older than I was (in their mid-forties and older), it became apparent that for those generations the project of recovering and making sense of their memories of the 1940s–1950s was an urgent task, relevant to finding a new sense of social belonging.

This occurrence coincided with the beginnings of the growth of "memory studies" in U.S. and parts of European academia. I was thus fortunate to begin making sense of this vibrant phenomenon in post-Communist culture in the company of insightful historians and other scholars. This study stands on the shoulders of important precursors that have inspired and challenged me to find my own answers to complicated questions. The work of Jay Winter, John Bodnar, John Gillis, Catherine Merridale, Nina Tumarkin, Gaines Foster, Robert Moeller, Vieda Skultans, Rubie Watson, and many others, has offered rich examples of ways in which memory is important not just as playground for politicians or as a psychological phenomenon, but also as a realm for making cultural meaning out of violence and destruction.[1] Their insights also challenged me to articulate where to situate the memory traces I was studying within a broader discourse about remembrance and identity in the modern world. Much of the literature on this topic took nationalism and the nation as crucial referents for how memory traces are emplotted and deployed in the cultural realm. Such an analysis struck me as somewhat simplistic, even where it seemed to speak to a local reality, as in France, for instance, in the aftermath of World War I.[2]

Though nationalism is in fact everywhere apparent in eastern Europe today, it is far from a self-evident force with a straightforward, easily identifiable meaning. The reality is far more complicated, and the more I read through the work of these prominent scholars, the more I wanted to be able to understand the complexity of commemorative experiences beyond a simple narrative of inventing traditions for the sake of political legitimacy, as Terence Ranger and Eric Hobsbawm suggested in their pioneering study, or constructing rituals to mobilize masses around the flag, as Paul Connerton showed in *How Societies Remember*.[3]

The research of anthropologists working on contemporary Europe and further afield became an important reference point for how I began to modify my understanding of commemorative processes and products in twentieth-century eastern Europe. In particular, the work of Katherine Verdery and Gail Kligman opened up important avenues to allow considering how people in an overwhelmingly rural environment, and with a low level of literacy until the second half of the twentieth century, articulated their identities in connection to the past and community-based memory traces. Verdery's study, *The Political Lives of Dead Bodies,* came out as I was starting to consider framing my study outside questions that focused primarily on nationalism.[4] Her theoretical insights into ancestor worship and her way of framing questions about rituals and discourses helped me find different questions and angles for my own project.

The work of historians of religion and anthropologists studying the cult of the dead also became important for understanding the kinds of diverse forces shaping choices that communities in Romania made to commemorate the war dead. Gail Kligman's work proved essential in this regard.[5] In addition to her *Wedding of the Dead,* I was able to use the work of Mircea Eliade, as well as studies by Bruce Lincoln, Loring Danforth, Simion Florea Marian, and Ştefan Dorondel.[6]

The scholarship published in the past decade by scholars of eastern Europe and Russia has been a useful framework to help contextualize the specificity of my case study. Catherine Merridale and Nina Tumarkin's work provided important points for considering relevant connections, but more often than not, differences between the Soviet case and that of eastern Europe in the twentieth century.[7] Some cultural connections pertained to the religious traditions among Orthodox populations in Russia and parts of eastern Europe. But many other differences separated these lands in both the pre-Communist and Communist periods, including the relationship between rulers and the ruled in terms of legitimacy, especially after World War II.

Historians working on Poland, from Jan Gross to Patrice Dabrowski and Christoph Mick have also helped me construct important points of reference with the Romanian case.[8] In particular, the question of remembering a war fought on both sides by the population of post-1918 Poland, and then the question of responsibility and victimization as reference points in remembering World War II, played themselves out somewhat similarly in the two countries. Still, as memory is always local, one can find important differences between the ways communities in Poland have articulated their emotional relationships to the two world wars and the approaches of various groups in Romania. For instance, no Romanian group could ever claim a Home Army or any kind of underground partisan activity during World War II of the sorts that came to dominate the imagination of many Poles after 1945. Nor did the heartland of Romania live with the death camps of World War II, as was the case with postwar Poland. A literature on the memory of the world wars has also started to grow in the rest of eastern Europe, and some of these studies have been important for offering comparative insights in my own work.[9]

An interesting related scholarly debate has been developing around the question of the periodization of World War II. Declarations of war or the signing of an armistice or peace treaty no longer demarcate when the war started and when it ended. The legal definition of wartime violence has come under criticism from social and cultural historians who look at World War II as a total war, where mass violence against civilian populations in fact preceded the official beginning of the war in certain areas, and where both civilians and soldiers were embroiled in violent conflict after the official end of the war. A few years ago, Jan Gross advanced a bold notion that the periodization of the Communist takeovers should be pushed back to the beginning of World War II.[10] In a recent book on the Communist takeover in Hungary, Peter Kenez makes the argument that the years 1945–1948 are a self-contained period. He positions himself in contradistinction both to Gross and to historians who see 1945–1948 as part of the Cold War, separate from World War II.[11]

I see this issue differently. In looking at the subjective self-representation of individuals' life stories in connection to World War II, one can view this conflict as extending from 1938 (and in the Romanian case, 1940) to 1953, when many deportees from Poland, the Baltics, Romania, and other places in eastern Europe to Siberian labor camps finally returned home. Because I take local cultural representations of wartime violence, and especially death, as important loci for considering the memory of the war (rather than tragedy writ large), this subjective dimension of periodization is quite important for my analysis. If inhabitants of a German village erected a plaque commemorating the people who had perished in World War II and dated it 1941–1946, one has to take such a self-representation of the wartime experience as truthful to their subjective remembrance of the war, rather than a faulty understanding of history. It is a particular, localized view of the war that doesn't easily fit into the official periodization, but which is essential for trying to understand how people in that place felt about the war and wanted to remember it: deportation was identified not as a Cold War issue, but rather as a World War II one.

This broader periodization challenges two other important categories for constructing the meaning and memory of World War II. First, the Holocaust stands within the larger context of violence against civilians that took place before and after the death camps were closed. The pogroms and deportations of Jews after they returned from death camps are taken as part of the anti-Semitic continuum of wartime violence, rather than something separate from it. By the same token, the deportations of other ethnic groups to labor camps are also to be integrated with the Holocaust in the wider picture of violence suffered by civilians during the war. Such integration doesn't deny the uniqueness of the Holocaust in its genocidal racist essential nature. On the contrary, it forces historians to consider the ways in which the anti-Semitic horrors of those years could be and *were* minimized by non-Jews.

Secondly, the period of anti-Communist resistance, which generally spans the years 1944 to 1953 (with the exception of a few lone figures who remained at large until the 1960s), cannot be viewed as separate from the war. This is important, because specific experiences in the war, as well as ideologies underpinning it, largely framed these anti-Communist partisan activities. In particular, the Romanian "crusade against Bolshevism," understood on the grounds of religion (as a legitimate Christian action, in some cases with implicit anti-Semitic elements), ethnicity (anti-Russian sentiment), and ideology (anti-Communism, as well as an overt endorsement of private property), was the widest framework that the Antonescu regime used to mobilize soldiers and civilians in the war. Many of those who went into the mountains after August 1944 did so not because of a great concern for democracy, but rather because of their desire to continue to fight in this (generally non-democratic) crusade. How such resistance was constructed and what it meant for those fighting against the Communists from 1944 onward cannot be understood as something initially separate from the experience of the war.

In addition to this challenge to the periodization of World War II and implicitly its relationship to the Cold War, my analysis also adds new dimensions to the understanding of the Cold War period itself in the scholarship on eastern Europe, especially in the realm of cultural policy making and implementation. Even as some historians of eastern Europe have recently challenged the notion that the Communist bloc lived under totalitarian rule at any time during the forty-five years of Communism, others see evidence of at least Romania living in a frozen Stalinist nightmare.[12] If the picture of Romanian Communism viewed from the inner sanctum of the Politburo in Bucharest is one of unchanging authoritarianism with grotesque elements of a cult of personality, this angle provides very little insight into how people lived it.[13] My chapters dealing with the state policies toward wartime commemorations and the memory traces of those who lived through World War II and the Communist years emphasize the ways in which cultural politics at the local level never became frozen. People worked both within the system and outside or even against it to establish their own vision of how to properly honor the wartime dead. Some might consider this particular element a minor detail in the larger universe of the policies of oppression conducted by the Communist state in Romania. Yet I argue that the memory of the war dead was in fact an issue of great emotional valence for those who lived through the war and early Communist years, and helped establish their lack of trust toward the Communist regime.

✧✧

The heart of my analysis is intimately connected to the kinds of sources I sought out and to my methodology. For official efforts to remember the world wars, the documents of the Ministry of Defense and the Ministry of Culture and Education, as well as regional and municipal records, originating from Bucharest to Iaşi, Cluj, Sibiu, Braşov, and Satu Mare, constituted the bulk of my research data. By seeking out both central archives and regional and municipal ones, I was able to investigate questions of dialogue and tension between policy making in Bucharest and its implementation in various regions throughout the country. For most of the archival documents I investigated, I was the first researcher to look at them. A rich array of published sources—newspapers, written propaganda (pamphlets, performance programs, etc.), memoirs of prominent politicians, as well as documentary films produced by the state for propaganda purposes—also helped me better understand the distance between intentions and implementation of government commemorative cultural activities. Though by no means exhaustive, the points of regional reference on which I focused helped me map out the extent of variation at the local level vis-à-vis central claims for representativeness. I can only hope that subsequent studies of these phenomena will take this research as a point of departure for further developing nuances of this analysis of regional variance, from Chişinău to Constanţa.

For traces of local communal and individual voices, I had to look creatively inside official government sources and beyond them. There are journals, memoirs, and fictional autobiographical writings published in connection to both world wars. These materials were extremely useful for understanding the limits of educated self-representations of wartime remembrance. Though most of the autobiographical literature was read widely both in the interwar period and since 1989, when most of the World War II material was published, I have not found any serious engagement with these materials as historical sources, either in the realm of literary history or more widely as part of historical analyses of the two world wars and their remembrance.[14] And artistic renditions—whether in word, moving image, or stone—have not been the subject of attention by social and cultural historians seeking to understand the twentieth century.

This first attempt to cull such historical traces, from official government documents to poetry and film, is still somewhat limited, as these sources largely represent the voices of educated elites, especially with regard to World War I. For World War II, the issue of representativeness could be addressed only by taking into consideration the overt or indirect censorship of publishing under Communism. To what extent can materials published during the 1945–1989 period be considered unconstrained individual voices, rather than officially sanctioned (and thus manipulated) ones?[15] In my analysis of these texts, I took those not published during the Communist period as representative individual voices, but opted to view published memoirs and memorializing novels as voices that contributed to construct the official narratives.

For people who did not write about their suffering or their pain at losing loved ones in the world wars, I looked at localized efforts at memorializing the war dead. There are thousands of such memorials in Romania erected through local efforts, and I scoured the archives to find out how such monuments came into being, whether they were in fact the fruit of local labor, and to what extent they were part of any larger government-underwritten effort at commemorating the war dead. I also traveled extensively throughout Romania to view many of these monuments. The physical reality of the environment in which they were erected and how they look in that environment became essential elements that enabled me to identify the choices local communities made about remembering their war dead. Visibility and invisibility, resonance and silences, monumentality and smallness are all qualities better understood through ethnographic observation, rather than by simply considering aesthetic norms of the day or what monuments in Bucharest and Paris look like. This is particularly true for a society that until the 1990s still lived mostly in rural settings, where the largest building in a community would be the church or some other place of worship.

In addition to such research, I attended both official and community-based commemorations organized on the Heroes Day state holiday, from Bucharest to Cluj and remote villages in Maramureş. I also undertook several rounds (in 1999, 2000, 2001, and 2002) of oral history interviews, recording life stories of more than a hundred veterans and civilians who lived through the war (around fifty), as well as younger generations (around fifty), with sizeable representation among both genders in all these categories. In addition, I worked with a group of students at Transylvania University in Brașov, who taped a hundred more interviews in the summer of 2001.[16] These interviews were loosely structured around questionnaires regarding the war, but overall they followed a life-story method.

Finally, in trying to reconstruct rural religious rituals connected to the cult of the dead before 1918, I worked with the ethnographic research done by pioneering scholars at the turn of the century, especially Simion Marian.[17] Though clearly influenced by the contemporary Orientalist parameters of research and analysis prevalent in European ethno-anthropological research at that time, Marian is remarkably even-handed and precise in both description and annotation. Thus, although I question some of his analysis, I found his methodology and data very useful for reconstructing ritual practices.

For the recent post-1989 period, I added to my analysis the voices of the wider public as represented on the internet. I am fully aware that such material raises questions of reliability.[18] It is not clear who the people writing in an internet forum are— young, old, average Joes, political agents, living inside Romania, living abroad, etc. Be that as it may, a certain "tone" in postings about commemorative events linked to the world wars can be gleaned from various sites that have a range of participants. In addition, one has the advantage of seeing postings from a fairly stable group over a number of years, if we are to take email addresses as representing the same individual at different points in time. Without attempting to offer a systematic analysis of all opinions on the web, I still argue that such forums at least help us understand the opinions of some of the public who use the internet actively, but whose voices cannot be found elsewhere in published archives.

This wide array of sources and approaches has enabled me to bring into discussion memory traces and memory work that have not been the subject of much historical analysis to date. It is the goal of this book to suggest not just new important subjects of historical analysis, but also new ways of integrating the methodologies of several disciplines, from ethnography and anthropology to art history and literary criticism. My analysis takes, for instance, critical distance from the literary canon as it has been constructed to date, to suggest that categories of signification among literary texts should be constructed not simply by adhering to or contesting aesthetic parameters that are primarily the making of literary elites and their readers. Why and with what effect people who were not professional writers began to write and publish autobiographical writings after World War I is an important element necessary to better contextualize our understanding of literary production and reading during that period. Likewise, I insist on analyzing the building of visual markers as a process worthy of historical consideration, regardless of the size and "monumentality" of such markers. By moving among different disciplinary boundaries of what is to be viewed as meaningful and why, I was able to bring into conversation a new array of historical traces, and I hope to embolden other scholars to do the same. Finally, though primarily a work of cultural history, my analysis also takes the political and social realities in which cultural processes occur as extremely pertinent. This is in fact part of how I argue about the local quality of all memory work.

Acknowledgments

In the decade that has passed since I began work on this project, I have amassed so many institutional, intellectual, and personal debts in being able to arrive at this point that it is impossible to pay proper homage to all those who helped me along the way. The International Research and Exchanges Board helped me get started with an Individual Advanced Research grant in 1996 and 1997. Subsequently I benefited from a research grant from Fulbright-Hays between January and July 1999. A collaborative grant between the Aspera Foundation and Indiana University enabled me to conduct an oral history project related to this book in the summer of 2001 in Braşov. Indiana University also offered several travel and research grants that helped me return to Romania and also travel elsewhere (Poland, Hungary, Germany, Bulgaria) for comparative research.

I owe a debt of gratitude to numerous colleagues at my home institution, who have encouraged me along the way and have read and commented on this manuscript or papers connected to it: Jeff Wasserstrom, Marissa Moorman, Mark Roseman, Padraic Kenney, John Bodnar, David Ransel, Jeff Veidlinger, Christina Zarifopol, Sarah Phillips, Sarah Knott, and others. The members of the Poynter Center seminar titled "Memory: Ethics, Politics, Aesthetics" (2007–2008) were immensely helpful in helping me frame my questions and methodological approach from a richly interdisciplinary perspective that stretched from ethics and rhetorics to law and early-modern east Asian history. A special thanks goes out to the director of our seminar, Richard Miller, who has continued, even after it ended, to offer advice. Other wonderful colleagues around the world were generous in their intellectual fellowship, helping me engage tough questions and sharpen my arguments: Mihaela Miroiu, Liviu Rotman, Andrei Pleşu, Irina Livezeanu, Radu Ioanid, Krassimira Daskalova, Maria Todorova, Chad Bryant, Melissa Bokovoy, Nancy Wingfield, Jay Winter, Mark Cornwall, Marius Turda, Keith Hitchins, Ben Frommer, Katherine Verdery,

Doru Radosav, Meda Bârca, Mişu Gherman, Mihai Dinu Gheorghiu, Michael Shafir, Ştefan Ungureanu, Andrei Pippidi, Lidia Bradley, Maria Berza, Valeria Bălescu, Lucian Boia, Elena and Constantin Bărbulescu, Ioan Drăgan, Melinda Mitu, Radu Hriniuc, Valer Hossu, Sabina Ispas, Dinu Necula, Bujor Râpeanu, Virgil Mureşan, Mirela and Bogdan Murgescu, Rodica Palade, Marius Popa, Ioan Opriş, Carmen Popescu, Leon Volovici, Ilie Schipor, Pompiliu Teodor, Corina Turc, Smaranda Vultur, Vasile Crişan, Trandafir Vid, Alexandru Zub, and many others. And while I was traveling through Romania and elsewhere for research, many of these people offered me their friendship and hospitality as well. A special thanks goes to: Mom, Dad, Mary Lee, Mihaela, Adi, Elena, Doru, Oltea, Virgil, Lăcrămioara, Meda, Cleo, Tanti Vali, Rareş, and Şerban. Finally, this book would not be what it is without the thoughtful critiques it received from the Indiana University Press readers and editors. I am extremely grateful especially to Janet Rabinowitch and Candace McNulty for the detailed comments they provided for this project.

My deepest gratitude goes to those close to me who put up with my absences and visits and absences again, and who gave their love and support to me even when I was being difficult. Just as with all my other projects, I couldn't have done this one without *Buni* (my Romanian grandmother). Initially she was there in the background of my intellectual pursuits, ironing clothes and cooking meals, but gradually she became one of my subjects and a profound source of inspiration. Like other women in Romania from her generation (she was born in 1919), she started preparing for her funeral around the age of fifty. By the age of sixty she had acquired a veritable dowry that I used to laugh about before my family immigrated to the United States. In the time I spent with her from January 1997 until her death in April 2006, I came to understand much better the depth of this obsession as a cultural norm with which she identified as closely as many of the women I visited and spent time with from Iaşi to Cluj and villages in Maramureş. Thus, both in life and in her preparation to be reunited with loved ones she had long lost, *Buni* was a permanent reminder of the power of ritual and the profound ways in which specific religious beliefs and practices linked to death have a wide and lifelong impact on someone's life. This book would have been a very different exercise without having had the privilege to spend the last year of her life around her. Dumnezeu să o odihnească!

And as I began understanding the power of the cult of the dead in Romania, I also had the wonderful experience of becoming a mother. Dylan was with me in Romania from day one during my trip there in 2000, helping his mom along the way, even though he wasn't yet born. But he was my little guardian in the villages where people opened their doors more widely after seeing my protruding belly. Elvin came along a few years later and took me a bit further away from writing this book, but enabled me to think more about what the dead mean to future generations. And throughout all this, Danny has always been by my side—present in person or in my dreams, supportive and critical when it was needed. I wouldn't be half the human being I am without these three wonderful people. Thanks, boyz!

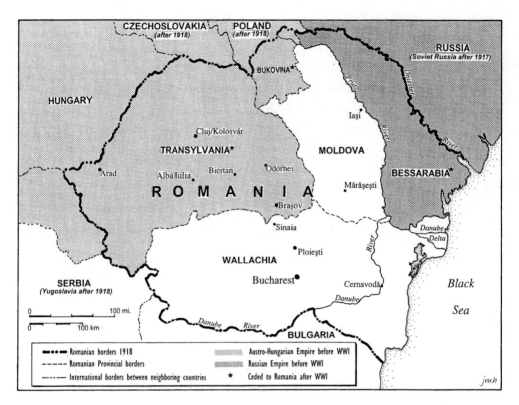

Map 1. Romania during and after World War I

Map 2. Romania during and after World War II

INTRODUCTION

Memory Traces: On Local Practices of Remembering and Commemorating

In 2006, the online journal *Eurozine* initiated a dialogue about the European memory of World War II. Enlightened public intellectuals from Europe and North America—philosophers, historians, sociologists, journalists, and psychologists—responded with various considerations about the meaning of the war in various places in Europe and at various points of time.[2] This dialogue revealed a major division between two groups: some respondents considered a common memory to be desirable, even if they acknowledged that such a memory doesn't exist and that there are serious obstacles to its creation. Unsurprisingly, these observers come from western Europe.[3] Other respondents, from both East and West (Europe and North America), did not think that a common memory is possible, given the way the European Union is constructed today; they pointed to problems with the very concept of a European memory of World

War II.[4] Their critique generally centered on the inability of the commemorative narratives about World War II written as "European" to represent the significance of that war for those who lived in the Communist bloc after 1945. Most surprising in this discussion was the lack of attention to how average people relate to this question. Although many respondents pointed out that memory is linked to locally grounded events and context, they did not articulate the ways in which place and community are in fact essential to how average people construct and recollect the meaning of specific events. Instead, differences and divergences were represented along broad national(ist) lines.

Beyond the Politics of "European Memory" of the World Wars

My study represents a response to the debate about memory culture with regard to the two world wars. This debate has focused insufficiently on the eastern front and has not considered the localized dimensions of commemoration and cultural production of rituals as central elements of how we need to understand the culture of remembrance in twentieth-century Europe. I challenge the prevailing views by shifting my focus and privileging the local, both chronologically and also conceptually. I also place the institutional, centralized, state attempts to mold commemorations on the receiving end of the process of constructing meaningful sites of memory and rituals to remember the two world wars. And by making memory the central concept for examining the production of cultural identity markers, I avail myself of a wide array of vantage points and memory traces that have been largely untouched as sources for writing a historical narrative of cultural practices in twentieth-century eastern Europe.

The novelty of my analysis (especially in the eastern European context) rests also in the claims I make for thinking of memory work not only in terms of permanent, monumental sites of memory, but especially through smaller funerary markers, rituals, and other manipulations of space (e.g., street names, plaques, use of particular spaces for specific rituals), as well as autobiographical writings, novels, and film. This wide array of memory traces implicitly and explicitly argues for placing small, marginal, and sometimes evanescent markers alongside solid and prominent ones, and inviting a revaluation of their everyday cultural meaning. My analysis ultimately seeks to privilege the seldom heard voice of average people at the local level, even while acknowledging that the state and other powerful institutions, such as religious establishments, have had greater resources and a continuous will to control the commemorations linked to the two world wars.

And by focusing on Romania, a country that was situated in the midst of the eastern front during both world wars, I also introduce an example that challenges the dominant narratives about the meaning and memory of the war dead in both world wars, constructed primarily around the German and French cases. My aim is to open up new avenues for thinking about the diversity in wartime experience and especially its representation through the commemorative efforts that sprang up after the wars, both locally and subsequently more broadly at the national level. The politicization and institutionalization of such commemorative events has led to a devaluation of understanding how these rituals came about, as well as how they have continued to be both challenged and simply made meaningful in diverse and specific ways that are always contingent on local communities' particular understanding of the wars. It is this continued negotiation and diversity that my study seeks to bring forth by analyzing how people in Romania dealt with the memory of the two world wars since 1918.

The argument that memory is *always* local is central to my analysis of remembering the world wars in Europe. Indeed, we cannot understand the history of Europe in the twentieth century without paying greater attention to eastern Europe, and we cannot fully understand the history of eastern Europe during the twentieth century without paying closer attention to how average people engaged with the ideologies and processes set in place by political elites. This is not a novel idea, but it is one that has not been taken to heart by most historians working on eastern Europe.[5] In these pages I follow the dialogues, debates, and often parallel (if disjointed) paths that social and personal remembering of the two world wars took in Romania after 1918. My aim is to show how such cultural processes have helped shape the way individuals and communities came to understand themselves both locally and in relation to the state in this country at the edge of Europe.

The "edginess" of my approach consists, then, in demonstrating that the experience of a purportedly marginal country like Romania, often viewed as anomalous in terms of its political trajectory during the twentieth century, can be important to the overall narrative of modern Europe. The Romanian experience presents a powerful case study for reconsidering how cultural commemorative practices connected to the two world wars were articulated and have been rendered significant since then at both the local and the national level. Disrupting the standard narratives of wartime remembrances in twentieth-century Europe is ultimately one of the important aims of this book.

My analysis focuses essentially on both dialogue and disjunction between vernacular and official voices of remembering.[6] I see some modern states in Europe as far less successful in constructing a cohesive, stable narrative about their legitimacy, control, and continuity than many historians have claimed is the case, at least implicitly.[7] While Pierre Nora asserted the centrality of various *lieux de mémoire* in modern France as evidence of both the stability of the French nation and the French state's effectiveness in representing it, no such claim can be made for eastern European states that came into being from the nineteenth century onward. And yet, by focusing on sources linked to institutional national politics and by asking questions about nationalist discourses, historians of eastern Europe have contributed to constructing an image of this region in the twentieth century implying that states successfully controlled the fate of their citizens. As Rogers Brubaker and Jeremy King have shown, this image is connected to an unreflexive view of nationalism and of national communities that represents them as somehow naturally existing, ready to be "molded" into cohesive states by politicians and governments, rather than contested and rearticulated with each passing generation.[8]

However, my narrative is not focused solely on the failure of the Romanian state and on public resistance to its policies. When I speak of disjunction, I mean simply a disconnectedness that should not always be interpreted as resistance. Some communities, such as the Hungarians in Transylvania during the interwar period, abstained from involvement in official commemorative events in which they would have participated when they were a part of the Austro-Hungarian state prior to 1918. In that case one can easily interpret their disconnect as a form of resistance against the Romanianization of public culture. But what is one to make of the lack of participation by Catholics (ethnic Romanians) in the same official commemorations during the interwar period? That case is not so clearly a form of resistance. Often state policies were ineffective because they did not reach their intended audience and were not viewed as representing a legitimate authority. Local populations did not recognize the kind of official nationalism that these policies sought to embody. Yet non-recognition was a failure in communication, rather than necessarily a form of resistance.

A word should be said about the image of the Romanian state that emerges in these pages. Though it was by no means monolithic (on the contrary, its institutional weaknesses and inability to carry through its goals are an important reason for its failure to successfully enact its commemorative policies), in matters pertaining to commemorations the executive played a rather straightforward top-down role. There were no parliamentary debates, no policy of delegating authority to local representatives of the government to interpret executive orders issued in Bucharest in a locally resonant fashion. Instead, in the interwar period the king, the government, and representatives of the army acted in a highly centralized way to dictate exact policies regarding commemorations. During the Communist period this centralizing tendency continued under the guidance of the Politburo.

When local authorities dissented, they did so as members of the local communities. For instance, during World War II representatives of the local government in a village near Alba Iulia, a Romanian city close to the border with Hungary after the Vienna Award of 1940, participated in the inauguration of a cemetery for the soldiers who had died on the eastern front, in complete violation of the rules decreed by Ion Antonescu (1882–1946), the Romanian wartime military dictator. But they did not notify the central government of this violation. Instead, we learn about this action from a village historian, who kept some documentation from the inauguration of the cemetery. The presence of local bureaucrats was thus a violation of their official duties, as they disobeyed regulations established by the highest state authorities. At the same time, through their presence as self-identified state representatives (rather than as private citizens), these officials also led the local population into believing the state endorsed these commemorative efforts. It was thus the localized form of embodying officialdom that counted for the local population, while ignoring the full array of policies passed in Bucharest.

Looking at how people reacted to the horrors of World War I, which brought many of the eastern European states into existence as independent units (Czechoslovakia, Poland, Hungary, and Yugoslavia), or created a drastically new context for existing countries (Romania, Bulgaria, Greece, Albania, and Russia), it becomes readily apparent that these states were far less stable and legitimate than they claimed to be. Yet in most areas of public life, average people did not speak out, so we are generally unable to see clear and continuous evidence of dissonance between what governments claimed to control and what was happening locally. Overall, historians of eastern Europe have been uninterested in the silences embedded in the recorded historical traces of the modern period.[9] Yet in the area of war commemorations and remembrance, there is in fact ample evidence witnessing not only how people were ahead of the state in constructing their narratives about the meaning of the war writ small (regarding the local community's dead), but also how they continued to assert their own concepts of what it meant to properly honor the war dead even as the state attempted to create its rituals.[10] These phenomena were present and have been studied to some extent also in Poland, Yugoslavia, Hungary, Bulgaria, and Czechoslovakia in recent years.[11] This book builds on these works by applying their insights to the longer durée, encompassing the entire twentieth century.

My study doesn't deny that the politics of commemoration had a role in shaping the narratives of remembering the two world wars in Romania (and by extension, more broadly in eastern Europe). I accept that nationalism was a major filter through which individuals and local communities came to see death in the two world wars. But I do not consider the role of the state and politics as *the* central force in commemorative discourses, either during the early post-1918 years or even at the height of Communist dictatorship. Nor was nationalism the primal or ultimate lens through which people articulated their memory of wartime violence. Instead, the state participated in (or stayed out of) local commemorations, and communities negotiated their responses to state initiatives or dictates from a position that combined a variety of contexts: local traditions with regard to the cult of the dead; whether the dead had perished on the battlefield or in civilian life; in which army the deceased had served; when, during the war, they had met their death; and what communities with divergent experiences of the war were located nearby. Religious, ethnic, economic, regional, and gender elements of a community's traditions all played a role in how war violence was understood at the local level and how people chose to construct its remembrance. Whether people participated in state-sponsored commemorations, abstained from doing so, or orchestrated their own parallel ones, they made choices informed by this more immediate local context. Ideology and state institutions played a role in constructing the limits of commemorative imagination but never fully controlled these cultural processes, many of which simply took place outside any official definitions of "proper" means of honoring the dead, to the frustration of politicians, nationalist intellectuals, and bureaucrats.

Why Romania?

It is difficult to claim that a minor power in Europe could be in any way exemplary of broad trends on the continent, especially as I am questioning the very notion that it is possible to narrate a "European memory" of the world wars. In this regard, for purposes of contesting the established narratives about remembering the world wars in Europe, other cases would demonstrate just as clearly the ways in which memory is always local. Is Romania, then, at least exemplary for eastern Europe? I claim it is a good case study, less well known than others, but quite as rich and possibly uniquely complex in the array of different traditions it encompasses. The ethnic and religious diversity in Romania, as well as the diverse political pasts of its various regions, render this state a transnational case study of a sort comparable to Poland, Czechoslovakia, Yugoslavia, or Hungary. Because of this, Romania is in fact an excellent example of the ways in which local cultural practices engaged critically with state policy in constructing memorials to the two world wars. Therefore, this analysis is offered as a relevant case study for all who reflect on remembering the world wars in eastern Europe.

A brief outline of Romania's experience in the two world wars will help bring into greater focus the unique as well as broadly relevant aspects of this case study. Established as an independent state with all the trappings of modernity after the Treaty of Berlin in 1878, the Romanian Kingdom represented a buffer state between Russia and Austria-Hungary. By the beginning of the twentieth century, Romanian leaders had come to see their state as an important player in regional politics, especially with regard to the unstable Balkans. Romania's central role as a negotiator and the involvement of Romanian troops in the Balkan Wars of 1912 and 1913 reinforced the self-assurance of the Romanian army in its abilities.

The experience of World War I proved it wrong. Between 1914 and 1916 Romania stayed out of the war, principally because of the loyalty that King Charles I (r. 1866–1914) had for his old German allies and the territorial guarantees that Romanian political leaders wanted to receive for joining the war on the side of the Entente. In August 1916 the Romanians finally joined the Entente and attacked Austria-Hungary in Transylvania, where they scored a few quick and easy victories. Within weeks, however, the Central Powers attacked Romania from both south and northwest and succeeded in occupying the entire southern half of the country, pushing the king, queen, and government in exile to the Moldavian city of Iași. Bucharest, the capital, was left under German occupation for over a year.

The Romanian casualties, both military and civilian (due to harsh conditions and especially a violent typhoid fever epidemic), were staggering. The economy was in shambles and supplies difficult to come by. In addition, the Russian allies proved to be a liability, in terms of both military strength and morale. The Romanian government in exile felt compelled to promise wide-ranging land enfranchisement to the peasants in uniform in order to prevent them from adhering to the new Bolshevik ideas that circulated through the rank and file of the Russian troops.

It was only in the fall of 1918 that the Romanian leadership began to see some dividends from their costly involvement in the war. With the Entente victorious in the west and other fronts, King Ferdinand (r. 1914–1927), Queen Marie (r. 1914–1938), and the Romanian government were able to return to Bucharest with promises not only of restoring the old boundaries, but also of acquiring new territories, from Russian-ruled Bessarabia to several Austro-Hungarian areas (Transylvania, the Banat, and Bukovina). After Versailles Romania gained forty percent more territory than it had in 1916, most importantly the much prized and contentious Transylvania. The new Romanian geography proved to be both a boon and a tremendous challenge, as the diversity of the population, of the administrative set-up, and of the economic infra-structure of the new territories were often overwhelming obstacles against the dream of Bucharest authorities to create a unified Greater Romania.[12]

Given the change of most eastern European states from democratic parliamen-tarism toward illiberal autocracy over the interwar years, Romania's eventual siding with the Axis might seem like a foregone conclusion. Yet the road from Versailles to World War II was a matter of contingency and involved difficult choices to serve the ideal of preserving Romania's borders against revisionist threats. Foremost among these were the Soviet threat on the east, which was perceived also as a grave ideological concern, and the Hungarian threat on the west. King Charles II (r. 1930–1940) tried to remain neutral at the beginning of the war, but lost important territories to the Soviets in the east in July 1940, to the Hungarians in August, and to the Bulgarians in September. By September the king was forced to abdicate, and a radical fascist government came to power under the formal leadership of Marshal Ion Antonescu and the shadow authority of Horia Sima (1907–1993), the leader of the Iron Guard, the Nazi-sympathizing Romanian fascist movement.

Romania spent most of World War II (June 1941 to August 1944) on the side of the Axis, in what Antonescu identified as the "sacred crusade against Bolshevism." This alliance was partly pragmatic (especially after the Nazis invaded the Soviet Union) and aimed against the Russians, and partly ideological, as the Romanian wartime government shared some of the anti-Semitic and anti-democratic convictions of the Nazis. There was no Romanian "Final Solution," but the Romanian government undertook its own path of isolating, impoverishing, and decimating the Jewish population, especially in the territories it (re)gained from the Soviet Union and went on to control for most of the war (especially Transnistria). As historians have observed, the Romanian Holocaust did not rise to the level of the Nazi practice mainly because of the inefficiency of the policies of the Romanian government with regard to the Jews. The survival of a large numbers of Jews in territories controlled by the Romanian government was due primarily to the inability, rather than unwillingness on the part of state representatives, to complete this goal. The slowing down of the policy of extermination was also a pragmatic response by the Antonescu regime to the losses incurred by the Axis powers and the growing likelihood that the Allies would be victorious.

The losses incurred by Romania during the first three years of war, up to July 1944, took place primarily outside the borders of wartime Romania. The Romanian army suffered great losses on the way to Stalingrad and during the blockade of that city (almost 160,000 people). Civilian deaths were especially high among Jews, as 280,000–380,000 were killed by Romanian officials. The pre-war Romanian territories were affected primarily through the bombing of the oil fields around Ploieşti, but casualties were rather low, and the primary losses were economic.

After August 1944 Romania belatedly switched sides in the hope of receiving better treatment from the Soviet troops advancing over Romanian territory, and in the hope of recovering northern Transylvania from their Hungarian Axis allies. This turnaround meant that the Romanian troops were the front lines of the allied troops fighting to push the Nazis out of eastern Europe. The Romanians suffered great losses at the hands of their old allies, around 167,000 out of the total 538,000 (over 31 percent). Many civilians on Romanian soil suffered human and material losses at the hands of the Soviet troops.

By the end of October 1944 the Romanian troops (with assistance from the Soviet Union) were back in control of the entire territory of Transylvania. After the peace treaties Romania regained most of the land it had lost during World War II, save for Northern Bukovina and Bessarabia, which remained part of the Soviet Union, and southern Dobrodgea. This victory came, however, at a high cost, as Romania became part of the Soviet bloc. Its borders were "protected" by the presence of Soviet troops and advisors on Romanian territory until 1957.

These details render Romania a rich and complex site for researching the diverse and often divergent ways in which people living close to each other maintained different discourses of remembrance and commemorative rituals over the twentieth century. Though by no means exemplary in every facet of wartime experience in eastern Europe, Romania does have important commonalities with each of the countries that became part of the post-Versailles eastern European landscape and the Soviet bloc after World War II.

Remembering and Self-Identification:
On the Limited Use of "Collective Memory"

This study aims to present original arguments in the growing scholarship on memory. Within this vast literature, I am interested in discourses of remembrance, whether factual or fictional. Although it is important to differentiate between the two, what interests me most is how people invoke such discourses in order to identify with past events and experiences. Thus, I see memory as both a process and a product. As a process, remembering is always social and cultural, as well as physiological. Remembering enables people to function in daily life (walk, open doors, ride a bike, speak, etc.).[13] At the same time, as a social and cultural process, remembering helps to inhibit certain instinctual responses while allowing others to occur.[14] Suppression and forgetting are integral parts of remembering in the physiological, psychological, and cultural realms.[15] Therefore, I see memory not as a discrete topic that can be investigated as one aspect of wider social and cultural phenomena, but rather as a fundamental building block for anyone trying to understand social and cultural history, especially if questions such as identity politics and self-representation are important to a historian's arsenal of investigative angles.

As a product, memory is an individual synthesis that results from the social process of recollecting and discarding. Because of this important distinction between product and process, I do not employ the concept of "collective memory."[16] Collective memory can at best be viewed as a metaphor for the process of remembering in its social context. Yet there is no stable product one can identify as "collective memory."

Rituals, commemorations, and other outcomes of discourses of public remembrance cannot be defined as memory per se. They may become memory triggers for individuals, but they do not encapsulate in a stable, solid form, the essence of a past event remembered.

Instead, I view political elites in modern states as constantly attempting to employ narratives and rituals about the past to gain political legitimacy. I identify these processes as commemorative discourses. They seek to appropriate memories by mobilizing remembering in a social politicized context, but they do not reflect memories. When this process is successful, the people whose memories are engaged in commemorations identify with the institutional efforts. Yet more often than not, especially in the case analyzed here, a distance exists between institutional intentions and the people who are to be mobilized by these commemorative rituals. This tension marks precisely the important difference between memories as individually bound products, and commemorative discourses as their politicized social re-articulation.

A middle ground between these two poles is the community in which a person shapes her or his formative memories, what James Fentress and Chris Wickham identify as "social memory."[17] In their articulation, social memory represents the product of socialization into the immediate kinship community through a process of invoking identification with various elements of the past—feelings, events, and signification of processes. Though possibly just as politicized and sometimes manipulative (as well as willfully forgetful of certain aspects about the past), familial networks and small rural communities often play a crucial role in directing how new generations identify with events from the past. My study exposes the results of these processes of identification and distancing between the individual, the familial/community, and wider social contexts of remembering and commemorating.

My own definition of remembering as a social phenomenon is linked to one essential concept: identification.[18] People construct selves in relation to the world through a learning process that includes aspects of both rational thought and spontaneous or emotive forms of remembering from past experiences. The significance of such memories is in fact highly dependent on the larger cultural environment in which a person grows up. Fears and phobias develop not just out of painful personal experiences, but also from learning taboos. For an individual, the meaning of specific forms of learning is different if they are acquired as memory, rather than taught as simple fact. In the modern world, people may tend to value more highly what they think they remember than what they learn as given knowledge.[19] For instance, trauma cannot be generated by acquired knowledge that is subjectively processed *as* knowledge. Yet, when someone experiences a learned trauma as his or her own memories (regardless of whether the traumatic events actually happened to the individual), the associative relationship between consciously learned facts and personalized information is one of identification and remembrance, and the effects can be as strong as if that trauma had actually happened to that person.[20] For instance, generations of Soviet citizens who grew up after the Great Purges in the 1930s were affected deeply by the "post-memory" of those traumatic years as a remembered event, even when they were born after those years.

This study offers new reflections about the theoretical underpinnings of memory studies in a few specific areas. To begin, I use "commemoration" both in straight-forward descriptions of events planned by individuals and small local groups or at the highest official level, as well as discursively, to draw attention to the attempt to mobilize various participants to act. To commemorate means literally to remember together; but what does remembering together involve? Who is to do the remembering together? Individuals? Communities? How is one to measure the degree of together-ness? Does it imply a spontaneous coming together or, on the contrary, the need for some authority (individual, institution) to coordinate this process? All these possibili-ties are encapsulated in the word "commemoration," and the analysis below bears out the various interpretations of the word by different historical actors, opening up a rich and contested use of the term. It suggests that cohesion and tension are forces that turn commemorative policies into living, performative historical events worthy of notice.

Another topic to which I bring a new perspective is post-memory. Some scholars have contested the notion that post-memory, recollecting an event in which one has not participated, can be in fact considered a process of remembrance.[21] Recently, however, following up on works by Marianne Hirsch and others, cultural critics have taken post-memory or prosthetic memory to mean a specific kind of identification discourse, in which a person constructs her or his self in relation to "remembered" events through which that person has not lived.[22] This scholarship in fact problema-tizes the very notion of "experience" as somehow essential for grounding meaning and authenticity, echoing criticisms that Joan Scott advanced in her deconstruction of "experientialism" as a privileged position for creating discourses about the past.[23] My own position in this debate about the usefulness of the term post-memory in connec-tion to the two world wars is situated somewhere between Scott's outright rejection that experience has any claim to a privileged position in constructing meaning out of the past, and the neuroscientists who define memory strictly in terms of physiological processes of storing and recovering information to one's own physical and emotional experiences.

If identities are constructed through a process that is subjectively understood as remembering (though it might not strictly mean remembering one's *own* previous experiences), then post-memory is the identification, by someone in a generation that has not lived through a particular event, with that event in ways that help construct the self-understanding of this later generation. This definition comes closest to acknowledging the insights about social memory offered by Maurice Halbwachs.[24] But while Halbwachs was not particularly able to identify the mechanisms by which memory traces become a social good, a building block that individuals in subsequent generations use to define themselves, other scholars have subsequently explored these processes more thoroughly, especially in connection to the traumas of the Holocaust among survivors and their children and grandchildren.

The particularity of post-memory in being associated with remembrance is the subjective stance of "heirs" to such memories that they possess a privileged relationship with those memory traces. They often claim an emotional closeness that comes out of hearing stories about the events narrated in the intimacy of the home, of trust and love, as well as relived traumas and renewed pain. Having direct access to the intense emotional aspects of these memories on a repeated basis, the younger generations of those who experienced the violence of the world wars see themselves as responsible for keeping alive these poignant truths, which cannot be rendered fully meaningful by historical analysis of those events. Yet the position of authority that post-memory generations claim also acknowledges, in part, the importance of historical analysis of the remembered events: historical knowledge is useful for making their remembrance relevant to a wider public. Thus, for these generations it is important both to acknowledge historical knowledge and also to separate it from their own remembrances, which are to be held as a more intimate type of knowledge, more readily transferring into identification with a community than into historical analysis.

The distinction and the tenuous relationship between post-memory and historical knowledge allow us to understand the extent to which generations ranging from those who grew up in the 1950s to generations coming of age today are still beholden to the events of World War II in defining their own relationships to certain communities and sets of concerns. If learning about the Holocaust in school had the same effect as learning at home about the suffering of one's grand- and great-grandparents in World War II, then there would be no difference between the two. In reality, since World War II, different meanings have been ascribed to official narratives about the war by people in the intimacy of their homes and by local communities than in a wider public context.

Gender and Remembrance of Wartime Violence

I am concerned also with the gendered nature of remembering, especially with regard to how memories are narrated and represented to others. In this study, gender appears both as an overt, constitutive element of how people and institutions define wartime experiences, and as a silence or blind spot. Most people do not reflect directly about the gendered nature of their remembrance. The rare instances when people address gender issues enable us to see with great clarity the ways assumptions about gender roles always shape recollections about war. What is important to a person to remember about life during wartime (politics, violence, loss, food, childcare, military equipment, etc.), and what is considered representative of wider society, depend a great deal on that person's identification with specific gender norms and practices.[25] The meaning attributed to specific narrated events is also gendered. What is to be considered heroic rather than banal suffering? What does it mean to remain virtuous? Who can claim to be a war victim, and on what grounds? Answers to these questions are often not explicitly posed in gendered terms, nor are they entirely polarized in a male-female dichotomy. Yet a careful reading reveals a great deal of difference between the ways in which men remember and forget, and women recollect and discard, their experiences of war, and how their narratives often reinforce gender norms and rarely pose self-conscious challenges to them. Likewise, heteronormativity is generally implied in such narratives.

What is *not* talked about and is forcefully forgotten is also a matter of gendered assumptions about what is publicly significant and what one can in fact speak about. Stories about sexual victimization are almost entirely absent from any personal narratives about World War I and II in Romania. Women almost never talk about this, as they generally didn't in many other settings after the two world wars.[26] Men sometimes bring up the subject, but either in speaking about others or by retelling their sexual liaisons with women in terms that represent them as consensual. Overall, rape remains generally unaccounted for as a form of wartime victimization, and the memory of such wartime experiences seems to have been buried deeply through fear of shame.

Generally speaking, neither men nor women saw sexual violence as an important and representative form of victimization in Romanian society at large. However, their reasons differed. Men either didn't think the issue concerned them or saw it as irrelevant to the public significance of the war, whether or not they viewed or participated in sexually licentious liaisons during the war. Women generally viewed their experiences of sexual violence as not representative of the society at large and thus not worthy of public remembrance.[27]

In addition, as anthropologists, sociologists, and linguists have shown, narrative styles and forms of speech are gender specific. According to gender analyses of self-representation, women tend to relate stories about others rather than placing themselves at the center of stories about the past.[28] In my own interviews I saw some evidence of this tendency, but I also found examples where women did not fit this narrative strategy.[29] Overall, however, women were more likely to behave as vectors of remembering than as subjects of the recollections they participated in. This tendency reinforced the exclusive (though mostly implicit) identification of heroism and victimization with masculine experiences of war.

The masculinization of wartime victimization and heroism is just as prominent in the post-memory discourses developed among the generations after 1945. These younger men and women have tended to privilege the war stories of their fathers and grandfathers, even when these were stories of familial (male and female) suffering, as in the case of deportations.[30] And when women's stories differed from men's, the silencing, in official narratives, of the military experiences on the eastern front after World War II also lent an exclusive aura of heroism to these male counter-memories, placing them at the center of familial narratives, often at the expense of any description of women's experiences. Yet women have been and remain at the center of the cult of the dead in Romania, something so obvious that most people don't consider it as a culturally bound, learned, and thus important element in considering how remembering as a social phenomenon actually takes place.[31]

The Local Contingencies of Remembering War

While offering new insights into post-memory and the gendered aspects of memory, my main contribution to the literature on memory is in showing *how* memory is locally contingent. Examining the specific ways some traditions are locally and individually deployed to remember the war dead while others are discarded, and the ways people respond selectively to new state policies, forms the inner core of my analysis. My goal is to destabilize any impression that commemorative discourses somehow flow from the center to the margins, or that there is in fact a valid distinction between central commemorations and marginal ones, in terms of their overall cultural-social significance. What I claim is that after World War I the Romanian state's nationally staged commemorations were unsuccessful in constructing widely embraced narratives of remembrance.

The post–World War II period is more complicated. Under Communist rule, war commemorations were strictly controlled by the state, but subterraneous counter-memories developed and became extremely effective in negating allegiance to the narratives developed by the state. I define "counter-memories" as memorializing narratives that were articulated sometimes in stark opposition to the official narratives of the wars and often separate from them, even when these two apparently antithetical discourses actually shared some elements, such as nationalist or victimist sensibilities. One can speak about the Communist regime as effective in limiting the imagination of the postwar generation to think of wartime violence outside the officially defined discourse. There is rich evidence, however, that counter-memories developed all over the Communist bloc and were passed down from the wartime generation to younger ones. Thus the Communist regimes played a central role in polarizing the notion of what could be considered "truthful" memories of the war. Nonetheless, local communities and individuals still developed their own narratives about the war, emphasizing selectively their own persecution at the hands of others. These remembrances of wartime victimization painted specific communities as uniquely harmed by the war, their suffering unparalleled by that of any other groups. Therefore, I reject the notion that the Communist regimes in eastern Europe succeeded, on the whole, in indoctrinating their citizens with a Communist remembrance of World War II.[32]

My analysis of official and other public and personal discourses about the memory of the two world wars reveals a picture of selective remembering and forgetting that exclusively foregrounds victimhood during both world wars, even among aggressor populations, combined with a self-image of heroism through sacrifice and death. The official commemorative discourses after 1918 and 1945 painted Romania's participation in those wars as protecting its legitimate claims over territories and people. The Romanian soldiers who perished in these wars were heroes who had died defending their country, even when most of them fell outside of Romania's borders. For civilians, the memory of the world wars registered as a period of suffering, occupation, and sacrifice. Who the perpetrators were shifted along the lines of which community was remembering wartime violence; and sometimes discourses about guilt and responsibility were self-contradictory. Overall, there has been little self-reflection about responsibility for wartime violence. The kind of self-examination that took place in West Germany after 1945, which allowed for a fuller, if more painful, memory of the Nazi past, has never occurred in Romania or more broadly in eastern Europe, with the exception of Poland in recent years.[33] My analysis underscores the ways in which the particularities of the wartime experience and the related postwar experiences of communities inside Romania account for a great deal of this vacuum of accountability.

It is impossible to understand the "return" or "arrival" of the post-Communist countries to the wider European home without understanding this polarized culture of war remembrance. How Poles, Czechs, Slovaks, Hungarians, Romanians, Croats, Serbs, Bulgarians, Estonians, Latvians, Lithuanians, Macedonians, Bosnians, Slovenes, Ukrainians, and Albanians after the fall of Communism reacted to certain narratives that claimed to be truthful memories of the two world wars cannot be understood in the context of prevailing Western-centric views of World War I and World War II. While World War I is painted in the West as a tragic end to the long period of growth, most people in eastern Europe see 1918 as a moment of promise and beginning. The narrative that emphasizes the triumph of democracy in Europe after 1945 erases the history of a half century of imperialist oppression at the hands of the Soviet Union in the Communist bloc. Euroskepticism among the new EU members comes in part from belief in the lack of empathy on the part of intellectuals and politicians in the West that would dispose them to a proper understanding of the nature of lived Communism. The counter-memory of suffering and oppression still holds sway over the emotions of people living in the post-Communist states. That is a reality that the articles from *Eurozine,* as well as policy makers in Brussels who insist on celebrating Europe Day on 9 May, simply do not take as serious, legitimate problems that involve the EU at large, rather than just these individual populations at the edge of Europe. The idea of a unified Europe, in its self-image of the past as well as its imagined future, depends on taking these challenges more seriously and truly understanding the vastly different experiences and memories of the two world wars of the people who lived in eastern Europe.

A Map of the Book

A brief map of this study is helpful at the outset, since the organization of the book is intentionally tied to the arguments woven through it, eschewing any linear narrative line. Generally speaking, the chapters are structured to underscore the disjuncture between official and vernacular voices. I tried to let these different registers speak for themselves and interrogated their connections only after laying out their specific forms of engagement with commemorative discourses. I aimed to avoid creating an image that emphasizes the resistance of individuals and organic communities against a monolithic state. Instead, these two registers are juxtaposed as coexisting, sometimes in frustrating proximity and sometimes in complete mutual obliviousness. I suggest that such occurrences generate no overarching meaning, other than a mindfulness about the self-importance of narratives constructed at the center, which assume that phenomena at the local level (in this case, in the area of cultural production) are derivative of more important developments that take place at the center.

The book begins with a chapter focusing on the pre–World War I period, in order to establish what kinds of death rituals, both localized and religious as well as official, existed prior to World War I in the space that became Greater Romania after 1918. This chapter also sets up a detailed picture of the sorts of variables that defined both rural and urban populations in these spaces. Chapter 2 focuses on the specifics of this tragedy on the eastern front and more specifically in Romania, looking first into the mourning processes that took place right after the war and the subsequent local-ized efforts at memorializing the war dead. The focus here is on the great diversity of responses of various communities and on the communities' lack of felt need to follow any lead in these actions, which were primarily steeped in preexisting traditions having to do with the cult of the dead. Chapter 3 follows the attempts of the state to control the commemorations springing up everywhere. From legislation to school policies and funding building projects, the interwar Romanian state played catch-up with individuals and communities who had already found their own ways of remembering the war. My focus is on both events, such as the establishment of Heroes Day and other national holidays linked to World War I, as well as spaces that were constructed to embody remembrances of the war.

The second part of the book shifts perspective to focus first on the role of the state vis-à-vis local initiatives. Chapter 4 demonstrates that one cannot in fact understand post–World War II war remembrances in Romania without a good grasp of the policies and processes in place during the interwar period. This discussion identifies several factors as important in shaping official commemorations starting in 1941: the interwar experience of the Romanian state with commemorations of the Great War; the experience of World War II, especially Romania's participation on both sides of the conflict; the war crime trials at the war's end; and the ideologies first of straight and narrow Soviet subservience and eventually of outright nationalism by the 1960s. This chapter also foregrounds the development of the victimist-heroic self-image in post–World War II Romania, which came to dominate both state and vernacular commemorative discourses. Chapter 5 considers the individual voices of those who found themselves unrepresented by the official commemorative discourses. Counter-memories or counter-myths are a central theme of this chapter.

In chapter 6, I bring these two strands—official and vernacular—back together, to show the transformations of the commemorative discourses regarding the world wars since the fall of Communism. The world of post-Communist democracy is proving, however, far more complicated and non-democratic when it comes to remembering the war dead than political elites would want. How these commemorative discourses change in the next few years will attest to what extent remembering Europe's world wars can become a non-antagonistic local and continental effort. For now, the tension between these two levels of framing the tragedy of World War II leaves little room for imagining a space for reconciliation.

1

DEATH AND RITUAL

Mourning and Commemorative Practices before 1914

In the elaborate burial rituals observed for many centuries by the mostly Orthodox populations of southeastern Europe, mourning was a central element, and the prescriptions for who could perform the task were precise:

> The wailers [would be] women, or girls, because only they are entitled by custom to cry for the dead, usually the closest or more removed relatives of the departed: mothers, wives, sisters, cousins, sisters-in-law, goddaughters, and the godmothers of one's child, as well as those who had remained in amicable relations with the dead. But the first in line are always the mothers and wives. If the dead doesn't have any close relatives versed in the *art of wailing* to cry for him, then women from the village who have made a *profession* out of this, and who deserve the real title of mourners, wailers, or incense burners will be hired.[2]

After the body was interred, for six weeks "a girl would be hired to bring water to different houses, for the soul of the departed."[3] At the six week mark, "when the second almsgiving [*pomană*] for the dead is to take place, the mother, sister, cousin, or another woman from the family takes an offering of warm bread, a black rooster or hen, then a few hot embers in a small container, together with some incense, a scarf in whose corners she ties a few coins, as well as a wax candle and then goes to the well" to offer them to the girl who had been hired to commemorate the soul of the departed by bringing water to neighbors.[4] An elaborate almsgiving meal and ceremony would follow, and for seven years after the death of a family member, families, especially women, would continue to perform specific rituals to ensure the peaceful passage of the dead into the afterlife. After that, the memory of dead ones would be kept alive by visits to the grave throughout the year and almsgiving in their name during religious ceremonies dedicated to the memory of the dead.[5]

I offer this extended description of burial rituals by way of suggesting two important components of mourning and commemorating the dead among Romanians and other populations in eastern Europe: the cult of the dead was a central component of these cultures and societies, especially among the Orthodox, and included both religious and semi-pagan elements so elaborate as to suggest a life-long learning process in order to master them; and funerary rituals were fundamentally gendered, with women playing specific gender roles at every step of the way not only as followers, but also as central gatekeepers of the passage into afterlife.

This chapter describes the context that framed the cultural practices of burial, mourning, and commemorating that developed after World War I. Though there were unprecedented developments in the realm of mourning and commemorating the dead all over Europe after 1918, I contend that they were fundamentally shaped by the types of traditional practices described here. This is not a startling claim in itself, as Jay Winter, for instance, made the notion of continuity rather than break a central component in his argument in *Sites of Memory*.[6] The difference rests in the actual traditions discussed here, as well as their relationship with efforts by monarchs and other state representatives to coax such traditions into mobilizing practices on behalf of either the nation or the empire. The localized and centralized actions I focus on are far less interconnected than was the case in Great Britain or France, for instance. Burial, mourning, and death rituals were a site of intense, constant cultural production and reproduction in the mostly rural societies of eastern Europe before the twentieth century, contrasting and competing with newly emerging nationalist and imperial ones, which attempted to construct new bonds of loyalty and legitimacy between rulers and the ruled. The two realms of commemorative practices coexisted, largely unconnected at the local level, with the state pursuing certain symbols and practices, while local communities followed their own traditional practices or offered local inflections on new commemorative symbols.

The Religious Landscape

Death was a central reality and cultural leitmotif in the life of the people inhabiting eastern Europe, and especially, my main focus here, in what became Romania starting in the late nineteenth century.[7] This is not an unusual feature for an overwhelmingly rural and greatly religious population. In cultures with an experience of short life spans and great earthly hardships, religious beliefs and rituals surrounding death have played a prominent role to provide relief in the face of frequent death and the hope for a better afterlife.[8] Some scholars have gone so far as to say that "what we call culture is nothing else than an ensemble of beliefs and rituals created to fight the subversive effects of individual or collective death."[9] Louis-Vincent's statement above, though hyperbolic in its claims, does reflect the intense obsession of rural populations in eastern Europe with the cult of the dead. In the pages below I assert that death rituals and other means communities employed to keep alive the memory of beloved dead ones give us important insights into how people dealt with violent death during the world wars of the twentieth century.

In this broader context the specifics of Romania are worth remembering for their complexity, which renders this case comparable with others in Europe, while underscoring its uniqueness. At the turn of the twentieth century, over 85 percent of the population of Romania and Transylvania lived in villages lacking most modern amenities and services, from running water to schools and healthcare. This picture holds true more for ethnic Romanians, who were more likely to live in such rural settings, than for Hungarians, Germans, and Jews.[10] These populations also had their share of rural living (over 50 percent) but had become more urbanized than ethnic Romanians. Still, the vast majority of people inhabiting the future Greater Romania lived much closer to the cyclical rhythms of agriculture and to the core values of their religious identity than to the more cosmopolitan and secular culture developing in cities.[11] This is also true for most of eastern Europe, broadly speaking, with the exception of the more urbanized Bohemian lands in the Habsburg empire.[12]

The core cultural practices of these populations varied over the territory that became Greater Romania after 1918. They generally reflected local understandings of the religious identification of the inhabitants, spanning Orthodox Christianity, Catholicism, Greek Catholicism (the Uniates), Protestantism of various kinds (especially Calvinist, Unitarian, and Lutheran), Judaism of various degrees of orthodoxy, and even some remnants of Islam.[13] Almost all ethnic Romanians were Orthodox or Greek-Catholic Christians, and the rural population was overwhelmingly illiterate, including the clergy. This meant that their religious practices were closely connected to local popular interpretations of the religious dogma, which often included many elements of pagan ritual.[14] There were great similarities in this regard between these populations and other Orthodox Christians living in the Russian and Habsburg empires, Serbia, Bulgaria, and Greece. In addition, a sizeable fraction of the ethnic Romanians in Transylvania were Greek Catholic and adhered to some Orthodox Christian dogma, with the changes that had been introduced with the creation of this institution of religious compromise in the seventeenth century—mostly liturgical and theological.[15] In fact, the descriptions of the rituals regarding burial and remembering the dead offered above encompass the practices of the Greek-Catholics in this area as well. Similarities in this regard could be found in the Ukrainian regions that had embraced the Uniate Church during the same period.[16]

The large Hungarian minority that lived in Transylvania[17] was divided between Catholics and Protestants, with an additional small but growing section of acculturated Hungarian-speaking Jews, who in the nineteenth century either were converting religiously, or at least taking up some Hungarian cultural practices, embracing Magyarization more readily than Slovaks and Romanians.[18] Transylvania had been a stronghold of Calvinism in the early modern period and remained so in part until the twentieth century. Hungarians also tended to be better educated and to remain more closely observant of their churches' strict dogma, for various reasons—the clergy were more educated, and the Catholic Church in particular had played a major role in secular education, thus ensuring that successive generations of believers possessed a good theological foundation for their religious beliefs and practices, something that was similar to Catholic Poles.[19] Overall, both the Protestant churches, due to their specific theological underpinnings, and the Catholic Church, especially after the counter-Reformation, were more preoccupied with retaining a greater degree of adherence to their dogma than the Orthodox Church.[20] Yet especially in rural areas, Hungarians developed their own elaborate rituals linked to death. Funerary markers in parts of Transylvania were erected to represent the life story of the buried person, a kind of transposition of that individual into a moral typology of the eternal.[21] Some burial rituals also embodied some of the complexity of practices observed more often among the Orthodox; the burial of young maidens as brides was similar to the practice best described in Kligman's *Wedding of the Dead*.

A smaller German-speaking minority also comprised a mix of Protestants (especially Lutherans) and Catholics, most of whom lived in self-enclosed communities, alongside rather than in direct communication with their Hungarian coreligionists, and even more isolated (in terms of identity and cultural practices) from their

Romanian neighbors. These German populations were located in a few of the larger cities in Transylvania (Hermannstadt/Nagyszeben/Sibiu, Kronstadt/Brassó/Braşov, and Temesvár/Temeswar/Timişoara), and also in small rural communities on the edge of the Carpathians. The burial rituals among the German Lutherans remained simple; one cannot speak of a rich ritualistic cult of the dead in these communities.

Catholics, both German and others (Hungarian, Romanian, and Csango), remained more dedicated in their cult of the dead than Protestants, much as in the rest of the world. The Day of the Dead, 1 November, remained dedicated to the annual remembrance of the dead, and Catholics would often celebrate this holiday through cemetery visits, special alms to the poor, and offerings of food with biblical connotations.[22] Women were almost always those who prepared these offerings, but both men and women participated in the ceremonies. Catholic cultural practices were less elaborate and showed less ritualistic preoccupation with remembering the dead than the Orthodox, as observers of Catholic and Orthodox communities have commented.[23]

Finally, there was a large and growing presence of followers of Judaism,[24] who varied in their degree of assimilation in the host communities (much greater in urban Transylvania among Hungarian speakers than anywhere else), as well as in specific observance of orthodox beliefs and practices of their religion.[25] There were strictly Orthodox Jewish shtetls in proximity to reformed communities. In addition, there was also a mix of Sephardic Jews in the south and Ashkenazis in the north, who differed from each other in some of their practices and traditions. The Jewish population of Romania and Transylvania encompassed some of the best-educated and most secularized individuals to grace the urban landscape, along with tiny and isolated rural communities, much as in the Habsburg and Russian empires, in the territories of partitioned Poland, Bohemia, and Hungary.[26]

Jewish commemorations of the dead were framed by the Torah and rabbinical authority, but they also took on local color. The rituals surrounding sitting shivah and saying Kaddish for a dearly departed also involved performative elements strictly delineated, from embalming the corpse and presenting it by the mourners to dress (e.g., cutting of the lapel/tie for men) and actions to be taken by the mourners, and finally to the burial itself.[27] In Jewish communities in both the Habsburg empire and the Romanian state, various *chevra kadisha* societies were entrusted with taking care of these details.[28] These were tasks to be performed in strict accordance with rabbinical authority, and men were exclusively both the authority figures and the performers of most tasks. Women also played a vocal, albeit secondary role in this ritual, as they were the mourners.

In addition, in Judaism, religious holidays have a core commemorative element. Therefore, though not strictly commemorating one's dead, all holidays from Rosh

Hashanah to Yom Kippur were occasions for remembering both events and ancestors from the distant past and also one's own kin.[29] The emphasis of Judaism on remembrance and identification with one's ancestors was unique among the religious practices in the area. The Orthodox cult of the dead was somewhat similar to it, though the emphasis in Orthodoxy was much more on allowing the dead to depart peacefully into the afterlife than on maintaining an active memory of one's remote ancestors.

Taken separately, the features of each of these ethnic and religious communities resemble others across Europe. But it is their close juxtaposition in this Babel's Tower of religious and ethnic identities that makes the context of territories to be controlled by Romania after 1918 in a way illustrative, but also unique. This religious diversity suggests that practices related to mourning and burial varied across this territory, largely dependent on the religious and other traditions of each local community.

An important additional factor for understanding the commemorative/death practices in this area is the privileged official role granted to some religions in the different states that controlled these territories. In the Habsburg empire, which controlled Transylvania, the Banat, and Bukovina, Catholicism remained the most important religion, for the Habsburg emperor had also been the Holy Roman emperor for centuries, a purely symbolic title but one that reflected the desire of the Habsburg emperors to fashion themselves protectors of Catholics everywhere.[30] However, Protestant denominations were also considered accepted religions, and in Transylvania they received full recognition and financial support from Budapest, unlike the Orthodox Church, for instance.[31] In the Russian empire (the relevant area here is Bessarabia) it was Orthodoxy that reigned supreme, at the expense of Protestants, Catholics, Muslims, and especially Jews.[32] In the areas under the control of the young Romanian state, though headed by a Catholic king (Charles I), the Orthodox Church had established itself securely as the official religion, pursuing severely prohibitive policies toward other religions, especially Judaism.[33]

Given the antagonistic policies of these states toward some of their religious minorities, as well as tense relations on the ground among these different ethno-religious groups, adhering to one's specific religious practices was a valuable form of preserving one's self-identification with the immediate community. Burial practices were central among these rituals. For most religions, those closest to the dead (kinfolk and close friends) rather than a more widely sanctioned entity had to take care of these needs. These conditions generally ensured that in the countryside, burial and mourning practices remained largely unchanged for the early modern to modern period until World War I, when abrupt and vast changes in the political geography of this area, as well as the mass experience of violent death, forced important changes in the ways rural communities related to the state in terms of the cult of the dead.

Political Background and Royal Commemorative Practices

A brief background of the political and social geography of these territories at the turn of the twentieth century is also in order, before delving into the specifics of the burial and commemorative practices at that time. Over the nineteenth century, official practices attempted to establish state-sponsored rituals that would incorporate religious traditions into a new register of mobilizing citizens in the service of the state (most often in the person of the monarch or emperor). What developed after 1918 in the realm of official commemorative discourses was, in the case of the Romanian state, a continuation of these practices and, in some cases in Habsburg Transylvania and Bukovina, the most important parts of what became Romania in the twentieth century, a rejection. In this section I focus on the young Romanian kingdom itself, Austria-Hungary, and Russia.

Romania became a state after the 1856 Paris peace conference held at the end of the Crimean War. As a sidebar to the scuffle among the Great Powers, two Ottoman empire vassal principalities, Walachia and Moldavia (also known as the Romanian Principalities), came under discussion. The Russian empire had been extending its indirect but powerful influence into the Romanian Principalities since the 1830s, and the Romanians had become anxious to step back from this tight embrace. The Romanian Principalities as a joint venture ruled by Alexandru Ioan Cuza (1820–1870) emerged on 24 January 1859.

A Romanian state proper came into being only after 1866, when Cuza was overthrown by a combination of old supporters and enemies, who came to see him as a stumbling block for the further progress of Romania's (and their own) political interests.[34] In search of a respectable European pedigree in the form of a royal ruler, the liberal politician Ion C. Brătianu (1821–1891) traveled throughout Europe, knocking on royal and princely doors, most prominently those of Belgium (far away and without direct interests in Romania) and the German Confederation. The courtship with Philippe of Flanders (1937–1905) did not bear fruit, so Brătianu turned to the Hohenzollern-Sigmaringen house, and Charles (1839–1914), a cousin of the future German Kaiser Wilhelm II (1859–1941), accepted the throne.[35]

Romania was still a tributary to the Ottoman empire in 1866, when Charles I arrived in Bucharest to assume the position of prince, and it was only after the Russo-Turkish War (1877–1878) and the Congress of Berlin (1878) that Romania finally gained international recognition of its independence (1881). During his long reign (1866–1914), Charles I became in many ways the embodiment of the modern Romanian state, even though he ruled from day one according to a constitution (1866) that limited his royal powers and obligated him to work with the Parliament and through clear limitations with regard to taxation, government spending, and individual rights.[36] Romania saw economic growth and the development of many components of a modern state, from government institutions to the administrative infrastructure that encompassed the entire country, and a strong army that proved quite successful in 1877–1878 and in 1913 (the Second Balkan War). It was an executive-driven state, with a weak and generally non-democratically elected Parliament, as well as a state that had weak attributes in matters of culture and education.

In terms of the general wellbeing, Charles I's success was less stellar. The vast majority of the population, the peasants who were the subject of my opening anecdotes, lived in abject poverty. A mass peasant uprising in 1907 revealed the depth of their misery and desperation. Few efforts and fewer successes marked the government's attempts to actually recognize and deal with this problem.[37] It was only after the government armed these peasants and became the grateful recipient of their mass sacrifices in World War I that politicians finally sat down to consider serious political and land reforms.[38]

The growing Jewish population of Romania was also treated as a class of tolerated pariahs, rather than tax-paying inhabitants. Jews could gain Romanian citizenship only on the basis of a complicated and highly selective process.[39] As a result, most Jews in the country remained non-citizens and were refused basic protections and civil rights, including the right to own property. By 1914, the Jewish community of Romania numbered over 250,000 out of the total eight million inhabitants in the country,[40] and though many lived among ethnic Romanians in large cities such as Bucharest, Focşani, Suceava, and especially Iaşi, they remained quite isolated because of their non-citizen status. A growing number were trying to take advantage of new opportunities opened up especially in education and new professions, such as medicine, engineering, law, and architecture.[41] But, by and large, the Jewish population had to rely on its own community's resources for advancement, remaining both marginal to the Romanian official cultural landscape and marginally involved in it.[42] This was even truer for the population living concentrated in smaller rural Jewish communities, which encompassed the majority of Jews in Romania.

Another important "other" to the "haves" of the young Romanian state were 51 percent of the population, women, who were denied full citizenship rights (both civil and political) until 1945.[43] Before World War I women didn't have the same rights as men to own property or have guardianship over their legitimate children, according to the Civil Code adopted in 1866, which mirrored the Napoleonic Code in vogue in much of Europe at that time.[44] Romania was in no way exceptional in Europe in this regard; its aggressively anti-Jewish stance, however, was remarkable in its unwillingness to curb anti-Semitism, something Romanian politicians touted as a mark of their independence in Europe. While the Great Powers had insisted at the Congress of Berlin (1878) on making the Romanians' independence contingent upon granting Jews the same rights as ethnic Romanians, these states generally had the same exclusionary position toward their own female inhabitants. None was willing to force the hand of the Romanian state in the direction of gender empowerment, and the feminist movement was still weak inside Romania in its political demands.[45]

To construct an image of unity and legitimacy despite the many fractures and tensions present in Romanian society and politics, Charles I adopted, like other monarchs of late nineteenth-century Europe, the trappings of both personal panache and holidays and celebrations to entertain and mobilize the population.[46] Taking their cues from Queen Victoria's masterful use of these cultural techniques, other princes and monarchs throughout Europe began to turn their own households into window-displays for the values they wanted their subjects to espouse.[47] From building a proper residence in Bucharest and an even more remarkable summer palace, Peleş (1883), in the Carpathian town of Sinaia, to constructing monumental projects to commemorate important moments in the history of Romania and the king's own central role in them, Charles I marked his presence through space and spectacle.[48]

Although commemorative monuments designed to connect a glorious past with the current Romanian state began to sprout during Charles I's reign, they were never part of a concerted, massive memorializing campaign by the king or central government. Of the fifty-sixty such markers erected during his reign, a majority were local efforts by city planners or local enthusiasts, and only around twenty made reference to events that took place during the king's own rule.[49] In Iaşi, for instance, which was then deemed a second capital of the country, virtually all statues erected during Charles I's reign to commemorate historic figures, battles, and other events of public interest referred directly to political, military, and intellectual figures from that city, with no reference to the king. There was no rush by either community-based groups or government representatives to erect statues to the king or other distant representatives of the state.

Even in Bucharest the king was relatively modest in crafting a monumental self-image, by comparison with his counterparts in Vienna, Paris, and London as well as future leaders of Romania. All statues erected during his reign represented other rulers (e.g., Michael the Brave) or cultural figures (e.g., Ion Heliade Rădulescu). These monuments, most of them placed in a small area downtown, were efforts by nongovernment committees. The monument to Michael the Brave (1558–1601) was the closest representation of an abstract nationalist ideal of the legitimacy to rule over all territories where ethnic Romanians lived, rather than a funerary monument. But most others, for instance the nearby large statue of Heliade Rădulescu (1802–1872), were built as commemorative memorials to those individuals after their death.[50] There was no "monument mania" to speak of during this period in Romania, by contrast with the frenzy that seemed to grip many Habsburg territories.[51] Overall, Charles I was untouched by some of the more autocratic tendencies of his neighbors to the south and remained a man of self-discipline and high expectations regarding those surrounding him, with a penchant for military pomp.[52] His building projects combined a desire to display power with a self-conscious need for functional justification, best exemplified through the Cernavodă Bridge discussed below.

During his reign, especially after the 1877–1878 War of Independence, many communities raised funds to build monuments that marked this great military victory over the Ottomans. One such monument will serve as an example of the transition taking place during this period from a traditional religious symbolic vocabulary toward one influenced by the neo-classical and imperialist trends in vogue at that time elsewhere in Europe. In the large city of Ploieşti, the monumental Hunters' Statue was built through the financial and planning efforts of a local committee and unveiled in 1897. Centrally located and tall, over thirty-five feet high, this monument was easily visible to both locals and visitors on foot and by carriage. It featured a large obelisk with four soldiers keeping guard on each corner of the ensemble, slightly larger than life size and depicted realistically in a resolute but not overly aggressive posture. An oak wreath (symbol of the Romanian nation), a flag, and an eagle decorated the higher parts of the obelisk, while two bas-reliefs at the base of the obelisk depicted the battle of Griviţa and an allegory of victory, represented as a woman, reminiscent of the ancient Greek goddess Nike, being received by the city's joyful inhabitants.

These visual elements—the obelisk, the realistic virile soldier, the eagle, the flag, the oak wreath, and the presence of an allegoric female figure—were building blocks of the modern secular grammar of nationalist commemoration and were largely copied from the general stock of commemorative symbols in Europe at that time. The obelisk as funerary piece had come back into fashion since the early nineteenth century, when Napoleon traveled to Egypt.[53] The allegorical symbol of the country or victory as a woman dressed in flowing robes reminiscent of the bas-reliefs on the Parthenon had also become common over the nineteenth century, after French, German, and British museums had started to plunder ancient Greek and Roman sites in their relentless quest to liberate the Greeks.[54]

It is difficult to pinpoint how local committees in young Romania became so inspired by these symbols not present in the local memorial landscape in the past.[55] Crosses, rather than obelisks, and heavily ornate non-figurative symbols had been the mainstay of monumental statues. This transition to symbols connected to classical antiquity via the colonial European powers indicates a familiarity among Romanian

Figure 1.1. The Ploieşti Hunters' statue. Photo Maria Bucur.

artists and interested members of the public with this new vocabulary (through travel and portable images—photographs, drawings, paintings), as well as a desire to emulate them.[56] Such images, rather than the more traditional Orthodox crosses prominent in the past, seemed to represent more suitably the sentiments of piety and nationalist fervor that animated some of the post-1877 committees that spent time and money to put up such monuments.[57]

The eagle, flag, and oak wreath seem more straightforward symbols, with a longer history within the Romanian lands. A vulture used to grace the official princely seal of Walachia,[58] used on many plaques, large and small seals, architectural details in palaces and churches, and on the tombstones of medieval voivodes.[59] The flag as a symbol of military victory had been used in Christian iconography since the Middle Ages, most prominently in depicting the popular St. George slaying the dragon. Oak leaves and wreaths had been used often on funerary crosses and tombstones of voivodes, most famously by Constantin Brâncoveanu, who made it a basic leitmotif of Walachian baroque art and architecture.[60] But these symbols themselves had been recast in the realistic-naturalist style of the second half of the nineteenth century. They represented transitional symbols, introducing a new Western-looking aesthetic inflection in the familiar commemorative vocabulary.

Other monuments built around this time offered similar, sometimes grandiose, but most often more modest combinations of the same symbols. For instance, in the small village of Suraia, in Vrancea, far away from any of the battlefields of the War of Independence, local inhabitants commissioned a modest, twelve-foot monument, in the shape of an obelisk, to mark the death of five men from the village in the 1877–1878 war. Like most other such monuments built with local funds in small communities, this was more of a funerary marker, mourning the death of people known to the inhabitants of the village, than a proud monumental symbol of heroism. Its modest size, to be sure, was less awe-inspiring than the Ploieşti monument. But a reference to the local men's death "for the country in the War of Independence of 1877–78," also made a connection between the tragic disappearance of individuals known and presumably loved in the community, and broader, more abstract ideals—for the country, for independence.[61]

The most monumental of the projects connected to remembering the War of Independence was the Charles I/Saligny Bridge, commissioned by the king and directly embodying his idea of commemorating the war.[62] The bridge crossed the Danube River at a point where the waters of this most European of all flowing waters on the continent had an impressive width, and where hills descended onto a broad valley, as one moved from Walachia proper to Dobrodgea, the prized territorial acquisition of Romania in the War of Independence. The Charles I Bridge represented a tie, literally and symbolically, between the past and the future, and embodied progress—for it was a railroad bridge (the longest in Europe at the time of its inauguration in 1895), which most significantly connected land transportation and especially trade with the port of Constanţa, the jewel of Dobrodgea. With this new territorial acquisition in 1878, Romania had become a "respectable" European state: it had a seaside and a comfortable, modern way to travel to it. Through its beauty and monumentality, the Charles I Bridge was a permanent reminder, visible to both train engineers and passengers, that Charles I had brought independence and great progress to the country and all its inhabitants. Stone-carved soldiers at both ends of the bridge reminded all travelers that progress was in fact secured through the sacrifice of real men.

Charles I operated at both the monumental and the micro-level of pomp and circumstance. Stamps and medals, strictly military as well as civilian and memorial, were inaugurated over his long rule, marking his personal style and preferences more directly than any other commemorative projects. After all, the king had ultimate veto power over symbols to represent his rule. The first decoration created was the Star of Romania; this was also one of the first independent state actions of Charles I on the day Romania declared its independence, 10 May 1877.[63] The elaborate decoration featured four Orthodox/Byzantine crosses; the royal crown; two swords; the initials of the king in the center, surrounded by a circular wreath of oak leaves; the Latin inscription *Genere et corde fraters* [Brothers in blood and heart]; and sun rays in the background.[64] The overall look, especially with the sun rays, was baroque. Equally important was the combination of religious and secular symbols of power, tied together by the nationalist symbol (the oak wreath) of unity and strength.

Inaugurated on 10 May 1881, the Crown of Romania was the second highest decoration Charles I offered. The symbology of this decoration was slightly, though significantly, different from that of the Star of Romania. Instead of the Orthodox/ Byzantine Cross, this one featured a Maltese Cross, closer to the heart of the devoutly Catholic Charles I. Instead of a Latin inscription, it featured a Romanian one, "*Prin noi înșine*" [Through ourselves], which had become a mantra of Romanian nationalism by 1881. With this decoration, Charles I established himself as *the* legitimate representative and even arbiter of the interests of independent Romania, as he was the person to decide to whom the decoration was to be given. The decoration also reflected his ability to successfully stand his ground as a non-Orthodox ruler in a land of deep Orthodox devotion.

Charles I's formidable partner in his endeavor to paint himself the legitimate representative of the Romanian state and nation was Queen Elisabeth (1843–1916), who took to being the first queen of Romania with great flair.[65] She coined her own decoration, the Elisabeth Cross, in October 1878, for women who served during the War of Independence in the medical field.[66] In the shape of an Orthodox cross, the medal featured the Romanian motto "Relief and Tenderness, 1877–78," an appropriately gender-specific text from a queen who wanted to celebrate women's contribution to public life by underlining their femininity. Elisabeth herself became the image at the center of the Sanitary Merit Cross coined in 1913, which was to be offered to medical personnel who had distinguished themselves during the cholera epidemic of the Second Balkan War.

In general, the Hohenzollern-Sigmaringens remained somewhat restrained in their use of public spectacle to celebrate their rule. Initially identified with the Declaration of Independence in 1877, 10 May became the national holiday, subsequently morphing into a celebration of the king's rule with parades, religious sermons, and the laying of wreaths at monuments that commemorated the War of Independence. These mild commemorative attempts offer a different picture than obtained in the lands south of the Danube.

In Bulgaria, 1877–1878 came to be viewed as a more important political moment.[67] A massive commemorative effort began to unfold in both Bulgaria and Serbia after the Balkan Wars of 1912–1913.[68] While for Romania these wars represented a minor reason for concern about their own borders and security, they were traumatic events for many civilians and soldiers stationed in Bulgaria, Serbia, and Macedonia.[69] The tense contest among Bulgaria, Serbia, Greece, and the Ottoman empire over territories and populations in Macedonia gave rise to both cruel treatment of people in those areas, as well as renaming places, mourning traumatic human losses, and erecting monuments on behalf of the victorious armies of all sides.[70] Thus, by 1914 two episodes of struggle to mark places of great violence and massive death had just ended south of the Danube. By contrast, in Romania milder commemorations on behalf of the War of Independence acted as more distant reminders of the heroic victory over a past enemy, rather than current threats.

In these commemorations, the participation of the public was still somewhat unimpressive. This was the age of the state trying to make itself visible to its subjects and impress average citizens with its military and political prowess, with the glitter of power and privilege.[71] This was indeed a new experience for most people living in the Romanian, Bulgarian, or Serbian states, as they had not been able to look up to any authority figure as a "beloved king" in the recent past. But most of these average subjects did not in fact view or become impressed with their king directly. The image of the king appeared in history books and surfaced in stories about the wars of independence.[72] But even that interaction was limited to a minority of the population, mostly urban inhabitants, as rural residents remained largely illiterate before World War I.[73]

Imperial Commemorative Legacies: Austria-Hungary and Russia

The second-largest portion of what became the Romanian state after World War I was part of the Habsburg empire (Transylvania, the Banat, and Bukovina) until 1918. The political and cultural legacies of this state were vastly different from those of newly established Romania. Since the early modern period the Habsburg emperor had worked continuously to maintain the claim that the title of Holy Roman Emperor represented a special relationship between the secular authority of the emperor and the Catholic Church. By the nineteenth century this claim had become merely cultural and to some extent political, in the new context of fashioning modern citizenship and state institutions, as Dan Unowsky successfully shows in a recent study.[74] A pressing issue for the Habsburg empire in the second half of the nineteenth century was its diminishing prestige among the Great Powers in Europe. Great Britain, Russia, and France all had made successful bids for imperial conquest or at least maintenance of interests outside Europe, while the Habsburgs found themselves becoming junior partners and unsuccessful competitors to the rising Prussian power to the north.

In addition to external strains felt especially starting in 1848, the Habsburgs had to contend with important internal tensions, especially the nationalism that threatened to pull the empire apart in 1848–1849. After pulling back from the brink of dissolution, partly with the help of the conservative Russian empire, the Habsburg empire underwent a thorough self-examination of its structure, identity (or, better said, multiple identities), and underlying ruling principles, and after almost two decades emerged transformed in 1867 as the Austro-Hungarian Dualist empire.[75]

The toughest problem proved to be nationalism, most importantly the well-articulated claims of the Hungarian Crown. The Hungarian lands (inclusive of Transylvania and the Banat) boasted large socioeconomic elites with high political aspirations of becoming either independent or at least full partners to their counterparts in the Austrian lands, and in full control of the people who lived within the lands of the Hungarian Crown. But the Croats, Poles, Czechs, Slovaks, Tyroleans, Ruthenians, Serbians, and Romanians also posed nationalist challenges to the existing structures of the empire and introduced new ideas of what loyalty to the state, as well as imperial and local community, meant. The rule of Francis Joseph (1848–1916) became dominated by practical concerns with retaining political stability and creating institutions to preserve the integrity of the state in the face of new nationalist challenges.

Francis Joseph also spent a great deal of effort in refashioning himself into a beloved emperor to all subjects. Under his rule, the Habsburg empire began to abound with festivals, ceremonies, anniversaries, and jubilees that both reinforced and challenged the unity of the state. Two avenues seemed to work best for the purposes of bringing most, if not all subjects of the emperor into the fold of loyalism—Catholicism and the army. Francis Joseph wished to retain legitimacy as a Catholic ruler among populations in Bohemia, Moravia, Galicia, Bukovina, Hungary, Transylvania, Slavonia, and Croatia. During his rule, Catholic religious holidays such as Corpus Christi were celebrated with great pomp, often featuring the presence of the emperor himself, not only in Vienna but even in more peripheral provinces such as Galicia.[76] Religious kitsch featuring the emperor became ubiquitous throughout empire, and it was apparently quite popular.[77]

But not all people living in the empire were Catholic. For Protestants, Orthodox Christians, and Jews, these festivals offered little reason for celebration or sentiments of loyalty. It should be said, however, that such events were not mandatory, nor was there any attempt to convert non-Catholics via such ceremonies. Still, from the perspective of these other religious believers, their sense of marginality was reinforced by Catholic cultural practices. A clearer statement of this marginality came through the second-class treatment of some religious denominations in terms of lack of state support for schools (or even official recognition of such schools as legitimate learning institutions), as well as the lack of support for the religious establishments themselves, some of which, especially Orthodox Christian and Jewish, were simply tolerated.[78]

Francis Joseph's fuzzy embrace of his subjects via Catholicism allowed people in the empire to craft various interpretations of this notion of Habsburg identity as primarily Catholic. Many didn't buy into it, and some overtly rejected it.

This rejection itself had local color. Jews were especially concerned about the tradition of Catholic anti-Semitism.[79] The Orthodox cared especially about the Magyarizing (both Protestant and Catholic) nationalist exclusivist legislation that was passed in Budapest after 1867 regarding the Hungarian Crown lands, which negatively affected Romanians, Ukrainians, and Serbs. For the Orthodox, Francis Joseph's Catholic rituals in Vienna seemed rather distant and less significant than changes undertaken in Budapest.[80]

By the same token, many Catholics used these rituals and events to simply build a non-Habsburg nationalist version of Catholicism. In Galicia in particular, a growing wave of Polish nationalism in the last few decades of the nineteenth century turned toward a combination of Romantic political visions of the Polish Commonwealth before the late-eighteenth century partitions and a more populist vision of Poland as a Catholic nation, the "Christ of nations," as the national poet Adam Mickiewicz (1798–1855) had dubbed it.[81] Pilgrimages to holy Catholic sites became popular during this period, some embracing the Viennese authorities, others completely separate and sometimes at odds with notions of loyalty to the empire. Ceremonies that gathered broad swaths of the population were sites for both constructing and contesting different versions of Catholicism and Polishness in relation to the Habsburg crown.[82] Hungarian and Bohemian/Czech Catholics also developed local, often nationalist inflections on their participation in mass Catholic celebrations.[83] The effectiveness of the Catholic festivals and rituals to preserve the unity of the empire seems to have been at best limited, as this unity was continuously both contested by non-Catholics and used for separatist nationalist purposes by Catholics themselves.[84]

Another important vehicle for constructing a sense of loyalty toward the emperor was military service, specifically army recruitment and parading the empire's multinational force.[85] The emperor himself sported a military uniform in most of his official appearances and spent a great deal of time visiting troops all over the empire. The strength of the Habsburg Army during this period might be questionable, as it didn't score any victories until 1878, when it peacefully occupied Bosnia-Herzegovina. But from a political and cultural point of view, the army became an important institution for bringing together different nationalities within a unified meritocracy. The extent to which this worked is again a matter of debate, as István Deák aptly shows in his important study on this topic.[86] An important site for building the prestige of the military was the public spectacle of the officers and troops, which Francis Joseph loved to display. Military parades were not a new feature of how the monarchy presented itself to the public. But they grew in frequency during this period, to the point that they became a central and even banal component of many public events, sometimes awe-inspiring and other times veering toward the ridiculous.[87]

In addition to these ritualized forms of popular mobilization in the name of the empire and commemorating the monarchy's strength, Francis Joseph was also interested in celebrating himself through statues, plaques, the renaming of squares and streets, and other spatial markers. These symbols were in line with the trend among Great Powers in Europe to mark the ruling dynasties as embodiments of civilization (by endowing art galleries, education institutions, and libraries with funds and placing their names atop such symbols), as well as progress (having the monarch's name or images pasted all over trains or train stations, à la Victoria Station in London). In that regard, Francis Joseph was just "keeping up with the Hohenzollerns." His efforts were more thoroughly spread throughout the land and in different areas of public activity than in the case of Romania for obvious reasons having to do with size, resources, and prestige.

With all these cultural practices on the rise, one would have expected that by 1914 Transylvania, the Banat, and Bukovina would have been dotted with symbols of Francis Joseph's rule. That was not the case. Transylvania and the Banat became part of Transleithania, the lands ruled by the Hungarian Crown from Budapest after 1867, and thus saw an increase of Hungarian symbols (for instance, monuments to the 1848–1849 Hungarian War of Independence, marking resistance against Habsburg rule that was tolerated with discomfort in Vienna).[88] The most important official holiday in Transleithania was 15 March, the day on which the Hungarians had declared independence from the Habsburgs in 1848.[89] This holiday did not sit as well with the Croats, Romanians, or Slovaks, who had seen their nationalist movements crushed in that same war, but they were powerless minorities. In Bukovina, still under direct control from Vienna until 1918 as part of Cisleithania, other local nationalist contests between Ruthenians/Ukrainians and Romanians colored the reaction to the imperial attempts to mark the region. Yet the emperor was less concerned with this peripheral area than with Galicia, a province closer, more populous, and also more active in terms of nationalist anti-Habsburg movements. Bukovina remained an imperial backwater, with few state resources going to the cultural imperial projects described above.[90]

The Habsburg provinces that came under Romanian rule after 1918 saw only faint echoes of the pomp and circumstance of Francis Joseph's rule. More regionally significant were the local inflections on these rituals, anniversaries, and markers, which seemed to take on an increasingly ethno-nationalist turn especially after 1867. Tensions between different nationalities living in the same areas marked these cultural practices, which became contested by 1914, and continued to do so during the war and afterward, when power relations between ethnic groups were inverted.[91] Such contests over public places and symbols should not be overstated, however. During this period there were also no wars or important military clashes that affected the local populations. A tense but peaceful life side by side and out of each other's way would be a more accurate depiction of how different ethnic and religious communities engaged with the politics of ritual mobilization and nationalist celebrations during the 1848–1914 period of the Habsburg empire.[92] In addition, the nationalist contestations described here involved mostly the educated populations of these nationalities, which were a minority (ranging from large in Bohemia to tiny in Bukovina).

And, most significantly for the background to what happened after 1918, there were no war memorials built during this period. A few commemorative ones recalled the 1848–1849 war along with cultural, political, and military individual figures from antiquity onward, but there were no recent moments of great collective mourning for mass deaths.[93] Francis Joseph's embarrassing loss to Bismarck in 1860 was not something the monarchy cared to commemorate through monuments, and the victory in Bosnia-Herzegovina had been a relatively peaceful turnover of power rather than a military victory, by contrast with the military gains Romania made in 1878.

The only important exception was the burial of Francis Joseph's wife, Empress Elisabeth (1837–1898), who was murdered in 1898. This offered the opportunity for staging an elaborate state funeral, and many people of all walks of life read or heard about it.[94] But this ritual remained focused on the loss for the dynasty and for the crown, rather than any broader abstract notion such as the nation or the vast community of all real or potential subjects of the empire. Commemorating the empire, the nation (among both minorities and Austrians alike), or ideals of independence and heroism through mourning did not become an integral part of the Austro-Hungarian empire's cultural practices until after 1914. In this regard, Romania between 1878 and 1914 had laid more groundwork in terms of commemorating the massive deaths that took place during 1914–1918.

Russia was the other imperial power that yielded some of its territory (Bessarabia) to Romania during the interwar period (1918–1940) and offered models for cultural practices surrounding death and mourning, most importantly because of its Orthodox Christian practices. In the late nineteenth century the Russian empire underwent its own struggle to maintain Great Power status in Europe, while nursing its colonial ambitions in the Near East and farther afield in Asia.[95] Even as the tsar, his advisers, and the emerging political elites were considering the geographic nature of Russianness—Western, Eastern, European, Eurasian, exceptional—few were questioning its cultural identity as Christian Orthodox.[96] Since the first bid of Catherine the Great to represent and protect Orthodox Christians in Europe in the eighteenth century, Russia had embraced this symbolic role, though with varying interpretations regarding its political, military, and religious commitments.[97] This self-understanding helped start the Crimean War in 1854 and the Russo-Turkish War of 1877–1878. Whether other Orthodox Christian populations welcomed this protection, as some Greeks did in the eighteenth century, or, like the Romanians in the 1830s and 1840s, did not, the self-image of the Russian empire was that Moscow was the Third Rome.[98] By the nineteenth century the Russian tsars saw themselves as the protectors of Orthodox people everywhere, since the Patriarch of Constantinople had ceased to play that role after the Ottoman victory in 1453.[99]

The Russian Orthodox Church paid perpetual tribute to the authority of the tsar through ritual references and visual markers. Every liturgy contained references to the tsar, to whom prayers and thanks were addressed alongside all the saints and leaders of the Church itself. Churches bore images of past tsars who had contributed to the building of these houses of worship as a permanent reminder of the alliance between caesar and the Orthodox Church. The extravagant ceremonies that comprised the funeral of Tsar Alexander III (1845–1894) offer, as Catherine Merridale argues, a revealing glimpse into the close identification of the tsar's authority with his image as divinely appointed and thus a protector of the Orthodox Church and flock.[100]

At the turn of the twentieth century, Tsar Nicholas II (1868–1918) and Tsarina Alexandra (1872–1918) proved staunch supporters of the Church, both of them given to great spectacles of religious piety and generosity. Nicholas II built his image similarly to Francis Joseph, through self-identification with the official religion of the state and militaristic rituals, spectacles, and military contests. Yet, unlike Francis Joseph, who ruled as a constitutional monarch after 1867, Nicholas II still professed to rule as a divinely appointed autocrat. The Orthodox Church and its spectacular rituals represented not just symbols, but the actual embodiment of this divine power.[101]

Like the Habsburgs, the Romanovs also saw internal contestations. In the case of Nicholas II, however, political non-nationalist challenges arising from dire poverty and from the radical left created the most pressing problems.[102] In his case, an attempt to show strength through military conquest in the East in 1904 against Japan brought about great disappointment and even embarrassment, against which parades had little relief to offer. The losses in that war could not be commemorated within the usual celebratory vocabulary of state rituals of the nineteenth century. Parents and close communities mourned their dead in traditional fashion, through Orthodox Christian rituals, but the practice of placing markers for these war dead was not taken up for a war that offered little occasion for pride.[103] Russia's internal problems could not be solved through symbolic actions and cultural rituals, as poverty and violence at the local level could not be overturned through symbolic acts. In their immediate communities people continued to use the cultural rituals that helped them deal with loss and death, but were not persuaded that these deaths were necessary sacrifices for a noble, greater cause.

All three contexts presented above—Habsburg, Russian, post-Ottoman—shared important general approaches to how states engaged in ceremonials of self-glorification vis-à-vis their citizens, approaches that appear clearer when contrasted with the better studied British and French cases. As Pierre Nora, Jay Winter, Eric Hobsbawm, and others have shown, the invention of national tradition was largely a success story in these western European states by the beginning of World War I.[104] The monarchies atop their governments went to great lengths to build up an impressive image of naked power alongside civilizing efforts, an image designed to awe their subjects. Scholars have held Victoria's endeavors as the most successful example of such spectacles of bread and circus in a modern nationalist idiom.[105]

These cultural practices on the part of state leaders have to be understood, however, alongside other important institutional and cultural contexts: subjecthood and citizenship had come to be identified quite closely with nationalist aspirations of states on behalf of these communities. In the case of France and Britain, imperial aspirations in the capital successfully engaged many average people far from Paris and London in fighting on behalf of their leaders and nation and shaping their daily lives in accordance with the consumer aspects of national/imperial authenticity.[106] To be sure, there was opposition to these aspirations as well, most prominently from anti-colonial movements on the periphery of the empires and from socialist groups in the metropole.[107] But with the exception of the internationalist wing of the socialists, these movements spoke within the same idiom of nationalism.

Nationalism had been so successful due to many factors, chief among them being educational institutions and cultural practices that had come to encompass most of the population, rich and poor, urban and rural.[108] By the beginning of World War I most people in western Europe were literate and had access to the mass media, which partook of a mostly nationalist flavor, whether favoring or opposing the government.[109] Military contests, whether defeats or victories, were successfully packaged in this new idiom as sites of national pride or humiliation, with much fanfare to accompany them. By 1914, while increasingly prosperous, the French and British publics had also become used to the militaristic nationalist mobilizing discourse uttered daily in the newspapers by both politicians and journalists.[110] Whether these discourses were the product of mass movements or political elites, they were popularly understood and accepted as legitimate. When people reacted to the war declaration in 1914 with spontaneous joy and well articulated forms of nationalist celebration en masse, it was proof of the extent to which nationalist ideas had become internalized as cultural daily practices.

People on the street recognized and knew how to engage in them as normal forms of communication, rather than government propaganda.[111]

This level of easy recognition and mobilization along the lines of nationalist cultural practices did not characterize the average subject in the Austro-Hungarian and Russian empires, or the post-Ottoman states.[112] Mass education and cultural enterprises by the state to "mark its territory" had been far more limited in size and less successful. Attempts by educated populations with political aspirations to construct a popular public culture along nationalist lines were limited in reach and resources, especially in places like Transylvania and Bessarabia.[113] The fall of the Habsburgs and Romanovs by the end of the war can be taken in part as a sign of this failure. But, even long before 1917, their limited success in the realm of cultural practices is clear to see. As Dan Unowsky, Steven Beller, Aviel Roshwald, and others have shown, the Habsburg imperial attempts to fashion a popular, legitimate type of nationalist-imperial discourse was ultimately unsuccessful.[114] In Russia, the work of the state to educate and modernize on behalf of the national idea also came too little, too late.

In the case of the Romanian state, the limited resources and difficult challenges of putting together a fully functioning modern state meant that Charles I had to make tough choices in terms of where to invest his efforts—political, military, economic, or cultural. Mass education was not among his chief achievements, and thus many of his subjects, especially the vast majority of illiterate peasants, remained untouched and unmoved by the spectacle of monarchical glory or military success (1877–1878 and 1913), as well as other modernizing projects (bridges, railroads, and large buildings in Bucharest). A similar disjuncture between the project of bringing their capitals and states up to "respectable" European standards and the general population's inability to recognize these markings characterized other newly minted post-Ottoman states in the Balkans.[115]

Popular Death Rituals and Gender Roles

To better understand how most average people dealt with loss in this period of growth of the state and of public culture, we need to return to the village. Death rituals in eastern Europe have a long history of complex cultural practices. Anthropological studies of tombs dating back to the ninth century AD at sites in Romania have uncovered both highly ritualized funerary practices, showing similarities to those identified with the late Roman empire, and also examples that are somewhat different. Cremation, in particular, seems to have been specific to these territories; Romanian historians were quick to identify it as a "Geto-Dacian" element of the local culture and thus proof of the continuity of that population on the territories where the Roman empire had briefly held control in the second century AD.[116]

These archeological findings are important in showing the presence of detailed customs, from the funerary stone to the disposal of the bodies and their placement inside the tombstone, all suggestive of an elaborate cult of the dead before the conversion to Christianity of the populations living in these areas. Most striking among these customs was the double burial of couples and sometimes their offspring. This custom seemed to be present among many Slavic populations and to affect women exclusively. Similar to the Hindu custom of widow-immolation, these double tombstones suggest that widows were viewed as worthless liabilities in life, more valuable as corpses next to their husbands. The sources cited by the authors describe these unnatural deaths as voluntary acts of women to follow their husbands. The authors never question the reliability of such conclusions in terms of gender assumptions about social customs and free will.[117] On the basis of more gender research and scholarship published since the 1970s, I would venture to speculate that such customs reflected, much as in Hindu society, a low level of respect for women's worth as individuals in the community, generally elevated through marriage and motherhood, and severely hampered through widowhood to the degree of approaching pariah or non-person status.[118]

These practices became more complex with the arrival of Christianity in the Middle Ages, but they continued to be shaped by local customs that seemed completely apart from the dogma of the Orthodox or Catholic churches. It is virtually impossible to speak in great detail about significant changes in death rituals over time, as there are no consistent sources across long periods, but we have a fairly good idea of what they looked like in the late nineteenth century.[119]

Eastern European rural cultural practices connected to dying have become legible to us through the work of ethnographers who, often in the spirit of nationalist fantasies, wished to uncover the authentic soul of their people in the countryside by watching and writing down what seemed fundamental spiritual practices linked to birth, marriage, and death. The descriptions of these rituals come to us mediated by eyes that viewed them with either exaltation at "discovering" the essence of the peasant élan vital, as did Vuk Karadžić (1787–1864) and Leo Tolstoy (1828–1910); or with fascinated consternation, à la Rebecca West (1892–1983) or Edith Durham (1863–1944). Still, their observations are the best window we have for reconstructing the cultural practices connected to death prevalent among the rural populations of eastern Europe.[120]

For the Romanian lands, a number of studies came out during the last few decades before World War I, rich in detail and broad in geographic and even demographic coverage, with the authors interested primarily but not exclusively in the Orthodox rural populations. From El. Sevastos's collection of travelogues by foreign observers (1888) to Vasile Alecsandri's collections of oral peasant folklore (1866) and a series of other collections or periodic publications such as *Șezătoarea* [The Gathering], a multitude of writers and budding ethnographers offered their own take on peasant culture.[121]

The most successful effort to synthesize these individual efforts was a three-volume work by Simion Florea Marian (1847–1907) on birth, marriage, and burial practices, published under the auspices of the Romanian Academy between 1890 and 1892.[122] Marian's work is remarkable in its conscious attempt to establish a transparent, well documented, and as far as possible comprehensive synthesis of all the studies others and he himself had undertaken in the nineteenth century. Virtually no other works of Romanian ethnography from that period make use of footnotes and critical references in the same way. His is a true model of modern professional social science scholarship, in contrast with the prevalent dilettante Romantic style preferred by many other ethnographers, including Westerners traveling through eastern Europe. Marian is not free from certain nationalist musings characteristic for that period, such as frequent characterizations of Roman burial practices as similar to those in Romanian Orthodox villages.[123] He is also quick to talk about commonalities between practices among the Romanians living in the Romanian state and those living in Transylvania, Bukovina, and Bessarabia, which at that time were not under Romanian rule, in a way that wishes to underscore the integrity of Romanian culture as a national cohesive unit. But Marian is also careful to point out local color and differences and to highlight both commonalities and differences among Orthodox, Catholic, and Jewish practices without implying superiority on the part of the Orthodox believers.

In reading these descriptions of death rituals, what most strikes the twenty-first-century reader is the level of detail and complexity in each gesture and symbol connected to various stages of dying, burial, mourning, and commemoration. The process of mourning and watching for signs of impending death started while the suffering person was ailing. The breaking of household items, the opening of doors, the meowing of cats, and other such signs seemed to point toward an imminent death, even when nobody was ill.[124]

Once an ill person arrived at a state of despondence, family members, close neighbors, and other friends would try to undo the evil that seemed to be visiting the ailing one through incantations, potions, or salves, such as garlic-infused oils, keeping guard over the sick one, and on occasion calling a priest to help along.[125] Though specific religious holidays would bear upon the choice of potions offered to the ailing person, and the priest might make an appearance, these rituals were constructed and sustained by lay people, specifically women. Their role would sometimes mimic that of the priest—for instance, the oiling of the dying person's body to protect it from evil/death.[126]

The description of the ritual offers only the possibility for speculating whether such mimicking had the role of substituting the priest's spiritual authority, or whether it was simple imitation. Last rites, after all, could only be administered by a priest: "If neither the incantations nor this means [a potion prepared by women from the root of a plant growing on the grave of a child, harvested on Good Friday] helped in any way, and if the ailing person is an older man or woman, for whom there is no getting better, they call the local priest for confession and last rites."[127] Yet the women in the community, especially family members, seemed to play a mediating role between the official religious authority of the priest on such matters and more traditional religious practices that engaged the lay community itself. It is also important to underscore that the priest, whose persona makes an occasional appearance, is the only non-kin/community authority to participate in these customs. Reading through the description of these rituals, one gets a sense of disconnectedness between rural communities and any state institutions.

Women's ritualistic role became even more prominent once the ailing person passed away. Washing the body was an important rite, after opening doors and windows and covering mirrors. The water and pot had to be clean, pure. The water had to come from a spring or well, rather than a pond, and the pot had to be new.[128] The cleansing of the body signified a cleansing of the soul of past sins, so that the dead person might properly arrive at heaven's gates. That lay people, and in particular women from the community, were those who had to undertake this task suggests that most believers had a broad view of authority and power when it came to religious ritual and spiritual matters. The priest was, to be sure, still an important figure, punctuating different stages of the process of laying to rest, interring, and watching over the peaceful passing of the deceased into the afterlife. But the community, especially women in the family, seemed to play an integral role, not simply as companions but also as guardians, knowledgeable and authoritative figures in matters of the peaceful laying to rest of the dead.

The complexity of burial rituals increased at the point of death. Some components were to be enacted by men and women together, but along gender lines. Pallbearers could be all men (for an adult male), all women (for an adult woman), or mixed (for a youth), with a preponderance of young women for a female, and the opposite for a male. While men had few exclusive tasks to fulfill—making the coffin and digging the grave[129]—most responsibilities fell specifically on women's shoulders. They did everything, from preparing the clothes for the dying person to gathering or making the food that was to be eaten and given away, gathering all the things that were to be given as alms, wailing, warding off the spirits at the gravesite, and carrying clean water in the village to help wash the sins of the departed.

Marian doesn't pay attention to the gender dimension of these rituals. He simply uses the grammatical form (pronoun or noun) that accurately describes the gender of those performing an action.[130] Thus, Marian might state that "they dress her same as a bride" [o gătesc ca pe o mireasă], making it impossible to discern without prior knowledge that it is women who are exclusively performing this task. Yet he also occasionally states that "as soon as they have bought them, several women who are present begin to cut and sew the necessary clothes and then dress the dead."[131] More recently, however, scholars have underscored the importance of these exclusive gender roles, and in particular women's work in enacting and preserving popular burial practices.[132]

The dead person had to be dressed in a particular way, in clothes that symbolized and reflected her or his identity and deeds—man or woman, young or old, married or single, rich or poor, saintly or sinner. Every detail, from the material used for the burial clothes to the thread used to sew that cloth, was carefully prescribed and essentially gendered. Women prepared this stage and watched over each other in the process. A young person was to be buried in clothes sewn with a thread that had not been knotted: "If a maiden dies, her shirt and the other clothes she is to wear *are to be sewn* with an unknotted thread, because if it is knotted, the belief is that the one [originally] destined to marry her will not be able to marry again."[133] The same held for the opposite sex, with clothes typically worn by a young lad.

Though the ethnographer makes no mention of this issue, one has to ask—who is to oversee this careful preparation of the clothing? Who are the clothes to be sewn by, if not the mother, sister, or other female relatives and friends of the deceased? In the countryside, where women were in charge of weaving and sewing, one can safely assume that they would have to sew such a dress or shirt and pants. I would venture to conclude that traditional rural communities entrusted women with the key (or needle) to releasing the dead from earth and ensuring future happiness for the living. Even during this early step in the burial rite, women performed the role of guardians of the dead spirits.

Another important role played exclusively by women was wailing for the departed:

> The wailers [would be] women, or girls, respectively, for tradition has established that only they can wail for the dead, and generally, the closest or further removed kin of the deceased, such as the mothers, wives, sisters, cousins, sisters-in-law, and goddaughters. If the dead doesn't have any close relatives who are well versed in the *art of wailing*, then some women from the village are hired to wail for him—those who made a profession of this and have gone on to become wailer, crier, or incense burner.[134]

There were different and specific wails for various stages in the mourning process, with lengthy and varied texts. One has to assume that such a skill would be passed down from one generation of women to another—learned orally from mother and mother-in-law by the next generation, as an integral component of their gender role in relation to the larger community. This is supported by the description above, which defined wailing as an art or even a profession.

It is not hard to imagine why only women were considered suitable for this role of displaying emotion, empathy, and distress. More significant is the fact that this was an important role in the funeral, punctuating each stage of the process of mourning like a chant, serving as both background to the viewing of the dead or the procession from the home to the cemetery, as well as cathartic moments of releasing pain and sadness. By contrast, the priest, though generally viewed as the spiritual and moral leader of the community, appeared only rarely in this complex set of rituals. His role seemed somewhat distant from that played by the family and community at large.[135] A comparative glance at other populations that combined popular rituals and Orthodox practices in their burial ceremonies shows that from Greece to Russia women tended to have a similarly prominent role at the local level.[136]

At a few crucial moments—the stages of the cross on the way to the church, the brief mass in church, and another brief mass in the cemetery—the priest sanctioned this elaborate process. Yet women had the most continuous presence, from preparing the body of the dead to preparing the meal to commemorate the deceased [parastas],[137] wailing, giving alms to the poor at the various stages of the cross and after the burial, revisiting the grave at established intervals to "watch over" the grave by burning incense over it, and in some cases making special incantations to keep the undead [strigoi] away from the dearly departed: "The oldest woman, or the most knowledgeable one, takes a knife in her right hand and goes around the grave three times, after which she places it in the ground by the cross at the deceased's head, making secret incantations, especially for the dead to walk only within the perimeter inscribed by the knife."[138]

How is one to interpret the relation described above between the patriarchal figure of the priest and the work done by women at the gravesite? Was it that the institutional authority of the priest conferred upon him a more central and important role in the ritual, despite his periodic and brief performance? Or was it that the presence of the community and especially of those who prepared and performed most of the rituals, albeit with a more subdued, even indirect role, counted as the most significant element of the ritual? In fact, both components are essential to the burial and commemorative rituals. Viewing burial practices as an amalgam of strictly religious (and exclusively masculine) practices and popular ones (almost exclusively feminine), such a position offers a more comprehensive view that challenges the assumed patriarchal authority of the priest and underscores the gendered qualities of the cult of the dead.

Another important aspect of women's role in remembering the dead pertains to the practice of patrilocality. During the period examined here, women tended to follow their husbands in terms of place of living.[139] Even in the case of urban marriages, it was more common for the young couple to move in with the husband's family, or for the wife to follow her husband. This was even more the case in rural settings. In Romania before 1932, when women gained the right to administer their property, this was true also for legal reasons: the husband controlled the wealth of the family, which usually resided in rights to land use and, after 1864, landownership.[140] Of course, these legal limitations both reflected and also helped construct a view of women's role in the family and more broadly in the rural world as secondary, lacking in power, and therefore cast in the role of "followers."

In practical terms, this meant that the young bride would often leave her village or neighborhood to follow her husband to his family's abode. As these young women moved to a new location, they were also assigned the role of learning the traditions and the family memory of their husband. They would learn to embroider in the style and with the patterns of their new village.[141] They would learn to bake and cook in the ways of their new family (that of their mother-in-law, usually). They might sometimes bring their own style and traditions to this task, but their obligation was to learn the traditions of their new community.

Most importantly for this study, young Orthodox Christian brides were to learn about their husbands' ancestors and to become the vectors of remembrance in their husbands' families. The Orthodox religious calendar has a large number of specific holidays on which some or all dead are to be remembered, and also a general practice of commemorating the dead on Saturday. On these days, during the liturgical services reserved specifically for such commemorative practices, lists of the dead were read and blessed through the priest's words, and thus brought back into memory, even while he prayed for their easy departure from earthly worries. In traditional practice, women were to keep these lists and write them out or utter them for the priest or another man, such as the deacon, more likely to be literate than the woman herself. Though married women could list their own birth kin among those to be remembered, they were charged with remembering the kin into which they married, their husbands' parents, godparents, grandparents, brothers and sisters, etc.

These learned lists represented an important component of becoming part of the kinship group into which women married and part of the village community that watched over the rituals. A woman's ability to appropriate what was not genealogically hers gave her status, enabling her acceptance by her in-laws. For married women, connecting with the collective remembrance of their husbands' dead ancestors represented an act of willful learning, rather than remembrance or traditions incorporated almost "by osmosis" as young children. They were, in effect, doing post-memory work, learning to identify emotionally with people and events they had not known personally, but were supposed to view as part of who they were inside their families. No men were asked to assume the same kind of memory work on behalf of their life partners. These gendered aspects of the cult of the dead and ancestor memory work are common to other Balkan societies, where patrilocality and the specific role of women in commemorating their families' dead ancestors were common.[142]

In other religious communities, even where the cult of the dead was strongly represented in religious practices, women played a less specific role as virtual carriers of the memory of the deceased. Among Catholics in eastern Europe, the role of the priest seems to have been more elaborate at the expense of the community, whose practices were more restricted by dogma and tradition. The cult of the dead was less elaborate and central to the religious rites of Protestants.[143] More similar to the Orthodox rituals of mourning and burial, as Marian himself observes, were Jewish practices, also gendered, but somewhat differently than Christian Orthodox ones. There are continuing debates over the actual rabbinical authority over women's traditional practices, such as covering all mirrors in the house of the dead or saying Kaddish. Yet there is no doubt that women participated in these actions and that the rituals connected to mourning in either public or private were segregated by gender to a great extent, with men playing the most prominent roles, while women also found ways to participate in gender-specific ways.[144] As mentioned above, women did play the role of mourners in Jewish communities, but this was restricted more clearly to the home. Men were exclusively in charge of performing most other tasks, both ritual and physical, of preparing the corpse and performing the burial ceremony.

These elaborate theatrical spectacles of the cult of the dead in small village communities contrast rather strongly with the spatial aspects of commemorations. While people spent a great deal of time and effort on specific actions, all carefully encoded with symbolic meanings meant to guide the soul of the dead and protect the community from the wrath of the undead, funerary markers were generally simple in shape and relatively unadorned. Class or socioeconomic standing and location did make a difference in terms of how people chose to mark the graves of their dead. In rural areas where Orthodox Christians lived, markers were made of wood, in the shape of a cross, bearing the name of the deceased and that person's dates of birth (if known) and death. Among Jewish populations, one finds exclusively stone funerary monuments, though it is known that wood was used at some point in the past. More frequently, one finds ornate wooden funerary memorials among Hungarian rural communities in Transylvania.

Occasionally, Orthodox markers would be accompanied by a small icon or have some engraving that bore local design styles. On occasion, such crosses would be larger and have a more complex shape, named *troika*.[145] These larger markers would often be placed by the road or at a crossroads where the person being commemorated had died. The choice of location represented an attempt to commemorate the deceased in the most public and evocative way for the local community, who would presumably be aware of that person's passing at the location of the marker.

Other markers were fountains or wells built in well-traveled public sites. A biblical verse, some epigraph, the name of the person, or some other evocative text might be placed by the fountain to remind users of the person being commemorated and encourage them to actively think of the deceased and thank him (rarely her) for the water. These memorial practices involving water were also part of a larger ensemble of beliefs about the purifying and life-giving symbolism and power of water, so that a fountain would represent a purification of the dead person's soul through the living who were using it, as well as an even more metaphysical concept, that dying was in fact life-affirming and life-giving. These markers were common especially in the areas of the Balkans under direct Ottoman control—Bulgaria, Macedonia, Serbia, and Albania. The building of wells and fountains as *waqf* practices had been a long standing tradition among Muslims, and it seems that the local Christian populations took to the tradition in their own modified fashion.[146] In general, public funerary markers were connected to the everyday use of a public space by the local inhabitants, rather than to the possible official significance of a space in institutional symbolic terms (for instance, the local school or offices of law enforcement, if they even existed). One exception to this was places of worship, which were indeed treated as institutions of authority in a strictly religious/spiritual sense.

Large markers were rare, as was the notion of building a marker outside the churchyard or consecrated cemetery, especially in the case of Jewish communities. Among other components of the cult of the dead, rural populations believed strongly in the notion that burying someone in the cemetery and placing a marker there was the only proper way both to allow the soul of that person to depart, and also to protect the living from the potential anger of those who had died. If placed in a cemetery or churchyard, the dead would stay put. If placed somewhere else, that soul might remain unsettled and come back to haunt the living.[147]

Exceptional funerary markers pertained to the death of people of elite social standing. Rulers and people of princely heritage wished to be buried with greater pomp and to create different, holier, and more permanent markers than the plebes. Much as in the rest of the Christian Europe, rulers and nobility in eastern Europe erected churches for such purposes, placing their likeness—in murals, sculptures, and written messages—inside these consecrated spaces, on their walls, ceilings, and sometimes floors.[148] They also built such churches to have a place where *they* would be buried, in the hope that such deeds would help them in the afterlife and ensure their memory would be kept alive. Marble or stone funerary stones adorn some of the most prominent churches in eastern Europe as a reminder of these noble, important lives. As in the rest of Europe, believers made pilgrimages to such tombs and churches as holy places.[149] But local, more modest practices seldom attempted to imitate the elaborate aesthetic of the elites. The awesome quality of the princely funerary markers was also an admonition, reinforcing the accepted taboo against comparing the death of humble Christians to the demise of elites.

The picture that emerges from the preceding pages is one of disconnect or juxtaposition of various rituals and elements of public commemorative culture. If this lack of connection seems frustrating, it might be because the picture doesn't fit well with the better-known narrative of states turning their subjects into active citizens (the "peasants into Frenchmen" narrative). But this lack of correspondence between the aims of the state and local cultural practices in matters of dying is an accurate representation of the situation in eastern Europe. The relationship that states and societies in eastern Europe had with death—mourning, burial, and commemoration—pertained in great measure to the precise location and religious beliefs of the predominant group living there. Rulers attempted to some extent to create a monarchical style of celebrating the successes (and sometimes commemorating the losses) of their rule through ceremonials. Yet these attempts to create national or imperial legitimate rituals connected to heroism and death were not particularly successful before 1918 in a broad sense, especially among the vast majority of the population, who lived far away from the urban places where such rituals were enacted. The reasons for this lack of correspondence can be found in the dizzying variety of local practices; the states' inability to devote the needed resources to do the work of nationalist imperial teaching, unlike, for instance, Britain during the same period; the youth and relative inexperience of some of the monarchies that had come to power just in the late nineteenth century (for instance, Romania and Bulgaria), with little to build upon from the recent effort to successfully legitimate themselves in a nationalist mode; and the strength of the existing religious practices that made a great deal more sense to the majority of people, living mostly in small communities, than any appeal to abstract concepts of nationalism and heroism. Equally important for my analysis are the gendered aspects of these commemorative rituals, which played a significant role after 1918 as well.

There were, of course, some changes in commemorative practices in response to state-driven initiatives, such as the responses of local communities to human losses and territorial gains in the Russo-Turkish War of 1877–1878 or the Balkan Wars of 1912–1913. These moments were commemorated in Romania, Serbia, and Bulgaria not only by the government but, most importantly, by local people raising money and placing markers without prodding from their capitals. These markers remained, however, relatively few and far between, and it is difficult to speak about a general new secularized vocabulary of nationalist mourning of the war dead, much less of cultural practices that combined existing beliefs and rituals with new nationalist symbols. The conceptualization of wartime suffering and victimization as heroic did not develop during this period; this shift happened only after World War I. How this change took place first at the local level and subsequently at the center is the subject of the next chapter.

With my heart filled with the tenderest gratitude,
I beg you to receive the expression of my most
profound appreciation for the immeasurable
good you did to me, by bringing back the
earthly remains of my unforgotten son, Lascăr
Luția. . . . Now I am happy, as I can always
go on pilgrimage to my precious grave.

—Teofila Luția (1922)[1]

MOURNING, BURYING, AND REMEMBERING THE WAR DEAD

How Communities Coped with the Memory of Wartime Violence, 1918–1940

The experience of total war between 1914 and 1918 was unmistakably life-altering for the populations of eastern Europe. The unprecedented magnitude of the front, the duration of the war, and the political outcomes confronted average people and elites with finding new means to cope with loss and make sense of death. These challenges became important battles for legitimating political regimes from 1918 to 1939. Just as importantly, the great human and material losses in the war dramatically transformed many small communities and innumerable individual lives. This chapter reconstructs the first attempts to deal with these losses at the local level, which is where the initial impact of coping with the dead in World War I took place.

By placing the story of these responses ahead of the discussion of how political elites attempted to capitalize on the massive deaths in World War I toward political ends, I want to accentuate the dialogical relationship between margins and the center in commemorative practices. My analysis questions the very centrality of what was happening in the capital, in large cities, and in the officially sanctioned commemorative practices linked to the war. Other historians, much like the cultural elites of the interwar period, have read the role of the government unproblematically as legitimate, rather than seeking legitimacy.[2] A closer look at what took place in the interwar period in rural and community-based commemorative practices reveals divergence and a fluid, two-way communication between official and vernacular practices, with the capital often playing the role of catching up to the quick commemorative initiatives that sprouted up elsewhere after the war. This decentered narrative then helps question the significance and specific meaning of nationalist cultural practices as viewed from the center, describing official commemorations more as reactive rather than *pro*active phenomena in relation to community-based and individual cultural practices. What nationalism and heroism came to mean in the twentieth century can only be understood in this unstable context, which underscores the relative and often secondary significance of central political/state institutions vis-à-vis more locally relevant practices and traditions. In this chapter and the next, I lay the groundwork for what it meant to communities and individuals to deal with the massive deaths and traumatic experiences of the war. In chapter 4, I turn to the institutionalized means of commemorating World War I.

The War in Eastern Europe

To understand the magnitude of the process of burying and mourning the dead, one has to first understand the nature of World War I in eastern Europe. In the United States and western Europe, the iconic symbol of the war is the trench in which soldiers lived, fought, rotted, and sometimes went mad. This static image, which many historians of Germany, France, and Britain have identified as quintessential for understanding the unprecedented nature and impact of World War I, is ill suited for understanding what happened to millions of soldiers from Vienna to Constantinople, in terms both of their experience and of the practices of burial and mourning when the casualties started to mount. The war in the East moved more unpredictably back and forth along thousands of miles. It was still a war of attrition of both lives and resources, but the wartime experiences of both soldiers and civilians were quite different from those on the western front.

The eastern European participants came into the war at different times, as early as the summer of 1914 and as late as June 1917 (Greece). Populations of different ethnic and linguistic groups fought side by side in the Habsburg and to some extent Russian empires. These soldiers sometimes found themselves facing enemy armies with which they shared more, culturally and linguistically, than with some soldiers in their own army. This was the case with Italians, Poles, Romanians, and Serbs in the Habsburg army. The front moved back and forth, and the Central and Allied powers moved through parts of Hungary, the Polish lands (under Habsburg, German, and Russian rule), Ukraine, Romania, Croatia, Serbia, Bulgaria, and Greece.

At its longest, the front stretched from the Baltic all the way down to the Adriatic, an area far larger than anything on the western front. Allies on both sides of the conflict also saw greater divergences among them on the ground than in the West. For instance, the Bulgarians were barely tolerated by their German allies; and there was a great deal of tension between the Romanians and Russians, one of the reasons for Romania's late entry (1916) into the war.

The number of troops involved in the conflict on the eastern front was around 33.03 million, compared to the roughly 32.7 million soldiers fighting in the West, including over four million Americans.[3] But the casualties in battle were much larger in the East. From the over nine million soldiers who died in the war, around six million perished in the East.[4] More significantly, from the point of view of understanding the devastation at the local level, the top four countries with the highest percentage of dead from among the men who served anywhere in Europe were all from the Balkans—Serbia (37 percent), Turkey (27 percent), Romania (26 percent), and Bulgaria (23 percent).[5] All these figures speak to the need to reconsider the existing narratives of the war in Europe and to integrate the eastern European experience more thoroughly and centrally in it. Yet the only well-known battle of the eastern front is the Allied disaster at Gallipoli.[6] We know much more about Verdun and the Somme; but, to give just one example, almost nobody outside Romania has heard of the Mărășești battle, which has mythical proportions in Romania's historiography and commemorative rites, in part because of the sheer size of the carnage, comparable to the Somme.[7]

The disparity between the narratives about the western and eastern fronts is more glaring when examining civilian experiences. The war was more destructive in the East than in the West: even before counting the Habsburg and Italian casualties, over six million civilians died in the East, while less than fifty thousand did in the West.[8] This suggests more strongly than any other statistic that World War I was a total conflict especially in the East. In France, Belgium, and Britain civilians, despite being deprived of many comforts and at times suffering complete destruction of their environment, by and large survived the war and were able to rebuild their living environment faster than communities in the East. The edge of Europe, in this regard, was also the heart of the devastation brought on by the war and truly needs to become the subject of more comparative attention by scholars interested in the history and memorializing of World War I in Europe.

A few other important differences shaped regional commemorative responses to the enormous numbers of war dead. Most of the soldiers who served in the East lived in small towns and villages, more so than in the West, where larger numbers among the men who served were urban dwellers. The largest civilian casualty counts in the East were, however, among urban dwellers. Some of the largest cities in eastern Europe were attacked early in the war (Bucharest), while others were heavily destroyed at the end of the war (Budapest). In addition, severe typhoid epidemics spread quickly in urban centers such as Iași in northern Romania, and many civilians perished due to the authorities' inability to control the spread of disease.[9] In the West, with the exception of Liege and a few other Belgian and French towns, the war left most of the urban landscape and especially the populations of urban centers alive and somewhat equipped to cope with the economic costs of the war.[10] At the end of the war most communities in the East had little, if any assistance from the state in trying to piece together their lives and bury their dead.

Another important difference has to be noted regarding civilians in the East. Switching gears to a wartime economy and taking full advantage of the available workforce was slower in the East than the West. The celebrated entry of women in factories and the service industries to serve their country was a reality in Britain, but didn't even become a dream in the Balkans.[11] Russia was one exception in the East, for women had become both better organized and more thoroughly integrated in the Russian workforce by 1914, and their employment trends continued during the war.[12]

Elsewhere in the East, women were largely asked to shoulder the difficulties of the war, such as caring for their families and looking after farms and businesses, without having much in the way of political or civil rights. In Romania, for instance, peasant women were by law obligated to manage (read "work") their husbands' land, but did not have the right to open bank accounts in their names or to use the profits of their work, unless they had written permission from their husbands to do so.[13] Mothers, wives, and daughters of those who were not independently wealthy (the vast majority of people in eastern Europe) made do during the war in dire straits, often unable to secure employment except as domestic servants.[14] Armies did a poor job of taking advantage of the interest shown by many women to volunteer as nurses, and hospitals

often suffered from understaffing.[15] Far from experiencing the economic empowerment of their counterparts in the West, most women who lived through the war on
the eastern front merely got by and experienced constant uncertainty. They greeted
the end of the war with relief.[16] This is an important aspect of World War I that has
also been insufficiently considered by historians of the women's movements in Europe
during the twentieth century.

The lack of thoughtfulness regarding women's wartime role and integration into
the workforce suggests in part why their participation in the war was subsequently not
considered historically significant and worth remembering.[17] Since women were not
regarded as legitimate partners in the war, their actions were not construed as heroic
and worthy of celebration either by most observers at the time or by historians and cultural producers after the war. Instead, their work of survival, imaginative, resourceful,
and courageous though it might have been, was generally discarded from any public
commemorations into the dustbin of official forgetting.

Burying the Dead

It is not difficult to realize why smaller communities, whether urban or rural, began to
deal with the memory of the dead before state authorities. The governments were still
in flux (in exile in Moldavia, in the case of Romania) while parents and spouses began
to search for ways of burying and commemorating their loved ones as soon as they
learned of their death. This process was itself tortuous and often riddled with uncertainty, because news about the war dead did not reach families in a timely or precise
way. With so many people illiterate, especially in the countryside where the bulk of the
fighting force came from, and with families having to flee from occupation, they had
a hard time keeping up with news about their loved ones in the army. Likewise, the
army had a difficult time connecting with families in exile or under occupation. This
gap in time between what happened on the front and the families' receiving the bad
news, compounded with the nature of the death, which was often violent and without
likelihood of retrieving the remains of the dead as integral corpses, also meant that
burials could not be performed according to traditional practices. Since the proper
burial of a loved one, as described in the previous chapter, was connected to specific
practices linked to the body itself, from washing to clothing, many families quickly
realized that they needed to find new ways of honoring tradition while dealing with
the brutal reality of the disappearance of the loved one far away from home, in lands
that were hard for the family to imagine, from France to Siberia.

Those who could not be buried properly, the tradition went, would remain
undead, unquiet, and could possibly come back to haunt the living.[18] For instance,

according to one belief among Orthodox Christians, "as long as the body is not buried, the soul of the dead wanders around the body and the home. Only when the body is buried can the soul move through the gateways to heaven or hell."[19] For deeply religious communities, the burial of the body only counted if properly performed, according to the rites observed by the family and community of the dead. If bones of the loved one remained strewn about a battlefield, many believed that his soul would remain restless, unable to find the gateways to depart from earth, and instead would haunt the world searching for its way back home. Such beliefs had deep roots in many villages; they kept communities embattled over the proper way to honor the dead and also lay them to rest. In general, on both sides of the war, among Orthodox Christians, as well as Jewish, Catholic, Protestant, or Muslim communities, the recovery of bodies was a great concern everywhere on the eastern front. With loved ones perishing in locations as far away as Siberia (for the Austro-Hungarians, for instance), or northern Germany (for Entente soldiers from the Balkans), families of all religious affiliations suffered at the thought of not being able to give proper burial to these soldiers.

Precedents for such problems in the modern period existed from the nineteenth century, especially the Russo-Turkish War of 1877–1878 in the case of Romania and the rest of the Balkans, and more recently the Balkan Wars. For communities that had seen fighting or large numbers of deaths, mothers and fathers, wives and daughters had already worked (sometimes with local philanthropic organizations or official bodies) to build monuments to the dead and to integrate the memorials into death commemorations traditionally observed in those communities, generally in connection with the calendar of saints and other religious holidays for the non-Christian populations.[20] But the number of unknown dead was much smaller in those wars than in World War I, and the front far more stable and limited in size, making it easier to find the bodies of the deceased and return them to their families.

The problem with World War I in the East was that the front kept moving more than in the West, where the static nature of trench warfare created a different problem of dealing with the dead. At Verdun and the Somme, with the front remaining in the same spot for months, give or take a few yards, giving proper burial was a matter of survival for the troops. Bodies had to be disposed of quickly and cleanly, so as not to contribute to the spread of communicable diseases.[21] Military cemeteries sprouted and then grew precipitously in these locations.[22] On the eastern front the battles were somewhat more dynamic, and the movement of troops took place over the dead bodies of the soldiers who had just perished in battle. Initial attempts to commemorate the dead were more furtive, especially when the casualties were those of a retreating army and thus more difficult to reconstitute after other armies and their dead had marked the same places. In addition, the Romanian army did not have clear policies in place with regard to this problem.

In some instances, especially where multiethnic and religious troops were fighting side by side, such as Protestant Hungarians next to Orthodox Romanians or Jewish Austrians, giving proper burial was next to impossible, because the appropriate religious authorities were unavailable to many soldiers. These repeated troubles created great morale problems among the troops, as evidenced by a story recounted by an Orthodox Christian Romanian officer of the Austro-Hungarian army at the end of the war:

> After the attack they proceeded with burying the bodies.
>
> On the terrain in front of us, from where we had retreated the previous day, there were over one hundred Romanian bodies left, largely leveled by the bullets of the Hungarian regiment, which was "protecting" our retreat, as they claimed.
>
> I remained a whole day with the victims of this massacre . . .
>
> After we all recited "God rest in peace," because the priest was partying [petrecea] far away from us, at the Hungarian General Quarters, out of nowhere came a few Russian soldiers and planted [on the communal grave] a large cross, on which teacher D . . . wrote in pencil "160 Romanian soldiers from Regiment no. 43"; but under order from Captain Gyárfás, he had to erase and write again in Hungarian and German: "Soldiers dead for the fatherland from the K.u.K. Rupprecht Gronprinz v. Bayern, no. 43 Regiment."[23]

This example, though likely an exaggeration framed by the author's own strong anti-Hungarian sentiments, shows the ways in which wartime experiences helped solidify walls between ethno-religious groups, rather than bringing about a broader solidarity of the soldiers all caught in the same terrible predicament.

This example also illustrates how not only the death of a soldier but his very burial helped render the story of his demise in a narrative of victimhood, rather than heroism. The retelling of the events refers to the battle as a "massacre," without naming the culprits (either the Entente or the leadership of the Central Powers) and focusing instead on the implicitly innocent (soldiers fighting with guns in their hands are generally not massacred, even when they die en masse, unless they were somehow tricked into taking the positions they had). The victimization of these dead soldiers is coded in ethno-nationalist terms, as the author recalls the order to erase their ethnic identity and to write down instead that they died for the "fatherland" in German. Finally, not being able to have a proper burial rendered those soldiers victims again, this time as human beings and Orthodox Christians in particular, who would thus be denied passage into the afterlife, despite their sacrifice.

After the end of the hostilities, communities began to gather the bones of those who had perished in the war. This was in part a locally based action, sometimes led by a religious or other local authority figure (a teacher or mayor) and generally supported by the families of those who had lost loved ones in the war. It was first and foremost at this level that the immediate emotional and ritual needs of those who lost dear ones in the war met in dialogue with representatives of the state. Crucial in this relationship was not so much the institutional role played by civilian authorities, but rather the closeness of these individuals to the community they were serving. Religious leaders, teachers, and mayors were there to assist the suffering families, rather than enforce any state-directed policies. In fact, these communities jealously guarded these findings as "their own," rather than belonging to the larger military establishment or the abstract nation. A memorandum signed by the local priest, the mayor, the teacher, the local policeman, and five war widows from the Orthodox Romanian village of Stoeneşti-Muscel emphatically stated, "We cannot accept for any reason whatsoever the wrong idea of taking these graves away from our village. On the contrary, keeping these bones among us [*printre noi*] constitutes the greatest pride for our community."[24] In this case, local officials tried to impose their own specific, locally based reason for noncompliance with a directive received from the central offices of the army in Bucharest, that the war dead would subsequently be placed in military cemeteries in order to be properly honored. That this group even wrote to the Bucharest officials reflects their desire to express their feelings and be heard, to dialogue with central authorities. But it is also clear that they were not ready to comply with the orders sent to them. In fact, this statement presents the dead as a permanent and almost living group in the community, to be kept not aside, in the care of the village, but rather among (in Romanian, the word literally means spread throughout, interspersed among) the living villagers.

It should be added that in many cases soldiers also assisted the work of locating and burying bodies (especially those of higher officers). On those occasions the funeral often turned into an extravagant public ritual, with religious, military, and government officials present and taking center stage in the events, at the expense of the families who were still mourning their loved ones.[25] But the central authorities did express in those moments some understanding for the localized commemorations underway, which sought to keep the memory of their dead close to home, rather than in a far-off cemetery.

If mothers, fathers, wives, and daughters could not retrieve the bodies of loved ones, they could at least honor them by retrieving bones of others who had died in the war. The first direct, palpable connection these communities had with the abstract notion of patriotism and the heroic brotherhood of self-sacrifice and military loyalty was thus through the bones of those killed in battle. Anonymous, maybe even mixed

Figure 2.1. Multidenominational cemetery for soldiers from the Romanian army in a rural area, 1920s. Photo courtesy of the National Military Museum.

with the enemy's, these bones were powerfully evocative for those who believed that honoring the dead meant first and foremost properly burying them.[26] In the Carpathian mountains, it became a tradition for the local population to begin their pilgrimages in search of bones as soon as snow first melted in the spring.[27] When battlefields or areas around a village were cleared, the local community sometimes took it upon itself to build a funerary monument or a cemetery for the soldiers.[28] Though military officials would often be called to inaugurate such commemorative sites, the tenor of the ritual was religious, and the intention was to properly tend to the dead through longstanding burial and commemorative traditions, and honor them in locally understood fashion.

In rare cases, families were able to find their own relatives and bury them in family plots in the local cemetery. When soldiers were identified by military officials in charge of recovering the war dead, their families were notified, and in some cases they received the body of the dead ones so they could bury them individually. These were exceptional situations, and the families, especially mothers of those who were recovered, openly expressed their gratitude at being able to properly bury their loved ones:

Figure 2.2. Men and women, parents and children help find bones of fallen soldiers in the village of Lerești-Muscel (1921). Figure from *Cultul eroilor noștri.*

> With my heart filled with the tenderest gratitude, I beg you to receive the expression of my most profound appreciation for the immeasurable good you did to me, by bringing back the earthly remains of my unforgotten son, Lascăr Luția, who died for the country . . . Without your help I wouldn't have been able to bring to life this dream, as I am a poor widow . . . Now I am happy, as I can always go on pilgrimage to my precious grave.[29]

This Romanian mother was thanking the Heroes Cult, an institution established in 1919 to oversee the commemoration of all war dead.[30] Though she acknowledged that her son died "for the country," Teofila Luția identified the grave as "*my* precious" one. To this mother, the memory of her son belonged first and foremost to her, and not his country. And though she expressed gratitude, one cannot sense much pride in the words of this mother. She depicted herself as a victim or at least a weak person ("poor widow"), rather than the proud parent of a soldier who fought for the fatherland, demanding recognition for his sacrifice.

Luția was indeed a "happy" case, while most other mothers were never able to properly mourn and bury their sons, seeking refuge sometimes in surrogate burials, such as the communal burial of mixed remains collected by locals from villages close to battlefields. If for Luția the thought of being able to visit her son's grave as often as she wished was the only source of comfort, one can only imagine the pain of a parent, child, or spouse at the thought of never being able to pray at the tombstone of a loved one who had died in the war.

Thus, coping with the dead often meant having to deal with the inability of fulfilling basic and well established traditions about burial and commemorating the dead. For most communities, the focus wasn't in finding wide recognition for the sacrifices of their loved ones in a nationalist idiom, as heroes who had fought for their country. Rather, these community-based and individual rituals revolved more directly around dealing with the pain of loss. Those with regular access to a priest/preacher/rabbi (people living in larger villages, wealthier communities, or cities) were able to find some solace in the presence of such religious representatives. But the regular life of religious communities was also disrupted by the war, so that people often had to make do without a priest, rabbi, or mufti, thus twice victimized, both in the loss of loved ones and in the inability to fulfill basic necessary rituals to lay these dead to rest.

Honoring the Dead

If families could not properly bury their loved ones, they could at least try to honor these lives properly, through rituals and markers. Here tradition played a strong role, and regional and religious differences had a great impact on the physical and performative components of commemorations. In addition to gathering the bones of the dead, families and larger communities also incorporated the remembrance of those who had perished in the war in the religious holidays linked to the remembrance of the dead.

The *parastas* was a first step in the process of remembering the dead among Orthodox Christians, and families held these commemorative funerary meals even in the absence of the funeral itself, beginning with the date when they learned of the death and continuing from then on to fulfill the calendar of commemorations indicated by Orthodox custom. These commemorative meals were also incorporated into the ritual of burying the bones of unknown soldiers in rural communities. By holding the traditional *parastas,* villagers were in fact trying to keep alive the memory of those whom they loved. Women played a central role in carrying out all elements of this ritual.[31] Since they had no knowledge of the food preferences of the unknown soldiers and did not have access to their belongings, women offered instead mementoes of their own dead soldiers, by feeding friends and strangers food that their own deceased had liked, and giving away some of their belongings.[32] This substitution also functioned as a powerful way of thinking of the dead soldiers as everyone's relatives. Parents could only hope, in the tradition of their religious upbringing, that someone somewhere else was washing the bones of their own child and giving them proper burial and honoring their memory. Of course, the limits of such empathy depended on the willingness of each community and family to step outside their own parochial loyalties—religious, regional, and national—and embrace those of other groups.

Remembering the war dead was also incorporated in other commemorative religious holidays: for Catholics All Saints' Day, for the Orthodox the "Moşi"[33] and every Saturday, as well as the Ascension (forty days after Easter), and for Jews Yom Kippur. The Sephardic community in Bucharest, through its New Life philanthropic organization, organized an annual commemoration of all "soldiers of Mosaic faith, dead in the 1916–1918 war, on the Romanian front."[34] But even here, though ecumenical with respect to religious divisions within the Jewish community itself, this service did draw a clear line between remembering those who fought *for* Romania and those who fought *against* it, as there had been many Jewish officers and soldiers in the armies of the Central Powers as well.

The war commemoration in the Bucharest Sephardic cemetery also included a memorial service at the grave of a father who died after learning that his only two sons had perished in the war.[35] This element added a more community-centered element to a ceremony with overwhelmingly political overtones, intended to bolster Jewish arguments for gaining citizenship in postwar Romania. By mourning the death of this man who had lost his sons in the war, the Sephardic community was mourning their own losses as parents, wives, children, of their loved ones. Though referring to the war dead as those who had sacrificed themselves for the country, these communities were also invested in simply mourning loved ones. Ultimately, these rituals focused on loss, rather than heroism and bravery. There was no explicit reference to specific ways Jews in Romania might have been victims during the war, but funerals such as this drew an arc between the loss of those who perished on the front and those who died as civilians in connection to these fallen soldiers.

Starting in 1920 the Romanian state initiated an official day for commemorating the dead, Heroes Day, which by decree was to be officiated on the Orthodox Christian holiday of the Ascension.[36] Yet local communities often pursued their own rituals apart from or in addition to the officially sanctioned ones. In fact, there were even some among the Orthodox population, those who refused to move to the new Gregorian calendar after 1918, who sometimes held their own commemorations on days that did not coincide to those of any other neighboring communities or the official one.[37] Especially in the first years after the end of the war, when families just wished to honor their dead in ways that were soothing and fit with existing religious traditions, the war dead were often incorporated into the larger community of all departed to be remembered by loved ones. In other words, even among those who welcomed new official commemorations, small communities often saw them as supplementary to existing rituals linked to the cult of the dead, rather than as days with greater symbolic weight in the public culture of each particular community.

The attitudes of Orthodox Romanians toward those who had died for Romania in the war but differed in religious affiliation ranged from benevolent tolerance to open animosity. Commemorations organized by Jewish communities were acknowledged in some publications, while ignored in others, but few Orthodox Romanians participated in such ceremonies.[38] In one rare case of commemorating Kiazim Abdulachim, a Muslim officer serving in the Romanian army who had died at Mărășești, the author of the piece ends with: "Even though we cannot pray for his soul, we can compensate for that through the admiration we will know how to show toward this hero."[39] If this statement represents an honest attempt at ecumenical generosity in terms of understanding sacrifice and heroism in the war in non-ethnic and non-religious nationalist terms, it also speaks to the limits of such ecumenism. The author, like other Orthodox believers, simply could not imagine a unitary comprehensive way to think about the war dead beyond religious identity. Religion remained a fundamental divisive element in imagining a national community of Romanian citizens.

Throughout the interwar period the Romanian government, at both regional and central levels, received numerous complaints from local authorities that people in their communities were not properly observing the officially designated Heroes Day. In Transylvania, Romanian police and mayors of multiethnic towns and villages complained that the Protestant communities (read "Hungarian and German") did not display the Romanian flag and toll their bells on this holiday, as they had been instructed.[40] Religious schools of the minorities would not give their students the day off, and so they would not be present at the parades and other commemorative celebrations for the war dead.[41] And government employees of denominations other than Orthodox were accused of "not respecting the national and religious legal holidays, but only their own."[42] In these actions (or inactions) of insubordination, the local officials saw rising signs of revisionism or anti-Romanian feelings.

This was not a strictly ethnic issue. In Moldavia, where there were patches of Catholic populations of Romanian ethnicity who had participated in the war on the side of the Entente, priests and local populations sent petitions to the Ministry of Education about having to take the day off on the Orthodox calendar day of the Ascension, but not being able to celebrate their own religious holidays in proper fashion. To these repeated pleas the ministry responded by undertaking an inquiry through local officials (all Orthodox Christians), who convinced the Bucharest offices that the Catholic priest was "attacking our state institutions, and undertaking propaganda to unite themselves with their Hungarian brothers."[43]

However, since Heroes Day fell on the Orthodox Christian religious holiday of Ascension, always a Thursday, it is entirely understandable why, regardless of any political overtones of such boycotts, a minority religious school wouldn't give students the day off.[44] What appeared as unpatriotic to the Romanian regime, with is own religiously and ethnically exclusivist vision of patriotism, was in fact a result of the strict cultural and religious limitations imposed by the government on this culturally diverse population. Hungarians might not have openly opposed the celebration of the Romanian war dead, but they also had no reason, according to their own longstanding religious practices as Catholics, Protestants, and Jews, to have the kind of religious ceremony dictated by the Romanian state on the Orthodox holiday of the Ascension.

It is also important to recall that these complaints regarded all religious groups, not just the Protestant and Catholic Hungarians who had not fought on the side of Romania during World War I. Ethnic Romanians of Catholic or Uniate rite, the Orthodox Christians who kept the old religious calendar, as well as Jews who had fought in the Romanian army during the war, all had different religious holidays, were part of communities with strong religious traditions separate from the official Orthodox Christian practice, and often wanted only to be acknowledged as part of the larger civic whole of the nation without having to give up their religious identities. In other words, they were open to a dialogue with the officials. But the selection of the date of this Orthodox Christian religious holiday for Heroes Day and the top-down directives mandating how to commemorate it made such coexistence of religiously inflected civic nationalism with religious diversity difficult to bring into being. (Chapter 4 presents more information on this topic.) Many opted to preserve their religious particularities rather than go along with the newly decreed official holiday, at least in the 1920s.

Memorials

Though the first efforts of recovering the dead had been most importantly about laying them to rest with other dead ancestors in the community, over time local communities decided by and large to mark these deaths through separate funerary monuments. These monument impulses might have been a reaction to the monument mania developing in other places (large cities and other countries that had participated in the war), especially since periodicals took to publishing news about commemorations elsewhere (from Bulgaria to France) in connection to their own as well as Romanian soldiers.[45] The military itself, through orders sent to all garrisons and active personnel throughout the territory of Romania, served as propaganda activists for such endeavors.[46] In other words, state authorities were not entirely absent from this local process, though they were not the motor behind local initiatives.

Figure 2.3. World War I
monument in rural area
(1920s). Photo courtesy
of the National Military
Museum.

Whatever the reason, in the first decade after the war over one thousand monuments sprouted on the territory of Greater Romania, undertaken by local communities independent of state institutions and overwhelmingly locally financed.[47] Most monuments were erected in villages and small towns, and the connection between the committees building and financing them, on the one hand, and those who were mourned/represented in the monument, on the other hand, was family or community based. These monuments did not commemorate some unknown great patriotic soldier or the fatherland. Those being remembered were local boys and men, their names often prominently displayed alongside standard lines about the patriotic fight they had been part of (see figure 2.3).

Listing individual soldiers' names became a typical occurrence, both in small villages, where the entire community knew the individuals identified on the monuments, and in cities, where the names would have been known only to a small part of those who regularly viewed the monument. Other historians, most prominently Daniel

Sherman and Thomas Laqueur, have identified this practice of listing names with the democratization of culture in the West and with the unprecedented number of dead in World War I.[48] In Romania, however, displaying the names of the dead soldiers has to be viewed in the context of the long-term burial rituals and politics of the communities who built the monuments. Among Orthodox Christians, the concept of keeping alive the memory of dead ancestors was closely tied to uttering their names out loud and making them publicly known, according to Orthodox traditions described in chapter 1. Engraving in stone the names of all the dead to be commemorated became an extension of the traditional lists kept by women in the community, now appropriated by the entire community in the process both of building the monument and of having it frequently viewed as part of a public space.

Catholic and Jewish communities also built monuments that prominently listed all the dead who were commemorated by that monument. For those communities, the monuments were generally located in their own religious cemeteries or close to places of worship, but did not mark actual graves. These names stood as markers for bodies that were not recovered. They also likely stood as symbols of loyalty of the dead to their own community, whether that community had fought on the side of the Allies or of the Central Powers. And in the case of the Jewish communities in Romania, these names became valuable political tools for a category of subjects who were struggling to gain full citizen rights by virtue of having fought bravely for the Romanian state.[49]

These local actions underscored the diversity of the population and wartime experience in Greater Romania in many ways. Some monuments prominently featured Christian Orthodox religious symbols (for instance, the troika), while others offered symbols more closely linked to Catholic commemorative traditions. Jewish communities placed plaques for the dead inside Jewish cemeteries, thereby circumscribing the publicness of these monuments, which were open to the wide public only on special occasions when non-Jews were invited to attend the commemorations. Sometimes these monuments prominently featured the Star of David (see figure 2.1).[50]

While these differences might only reflect divergent religious traditions and rituals, particularly with regard to the cult of the dead, other choices of locale and symbols underscored more directly antagonistic struggles over public spaces. Some ethnic communities, especially in multiethnic Transylvania, believed that their dead were entitled to a privileged space, while the dead of others were not welcomed alongside them. Transylvania's war dead were particularly tricky to commemorate communally, for some of the soldiers from the same town had fought on opposing sides. In particular, some ethnic Romanians had volunteered in the Romanian army. Though traitors in the eyes of the Habsburg army and Hungarian neighbors, ethnic Romanian communities considered these men true patriots.[51]

The overall question for communities where bodies from both sides were recovered was how to properly honor one's *own* dead. To separate them from the rest was in many ways impossible. Not to honor those of the opposite army also contravened the spirit of paying respect to the sacrifice of all soldiers. All the armies had already agreed to the international convention of burying the soldiers of enemy armies with the same respect as their own.[52] How individual communities responded to this conundrum was locally contingent and depended a great deal on interethnic relations in that locale before the war; the behavior of the different ethnic groups during the war; and how and where the local war dead had been recovered. Two contrasting examples illustrate the great differences in local choices about such monuments.

Sinaia is a mountain town in Walachia that saw a lot of action during World War I and was occupied by the Central Powers for part of the war. In Sinaia itself and in the surrounding villages and towns there are several points of interest regarding the war. To begin with, the Peleş Castle, where the German-born Charles I spent his summers, was where the king first decided to declare neutrality shortly before his death in 1914 and where, in the summer of 1916, his nephew and successor, King Ferdinand, finally decided to enter the war. The castle itself was thus a memorial to Romania's entry into the war, though it did not open to the public until after World War II. In the early 1920s several military cemeteries were built by the local communities in neighboring villages, such as Azuga. There the population was overwhelmingly ethnically Romanian and Orthodox Christian, and the locals, often led by the Orthodox priest or teacher, went on campaigns to gather the bones of the war dead, presumed to be Romanian.[53]

The most prominent war cemetery was built in the center of Sinaia, on the main route from the stylish Casino Royale (the cemetery is right across from it) to the Sinaia monastery and the Peleş Castle. Virtually anyone who wished to reach those destinations or to go farther up into the mountains for hiking or skiing had to walk, ride, or drive by the cemetery. The cemetery's most remarkable feature is its prominent display of various funerary stones, clearly identified by religious and ethnic affiliation. The Romanian war dead are in the center of the cemetery, identified with Orthodox crosses. The Maltese Catholic crosses of the German soldiers, with funerary inscriptions in gothic script, are also prominent. Plain (read "Protestant") funerary stones with Hungarian names are placed in the vicinity of the Germans. There are no markers for Jewish war dead, perhaps because none are buried in this cemetery, perhaps because of ignorance.

This cemetery went up without any great debates and was always well tended by local people and visitors. This might have been because it was close to the royal residence, which commanded great respect by the locals with regard to properly honoring all the war dead, especially since the first king of Romania had been German himself;

Figure 2.4. The Sinaia World War I Military Cemetery today. Photo Maria Bucur.

or it might be that the local community, almost exclusively ethnically Romanian, didn't feel personally invested in feelings of revenge vis-à-vis their Hungarian neighbors. The stones of the non-Romanian dead have not been replaced and are in poorer shape than the Romanian ones, some of which have been replaced over the years. But there are no signs of desecration of any of the Hungarian and German stones. This represents an ecumenical acceptance of the sacrifices of all soldiers in the war, regardless of their ethnicity, their religion, and the side on which they fought.

A contrasting example can be found in the town of Odorhei/Székelyudvarhely in the heart of the overwhelmingly Hungarian-inhabited part of Transylvania, where the dominant attitude was ethnic enmity along with an exclusivist understanding of whose sacrifices in the war were to be honored.[54] The city was dominated by Hungarian inhabitants (Szeklers) and the population in the city and surrounding areas had fought in the war on the side of the Habsburgs. Yet in the 1930s the local Romanian population wanted to erect a monument to King Ferdinand (he had died in 1928) in the center of town, to commemorate Romania's victory in the war and the sacrifice of many Romanians. Located in the main square, the monument would be maximally visible to the overwhelmingly Hungarian population, who had little faith in the authorities in Bucharest and had no fond memories of the king who had taken Transylvania away from Hungary and placed it under Romanian rule. In addition, the local planning committee wanted to place it in exactly the same spot where a millennium monument put up by the Hungarian authorities in 1896 stood. In other words, the Romanians wished their monument to literally erase a nationalist Hungarian symbol. Arguing for the legitimacy of such a monument, the committee described Odorhei as a city where "the yoke of centuries has left painful traces, through the Szekler-ization of all that had been Romanian on these ancestral territories [of ours]."[55]

In this area of multiethnic tensions, the war dead didn't speak to universal ideals of heroism and sacrifice, and ethnic communities did not extend their feelings of pain and loss empathetically toward their neighbors of other ethnicities. Revenge, rather than reconciliation, dominated some of these local commemorations. Nationalism became a point of mobilization in some places, depending on local historical particularities. This was the case for some Romanian communities in Transylvania, who recalled having been treated as second class citizens by the Hungarian authorities and had little desire to share their newly gained power with their Hungarian neighbors.[56]

Such feelings of revenge and entitlement were etched on many war monuments constructed by Romanian communities in rural areas of Transylvania during the interwar period. To a traveler from another region of Romania, the dates of the war on the funerary commemorative monuments in Transylvania often appear confusing. One sees 1914–1919 as the starting and ending dates (see figure 2.3). Yet to a Romanian from Walachia or Moldavia (and for most outsiders), Romania was in the war between 1916 and 1918. Not so for those who lived in Transylvania, which was embroiled in the war starting in 1914. But why 1919? For many communities in Transylvania this year marked the "true" end of the war, for they included not just the end of the hostilities in the Romanian territories, but also the campaign of the Romanian armies to defeat the Béla Kun regime in Budapest, in which many of the Romanian Transylvanians served and where significant numbers died. Only the most ultra-nationalist of the Romanians in the interwar government defined 1919 and the occupation (in Romanian nationalist parlance, the "liberation") of Budapest as the end of the war.[57] The 1919 date on these monuments was a reminder to Hungarian ethnics ("remember 1919"), along with marking the deaths of ethnically Romanian soldiers who served in World War I. Conversely, some of the local ethnic minorities wished to commemorate the deaths of their co-nationals who died after the November 1918 armistice alongside the rest of the soldiers who had fallen during the war.

Not all Romanian monuments and war cemeteries in Transylvania gave 1919 as the ending date of the war, which suggests that the meaning of the deaths of those who fought in it was locally contingent. Many Romanian communities did not wish to rake through the embers of the past and reignite conflicts, for they might have not experienced extreme anti-Romanian behavior, or didn't wish to continue the vicious cycle of enmity. It is close to impossible to identify the causes of such differences exactly, as in most cases no documents about the specific dates of the monuments remain, and the local population didn't speak overtly about interethnic relations. Only on rare

Michael Retter geb.1865
Karl Leonhardt, Mjr. " 1868
Karl Richter " 1869
Gottfried Roth " 1875
Martin Löw " 1879
Georg Welther " 1880
Johann Klusch " 1881
Undr. Wachsmann " 1883
Adolf Ungar " 1885
Julius Dietrich " 1885
Friedrich Girscht " 1885
Johann Thal " 1886
Martin Helwig " 1886
Johann Helwig " 1887
Karl Mattes " 1888

Sei getreu
bis in den Tod, so will ich
dir die Krone des Lebens geben

Den sächsischen Söhnen der Gemeinde
Birthälm die, ihrer Pflicht gehorchend, im
Weltkriege 1914-1918 starben in verehrungs-
voller Erinnerung gewidmet von den Glau-
bens- und Volksgenossen in der Heimat und
in Amerika.

Johann Schuster geb.1889
Andreas Horwath " 1889
Hans Maurer, Jnr. " 1890
Wilhelm Schuster " 1890
Martin Kloos " 1892
Friedrich Helwig " 1892
Karl Schuster " 1894
Johann Weinrich " 1895
Andreas Fleischer " 1895
Michael Kreftel " 1895
Karl Ungar " 1896
Joh. Landenberger " 1896
Edgar Kenst, Obit. " 1896
Johann Cremezi " 1898
Georg Krampf " 1883

Figure 2.5. War Memorial inside the Biertan German Lutheran church. Photo Maria Bucur.

prin WEIL RUDOLF által

Ezen emléktáblát a gyülekezet közadakozásából a hitközség 100a chewra-kadisa 71
e nőegylet 50 és a templom 25 éves fennállásának emlékére emeltetett.
1526 — 1926

על אלה אנחנו בוכים על בני קהלתנו חיקרים אבות על בנים
שנמלו ומתו במלחמת העולמית בשנים תרע'ד-תרע'ט לפ'ק תנצב'ה

IN MEMORIAM 1914 – 1918.

JAKAB JENŐ főhgy.	מוהר' יעקב בן ר' אברהם
GÉZA GÉZA hdgy.	ר' אהרן בן ר' בצלאל
KALMÁR JENŐ hdgy.	חב' יוסף בן ר' יצחק
MOSKOVITS IZSÓ hdgy.	מוהר' יצחק בן מוהר' אלי'עזר
ELEKES ERNŐ zls.	חב' אפרים בן ר' אהרן
INDIG ERNŐ zls.	חב' אברהם דוב בן ר' שמחה יהודה
MÉTH VILMOS örm.	ר' זאב בן ר' נחום
GOLDMANN ADOLF tizds.	חב' אברהם בן ר' אלכסנדר
GROSZ MANÓ klgny.	ר' מנחם בן ר' צבי מרדכי הלוי
RÓNA JÁNOS klgny.	חב' יוחנן בן ר' זעליג אשר
DEUTSCH BERNÁT klgny.	ר' דוב בן ר' יחיאל
BLAU SÁNDOR klgny.	חב' שמעיה בן ר' אברהם
UNGER ARTHUR zls.	חב' אברהם בן ר' משה

* — — — * ~ ~ ~ — — *

ÎN MEMORIA

MILIOANELOR DE BĂRBAȚI, FEMEI ȘI COPII SCHINGIUITI
ȘI UCIȘI ÎN EUROPA SECOLULUI XX PENTRU UNICA "VINA" DE A
FI FOST EVREI

AL KIDUȘ HAȘEM

לזכר מליוני היהודים. אנשים.נשים.
זקנים וטף. שעונו ונהרגו בזמן השואה
על קידוש השם

Figure 2.6. War Memorial inside Brașov synagogue. Photo Maria Bucur.

occasions of great animosity, as in the case of Odorhei, were nationalist antagonisms articulated so virulently through locally built and funded monuments.

Even for the populations who had been defeated in the war (Hungarians and Germans, as well as the Jewish populations from the Habsburg Empire who now lived on Romanian-controlled soil), the proper burial and commemoration of their war dead was possible. During the war, the Habsburg Empire worked to repatriate the bodies of those who had died in battle or in prisoner of war camps on foreign soil.[58] After the war this process continued mostly through international Red Cross support. In addition, the Protestant, Catholic, and Jewish communities in Transylvania (almost all of whom were not ethnic Romanians) wished to properly honor their dead, even when the bodies were not recovered. These efforts were more elaborate among Catholic and Jewish communities, who had a stronger cult of the dead in their religious rites than did Protestants. But Protestant communities also commemorated their war dead, possibly for nationalist reasons, since most Protestants in Transylvania were Hungarians, whose war dead were often not incorporated in Romanian-built monuments.[59]

These monuments frequently took emphatically religious symbology and were integrated in religious spaces (churches, synagogues, or cemeteries), where those who were not part of that particular religious denomination would seldom have reason or even permission to enter. These commemorative monuments thus served the purpose of properly honoring the dead for the members of that religious community. At the same time they remained invisible to the larger community and were only marginally (if at all) integrated into any civic commemorations. Though the intention was to protect the monuments from possible desecration by outsiders, the result was that the memory of these war dead remained marginalized, restricted to the ethnic and religious community to which the dead belonged. The heroism and sacrifice of those soldiers could only be remembered as tragic, failed (for the Central Powers lost the war and the Hungarians their rule in Transylvania), and ultimately a trauma not to be overcome but rather nourished by virtue of this marginalization of the memory of these sacrifices. (See figures 2.5 and 2.6.)

The spatial settings of the monuments also revealed important differences of meaning adhering to war monuments built by different communities. In small villages, memorials to World War I were often the first public markers to be other than strictly religious. Though often small in size, war monuments stood out not because of their monumentality, but because of their uniqueness. Their placement, often in the center of the village, also guaranteed that locals would pass by the monument frequently, and that even those who were passing through could spot them easily. Cultural critics of the interwar period and more recently historians have that claimed these monuments lacked monumentality, prominence, and grace.[60] Such judgments reflect a normative view of the aesthetics of memorial markers that does not take into account the crucial aspects of the physical space and cultural traditions present in the communities building these monuments. Such critics did not comprehend, much less fully appreciate, the local contingencies that endowed the markers with their full significance.

In urban settings, especially in cities, war monuments had to compete with many other preexisting markers that were monumental and already fully integrated in the visual and mental landscape of the inhabitants. Thus, for inhabitants of Odorhei, whether Romanians or Hungarians, the Hungarian millennium monument was a mark etched indelibly in local inhabitants' image of the city. The Romanians' attempt to replace it with the Ferdinand monument was premised on this familiarity and the strongly nationalist significations of the place.

In other cities, especially where there weren't the same sort of vengeful struggles over representing the war, committees tried to find places that were visible but that did not have some previous association with another historical event. Thus, it was quite difficult to think of a suitable place for a monument to World War I in Bucharest. The Triumphal Arch built in 1938 was located in a sparsely populated area, which had become a fashionable weekend boulevard in the previous decades. The location allowed the arch to be fully visible in a broad opening from close up and far away, giving it an impressive, monumental quality. Similarly, the Monument to the Sanitary Heroes, built on the shore of the Dîmbovița River, was placed in a recently developed fashionable quarter close to Queen Marie's Cotroceni Palace, the Law School, and the Medical School. The Tomb of the Unknown Soldier was erected in a park that was becoming fashionable in the interwar period, after having served as the grounds for a large exhibition a few years before the war. These monuments were not built in the central pedestrian areas in Bucharest, as those spaces were already crowded with monuments dating from before World War I.

The unavailability of suitable commemorative spaces was even more evident in old cities, such as Brașov or Cluj, where the urban landscape was already heavily populated by many prominent public monuments erected in the previous centuries. In Cluj, the heroes' monument and cemetery were located on a hill that at that time was outside the city. That remote location meant that the monument was not a prominent visual reminder of the war. It remained more marginal to the majority of the inhabitants of the city than a much smaller monument in a neighboring village would have been.

It is hard to imagine what war violence meant for the population of Romania as a whole in the interwar period, especially with this fragmented picture in mind. Though inscriptions honoring "the sacrifice of the sons to the fatherland" could be seen in many places and among all religious and ethnic denominations, they were not reflections of some unified or even consistent identification with a centrally driven sense of nationalism. It is uncontestable that many inhabitants had their own version of "patriotism" or "nationalism," and the war, with its tremendous carnage and the radical border changes it brought in this area, strengthened some of these sentiments. But abstract notions of fighting for the good of the country, for the nation, occupied a lesser place in the minds of the parents, wives, and children who were burying and trying to honor their war dead in the 1920s and 1930s than visceral emotions of pain and sorrow, and sometimes even revenge, writ local. Thus, the processes of building funerary/commemorative monuments and remembering their dead were initially much more closely connected with these local needs than with the agenda of the state to legitimate its rule by memorializing the sacrifices of its soldiers during the war. These monuments and commemorations were quite possibly multifunctional and cannot be understood as simple markers of nationalist victory in the war. Heroism was seldom represented on these markers by martial symbols that would connect the soldiers to battle. More often, traditional religious vocabulary of loss and suffering was used to commemorate the dead.

The loss of millions of men in battle had similar transformative effects in other eastern European societies. In Yugoslavia, losses in World War I were a continuation, albeit on a much greater scale, of the conflicts in which Serbia had fought since 1912. In fact, most monuments built after 1918 grouped the war dead in a 1912–1918 periodization of the three Balkan Wars.[61] As in Romania, women were the primary caretakers of mourning and remembrance rituals in the countryside. And similarly to Romania, the ethno-religious differences of the varied populations of Yugoslavia became reflected in the way traditional mourning and commemorative rituals were incorporated (Serbian-Orthodox) or omitted (Croat and Slovene Catholic, Bosnian Muslim, and Jewish) in national commemorations.

In Poland, where soldiers also fought on both sides of the war, and where the war lasted until 1918 in some places and until 1921 in others, burial, mourning, and commemorations also varied from place to place. Here, however, Catholic religious rituals, together with revived political ones from the pre-partition period, played a prominent role in how local communities remembered the war dead. Those placed at a disadvantage by these rituals were Jews, Orthodox and Uniate Ukrainians, and Protestant Germans. In Poland, who was to be commemorated as war heroes (and implicitly who would *not*) had wide implications for the ideological future of the state. Were Poles to celebrate those who had fought on the side of the Germans as the socialist Józef Piłsudski had done, or on the side of the Russians as the right-wing nationalist Roman Dmowski favored? Though Piłsudski became a venerated figure, veterans and families of war dead who had not been part of the Polish Legion found themselves often marginalized in public commemorative events.[62] Therefore, one can speak of divergence and fragmented narratives about sacrifice in the war in a traditional vocabulary of loss and mourning in many other places in eastern Europe, not just in Romania.

The vernacular processes to bury, mourn, and remember the dead in the war emerged in the territories that became Greater Romania in 1919 as soon as the conflict ended. There was little that unified them, other than overwhelming sentiments of loss and pain. Initially, the work of finding the dead and burying them acted to unify local communities in common endeavors. Few, however, reached beyond their own villages, for instance, to help others, especially across ethnic and religious lines. As time passed, some communities and participants, predominantly the Orthodox Romanians, had greater opportunities to represent their own dead as emblematic for wartime heroism and most worthy of being remembered. But this did not stop other communities of non-Orthodox Romanians, as well as those who were not ethnic Romanians, from constructing their own commemorative endeavors and monuments. In these localized initiatives, families and communities followed their own traditions and only occasionally worked together with official commemorations. Even in cases when they did, the reasons for the local efforts were often not linked to the agenda of the state, but remained bound to their own local context, even in terms of ethno-nationalist contests.

The following chapter continues an analysis of such endeavors, focusing on individual forms of remembrance through literary autobiographical texts. The marginalization of narratives by non-ethnic Romanians in the literary arena is an important part of my focus. My analysis also underscores the divergent ways in which gendered assumptions about courage, heroism, and self-sacrifice lent themselves to a contest over what counted as publicly significant and memorable (i.e., worthy of remembrance) among the multitude of wartime experiences recounted in the interwar period.

All this humiliation . . . you witnessed with your own eyes. Of course for you
this spectacle remains a great, indescribable pain. . . . You did well to bring to
light all that you saw. Others should do the same. . . . Our Calvary will not be
fully told if we don't also know these horrors. . . . When all is known, the virtues
of our people who produced today's Romania will appear even more brilliant.

—Take Ionescu (1921)[1]

If I dare bring to light my modest war Journal after so much time,
it is because I kept waiting for others more capable than me, more
competent at writing, to speak and remember those who fulfilled their
duty under the folds of the holy Flag of the Red Cross, raised here
by the greatest and dignified Queen of our days. I waited, I searched,
but I did not find more than two-three lines here and there.

—Jeana Col. Fodoreanu (1928)[2]

REMEMBERING THE GREAT WAR
THROUGH AUTOBIOGRAPHICAL
NARRATIVES

Remembering World War I was only in part a matter of mourning the dead and
coping with loss. While some worked to lay to rest their loved ones, others worked
through their own remembrances of the war. In the interwar period Romania saw an
explosion in autobiographical writing, much of it centered on the 1914–1918 period.
Everything from poetry to theater and from correspondence to journals was put into
print. Soldiers, civilians, men, women, professional writers and first-time writers, and

people of every creed and linguistic group put pen to paper and saw fit to share their impressions with a wider public. Remembering World War I thus became powerfully shaped by these individual voices and their reception, especially in the literary circles of interwar Romania. The early canonization of certain writers such as Camil Petrescu (1894–1957) and Liviu Rebreanu (1885–1944), who focused on the experience of the average soldier and officer of the Romanian army, at the expense of others who focused on different subjects (e.g., women and non-Romanians) and experiences (e.g., pacifism) led to powerful narratives about whose experiences mattered and how heroism and self-sacrifice were to be valued and remembered, both in the interwar generation and since then. The present chapter represents a critical reexamination of these narratives.

Commemorative Discourses in Word: Autobiographical Writing

Eastern Europe was much like the rest of the continent in the flourishing of autobiographical memoir literature it experienced after the war.[3] Romania was no exception; but in this case, literary critics did not view war-related writing as an important artistic development. From the beginning, much criticism surrounded its production. A great deal of this writing has remained marginal, if present at all, in the historical accounts of Romanian literature of the twentieth century.[4] Yet despite the mixed and generally dismissive response from the literary establishment, people continued to write and attempted to publish war-related writings.

These neglected sources need to be integrated into our understanding of the commemorative discourses that developed after World War I. When their writers made public the intimate and painful images of the wartime years, these authors were in fact claiming a kind of personal knowledge they believed to be a truthful representation of the war. Authors were aware they were speaking about events everyone in the country had lived through, so that their words did not aim at creating an imaginary universe, even in the case of fiction writing, but rather worked to evoke memories of experiences the writers shared at some level with their imagined public. Conversely, though today it is possible to read these texts as purely literary creations, the people who picked up these publications in the 1920s and 1930s did so fully understanding that these were pieces evocative of the war, and would likely function as triggers for their own memories. It is difficult to understand both intentionality and broad readership interpretation for literature where there is a thin record of readers' responses, as was the case with Romania. But, as I show in the following pages, there was in fact a lively interaction among authors and even between authors and readers of these texts, which suggests that literature about the war was an important locus for thinking publicly (albeit on the individual level) about how the war was to be remembered and represented.

I group these writings into two broad categories: autobiographical and fictional. Though there are examples of ways in which autobiographical writings verged on the fictional and even more cases where fictional writings were openly autobiographical, from the point of view of making specific claims to represent the reality of the war for subsequent generations, these two genres can be construed as intentionally different. The authors of autobiographical writings—be these diaries, letters, or memoirs— aimed to directly record events they had witnessed. Their initial impulse was generally to bear witness (especially in the case of diaries); to render visible for those not present there the reality of the war's horrors (especially in letters); or to bring back to life the experiences of the war for those who didn't live through it (especially in memoirs).

Autobiographical writing had developed sparsely in Romania before 1918 by comparison with other European languages, from French to Russian.[5] Few memoirs, whether by literary figures or politicians, were published before 1918. The reason for the late development of this type of writing might have to do with the particularities of literary creation in Romanian. The literature produced by religious (Orthodox) intel-lectuals and authors before the rise of modern literary writing did not take the kind of path of individualist examinations of the self present among Catholic cultures in Europe, whose most important precursor was St. Augustine.[6] These kinds of medita-tions on the self, which gave rise to a trend in Western thought and writing centering on the metaphysics of individual identity and the relation between the individual and divinity, were not to be found among theological writings in the Orthodox tradition, which focused much more on the link between the self and the community, and on the need to deny individual needs and foci for the sake of the community and the afterlife. A focus on death and resurrection was also a more important tradition in Orthodox theology than in Catholic writings.[7]

In fact, World War I represented a watershed for autobiographical writing in Romania. Because of the particularities of this case, the existing literature that exam-ines autobiographical writing as a site for forming and representing the individual self is only somewhat relevant, as it tends to focus on western Europe.[8] Why people wrote diaries and memoirs is in fact something particular to wider cultural, social, and spe-cific literary elements of an environment. It would be hard to extrapolate the insights presented by Philippe LeJeune and other prominent scholars of autobiography, and identify Romania after World War I as a case of a literary culture that finally "arrived" at a point of self-reflection through autobiography along the lines of the analyses offered by these authors. My own reading of these texts speculates on the basis of the available analyses of literary culture and cultural identity in Romania, while taking a critical stance toward ahistorical explorations of the rise and significance of the autobiographical literary genre that dominate these analyses.

Fictional writing about the war in Romania—be it poetry, prose, or theater—aimed to represent writers' war memories with an eye to rendering the emotional, existential reality of those experiences. The force of such writings rested in their ability to evoke, sometimes to shock, and sometimes to soothe. The authors were generally more concerned with aesthetics than with historical authenticity. Yet given the traumatic experiences of the war, much of this writing slipped sometimes toward the journalistic and the melodramatic, and often lacked in the aesthetic modernist qualities much celebrated at that time. Literary writers ultimately aimed toward an aestheticized version of war experiences, and their writings, as forms of war remembrance by those individuals, need to be measured against such claims.

The most important questions that drive my analysis pertain to the specific types of experiences, symbols, and meanings that the authors wished to attach to the war in their individual representations. How successful these attempts were in presenting evocatively and beautifully their wartime memories is less relevant here than exploring closely what these authors considered worthy of remembering (and by extension, what they shied away from focusing on). Equally important is the issue of *whose* remembrances were worthy of preserving and were taken as globally representative of the experience of the war.

There were no templates for describing the kind of experiences these authors had lived through. After the war, some had access to writings published in other countries, such as France and Britain.[9] Professional writers constructed their narratives in dialogue with or as or antithetical responses to other writers of the time, from both Romania and elsewhere. But most autobiographical writers put pen to paper for the first time after the war and viewed the process of writing rather as a form of direct communication between themselves and their imagined readers—their families, friends, the broader community of the nation, or in the case of diaries, their own imagined future selves.

The Canon: Brave Officers, Humiliated Politicians, and Patriotic Journalists

Given the paucity of news from the front that could be made public during the war due to censorship and occupation, Romanian publications compensated after 1918 by publishing a great deal of material especially by military and political officials who had played prominent public roles in the war. Some of the most famous and controversial figures were Alexandru Marghiloman (1854–1925), prime minister for part of the war, and Marshal Alexandru Averescu (1859–1938), the chief commander of the Romanian military operations in Moldavia. Averescu's *Daily War Notes* were published in part in 1920, and then fully as a volume in 1935, and were closely followed in the press.[10] Marghiloman's *Political Notes* came out in 1927, two years after their author had passed away, having given permission to three close friends to see to their publication.[11] Marghiloman's war diary in particular elicited explosive responses from political opponents and several newspapers across the political spectrum, such as *Adevărul* (a leftist paper) and *Cuvîntul* (a rightist paper). Both Averescu and Marghiloman wrote as men involved in the central decision-making processes linked to the fate of the war, and, despite the grumbling of politicians, the public voraciously consumed their writings.

Averescu's *Daily War Notes* offer an illuminating example of the kinds of insights readers would have gleaned about the experience of the war from the perspective of a military officer. Averescu's journal was unchanged, he contended when the book was published in 1935, as an assurance that the book represented the marshal's authentic experiences, as he wanted them remembered.[12] The author's explicit care for making this claim suggests that his intention was in a way to retain intact a certain remembrance of the war for his reading public (and presumably the historical record), so it has to be viewed as a commemorative discourse. The bulk of the notes pertain to tactical moves on the front: "Finally, on the night of 16 October, M.C. Gl. gives order no. 3224, from which it results that: 'The Nămăeşti Group in its retreat move will pivot on its right wing and will stop to occupy a position between the Târgului River and the Argeş River. This position will immediately be reinforced.'"[13] The information is understandable, but seems to have no significance whatsoever to anyone who was not directly involved on the battlefield.

Other segments offer generally cynical or snide remarks about political and strategic choices made by those around him, so that they are more a measure of Averescu's own positioning in the military and political elites of Romania than a description of the events: "Madam Cantacuzino told me . . . that the King would have told her he had given me the Crown of Romania medal. . . . Maybe, but I keep wondering and I am not rejoicing at all."[14] In many of these instances Averescu places himself as the all-knowing eye at the center of both action and representation. His is an omniscient voice, something that historians of gender have observed is particularly notable for male authors.[15]

Once in a while, we read actual descriptions of conditions in Romania:

> The population is dying of cold and hunger, something you see among all social strata. . . . The [typhoid fever] epidemic is spreading, however, because people from the front

Figure 3.1. "Difficult Winter. Soldiers Shoveling Snow." From Averescu's *War Notes,* 128.

come into contact with those who come from the interior, sent as reinforcements. The number of those ill is growing by the hour.[16]

Most evocative, however, are the many images that accompany the book, which include poetic and heroic, as well as gruesome, sights. Their content suggests hardships on the front that would have impacted the daily lives of soldiers beyond the trauma of fighting and seeing death on the battlefield. Averescu, however, never really engages with them, so we don't know how he understood them as evocations of the war. (See figure 3.1.)

Overall, the most vividly represented experiences of the war are the large movements of people, the sheer size of the military actions in which the Romanian army was engaged, and the kinds of decisions (in Averescu's opinion, mostly poor) made by the other military leaders and the civilian leadership. There is a sense of overwhelming misery, of instability, but the book captures little of the fear that most soldiers must have lived with permanently, as well as the despondency of death present all around. In this rendition, the war appears tragic, but with only faint echoes of the human condition. Most readers could not place themselves within this narrative of the war. Instead, this memoir placed the life of the men at the center of decision making during the war in a privileged position, to be understood as uniquely important and difficult—to be admired but not empathized with.

Lesser-known figures of the Romanian political and social elites also published their war memoirs in the first postwar years, both participants in the wartime campaigns and civilians caught in the difficulties of the war. Vasile Th. Cancicov, a lawyer and one-time member of parliament, published a two-volume tome, *Impressions and Personal Opinions from Romania's War: Daily Journal (13 August 1916–31 December 1918).*[17] Cancicov had spent most of the war as a civilian in Bucharest, under the occupation of the Central Powers. This type of war memoir was received with great interest by the press, the public, and some among the political elites, as the foreword by the prominent politician Take Ionescu (1858–1922) testified:

> All this humiliation [of occupation by the Central Powers] which we knew of from afar, you witnessed with your own eyes. Of course for you this spectacle remains a great, indescribable pain. But history gains [here] a document. You did well to bring to light all that you saw. Others should do the same. Romania was sufficiently heroic to not be sullied by the mud of a few degrading beings. But the history of our Calvary will not be fully told if we don't also know these horrors. . . . When all is known, the virtues of our people who produced today's Romania will appear even more brilliant.[18]

This brief yet passionate recommendation by Ionescu echoed the value that others saw in the publication of wartime memoirs.[19] His foreword underscored that the meaning of the war could not be fully constructed for political purposes without the voice of witnesses who experienced not just heroism, but also humiliation. In fact, as Ionescu asserted and others agreed, humiliation itself was an important component for reevaluating what could be construed as virtuous and heroic in the war. Though personal responses are only anecdotally visible, it seems that this memoir had a lasting shelf life. My own copy of it has two sets of notes by the original owner, one confirming the first reading "after an illness of fifteen days" on 13 January 1922, and another one confirming the same reader's second reading on 8 March 1938.[20]

The volume itself contained a fairly detailed description of the daily privations of civilians during the war, viewed from the perspective of a well-to-do, privileged man. Many of his comments in fact pertained to questions of political censorship; to the lack of news about the fighting front; and to the increasing prominence of the occupying forces in fashionable establishments the author had enjoyed before the war, such as the cafés on Calea Victoriei. Through the author's complaints about the offensive presence of the Germans, one learns quickly that Cancicov had been somewhat of a flâneur himself prior to the Central Powers' occupation. He emphatically resented being eliminated from that pleasurable role of social and cultural privilege:

We are in our second Sunday of occupation; those who have seen a third-class German city can imagine the look of our capital today. Soldiers, civilians, and dubious women, and, once in a while, an officer. Lots of Austrian and Hungarian soldiers, with a flower on their hat, arm in arm with a gaudily dressed woman; civilian suits and workers, almost all foreigners, accompany them. . . . The well-known feminine elegance of Calea Victoriei has disappeared; the view of a short dress and leggy boot has become rare.[21]

The author decries the loss of elegance on the streets of Bucharest in ways that evoke similar identifications of elegance with the identity of a better known European capital, Paris, with which many Romanian writers and their voyeuristic readers liked to identify.

His acrid pen offers, by contrast, a harsh view of "foreigners," not only the soldiers of the Central Powers, but also civilians and "gaudily dressed women" (at best, female escorts; at worst, prostitutes). Were these citizens of other countries who traveled to Romania during the war? Not likely. After 1878, most Jews had been unable to gain citizenship in Romania, despite promises to the contrary on the part of the Romanian government after its independence was conditionally recognized by the Great Powers in the Treaty of Berlin. Thus, "foreigners" was in part a euphemism for "Jews."

Cancicov's anti-Semitic views were broadly echoed in other memoirs of the time, most prominently that of Constantin Bacalbașa, a journalist who authored another popular memoir of life in wartime Bucharest, *Bucharest in the Time of German Occupation*. Describing the arrival of the German troops in Bucharest in 1916, Bacalbașa declared: "The whole foreign population is in the streets . . . throwing flowers and offering cigarettes."[22] Women authors also expressed openly anti-Semitic views. In her memoir of the war, Sabina Cantacuzino, sister of one of the leading figures of the National Liberal Party, wrote: "My mother arrived in Mihăești . . . dead tired. They had been ten in a compartment [on the train], and, of course, eight were Jews, because they were the only ones able to travel without restraints."[23] It is unclear how the author would have known without a doubt the religious identity of those traveling companions. Rather, her statement reflected the assumptions of her mother and Cantacuzino herself about the collaboration between the Jewish population and the German occupiers.

Cancicov's and Bacalbașa's memoirs have been quoted widely as important testimonials of the wartime experience by both contemporaries and, more recently, in scholarship about the war, but no work to date has examined closely the deeply anti-Semitic sentiments of these memoirs. For instance, even a volume attempting to recover the heroic role of Jews in the war, such as *The Jews in Romania in the War for the Country's Reunification, 1916–1919* (published with the support of the Federation of the Jewish Communities in Romania), praises interwar historian Constantin Kirițescu as a "great historian of the war." Yet Kirițescu was the first to reproduce in a historical "objective" narrative the typology of the unpatriotic "foreigner" as found in the memoirs of Cantacuzino, Bacalbașa, and others. Describing the arrival of the German troops in Bucharest in November 1916, Kirițescu identifies those who remained in the capital as the tragically "resigned," the "courageous," those "tied to their homes and families," the bureaucrats who felt "it was their duty—with all the risks implied" to continue their work. He then contrasts another category of people to these brave patriots: "The foreigners stayed; the whole Jewdom [*evreimea*] of the capital."[24]

In the next paragraph Kirițescu goes even further in suggesting that Jews were collaborators and acted out of unpatriotic revenge in seeking the incarceration of anti-Semites.[25] Implied in this description, which broadly focuses on opportunism among the civilian population under the German occupation, is the notion that anti-Semitism was a known fact in the Romanian public life of the time, acknowledged de facto by Kirițescu. But, according to this author, trying to eliminate anti-Semites from public functions and the government was an unpatriotic, opportunistic attitude, rather than in the public interest. Despite this, Kirițescu has remained an uncontested classic of the Romanian historiography on World War I, broadly quoted as an authority in virtually every book that focuses on the war.[26]

Cancicov's memoirs turned away from praising "true" patriots and vilifying "foreigners" on the streets of Bucharest, to focus more on his own everyday physical survival when the author was arrested and briefly put in a jail for a couple of months. Food, water, light, the ability to move, the comforts (or lack thereof) of his room and bed loom over any other considerations about the war, yet are still shaped by his privileged worldview:

> We are given neither glasses, nor napkins, nor tablecloths. . . . Dinner consists now of two kinds of food: a false sour soup is inevitable, a bean, beet, or potato soup; very rarely we would get soup with meat. The other dish is some vegetable stew, and rarely horse meat. . . . Only after a week were we allowed to order a glass of wine or beer.[27]

Such treatment was a privation only to someone who had lived in luxury before the war. Still, the reality of the author's suffering should not be ignored, for it was sincere, if potentially laughable to some of the working class people he himself criticized for being too friendly to the Germans.

During the months of incarceration, the author no longer bothered to talk about the censored news and noisy German vehicles ever present in downtown Bucharest. But as soon as he was freed, Cancicov went back to making remarks predominantly

about government and military affairs, rather than any quotidian problems of surviving the war: "At Verdun the French were luckier. . . . In Russia great activity on
the whole front. . . . In Moldavia, the Russo-Romanian troops, though superior
numerically, attack without result on the Șușița valley."[28]

Missing almost entirely from this lengthy diary (the two volumes are over 1,300
pages) are references to the author's family, despite his overt intention to have written and published the book for his daughter, Sonia, and for her children: "I dedicate
these words to you, for the time when I will no longer be alive, so you can read and
remember my joys and suffering."[29] There was in fact little for Sonia and her children
to learn about her own family's life during the war. If all of the author's joys and sor-
rows were in fact recorded with the intention of passing down to the next generations
what was significant about the experience of the war, it appeared that the German
occupation, the military operations of the Romanians, the actions of the Romanian
government in exile, and the author's own imprisonment were indeed the only things
worth remembering.[30]

Gender and Wartime Remembrance

Like the memoirs of Marghiloman, Averescu, and a host of other military and political leaders, Cancicov's diary offers an entirely masculinist (and masculinized) version
of what it meant to live through the war as a civilian and what the significance of
those experiences was, as reconfirmed by Ionescu's weighty opening remarks to the
two-volume memoir. From any of these autobiographical writings it is impossible
to imagine and reconstruct what it meant to live as a woman, without the economic
means of men (even for those who were well-to-do but didn't have the property rights
of their husbands), and to try to care for a family in the absence of any steady income
or even reliable availability of the basic goods for survival, from firewood to bread.

This is not surprising, especially in the case of military personnel. The military
leaders and lower ranking officers who wrote about their experiences after the war
presented a gender-exclusive picture of the trauma and the heroism of the battlefield.
Few of them ever mentioned their experiences in hospitals, for instance (though the
number of wounded in the army was over 200,000), where much of the personnel were
female. In the few existing examples of such narratives we are able to read evocatively
about the gendered nature of these experiences. Nicolae Russu Ardeleanu (1891–?),
who wrote a number of extremely popular books about his wartime experiences as a
combatant and prisoner of war, presented detailed portraits of the women volunteering for the Red Cross in Bucharest and elsewhere.[31] Whether he wrote about nobility
(women such as Princess Ghika, who was one of the leading figures in the Cantacuzino

hospital for prisoners of war in Bucharest) or mentioned anonymous simple volunteers, Russu Ardeleanu returned many times to the images of these women as selfless, courageous, and in general an example of patriotism, even (or especially) when they were working under the occupation of the Central Powers: "The ladies from the Red Cross I met [in the hospital] had a remarkable Romanian soul. Devoted and ready to sacrifice themselves for any Romanian prisoner, they stubbornly and painfully kept an attitude of dignity before the enemy."[32]

Most of the male writers of wartime memoirs, just like most male writers of that time in general, structured their narratives as gender neutral and universalistic. Their critics and historians of the time seemed to agree. Averescu, Cancicov, and Bacalbașa were viewed as authors who spoke of the Romanian experience of the war, accurately and vividly representing those around them. The strong impact of this un-self-reflexive and uncritical reading of the memoirs on the historical narrative of the war, from the early 1920s and until today, is indeed remarkable.[33]

This kind of war memorializing did provoke criticisms at the time. People who had fought on the side of the Habsburgs resented the veil of silence with regard to their own experience of violence and heroism. This was in fact the case even for ethnic Romanians fighting in the Habsburg army during the war, and more so for ethnic Hungarians and Germans.[34] It was as if the traumas of total war on one side could speak for the traumas on the other side, even when, in the case of some of these memoirs, including Bacalbașa's, the experience of the war was marked as anti-Hungarian, anti-German, and anti-Semitic. Hungarian and German language publications, as well as periodical publications of the Jewish communities in Romania (whether in Romanian or Yiddish), did publish fragments of memoirs from the war. But such testimonies were read within their own linguistic-ethnic communities, with virtually no echo among ethnic Romanians, with the exception of the rare breed of intellectually curious reader, such as Ion Chinezu vis-à-vis Hungarian interwar publications, for instance.[35]

Romanian women who had lived the war on the side of the Allies did have, however, an opportunity to express more widely their disjunction from the male-centered and universalizing representation of the war. In the 1930s, especially, a number of women's autobiographical narratives, mostly in the form of memoirs, were published.[36] This grouping is remarkable in two respects. To begin with, it was unprecedented in Romania for so many women non-writers to produce such substantial autobiographical writings. One can certainly identify the interwar period as an important moment in women's writing in Romania, though it seems to have remained entirely unobserved by the literary and cultural scholars of this period.[37] This phenomenon is paralleled in other eastern European societies, for instance in Bulgaria and Yugoslavia.[38]

As in these other neighboring countries, women in Romania who put pen to paper and published their memoirs tended to be relatively well-educated (whether through formal schooling or private tutoring), well-to-do (with one exception in the group I looked at, Nelli Cornea), and generally from the upper classes, if not outright aristocracy. Therefore, their own voices reflected not so much a cross-section of all women's wartime experiences as a specifically gendered representation of an economically and socially privileged existence. That is not to say that these women didn't suffer great privations. Their experiences in fact reflected many sufferings and grave losses with which anyone who lived through the war, man or woman, could identify. Yet they had forms of protecting themselves and their families from the war (especially through financial resources), which allowed them a distance from the most dehumanizing daily privations—from hunger and filth to lack of personal safety against theft and violence. Still, these memoirs offer a broad array of perspectives and reactions, and deeply enrich our understanding of how the war experience was represented differently by women than by men, and thus how remembrances of the war were in fact structured in gendered ways through the printed word already in the 1920s.

Another important aspect of these memoirs is that they engaged with each other and with the autobiographical literature of the period in a lively and even combative way. For instance, Sabina Cantacuzino, in a volume of memoirs she published in 1937 that included the war years, lambasted the high-society women who responded to the war, according to the author, in a cowardly and unpatriotic fashion, worried about their own skin before that of the soldiers fighting on the front, and making a show of empathy only when they were in a secure relationship with the German occupiers: "Such spectacles on the part of Didina [Alexandrina] Cantacuzino were staged as advertisement; she didn't miss a chance to make a speech or make herself publicly visible. Under those circumstances, only she could make such a public show, given the credit that Grigore Cantacuzino [Didina's husband] had gained with the Germans."[39]

Cantacuzino herself was attacked by some of her contemporaries for her biased recounting of the war, most prominently by Alexandrina Fălcoianu, who also sued Cantacuzino for slander. Fălcoianu began her *Examination of Conscience and an Answer* by declaring it to be "my supreme confession, which I humbly offer to the public opinion and those who have seen my work." Fălcoianu accused Sabina Cantacuzino of maliciously and untruthfully trying to "convince [public opinion] that only the Brătianus performed their duties vis-à-vis the country, that they have a monopoly on patriotism."[40]

In addition to such polemics that used war remembrances to settle what seemed like personal and political scores of high society, there were many other autobiographical writings by women who did engage with each other and the rest of wartime memoirs. They offer us thus an idea of the grip that wartime remembrance had on the Romanian public in the late 1920s, and the extent to which politicians and the wider public, military and civilian, men and women, professional and non-professional writers were personally invested in these debates. One author of a moving memoir from this group of publications was Jeana Col. Fodoreanu, who in 1928 stated in the opening page of her book, *The Woman-Soldier:*

> If I dare bring to light my modest war Journal after so much time, it is because I kept waiting for others more capable than me, more competent at writing, to speak and remember those who fulfilled their duty under the folds of the holy Flag of the Red Cross, raised here by the greatest and dignified Queen of our days. I waited, I searched, but I did not find more than two or three lines here and there.[41]

Apparently self-effacing, Fodoreanu's words and title in fact stated emphatically that she didn't consider herself and her traumatic experiences during the war (she lost her father and a brother, and she herself served in various hospitals and on the front, with the troops, as a volunteer nurse) as secondary to those of the male soldiers. Fodoreanu's imagined interlocutors were not the women of high society or personal enemies, as it seems was the case with Cantacuzino. Fodoreanu's book was a direct response to the wide breadth of wartime memoirs, journals, and literature that had appeared between 1918 and 1928. Her goal was to correct the near silence about women's experiences in the war—their heroism and pain, their losses and sacrifices, their patriotism. Her audience was the Averescus, the Cancicovs, the Bacalbașas, and the Kirițescus of the day.

Though Fodoreanu nowhere espoused any self-identified feminist perspective on the war, her dedication of the book to Queen Marie, rather than King Ferdinand, for instance, seems more than a mere polite and diplomatic nod to the honorary leader of the Red Cross in Romania. The heartfelt and ritualized actions of the queen during the war, on the front, in hospitals, in political and diplomatic circles, and among philanthropic groups created a virtual myth of Marie as a "mother of the wounded" and the ultimate feminine symbol of selflessness during the war. As I have noted elsewhere, this myth acted to establish an unbridgeable distance in much of the Romanian postwar public opinion between this super-heroic feminine presence and the kind of work other women did during the war: there was only one mother of the wounded, only one such saint, and no other real-life woman could even aspire to reaching such a lofty, idealized image.[42] In this foreboding context, Fodoreanu cleverly deployed the queen as a doubly useful symbol: of the highest form of feminine self-sacrifice and patriotism, and also as a representative of other real heroines of the war, whose actions were in fact within the same realm of heroism as those of the queen.

In her remarkable memoir, Fodoreanu made no secret of her strong views that women had performed services to the country on a par with those of soldiers, at times exceeding the courage of their male counterparts. Starting with the title, *The Soldier-Woman,* she unabashedly situated herself alongside male soldiers, though she was never officially part of the Romanian army, as women were not allowed to enlist. In the narrative itself, she provided numerous examples of doctors and nurses working bravely side by side on the firing line during battles, as well as evidence of the nurses' greater courage than enlisted officers' in such situations.

Her tone was sometimes competitive, trying to reinforce the notion that women were in no way less deserving than men of admiration for their heroism, but Fodoreanu was also just as quick to focus closely on the gendered nature of her own way of dealing with loss and suffering. After she lost her father and brother in the war, the triumphal return of the king and queen to Bucharest at the end of the war rang hollow with her: "I am not going to the parade. I am no longer anything more than a poor woman who lost her father, mother, brothers, relatives, friends. . . . I will remain between these walls where I was born to cry out my pain."[43] This statement might be viewed at first as an acknowledgment of her weakness as a woman, since the author identifies herself as "no longer anything more than a poor woman." But I view this more as an account, neither humble nor proud, but rather all-embracing, of the complexity of feelings, reactions, and attitudes of women in the war qua women. For Fodoreanu, staying home was a painful choice, but one which she felt she owed her family: to mourn her lost ones on behalf of her kin, which was women's first specific duty in the Orthodox tradition of remembering the dead. No feelings of self-pity and images of victimhood, like the ones found in Cancicov's memoirs about his days spent in prison, are to be found in this journal.

Though focusing on heroism a great deal of the time, this emphasis sometimes took a back seat to crying for the loved ones recently lost, even in the heart of someone as committed to the war as Fodoreanu was. In a way, the publication of the journal in 1928, ten years after the end of the war, represented a moment of moving from private mourning to acknowledgment and accounting of personal experiences and feelings as publicly significant precisely because their gendered qualities, which, she strongly felt, were representative of other women's experiences. Fodoreanu gave voice to other women's frustrations about the gender-exclusive way in which the remembrance of the war tended to be represented, rendering the male version of combat and civilian life universal while hiding, and thus rendering insignificant, women's own specific experiences and recollections.

The tone of women's recollections was different from that of the soldiers and male civilians who were hailed as representing the voice of the people. Though some, like Cantacuzino, commented repeatedly on political and even military events, most women's memoirs and diaries concentrated on daily survival, confronting the constant fear of living under occupation, and the stress of finding food for their families and keeping everyone protected from harm. Generally these narratives place the author at the center of the action, rather than as an impartial observer, as was the case with Bacalbaşa and Cancicov. The reader has an immediate sense of the subjective, highly stressful quality of living under military occupation.

Although remarking on their particular weaknesses as women (material, emotional, physical), women's memoirs do not present an overarching narrative of victimhood vis-à-vis the Central Powers. The source of women's vulnerability is identified with the Romanian state's and society's disregard for women as citizens of the country. One extremely evocative journal is Nelli Cornea's *Wartime Notes: A Journal* (1921).[44] Though nominally a rendition of her wartime journal, the text, much like Averescu's *Notes,* bears the imprint of a subsequent rereading and rewriting after the war. In this respect it functions as a memory trace, made public and worked over through the author's recollections of the events of the war after its end.

Cornea's journal is particularly interesting as it represents her immediate reactions to the onslaught of violence from the perspective of someone caught psychologically and logistically unprepared at the beginning of the war. Cornea was conflicted about the war from the very start. To begin with, she had two sons serving in the army. Toward the start of the journal she states that "the pen is falling out of my hand" at the thought of the possibility that her sons might have perished in a battle in the Carpathian Mountains.[45] She also confesses to getting caught up in the enthusiasm of the beginning of the war, together with everyone else, despite this personal cost and also despite her staunchly pacifist convictions:

> The entire population, from the high and mighty in the palace to those living in the smallest hut, was caught in the enthusiasm [of the hour]; they were heart and soul behind fulfilling without delay the national ideal. . . . I was, however, a convinced pacifist fighting for a long time through writing and speech. . . . But who can stop the normal development of things.[46]

The last two sentences suggest that Cornea inserted this remark about pacifism later, to somehow distance herself from the majority of those surrounding her, while still allowing herself to be identified with the nationalist fervor of the time (she didn't alter the nationalist cliché "national ideal," which suggests that she looked somewhat un-self-reflexively upon it and was still caught up in these sentiments at the time of her more bitter recollections in 1921).[47] At one point, Cornea contemplates her own feelings about the enemy: "A terrible hatred seems to grow in me against them [the

Germanophiles]. . . . But it doesn't turn into thirst for revenge." Further on, she writes about her growing depression, in part connected to a sense of powerlessness and in part to these feelings of animosity that seemed to engulf her, a self-avowed pacifist.[48] I have found no parallel self-examinations about their sentiments during the war in any of the autobiographical texts written by male authors.

Like other women authors, Cornea showed no sense of sisterhood with all women. Rather, she was eager to separate herself from what she considered to be the dishonorable attitude of many women.[49] In several instances, Cornea carefully differentiated between nurses who gave their all and those who refused to help or held back. Yet in the same breath she stated with frustration: "This [the administration of the hospital] will not prosper until it falls into women's hands."[50] She ultimately seemed to instinctively trust women more than men as caregivers.

By the summer of 1918, Cornea's frustration and powerlessness became overwhelming: "Our country, whose fate was in the balance [at the beginning of the war], is now lost."[51] She dwelled a great deal on her misfortunes as a woman. During the war Cornea lost her husband and saw her material situation deteriorate to the point becoming penniless and suicidal. A staunch feminist, she rebounded by shouting against the injustices done to all women in her predicament: "Women have no rights, widows even less. After widows are squashed like a lemon, they are thrown out in the street by the law. . . . Democracy, democracy, when will your time come, to rule here like in France and America, so that a person could win based on merit, work, and talent, and not inheritance."[52] Here the source of women's victimization is not the wartime occupation, but the undemocratic Romanian state.

Still, in December 1918 she was able to bounce back and rejoice with a sense of revenge and righteousness: "The messengers of victory were arriving. Our brothers, beautiful, as the Latins are supple, after the heavy trunks, the sinister Teutons [Germans]. . . . The noble army of our allies, the liberators of the world!"[53] Yet even at that point she returned to her focus on the need for gender equality as the only outcome of the war that would truly change life for women in Romania: "While bandaging its wounds, humanity should sift from all this suffering in the war a great lesson: Justice and equality for all individuals, including women."[54] These words, most likely written after the end of the war and after the euphoria of December 1918 had worn off, betrayed a more embittered view of the great lesson of the war: "From that terrible bloody tragedy we lived through, nobody learned any lesson. The powerful of the day, especially, have kept the same habits, denigrating [the concept of] justice and careless toward anyone else's suffering."[55] Indeed, women's specific experiences of vulnerability and victimization during the war became silenced and were considered unrepresentative of the broader experiences of the civilian population. When feminists tried to use the argument of women's wartime activities in keeping the home fires burning on behalf of their husbands at the front as a means to gain political rights, virtually all politicians rebuffed them.[56] The voices of Cornea and Fodoreanu were generally not viewed as broadly relevant or representative.

The richness of these personal recollections about the war well complement men's autobiographical writings. Women's narratives also bring into question the equation of courage and heroism exclusively with combat. Conversely, what it meant to be a victim or to incur specific forms of wartime humiliation seems more complicated than the picture that emerges from reading memoirs such as Cancicov's. The dangers and hardships women faced throughout the war confronted them with the necessity of becoming resourceful, brave, and steadfast in their efforts to survive. In order to smuggle food for hospitals and other philanthropic institutions, women "had organized a whole system: meat in caskets, with women crying behind the carts . . . and lambs wrapped as children."[57] Those who worked as nurses had displayed even more courage and spirit of self-sacrifice, some working under fire close to the front (Fodoreanu), others close to the source of typhoid fever infection (Cornea), and a few even helping some Romanian prisoners escape (Alexandrina Cantacuzino). But these voices have generally been silenced in collective commemorations of the war, whether vernacular or official.

Fictionalized Representations of the War

The war occasioned not only an explosion of memoirs, journals, and other forms of autobiographies. It also became the ground for creating a different literature. My analysis here focuses on literary works that dealt directly with the war and offered their own narrative avenues for remembering and commemorating the war on the part of the author or readership, respectively. The wide array of such literary products included poetry, drama, and especially prose, either short stories or novels. Despite the multitude of such works, literary critics and historians do not view the Great War as a watershed in the literature published in Romania. In George Călinescu's (1899–1965) canonical *History of Romanian Literature,* we find several chapters that extend to 1916 but are organized by genre or aesthetic orientation, rather than themes ("Directions toward Classicism," or "Eclectic Literature"). The chronological order seems to skip over the war altogether, resuming in 1919/1920 and then similarly focusing on different genres or aesthetic groupings ("The Novelists," "The Modernists," etc.). There is a "1919 Moment" and a "1920 Moment," but neither focuses on the war as more than a chronological bookend or caesura.[58]

Still, all literary critics who view the war as a bookend also identify a number of novels focusing on the war as classics of Romanian literature, most prominently Liviu

Rebreanu's *Forest of the Hanged* (1922) and Camil Petrescu's *Last Night of Love, First Night of War* (1930). These two books have remained required reading for school-age children until today. In my reading of these works, I focus especially on their context and themes, deeply connected to the experience and remembrance of the war, as central aspects that help us understand their significance and appeal during the interwar period, challenging the ways in which the historical context has been silenced in the literary histories of this writing.

Rebreanu is generally viewed as the most important Romanian novelist of the interwar period, the creator of the "mature Romanian novel." *Forest of the Hanged* is considered his masterpiece.[59] The novel is less a memoir and more a psychological investigation of a type of fallen hero, Apostol Bologa, an ethnic Romanian officer forced by his Austro-Hungarian superiors to fight in World War I against the Romanian army. When asked to execute ethnic Romanian civilians, Bologa finally decides he has to desert, but he is caught, almost willingly. He is hanged, a fate he receives with relief, almost with delight.

The portrait offered here is a typology of the tragic fate of ethnic Romanians in Habsburg-ruled Transylvania, a theme central to another important novel by Rebreanu, *Ion.*[60] Published only three years after the end of the war, *Forest of the Hanged* offers a dramatic picture of the experience of the war for those who fought opposite the victorious Entente, a view that is neither sympathetic nor moralizing. Instead, Rebreanu lays out the complex choices of this typological character as a rehearsal for thinking more broadly about the behavior of all Romanians—civilians and soldiers—during the war. Though entirely fictional and not based on Rebreanu's or anyone else's exact remembrances of the war, *Forest of the Hanged* occasioned a brutal and compelling reexamination for those who went into battle by choice, giving "heroism" a different meaning vis-à-vis nationalist considerations: Bologa refuses to kill ethnic Romanian peasants, but flees instead of confronting his superiors; he breaks his engagement to a Romanian girl friendly to the Hungarians, but ends up becoming engaged to a Hungarian peasant girl himself. He can thus be viewed as both hero and victim: he is to admired for his conscious decision to uphold his beliefs, while fully aware that he is to become a victim of the wider political context of the war.

The prominent critic Eugen Lovinescu (1881–1943) identified Rebreanu's novel in his *History of Contemporary Romanian Literature* (1928) as a "granite-like" product of the war: "The war, about whose lack of real influence on our literature so much has been written, . . . gave us also this solid *Forest of the Hanged,* of granite-like blocks, wrapped in the gray scroll of the start of another day."[61] Lovinescu's poetic description is a tribute to Rebreanu's own portraiture of Bologa as a complex, embattled, and ultimately anti-heroic character—an important perspective on recollecting the experiences of the war for the generation of the 1920s. Like German and French critics reacting to the war novels of Erich Maria Remarque (1898–1970) and Henri Barbusse (1873–1935), Lovinescu finds the grays and granite-like qualities in *Forest of the Hanged*, rather than any grand patriotic ideology, to be commended.

Also celebrated and more directly connected to remembering the war is *Last Night of Love*, an autobiographical novel by Camil Petrescu, who served as an officer in the Romanian army. The author himself acknowledged that "the second part of the book, which begins with the first night of war, is constructed using [my] front journal."[62] The book appeared over a decade after the end of the war, but can be defined partially as memory work and partially as psychological erotic novel. In fact, Petrescu was openly and profoundly under the influence of the writing of Marcel Proust (1871–1922), as both his style and themes show: "I will simply let the flow of memories take its course. But what if, while I'm narrating a story, I remember something else, starting from a word? No problem, I'll make a kind of parenthesis."[63]

The novel is emphatically memory work; the fictionalized first part deals with the internal struggles of the main character, an officer named Ştefan Gheorghidiu, to come to terms with his feelings for his ex-wife; the second part retells in journal-like format the horrors of daily life at the front and the gradual psychological collapse of the protagonist. While the first part is more clearly fictionalized, it uses as a technique the Proustian style of recollection in order to represent Gheorghidiu's interior emotional states, thereby introducing memory work as an important stylistic component of prose writing:

> It's impossible for me to write down all the trials I went through, the chaotic avalanche of thoughts I confronted. . . . I wished this had been a dream, so I could wake up, but it was only the encrusted reality. . . . My entire past now seemed to have an entirely different meaning compared to what I had gotten used to.[64]

The second part is even more directly connected to remembering the war, though here the author shifts away from the past tense of part 1, which had underscored the kind of memory work Gheorghidiu and, indirectly, Petrescu were undertaking. The front journal is written in the active present tense, placing the author, narrator, and reader at the scene of the battle, forcing the reader to follow the troops step by step and to (re)live with them the horrors of the war. Petrescu resumes his narration in the past tense only in the brief last chapter of the book, an effective reminder of the post-front reality, serving only to underscore the unbridgeable gap between that experience and all that came after.

The novel was immediately identified as an "absolute premiere" in Romanian literature and was widely read. By contrast with Rebreanu's narration of the front experience, Petrescu used his own ordeals directly, narrating the novel in the first person, identifying completely with his main hero, the officer Ştefan Gheorghidiu. The transformation of the hero through the wartime experience was similar to that of Petrescu himself and with the drama lived by the wartime generation: confrontation with death in horrific ways on a daily basis brought about his fundamental abandonment of any absolute values and a sort of moral suicide, though not a physical one, so that the scars of this decay remain as the permanent memory trace of the experience of the front. Ultimately, Petrescu/Gheorghidiu was not a hero, but rather a survivor, and in fact a victim. The juxtaposition of the existential drama narrated in the first half, where Gheorghidiu is rendered the victim of his wife's betrayal, and the traumatic horrors experienced as almost banal existence on the front, suggest both the meaninglessness of this war and also the kind of cruelty it embodies, which has nothing to do with grandiose, heroic war goals—that can in fact ruin or at least emotionally cripple a person's life.

These novels, and a number of other writings that have retained a lesser position in the history of Romanian literature, deal almost exclusively with the perspective of the ethnic Romanian (male) soldier at the front. They represent remembrances of the war as traumatic, devoid of heroism. Even with the perspective of over a decade after the end of the war in which Romania was victorious, at a time when it had doubled in size and had become Greater Romania beyond the dreams of ardent nationalists, the wartime generation exemplified by Rebreanu and Petrescu seemed consumed much more by the psychological traces of war trauma than by any sense of great affirmation of patriotic ideals or the sense that soldiers performed their sacred duty toward the country in a patriotic fashion. Poetry written both at the front and afterward and published in the decades after the war reinforces this vision of the wartime experience:

It's raining again and the wounded moan, crushing your hearing. . . .
The sky and earth are crying; the convoys flow in rows. . . .
An injured man left behind, to bind his wound under an acacia tree;
A shell breaks the trunk to make a cross at his head.[65]

One important exception to this picture of Romanian postwar literature are the works published in *The Cult of Our Heroes* (later entitled *Heroic Romania*), a monthly journal published by a veterans' association, the Heroes Cult, and having as its editor-in-chief a now largely forgotten writer, Ion Dragolsav. In his large synthesis of Romanian literature, Călinescu describes Dragoslav's work in two brief paragraphs, declaring that he "is far from being a writer," though the critic describes him as a picturesque character who died of alcoholism in a Bucharest hospital.[66] Yet Călinescu makes no mention of Dragoslav's editorial work, which was intense and long lasting, a labor of dedication to his veteran "brothers." Given the absence of *Heroic Romania* from any histories of Romanian literature, it is safe to assume that the readership of that journal did not include the prominent literary critics of the day, nor celebrated writers like Rebreanu and Petrescu, who would have glanced at and engaged with the avant-garde and established literary journals such as *Literary Life, Literary Journal, The Journal of the Royal Foundations,* but most likely were unaware of the existence of *Heroic Romania.*

Such a disjuncture is not surprising and underscores my larger point in this book, that cultural production in interwar Romania was vibrant but by no means cohesive. On the contrary, disparate social, cultural, ethnic, religious, and regional trends were represented in disparate literary works. Should one consider *Heroic Romania* secondary because Călinescu does not mention it in his encyclopedic *History of Romanian Literature?* The publication is in fact absent from the *Dictionary of Romanian Literary Press* (1987), though it received brief mention in the *"Thought" Encyclopedia* (1940).[67] In my view *Heroic Romania* represents an important case study of both individual and institutional preservation in remembering the war.[68] Thus I consider it worthy of attention as an important site for cultural work, regardless of the inherent aesthetic qualities of the material published there.

Even a cursory glance at *Heroic Romania* over its decade-long publication life shows that, even though Dragoslav was the main animator of this work, he had numerous collaborators, veterans eager to have their war poetry, short stories, and autobiographical texts printed. In addition, the numerous and varied letters printed in the journal also testify to its active readership. Similarly impressive is the geographic breadth of the remembrances recorded in the journal and the letters. They range from Bucharest and its surroundings to places throughout Walachia, Moldavia, and Transylvania, such as Bocşa Montana, Godineşti (Gorj County), Oradea, Bârlad, Vida (Vlaşca County), and as far as Cleveland, Ohio.[69] The publication reached a specific niche—veterans and their families—but that community was numerically significant, and it also comprised active readers, who, based on the reports and letters printed in the journal, were intensely engaged in other forms of remembering the war, through monument building and commemorations.

It would be easy to dismiss *Heroic Romania* as propaganda of the Romanian military establishment through the Heroes Cult. Undoubtedly, there is a heavily pedagogical, nationalist, and openly xenophobic (predominantly anti-Hungarian) element to it in terms of choices of historical moments to recall.[70] Yet the journal also acted as a conduit for active local veteran associations and individuals to have their voices heard, from sending in poems and short stories to offering descriptions of commemorative events and making requests for information about missing loved ones (especially in the first few issues of the journal). It is impossible to determine what kinds of editorial choices were made in creating the final product, since there is no archive of the submitted manuscripts. Yet the unsolicited readers' materials that appear in the journal reinforce the positive view of the army as an institution of patriotic devotion and integrity. The war remembrances represented here acknowledge the pain of having lost loved ones, but insist on connecting this loss to loftier abstract notions of sacrifice for the country, and of age-old traditions that are an integral part of the national fiber of all Romanians:

> War hasn't been around for a century or three,
> It is an ancient tradition
> We don't have women's souls. . . .
> We dance the *hora* with gladness!
> . . . .
> When finally it is our turn,
> And we know that we'll have much to fight,
> Still we have no fear:
> War was left to us by our elders![71]

Silenced Remembrances: Pacifists, Civilians, Women, and Non-Romanians

These literary renditions of the war have the same gaps as the memoirs. Whether traumatic and unheroic, as with Petrescu, or dramatic and heroic, as with *Heroic Romania,* the literature of war remembrance focuses almost exclusively on the frontline experience of ethnic Romanian soldiers, all men. From this picture, some important elements are missing. The experience of civilians in the war is relegated to background for the dramas happening at the front, and thus women's remembrances are once again represented as secondary to the larger dramas of the main male characters. Some of these writings go even further in their gender exclusivity, defining and depicting male heroism and the experience of the front in positive colors in contrast to women's experiences, as the poem above does, for instance.

Pacifists, though they are present in some writings—for instance, in *1916,* by Felix Aderca (1891–1962)—are repeatedly represented by critics as lacking both integrity (in a moral sense) and also depth (in a literary sense).[72] Călinescu is merciless toward Aderca:

Like most other Jewish writers, F. Aderca is obsessed with humanitarianism, pacifism, and all the other features of internationalism. . . . In fact this bizarre mentality belongs only to Jews and therein remains their tragedy. They do not understand that national instinct is a fundamental coordinate of our soul and territory.[73]

The pacifist view of the war and an internationalist postwar perspective is, of course, not represented in publications such as *Heroic Romania* either. Nelli Cornea is another rather singular figure among the autobiographers who proudly considered herself both a pacifist and a patriot.

The perspective of those who had been on the opposite side of the war is also absent from the literary representations of wartime experiences, with the prominent exception of *Forest of the Hanged*. The experiences of ethnic Hungarians and Germans are, however, absent from Romanian-language publications. The remembrances of these groups remained limited not only regionally, mainly to Transylvania and Bukovina, but also linguistically to their own ethnic groups, with the exception of the rare cross-linguistic readers.

One remarkable example of such a blind spot in the literature produced in Romania in the interwar period is the autobiographical war novel *Black Monastery* (1931), the remarkable chef d'oeuvre of the Transylvanian Hungarian writer Aladár Kuncz (1886–1931).[74] Born in Kolozsvár, he undertook his postgraduate studies in Budapest and traveled to France on many occasions, as a passionate reader and literary critic. The beginning of the war found him there, and he was made a prisoner of war, spending the next five years incarcerated in La Noirmoutier and Île d'Yeu. Upon his return to Budapest in 1919, he found the capital greatly changed by the post–Béla Kun white terror and moved back to his native town, now called Cluj, a choice few other Hungarians made during that period. Kuncz spent the next decade writing *Black Monastery*, which was published in 1931, shortly before his death. Compared in literary quality and thematic focus with Thomas Mann's (1875–1955) *The Magic Mountain* and Franz Kafka's (1883–1924) *The Trial*,[75] Kuncz's masterpiece was read and commented on broadly in Hungarian periodicals, such as *Korunk* and *Nyugat*.[76] However, the book received no attention from the Romanian press and was translated into Romanian only in 1971.[77]

The book itself offered a sobering, pacifist, and deeply democratic-humanist view of violence and incarceration, focusing on the psychological trauma of this experience. No jingoistic sentiments, or even broadly pro-Hungarian or pro-Habsburg (in other words, anti-Entente or anti-Romanian) perspectives, are expressed in this poignant wartime autobiographical novel. Still, in the Romanian cultural landscape of the interwar period this literary masterpiece was not deemed a significant witness to the experience of World War I, whereas, for instance, Cancicov's narration of his much briefer and less traumatic incarceration by the Central Powers in Bucharest was broadly read and praised. Individual attempts to recollect and bring into public consciousness victimhood as a multifaceted concept had a public presence in the interwar period. Yet these nuanced and varied significations did not leave a broad social imprint in many cases. Their attempt to become part of the commemorative discourse of the war had limited results.

The success or failure of autobiographical writings about wartime experiences to contribute to shaping commemorative discourses about the war is generally hard to measure. We know that these works sold well and thus must have been read by many people. We also know that literary critics and political commentators wrote about some of these works, if only to dismiss many of them as insufficiently elevated from an aesthetic point of view. Yet we do not know how the average reader responded to them, especially if one is to consider the large numbers of non-Romanian speakers in that country in the 1920s and 1930s, as well as the persisting high rate of illiteracy. So, in the case of these individual voices, what we can decipher at best is the intention of the authors and some faint echoes from their readers. The kind of clear, active engagement of groups of people in commemorative processes, as we observed in the case of burying and mourning the war dead, is impossible to sense in these individual voices. But they represent important departures: they offered unvarnished and unheroic public representations of the war (as was the case with Petrescu), and unprecedented narratives of women' specific experiences (as was the case with women's memoirs published in the 1920s and 1930s).

Still, autobiographical texts about the war were marked by a great disparity between men and women in terms of whose actions were held worthy of public remembrance and thus, worthy of being represented in memorials. This was especially the case with the publication of memoirs and memorialistic war literature. Though women suffered the brunt of the civilian plight and painful occupation by foreign troops, their experiences in the war were generally not viewed as courageous enough to represent publicly as remarkable or memorable. Even in the case of the nurses who risked their lives as volunteers at the front or in hospitals under foreign occupation (as was the case with the Cantacuzino hospital in Bucharest), their bravery and patriotism was recorded by some of their patients but later easily forgotten, when projects for monuments were mushrooming everywhere and histories of the war were published. Nor were women's specific forms of victimization represented as worthy of public attention among historians of the war or literary critics.

As Fodoreanu's memoir shows, however, women did not accept this silence passively. Instead, women's autobiographical wartime writings flourished after the war, in part as a reaction against the masculinist amnesia of the postwar years. Though a nationalist fervor was present in many autobiographical writings penned after the war, these varied in the degree of their support for the state projects of the postwar period. Some even openly embraced pacifism, while others laid out the still bleeding psychological wounds of the war. Somehow, though, these voices that gave richness and a humane texture to the nationalist discourse of the day have generally remained at best marginal among the visible memory traces of the war, twice forgotten—by contemporaries with a different political agenda, and more recently by scholars.

Equally important is the variety in how literary texts defined heroism and victimization as components of the wartime experience. These elements helped frame the memory of the war for both authors and their readers in ways that departed from the official representations of the war's glorious significance. Readers had a chance to find consoling or, alternatively, traumatic echoes of their own memories of the war. And for the generation coming of age in the decades after the war, these public individual renditions of wartime experiences helped keep alive thorny questions that could not be found in the official commemorative landscape. It is toward this contrasting narrative that I turn in chapter 4.

Only we [soldiers], and nobody else, have the right to take care
of the remains of our comrades and their commemoration.

—The Heroes Cult (1919)[1]

In different places in the country, to commemorate our Heroes
and historic deeds, various monuments are raised that lack
in beauty and greatness; instead of reinforcing sentiments of
piety and national uplifting, they diminish [such sentiments].

—The Heroes Cult (1938)[2]

4

THE POLITICS OF COMMEMORATION
IN INTERWAR ROMANIA, 1919–1940

Dialogues and Conflicts

On a brilliant fall day, on the morning of 18 September 1938, a multitude of people
descended upon the little town of Mărășești. Thousands of peasants, working
class people, schoolchildren, middle-aged women, soldiers, priests, along with numerous representatives of political parties and the government, all holding flowers and
flags, awaited the arrival of King Charles II (1893–1953) for the inauguration of the
Mărășești Mausoleum, which stood majestically in the background. The day was filled
with emotion—pain, honor, sadness, rejoicing, and even resentment among some.
The festivities were stupendous, with parades and processions, pompous speeches and

grand gestures, with religious and military rituals to elevate the event to a high level of spirituality and awe, and with a feast and cultural spectacle to end the evening.³ Among the speakers, though not first, stood proudly Alexandrina Cantacuzino (1876–1944), President of the National Orthodox Society of Romanian Women and initiator of the monument:

> After almost a quarter of a century, we, humble workers, who were called here to fulfill the sentiments of pious remembrance on the part of the entire nation toward those who rest here, are able to see with great satisfaction the blessing of this great Monument for the eternal remembrance of Romanian courage. . . . All the hardships we had to overcome over the years, all the injustices, the lack of appreciation of many people, all the bitter memories have now vanished in these moments of meditation when the King, Symbol of the Fatherland, is welcomed here on the Field of Mărăşeşti by the Soul among Souls, the One Who, having received the Crown of Romania, vowed in [a few] words, which became the guiding light of a short, but Glorious Reign: "I will be a good Romanian."⁴

Careful to identify herself as humble, Cantacuzino went on for over ten minutes to remind everyone about the important work her organization had done for the monument. She diplomatically bowed before the monarchy, while underlining the lack of support she and her organization had to overcome in their efforts to raise money, secure the land, and get cooperation from the military and civilian authorities for the mausoleum plans. Even as she claimed that "all the bitter memories have now vanished," Cantacuzino resurrected those memories and insisted on reminding everyone about her struggles. She also spoke, rather brazenly, to King Charles II as if to a young man (she was almost sixty at that time) and reminded him of the bravery of his father, King Ferdinand ("Soul among Souls"). As people of her generation easily remembered, Charles II had deserted during World War I, fleeing to Odessa with an older woman, whom he briefly married. Cantacuzino's words, though coated in praise, had an unmistakably sharp and unforgiving undertone. As she spoke, Cantacuzino glanced with heavy eyes toward the representatives of the Heroes Cult, her main competitor in the two-decade struggle to become the custodian of the public remembrance of the war.

Though greatly celebrated during its inauguration, the Mărăşeşti Mausoleum, the most monumental Romanian commemorative marker to the Great War, was completed only two years before the country's entry in the next world war and a full generation after the battle it was marking (Mărăşeşti, August 1917). Why such a delay? Was this an exceptional instance or something more typical of official war commemorations? This chapter follows the struggles of the state to construct a cohesive and unitary commemorative discourse around the Great War, examining both successful campaigns, especially in the realm of educational commemorative events, and failures, most prominently in the realm of memorial building.

The Romanian state struggled with its own success at the postwar negotiation table. Having nearly doubled in size, Romania had to contend with a multiplicity of existing traditions and institutions in all areas of government, especially within the explicitly centralizing position it took in all areas of public policy making, from administration and legal responsibility to taxation. Commemorating the war and properly honoring the dead were not at the top of the official agenda; still, they did constitute a permanent preoccupation for both the monarchy (initially especially for Queen Marie, and subsequently for her son, Charles II), as well as the government, from political parties to military authorities. Arduous though they might have been, these activities made slow inroads into the cultural practices of most people living in Romania. The dialogue and struggle between official initiatives, and the support as well as the opposition they encountered in many communities across the ethnic, cultural, and religious divisions already identified in this study, are the subject of this chapter.

Heroes Day and the Heroes Cult: Initial Efforts to Create National Commemorative Rituals

The person responsible for designating an official day for commemorating the war dead was Queen Marie, who as early as 1919 declared that a special day needed to be set aside for properly honoring the dead, a spring day, when flowers bloomed and the earth rejoiced in its ability to be reborn.[5] It is unclear whether Marie herself came up with the holiday of the Ascension as a designated day for the holiday. But it was she who first proposed it in public, and her suggestion was immediately embraced by the parliament, which declared that this Orthodox religious holiday would become an official holiday.[6]

There are some hints as to the discussions that took place before that date was chosen and Marie took it upon herself to advocate for it. On 12 September 1919, King Ferdinand signed a royal decree that laid the foundations for the creation of a society for the graves of the fallen soldiers, which subsequently took on the name Heroes Cult.[7] Among the duties of this new organization, the decree called upon its members "to commemorate each year the heroes of this nation who, just like those who have survived . . . , contributed in large part to the unification of our nation."[8] As expressed here, Ferdinand's reason for remembering the dead soldiers had to do with the ultimate political and concrete outcome of the war, the enlargement of Romania, and not with their sacrifice for the fatherland in an abstract sense. The wording of the decree also indirectly reminded people that the soldiers were only "in part" responsible, implying that the monarchy should be given most credit for Romania's great success at Versailles. The initiative to construct a commemorative discourse about the war was launched at the highest level of policy making in the Romanian state, and it privileged a martial, centralized vision of such a discourse.

The Heroes Cult emerged in 1919 as a complex organization—partly state driven and partly a volunteer effort. The main initiator was the king, through his royal decree of 12 September 1919. But the most important animators were the veterans, who wanted to keep alive the memory of the war and of their dead comrades in a fashion similar to military forces elsewhere in the world.[9] The most active among them were commissioned officers, still in the service of the Ministry of War. Though they did not act as direct representatives of the Romanian government, these initiators drew on resources of the Ministry of War and of the military in general throughout the entire period of the organization's existence. So, even though the Heroes Cult answered directly to its own board, which included private citizens (for instance, war widows of prominent officers, especially generals),[10] the organization's main operating budget and personnel came directly from the military.[11] Given its complex identity and responsibilities, the Heroes Cult represented the site of the most constant dialogue between the intentions of the government to articulate a unified commemorative war discourse, and the desires of the veterans and other individuals who sat on the governing board to reflect what *they* believed were suitable war commemorations.

When the Heroes Cult met in December 1919 to discuss for the first time the possible dates on which to commemorate the war heroes, the conversation touched on the traditional role of the Orthodox Church in preserving the memory of dead ancestors. The first proposition, apparently voiced by representatives of the National Orthodox Society of Romanian Women, was to hold the commemoration on the second day of Easter.[12] Since all board members were ethnic Romanians and Orthodox Christians, this proposal is unsurprising. Moreover, given the ample involvement of the National Orthodox Society of Romanian Women in maintaining Orthodox traditions in the urban environment and also preserving women's specific role in Orthodox rituals, it is no wonder that they suggested both a holiday and, implicitly, a commemorative ritual familiar to them and in which they could play an essential role. In keeping with traditional commemorative and mourning traditions, the representatives of this women's organization proposed priests as the leading authorities in these commemorations.[13]

A related topic at that important meeting was the definition of the heroes to be commemorated. Ferdinand's decree left it rather open for the Heroes Cult to decide who would be included among "the heroes of this nation who, just like those who have survived . . . , contributed in large part to the unification of our nation." Among the documents preserved from the meeting is a copy of the French law that had the similar aim of preserving the memory of those who had perished heroically for the country. The law included one article that became the subject of discussion at the meeting of the Heroes Cult in December 1919: it stipulated that among those to be included in the registers of heroes at the Pantheon should be those who died in the war at the hand of the enemy while serving as public workers in their duties as citizens. In other words, the definition of heroism would include broad swaths of civilians, and not just the rank and file of the army and high members of the government.

That Romanians were already looking abroad, and especially toward France, as a model for war commemorations reflects a high emotional investment in French culture. Throughout the 1920s and 1930s the Heroes Cult and other interwar organizations continued to hold up France as an appropriate model.[14] Despite political sympathies for other countries, especially Mussolini's Fascist Italy and later Hitler's Nazi Germany, most educated Romanians still looked toward Paris as the epitome of elegant, culturally resonant patriotism. Yet in this case the choice was *not* to follow the French model.[15]

In this regard, the organization was dominated by the views of the veterans, who considered their experience and remembrance of the battlefield as unparalleled and incomparably more painful and heroic than anything civilians had lived through, and the most central component for the war commemorative discourse. Subsequent attempts to broaden the definition of heroism and especially to include civilian and volunteer acts (for instance, the actions of volunteer nurses who served on the front but were never officially enlisted, as they were not allowed to by law), were met with harsh negative responses: "Only we [soldiers], and nobody else, have the right to take care of the remains of our comrades and their commemoration."[16] From day one, the Heroes Cult remained committed to an exclusively martial view of remembering war heroism and suffering.[17] This vision also fundamentally silenced any representations of victimhood—military or civilian.

By the time of Marie's and the parliament's official pronouncements about Heroes Day, the important decisions about the religious identification of the date with the Orthodox calendar and about strictly limiting those to be commemorated to soldiers had already been reached behind the closed doors of the Heroes Cult. The religious nature of the holiday posed some important problems for the diverse population of postwar Romania. Being always defined by the Orthodox calendar meant that the date of the holiday would vary each year; the Heroes Day would not be logically and easily marked for the population who were not Orthodox (or for Orthodox believers who followed the "old" calendar).[18] Those who attended private schools, as did many Jews, Hungarians, and Germans in the interwar period, had an even weaker connection to this new and important official holiday.

It is hard to imagine that the queen would have been unaware of these important consequences of supporting the choice of an Orthodox religious holiday for the commemoration of war heroes. She had been raised Episcopalian herself and later converted to Orthodoxy, and she was surrounded by friends and family members who were not Orthodox. But Marie aimed to embody the image of the mother of her country, having already captured the hearts of many soldiers and war volunteers during the war as the "mother of the wounded."[19] She likely realized the boldness of her proposal, and she just embraced with aplomb (and with an unfortunate ignorance of their depth) the religious traditions she was romantically invoking. Just as important were the limitations of the leadership of the Heroes Cult, whose ethnic and religious homogeneity virtually guaranteed that the dialogue about the commemorative discourse would in fact express a unified position on the religious (and by extension ethnic) question. As with other cultural enterprises, by choosing to work with only one of the many diverse communities in Romania, government authorities conducted a dialogue that ignored many of their subjects. By never addressing these gaps, those whose voices were heard, such as the Heroes Cult and the National Orthodox Society of Romanian Women, contributed to silencing important aspects of remembering the war.

On 20 May 1920 the first Heroes Day celebration was held, setting the tone for future official commemorations of the dead in World War I and, between 1945 and 1948 and again after 1989, for the dead of both world wars. There was no direct precedent for these commemorations, but a variety of religious and secular rituals became the building blocks for the Heroes Day celebrations. The festivities commenced in the morning, with a liturgy performed in a designated Orthodox church. In Bucharest the liturgy was held at the Patriarchy in the presence of the king and queen, as well as high dignitaries of the government, church, and the military. In Iași, Romania's capital for part of the war and the seat of the Metropolitan of Moldavia, the *Te Deum* was held at the Metropolitan residence. A second religious ceremony was performed at the main Jewish temple. In other cities a central location, generally the largest Orthodox church, was designated as the official site of the commemorative liturgy.

Orthodox priests at other churches were instructed to perform similar rites in addition to their regular Ascension liturgy, though government officials made it clear that the traditional service should not interfere with the official plans to mobilize the entire population for the Heroes Day commemoration.[20] In other words, Orthodox churches were to accommodate the political goals of the government and monarchy in terms of timing and specific liturgical choices, in order to facilitate the transformation of this religious holiday into a more broadly civic one. Even as the Orthodox Church was to play a central role in the commemorative process, it was by no means in charge of the process. Instead, it had to bow to the secular administration's call for an atmosphere of piety, a religious spectacle meant to give popular legitimacy, and a sober tone to the commemorations. Regular priests and their parishioners actually had few choices with regard to commemorating their own dead. All lay people and clerics were to follow the instructions sent down by the Patriarchy, which were scripted in response to orders from the secular authorities (the military in collaboration with the royal house). Here, the state regulations left little room for dialogue, underscoring instead compliance.

Responses by local authorities in some areas did reflect specific interpretations that enlarged the meaning of the rituals to be allowed. There is no evidence that the Bucharest authorities made special efforts to mobilize other religious denominations for Heroes Day commemorations. In fact, the official notification about the liturgy to be held on 20 May at the Patriarchate called on "laymen and Christians," meaning here Orthodox Christians, to participate.[21] This statement implicitly excluded other religious denominations. The parallel Christian and Jewish commemorations in Iași were in fact more the result of local initiatives than of Bucharest directives. Like Bucharest, Iași had a large Jewish population, many of whom had taken part in the war as soldiers or as civilian volunteers, and who were invested in the promise of gaining full citizen rights as good Romanian patriots in the war.[22] Already in May 1919, the Choral Temple in Bucharest had taken upon itself to hold a special requiem for the heroes who perished in the war, even before the official designation of Heroes Day on the Orthodox holiday of the Ascension. The presence at the event of the Ministry of War and the Royal Court was important for the Jewish community; its leaders aimed at reminding their Romanian rulers that the behavior of the Jewish community during the war was far from the anti-Semitic clichés that circulated widely at that time. Rabbi Dr. Beck reminded his audience that the country "has not sufficiently rewarded these heroes," ending his speech with the hope that "everyone will realize what sacrifices Jews have made on the altar of the fatherland."[23] Notable here is that the state authorities were willing to entertain, on the receiving end, the beginnings of a commemorative dialogue (with clear political goals) that the Jewish community in Bucharest wanted to get across. But central state authorities were *not* interested in responding in kind to this initiative.

That the Choral Temple was not identified among the officially sanctioned commemorative events of Heroes Day in Bucharest in 1920 and later on in the interwar period comes as little surprise. Neither were any liturgies at Catholic and Protestant churches in the capital. More surprising is the accommodation made by officials in Iași.[24] The ecumenical spirit of the Iași local government should be taken as a reflection of local cultural-religious realities, at the expense of strictly following the instructions received from Bucharest.

The religious ceremony was followed by a *parastas* (in fact, three of them in Bucharest) prepared by local groups of Orthodox women, one held at the Patriarchy and two others at cemeteries that had large sections dedicated to the war dead.[25] The *parastas* at the cemetery on the anniversary of a person's death, and also on important religious holidays such as the Ascension, were typical commemorative rites for the Orthodox but entirely foreign to the other religious groups in Romania. There was no living memory of national funerals of prominent Orthodox personalities to create a precedent or public familiarization across all religions. In Transylvania Orthodoxy had been at best tolerated as a public religion by the other denominations, and in the Regat the recently deceased King Charles I and Queen Elisabeth were both Catholics.[26] The closest relevant Orthodox burial had been that of infant Prince Mircea (Queen Marie's son) at the beginning of World War I. But the circumstances of the war's beginnings and the age of the deceased restricted the performance of any lavish commemorations.

It is likely that some non-Orthodox people would have been somewhat familiar with the *parastas* in the countryside. But in a large city like Bucharest, Cluj or Iaşi, Catholics, Protestants, and Jews were not familiar with this custom. For them, attending such a ceremony must have been rather strange. Especially in Transylvania, to have Orthodoxy take center stage with entirely new rituals imposed a foreign and even bizarre spectacle for the majority non-Orthodox urban dwellers. This unique ritual reinforced an important gap: on the one side stood families who commemorated their dead through Orthodox rituals and who found those traditions now recognized and elevated to a higher level of official endorsement; on the other were those who found the memory of *their* dead silenced once more by a ritual that was foreign to their cultural milieu.

After more speeches and a short sermon during the *parastas,* the religious part of the ceremony ended, and a procession was to take place that included religious, governmental, military, philanthropic, boy scout, and educational institutions. All schoolchildren were to take part in the procession, regardless of whether they attended state or private institutions. In Bucharest the procession marched from Victory Square to University Square along the main boulevard in downtown Bucharest, which, even then, would have blocked circulation of traffic through the entire city. If indeed all schoolchildren did attend the procession, then onlookers saw a large motley crew of mostly boys and some girls, representing every ethnicity, religion, and class in Romania.[27] In the 1930s, when Charles II began to organize the *străjeri* organization, these paramilitary scouts groups came to represent youth leadership among the students who marched in the commemorations.[28] As the *străjeri* were to be both ethnic Romanian and religiously Orthodox, that organization reinforced the marginalization of other youth categories.

The procession could be regarded as encompassing all the diversity that existed in the country. But of course many of these children and young adults were taking part in something very strange to their eyes, if they were not themselves ethnic Romanians and especially Orthodox Christians, for at the head of the procession were the high prelates of the Orthodox Patriarchate, with their icons, flags, and incense, all unfamiliar to ethnic minorities (see figure 4.3). Most students were to follow these clerical figures and the military ones, without actually viewing the military cemeteries or, in fact, any memorial to the war dead.

Equally relevant is the choice of destination for the commemorative parade: the statue of Michael the Brave, who had fought against the Hungarian Crown. Michael the Brave had already become a fixture in the landscape of downtown Bucharest, utilized in nationalist demonstrations even before World War I.[29] As the statue was situated across the street from the University of Bucharest, participants in the parades, including schoolchildren, interacted with students attending the university, the up-and-coming intelligentsia of Bucharest. The statue, in a high traffic location large enough to accommodate big crowds, conveyed the kind of patriotic fervor the government wished to bring to Heroes Day commemorations. The administration thus used this older symbol as a stand-in for all the brave soldiers who had perished in the war.

But in fact, there was no obvious connection between Michael the Brave and the sacrifice of soldiers and civilians in World War I. Although he was a figure of myth among many (especially the educated), the rural populations, most of whom were illiterate and unschooled, had at best a spotty knowledge of Michael the Brave.[30] In addition, for those who were not ethnically Romanian, especially new inhabitants of Romania who had fought in World War I on the side of the Central Powers, if Michael the Brave meant anything at all, it was not heroism but rather aggressive disloyalty to the Habsburg Crown. Thus, a gathering of the entire Bucharest population, government representatives, clerics, officers, soldiers, and students, celebrating Michael the Brave as representative of all heroes who died in World War I was likely a signal that those who did not fight on the Romanian side were *not* to be regarded as heroes. The choice of this heavily ethno-nationalist symbol was at best a thoughtless, if pragmatic, choice for staging a large procession and gathering. At worst, it was an aggressive message to all in Romania about the government's intentions to craft commemorations of the war (and implicitly the future of the country) in ethno-nationalist exclusivist directions, and to identify heroism and patriotism with the kind of aggressive militarist legacy that Michael the Brave embodied.

In most urban settings Heroes Day continued with cultural performances of various sorts. In Bucharest, a number of free performances at the National Theater (in 1920, these included "In a Hiding Hole," a play about the war, long-since forgotten), the Athenaeum, and the Lyric Theater, offered the possibility of listening to patriotic verse, drama, choral music, or, for those who hadn't had enough nationalist propaganda for the day, talks on the topic of the war. The commemoration ended with a "torch retreat" at night.[31] This phenomenon of a night-time parade by torchlight seems to have been a secular tradition since before the war that continued into the interwar period, sometimes with more menacing political goals. The ritual, seemingly inspired by ancient Roman rites, evoked the purported Romanian link with Roman culture and civilization.[32] Similar evening cultural events and torch retreats took place in Iași.[33]

It is not clear whether this ritual was faithfully replicated in every town in Romania. But in Iași, with the exception of the dual religious ceremony, it appears to have mirrored the Bucharest commemoration quite closely. The choice of location for the gatherings and processions was, however, locally contingent and didn't seem to have been as laden with ethno-nationalist connotations as the Michael the Brave statue in Bucharest. Yet in Orthodox villages (over 85 percent of Romania's population lived in the countryside during the 1920s and 1930s) the Ascension remained the holiday it had always been, with a small nod to Heroes Day, and in Catholic, Protestant, and Jewish villages the day went unmarked.

In the first years after the war, gatherings of people Bucharest and Iași attended sermons and the *parastas* at a couple of military cemeteries, but in neither of those locations was there yet any actual permanent marker for the war dead. The two largest cities lagged behind the smallest villages in Romania in finding human and material resources to honor in stone and wood the dead of their communities. While Bucharest mothers and fathers, wives and sisters of soldiers who died in the war placed their flowers and candles at the statue of Michael the Brave, a ruler from the seventeenth century, the families and friends of dead soldiers who came from Câmpulung, a small town in Moldavia, celebrated Heroes Day by inaugurating a funerary monument to their deceased fathers, brothers, husbands, and sons.[34]

Over the interwar period Heroes Day became more elaborate and heavily scripted with elements that generally echoed those of the first commemoration—the religious liturgy, a procession, laying of flowers at the tombstones of the war dead or war memorials, military honors and sometimes parades, and cultural programs with a strong nationalist element in schools and various theatres or auditoria. A government order sent to all towns and villages in Romania proclaimed: "Heroes Day has to be celebrated down to the most modest village on the entire territory of Romania, with a distinguished, solemn tone. . . . Our instructions are to be followed exactly by all civilian, military, ecclesiastic, and educational authorities, for which they will be held responsible."[35] Local officials from smaller towns reported to their county prefects about the ceremonies and were to mention any "abnormalities" in the proceedings.

School administrators reported to the Ministry of Education to describe in detail the poems, speeches, and songs performed by schoolchildren in their school's cultural program.[36]

There were few opportunities for personalizing these festivities. Veterans representing the war dead made a personal, direct connection between the war and the present. But the rituals that were to involve the attendees as active participants actually cast most people as mere spectators. These rituals sought to craft identification with a normative—Orthodox Christian and ethnically Romanian—definition of the nation, and by extension, of the heroism that was to be commemorated on Heroes Day. Students were to bring flowers and bows, as well as candles, to the procession. The participants were to sing the national anthem at the start of the ceremony, and to commence the procession when the local churches tolled their bells. During the religious sermon, all attendees were to kneel.[37] While this was an almost automatic response for the Orthodox believers, for the rest of the population this became a way of making them stand out (if they refused to kneel) or intimidating them into engaging in a religious ritual foreign to their beliefs.

The visual and performative commemorative vocabulary constructed by the Bucharest authorities in the early interwar period became solidified over this period and came to shape the government's ideas of any other public commemorations linked to the war. Over time, the rules of the central authorities seemed to become stricter, to the exclusion of local color, rendering impossible any real dialogue between local communities and the state authorities in Bucharest.[38] In the mobilizing commemorative rituals, these communities were to simply fulfill a strictly defined role, to the detriment of any deep emotional identification through local cultural symbols and personalities. Variations in details as small as who would give speeches and when were to be eliminated. A circular the Ministry of Education sent out in May 1931 instructed all school directors that "[s]peeches should not be given on the day before [Heroes Day] and not by teachers; only one student alone, at school, will give a speech, on the day of the commemoration."[39] The Bucharest administration also sent clear warning statements about excluding non-ethnic Romanians from these commemorations:

> The character of this celebration has to be patriotic, however, without hurting the sentiments of the non-Romanian populations, as is the case in Transylvania, the Banat, and Bessarabia, but still glorifying the great sacrifices brought by our nation for the national cause, which has always identified with the cause of civilization, defended everywhere by all cultivated [read "civilized"] people of the world.[40]

This statement encapsulates well the conundrum of trying to build a national unitary state while attempting to persuade ethnic minorities to accept the version of patriotism served by the Romanian state during these commemorations. In these efforts the Romanian authorities were blindsided by their own narrow definitions of what it meant to properly honor the dead, which from the start prevented most minorities—ethnic and religious—from feeling represented.

Throughout the interwar period Heroes Day official commemorations continued to bring to life and streamline a certain recollection of the war—nationalist and Christian Orthodox—as much as they silenced many other versions of remembering the same events. There was room for everyone to take part, the state claimed, in these rituals—civilians and soldiers, ethnic Romanians and other nationalities, Christians and all other religious groups, men and women, veterans and students. But the narrowly scripted ceremonies in which they were to participate reinforced the official versions of this process of remembrance and forced those who didn't identify with this version to remain silent. The fruit of this work was mixed at best—successful maybe among younger ethnic Romanians, but likely frustrating for those of the generation who lived through the war and remembered it differently than they were urged to do in these sermons.

Paul Connerton has drawn attention to the importance of participatory, mobilizing rituals for understanding how modern ideologies have been powerful in turning subjects into active citizens.[41] In Romania, Heroes Day ceremonies were an important first attempt to turn all subjects of Romania into patriotically enthusiastic Romanians. Yet, given the religiously (and implicitly ethnically) exclusivist elements of these rituals, they served from day one not only to mobilize loyalism, but also to silence or possibly elicit active disloyalty on the part of marginalized minorities.

The exclusionary nature of these commemorations was not unique to Romania. The case presented here is illustrative of similar tensions among populations in ethno-religiously diverse countries in eastern Europe. Orthodox rituals in Yugoslavia occasioned the Croatian populations' viewing themselves as second-class citizens and their dead soldiers as unaccounted heroes in the war.[42] Conversely, in Poland the Catholic Church took center stage in commemorations, to the exclusion of Protestants and Jews.[43] Though not unique to eastern Europe, the tensions analyzed here played a more significant social, political, and cultural role in these newly minted states with old religious traditions than in the more secularized western European ones that have been taken as the exemplars for constructing the narratives regarding the "European" memory of the Great War. What Jay Winter remarked as a somewhat surprising resistance to change among communities in France, for instance, is no surprise at all when it comes to the post-imperial lands of eastern Europe.

A Crowded Commemorative Calendar: 24 January, 10 May, 8 June, 6 August, 1 December

Besides conflicts over the narrow signification of heroism and patriotism through Heroes Day commemorations, the Romanian state itself had to contend with its own attempts to designate a host of other days as national holidays linked to the creation of Greater Romania that would also serve for commemorating World War I. In this multitude of national holidays, Heroes Day had a difficult time standing out, though the celebrations organized on that day were generally more lavish than on other dates. Having these other dates as national holidays, however, enabled local communities to put their own imprint on what they considered most symbolically appropriate. Although officials in Bucharest insisted that all communities should respect the officially determined schedules and celebratory prescriptions, local communities usually responded with polite nods. These communities reminded the capital that their resources were limited, and that they could not afford to put on all the commemorations Bucharest requested, except on a limited scale. Unsurprisingly, at the local level, veterans organizations, priests, teachers, mayors, and any other people with resources and public authority preferred to focus on the dates and ceremonies that most resonant with their own local remembrances of the war.

Among the commemorative days with some broad public significance in Romania before 1919, 24 January, the date in 1859 when Walachia and Moldavia were united to lay the basis for modern Romania, held absolutely no significance for people who had lived in the Habsburg or Russian empire at that time but became part of Romania after the war. Yet, especially for Moldavians, the date evoked great pride in their leadership role in the creation of modern Romania. In that region the day continued to be commemorated in most schools and towns through secular and religious ceremonies, with homage being paid to World War I in the same celebration.[44] Yet for those in Transylvania and neighboring Bukovina, for instance, this date remained a locally insignificant official holiday when schoolchildren had the day off.

A date of great importance for the monarchy, as well as inhabitants of the Regat, was 10 May. Between 1877 and 1930, when Charles II returned to Romania, 10 May was a great national holiday,[45] broader in reach than commemorations of World War I, for it celebrated the entire reign of the Hohenzollern-Sigmaringen dynasty in Romania, from Charles I to Ferdinand and, after his death, of the regency and Queen Marie. On 10 May in 1877 Romania had declared independence, and Charles I was proclaimed king. Until 1919 this date was thus connected strictly and directly to Romania's independence and Charles I's personal achievements. No other national holidays competed with 10 May until after the war except 24 January, which was not linked to the monarchy in any fashion.

After the war, Ferdinand and Marie wished to make the monarchy theirs through both symbols and action. Greater Romania was militarily and diplomatically their achievement to a great extent: Ferdinand had been the commander of the fighting forces and Marie had been present on the front with the medical corps and subsequently worked assiduously in Paris on behalf of the postwar peace negotiations. Both the king and queen, especially Marie, were wildly popular after the war. In addition to using Heroes Day to celebrate their great achievements in World War I, the king and queen also turned 10 May into a national holiday that would reinforce the monarchy's vision of how to remember the war.

The same kinds of religious ceremonies (albeit dedicated to the king and the queen, rather than the multitudes of soldiers who had died), with parades of military troops, government leaders and other civilian state representatives, as well as religious authorities and school pupils, dominated 10 May celebrations. Starting in 1924 they also included a more significant element connected to World War I: laying wreaths, flowers, and candles at the Tomb of the Unknown Soldier.[46] Cultural events such as musical and theatrical performances at the Athenaeum and other large venues would end the official public celebrations of the day.

The greatest pomp displayed during the 10 May festivities took place in Bucharest, and the monarchs never made an effort to take the celebration on the road. They wanted to be feted in their seat of power, even when provincial areas were their great prize in the war (Transylvania) or had been temporarily their seat of power during the war (Iași). The Bucharest celebrations were mostly staged for the king and queen, even when they were not in attendance.[47] After 1919 there was a clear shift in size and scope of the 10 May festivities. Becoming leaders of Greater Romania emboldened Marie and Ferdinand to celebrate their reign in a more grandiose style than the reserved Charles I.

In the provinces, people had the day off and were to participate in similar ceremonies as those put on in Bucharest. But, as with 24 January, this holiday had vastly different meanings in Moldavia and Walachia compared to Transylvania, Bukovina, Bessarabia, and the Banat. In the newly incorporated territories, there was great ambivalence toward Ferdinand and Marie. While ethnic Romanians generally embraced them as liberators, the rest of the population had either a doubtful or a forthrightly antagonistic relationship with the Romanian monarchy.

In addition, Ferdinand and Marie had accompanied the Romanian troops to the Tisza, deep into Hungary, in 1919, to "liberate" that country from the Red Scare of Béla Kun. Thus, even as Marie cut a charismatic, beautiful figure for many, she represented, especially for Hungarians, the partner of the king who took away their status and made them second-class citizens in Transylvania. Then in October 1922 Ferdinand and Marie went to Alba Iulia for their coronation as king and queen of Greater Romania. The ceremony lacked any legal justification, but the king and queen wanted to mark this historic occasion with a magnificent ceremony.[48] They chose Alba Iulia because it had been the site of a popular meeting on 1 December 1918, where representatives from all over Transylvania had voted overwhelmingly for the unification of Transylvania with Romania. The 1 December 1918 referendum was not legally binding and it is unlikely it would have carried the day if it hadn't circumstantially coincided with the interests of the Great Powers. But it had great psychological significance for all Romanian nationalists in Transylvania and Romania, who held this meeting as the proof that Transylvania belonged to Romania on the basis of democratic principles.[49]

When the king and queen made their way to Alba Iulia in October 1922 it was a warm homecoming for the Romanians, and a menacing reminder for all others that Transylvania was indeed no longer *their* land. By staging the unnecessary coronation in Alba Iulia, the king and queen struck a different chord with those who took part than with those who stayed home but were made aware of every detail of the festivities. The ceremony was not only lavishly featured in every newspaper, with pages upon pages of images and adulatory articles by prominent writers and politicians. It was also filmed, and the short movie that resulted was shown as an opening feature in many movie theaters throughout the country.

After the coronation, the image of the king and queen became more prominently fixed in public spaces in Transylvania, as well as in the minds and hearts of people living there, reinforcing their sympathies or antipathies toward the monarchy. The 10 May celebrations reinforced these images and feelings. This holiday generally unified ethnic Romanians around the crown beyond regional differences, while it separated inhabitants of Romania along ethnic lines, especially between those living in Transylvania and those living in the Regat. For religious minorities such as the Jews, however, this day represented a different opportunity, in addition to Heroes Day, to remind their ethnic Romanian co-nationals that they had been loyal subjects of the monarchy and brave defenders of the king and queen in World War I. On the occasion of the coronation, the Bucharest synagogues held sermons "full of pure piety. . . . [O]ur prayers will rise to heaven for the well-being of the country and the king. . . . Alongside the whole of Romaniandom we fought and brought heavy sacrifices in the war for the unification of the nation."[50] No similar events were organized by Jewish communities in Transylvania.

In the 1930s, another date gradually overtook the 10 May celebrations. On 8 June 1930, Charles II returned to Romania under the cloak of darkness, against the wishes of his mother and the political leadership. The next day Charles II resumed his position as king, even though he had signed a document renouncing his rights to the crown. His mother was flabbergasted, the political leadership appalled, but Charles II had many supporters, especially in the army, and was able to resume his role as king. Charles II became obsessed with making good on his promise to take care of Romania's interests by designing extravagant programs for military and urban development and education reform, and by turning Romania into a country ready to fight against the territorial revisionism of its neighbors, most prominently Hungary and the Soviet Union. Charles II also loved pomp and circumstance, and he turned 8 June into the celebration of his reign. By moving the celebration of the monarchy from that associated with his predecessors, Charles II aimed to make the crown his own. Thus 8 June became a national holiday and included all the religious, military, and civilian events described above in relation to 10 May.

But Charles II wanted even more. He wished to replace memories of his disgraceful behavior in World War I with a different official image of the war.[51] He took it upon himself to become an avid supporter of war memorials, including the still unfinished Mărășești Mausoleum invoked at the beginning of this chapter. He also began to personally oversee the staging of military parades and commemorations of the war dead on Heroes Day and 8 June, not just in Bucharest but also in other places, such as sites that had been major battlefields during the war. For instance, he made sure that a commemoration of the war dead at Mărășești took place on 8 June, even though that date was not associated with the battle of Mărășești.

It is unclear to what extent this new holiday successfully generated greater popularity and legitimacy for Charles II. Students took part in the events because they had the day off and were supposed to participate. Likewise, the military, religious, and government employees participated because it was their duty. Newspapers did report about the lavish celebrations, including accounts of the great crowds that participated in these events. But by the late 1930s, there was a greater degree of cynicism and outright questioning of the political establishment, including the king's role in it, among many people.[52]

Starting in 1919, one other national holiday was added to the increasingly crowded commemorative calendar, 1 December.[53] More than any other national holiday instituted after World War I, 1 December came to divide people all over Romania along mostly ethnic, but also regional, lines. Romanians in Transylvania took pride in this holiday, but not all felt as supportive about it. For Romanian women from Transylvania, 1 December represented the failed promise of full political rights.[54] And, of course,

Hungarian and German ethnics did not participate in these celebrations willingly, or even in any manner. Their children enrolled in state schools were obligated to do so, but these communities did not go out of their way to mark 1 December with religious or secular cultural rituals of any kind.

For most ethnic Romanians, however, this date became another occasion for asserting the link between the sacrifices of Romanian soldiers and the achievements of Greater Romania. Initially in Transylvania, but gradually all over the country (though by no means in every village and town), on 1 December churches tolled their bells to mark the holiday and offered special liturgies honoring the king and queen, as well as the soldiers of the Romanian army who had died in World War I. Schools and cultural organizations with a strong nationalist background, like Astra in Transylvania and the Cultural League in the Regat, organized extravagant performances that included speeches by historians and politicians, as well as nationalist poetry and music recitals. Though outspoken in their nationalist ethos, the 1 December celebrations were quite different from the participatory commemorations of Heroes Day. Veterans were sometimes invited to speak, possibly the closest affective connection to personal remembrances of the war. But the names of the deceased and details about the tragedy of the war were generally left outside the frame of these celebrations; performances focused instead on glorifying the leadership of Romania during the war and afterward.[55]

In this growing cacophony of holidays and commemorative events for the war, a few that were more localized remained more evocatively linked to the events of the war, particularly the official dates of some of the bloodiest and most famous battles. The most well-known and best attended was Mărășești, whose official date was 6 August.[56] Throughout the interwar period, 6 August remained an important marking point for recalling the immense losses in the war for all Romanians.[57] The state played an important role in bringing growing attention to it, but the government was neither the initiator, nor the main promoter of the Mărășești commemorations. In fact, 6 August never became a national holiday or even a local school holiday. Instead, 6 August was promoted mostly by a number of non-governmental organizations and the army, through the Heroes Cult.

The initiator and most active force behind staging these commemorations was a women's organization, the National Orthodox Society of Romanian Women, and especially the group's president, Alexandrina Cantacuzino. Cantacuzino had been present at the founding of the Heroes Cult in 1919, and she had insisted from the beginning that her organization and Romanian Orthodox women in general had an important role to play in gathering the bones, offering proper burial, and keeping alive the memory of the dead heroes. In addition, she had volunteered during the war at a prominent hospital in Bucharest, and she had multiple family members who had fought on the front. In claiming a central role for her organization in the commemorative rituals, Cantacuzino spoke not only as an ambitious entrepreneur; she also aimed to bring attention to the important social role women played in Orthodox Christian religious culture and rituals, especially with regard to the cult of the dead. Like many other Orthodox women, Cantacuzino couldn't fathom giving proper burial and having a proper *parastas* without the direct and heavy involvement of women, who were in fact those with the expertise in all the details of this complex process.

Her suggestion was welcomed at best with mixed feelings. The other women who sat on the board of the Heroes Cult, all of them devout Orthodox Christians and widows of generals who had perished in the war, either agreed with her or did not object to this view. But the majority of the board was made up of army officers and war veterans, who believed that they, above anyone else, should in fact be the guardians of the memory of their brothers in arms: "Only we [soldiers] and no one else have the right to take care of the remains of our comrades-in-arms and their commemoration."[58] This attitude is as unsurprising as that of the women who claimed the expertise and right to organize the commemorative services. Soldiers had just undergone a horrific experience that created strong bonds of affection, which seemed as close as those they had with their families. Thus the struggle inside the Heroes Cult was of two emotionally bonded communities that claimed the dead soldiers as their own. Both did so in the name of patriotism. But both did so fundamentally out of a sense of profound attachment to specific traditions—religious versus military.

Though the Heroes Cult ultimately found Cantacuzino's claims too aggressive and unwelcome, she was not easily intimidated; the military leaders had to put up with her, largely because of her own actions during the war (she had served at a Romanian POW hospital in Bucharest and helped a number of officers and soldiers to escape to Moldavia). Moreover, she was married to a high-ranking officer in the Romanian army. So Cantacuzino remained on the board of the Heroes Cult, mostly to keep tabs on the actions this organization was undertaking, and also to retain a link with the National Orthodox Romanian Women's Society. One could say the two organizations were officially working together, but that doesn't seem to have been the spirit of their relationship. Instead, they remained competitive, becoming antagonistic in the 1930s.

For its part, the National Orthodox Romanian Women's Society decided to dedicate most of its commemorative work to the Mărăşeşti memorial and site, while the Heroes Cult was to oversee more broadly the proper care of monuments and commemorations of the war dead on the entire territory of Romania. At Mărăşeşti, Cantacuzino's organization also worked with other groups. The Mărăşeşti Veterans' Association was dedicated to remembering the battle and those who had fallen there. Since the battle produced 35,000 dead and many more wounded, and over 50,000 men who had participated in the battle were still alive, this organization had a broad demographic basis, but not much experience with commemorations. They provided the human resources and first-hand remembrances of soldiers' experiences in that battle. An additional organization that provided assistance was the Mărăşeşti Society, which was based in that town and mostly assisted with local logistical support for staging the commemorations, while raising money for its own goal of rebuilding the town.

With the support of these two groups, every year on 6 August, from 1919 to 1938, the National Orthodox Romanian Women's Society staged an annual *parastas* for all who had died in the Mărăşeşti battle. The organization's focus was on preserving Orthodox customs, and so they adhered to traditional rituals, making the religious component central to the commemoration.[59] The strength of the National Orthodox Romanian Women's Society was in their great connections with Orthodox communities throughout the country and also among the clergy. Cantacuzino was able to often call upon high representatives of the Church to perform the liturgy for the dead, including the Metropolitan of Moldavia (see figure 4.1). More importantly, the organization was able to get in touch with the families and friends of soldiers who died in the battle and spread the news of the *parastas,* so that communities from all over the Regat came together to remember their loved ones at the site where they had perished. The National Orthodox Romanian Women's Society was even able to offer some assistance for veterans and poor families to attend these services. Cantacuzino used these connections, as well as the press, to publicize the 6 August commemorations, which became a tradition that was featured in great detail in the major newspapers of the day, such as *Universul* and *Curentul.* The results were impressive; thousands of people attended every year, even though Mărăşeşti is a difficult place to reach, especially for people from the countryside, who made up the bulk of families that had lost loved ones in the famous battle.

The National Orthodox Romanian Women's Society also opened up a dialogue with educational institutions, trying to convince the Ministry of Education to facilitate school trips there by offering cheap train tickets and the day off for students to participate. There is no evidence, however, that the officials at the Ministry were generally responsive to these suggestions. Still, the Society was able to rely on its own resources for such initiatives: it had its own girls school in Bucharest and was in good relations with several other girls schools in the capital. Together, they successfully organized annual student pilgrimages to Mărăşeşti.[60] On one occasion, in the fall of 1938, over 150 students from one school participated in such a commemorative trip, lavishly praised in the press.[61]

At the request of the Ministry of War, the commemorations also came over time to include a growing dose of secular speechifying and military parading. Cantacuzino

Figure 4.1. Queen Marie at a Mărăşeşti commemoration in 1928.
Photo courtesy of the National Military Museum.

herself was present every year and, in addition to presiding over the ceremonies, always gave a speech to remind her audiences about the important role her organization had played in keeping the memory of the Mărăşeşti heroes alive:

> The members of the National Orthodox Romanian Women's Society, out of deep piety, took the initiative to raise this great Mausoleum, where 10,000 soldiers who fell here during the Great War rest, together with generals Eremia Grigorescu and Cristescu. . . . Romanian women, who fought for one thousand years to keep unaltered our spiritual patrimony, and who linked their name to this great Mausoleum of eternal remembrance and glory, we thank you for coming to kneel at this holy Altar.[62]

Any mention of the Heroes Cult or the army, other than as soldiers who had sacrificed themselves in the Mărăşeşti battle, rarely made it into Cantacuzino's speeches, betraying the tense relationship that continued between these organizations throughout the interwar period.

The 6 August commemorations were a great success, to judge by the continued interest in the press, the large numbers of people who attended, and the efforts made at bringing schoolchildren there. Most remarkable about these commemorations is that the state offered some support, financial and logistical, but generally in response to initiatives of non-governmental organizations such as the National Orthodox Romanian Women's Society, veterans groups, or the Mărășești Society. The Orthodox Church, though heavily involved in terms of the spectacle of the commemorations, was present at Mărășești at the initiative of a non-governmental organization, rather than the state itself. Their success can be generally credited to a strategy by the National Orthodox Romanian Women's Society to build on existing Orthodox rituals of commemorating the dead, rather than inventing new ones.

For families who lost loved ones in the Mărășești battle, remembering the dead on the day they had died and in the place where their bodies were buried represented something more familiar and comforting than any of the governmental commemorations at that time; and people responded by attending these events faithfully. During the first few years after 1918, the National Orthodox Romanian Women's Society also helped organize several campaigns for "cleaning" the Mărășești fields, collecting and washing bones from the large expanse where the battle had taken place, to be then placed into crypts that lay beneath what would eventually (1938) become the Mausoleum. Veterans' organizations and the Mărășești Society also helped with these efforts. But during the first few years, the *parastas* approximated traditional burial practices more closely than any other large-scale commemorations: the bones of soldiers who actually died in the battle were buried by the National Orthodox Romanian Women's Society with the assistance of the actual families of the dead.

This success was also why the military establishment and especially the Heroes Cult put up with the National Orthodox Romanian Women's Society, its main competitor for guardianship of the Mărășești war dead. But by 1938, when the monument was finally realized, the Heroes Cult completely took over the commemorations, relegating the National Orthodox Romanian Women's Society to the role of behind-the-scenes organizers. The Ministry of War coordinated the events, financed the commemorations, and issued the invitations to the festivities. The Society was no longer responsible for the commemorations, which also started to take on a more martial character they have retained to this day. The archives of the Society give the impression that Cantacuzino was generally unhappy to relinquish her organization's role and that her version of having a dialogue with the military authorities was rather trenchant, similar to the attitude of the military officers on the board of the Heroes Cult. But regardless of these internal struggles and despite never becoming an officially endorsed holiday, 6 August emerged as a beloved, much publicized, and successful festivity, more so than any date from the official commemorative calendar.

Monuments of Remembrance: The Tomb of the Unknown Soldier

Spatial commemorative efforts became as important for the government as temporal ones. At the first Heroes Day commemoration it had already become apparent that Romanians as a nation did not have a proper monument where they could lay their flowers and place candles in remembrance of the heroes of the nation. Most public monuments commemorated great historical figures, political, military, or cultural, but not the average soldiers who had paid the highest cost for their participation in the war. While small communities had no trouble assembling funerary monuments for their loved ones who died in the war, the government had to consider the matter on a national scale, being careful not to offend anyone and attempting to use such a monument to rouse the patriotic loyalty of its citizens.[63] This issue was a concern in all other states created out of the eastern European empires; there, as in Romania, the first move of the authorities was to link commemorative rituals to older, often pre-modern political and especially religious sites or monuments.

Gazing westward toward France, Belgium, and Great Britain, the Romanian government and army decided that the best symbol for the sacrifice of the 350,000 soldiers who perished in the war would be a Tomb of the Unknown Soldier. Initially, the army suggested Mărăşeşti as the best site to represent Romanian heroism on a national scale. But subsequently the choice became Bucharest. Logistical issues (the remoteness of Mărăşeşti) as well as political considerations (placing the Tomb close to the seat of power, so that the monument could be accessible for suitable occasions) played a role in this choice.

The committee charged with deciding the procedure for selection and the ritual, comprising principally bureaucrats from the ministries of War, Education, Arts and Religion, and Work and Social Protection, decided to combine the two locations, Mărăşeşti and Bucharest, through a symbolic trip of the Unknown Hero from the battlefield to the capital on Heroes Day in 1923.[64] It is worth pausing to reflect on the options considered by the selection committee for the placement of the Tomb in Bucharest in order to better understand how government representatives constructed the basic building blocks of the official commemorative discourses that developed subsequently. As with all other monuments erected after World War I, the space in which the monument was to be built was carefully considered. The ultimate choice reflects both a compromise of various visions and a particular articulation of what it meant to honor the war dead and keep their memory alive. To begin with, no indoor locations were considered. Unlike Great Britain, where the Unknown Soldier was laid in Westminster Abbey, the location was going to be outdoors, presumably to ensure maximum visibility and accessibility at all times. But what locations in Bucharest were considered? Where did the committee believe that the geography of the capital's urban plan allowed for a suitably grandiose and pious viewing of the Tomb? The four choices were:

1) Under or next to the statue of Michael the Brave.
2) On the square in front of the Military Circle.
3) In the Military Museum park (Charles I Park).
4) Under the Triumphal Arch.[65]

The second choice, though symbolically dear to the army because the Military Circle was their main club and place of gathering for officers in Bucharest, was dismissed first. Members of the planning committee and even the press considered the location unsuitable, as the Military Circle was often a place for joyful celebrations, such as weddings, and its location was on the fashionable Calea Victoriei, across the street from several famous cabaret theaters (Tănase) and cafes (Capşa)—in other words in the heart of the nightlife district. It was hard for many to imagine the kind of pious atmosphere suitable for such a monument, when bands and cheering could be heard nearby.[66]

More people leaned toward the Michael the Brave location or the Triumphal Arch. Both locations already included a well-established monument. The Michael the Brave statue had already been used in the first Heroes Day celebration, so officials were somewhat used to the idea of that location already. It was easily accessible, and one could count on large crowds taking part in the commemorations. But it was also close to a noisy part of downtown, where there was a great deal of traffic and bustle, and many restaurants nearby.

By contrast, the Triumphal Arch was not easily accessible to those who didn't have private means of transportation, and it was located in the middle of a large intersection that didn't provide easy pedestrian access and saw heavy traffic. The Triumphal Arch remained recognizable and visible from far away, but it had no power to evoke or provide a peaceful atmosphere that would encourage individuals to pray or offer their personal thanks at the Tomb.

The third choice, in front of the Military Museum in the Charles I Park, emerged as the best compromise for a peaceful setting under army oversight. Though less centrally located than choices one and two and difficult to access for those who didn't live in the neighborhood, this park held another important appeal. It was close to one of the largest cemeteries in Bucharest, Bellu, where many officers who had died in the war were buried, along with many politicians and other prominent political figures. So the Tomb of the Unknown Soldier would be relatively close for those who wanted

Figure 4.2. The Tomb of the Unknown Soldier during the 1930s.
Photo courtesy of the National Military Museum.

to stage combined commemorative ceremonies at the tomb of family members and connect them to the symbolism of the Tomb of the Unknown Soldier.

In addition, the park itself had been built up into a semipermanent exhibit to celebrate the reign of Charles I. In addition to planting a number of beautiful trees, bushes, and flowers, and creating ponds, fountains, and other elements of landscaping, in 1906 the monarchy celebrated its twenty-fifth anniversary by erecting a number of pavilions and buildings, such as the Military Museum and the Palace of the Arts, to recall the great achievements of Charles I's long reign. The exhibit was reminiscent in part of the *exposition universelle* trend in curatorial arts at that time. The Tomb of the Unknown Soldier itself was to reside outdoors, on a hill, halfway between the top, where the Military Museum offered a vista of the entire park, and the bottom, where a crystalline lake reflected the trees surrounding the hill. The view of the park and city from the Tomb of the Unknown Soldier was both grandiose and extremely peaceful, giving visitors the illusion that they were in a vast forest, with the city seen but not heard somewhere in the distance.

The Tomb was constructed rather hurriedly in the spring of 1923, in order to have the site ready for the Heroes Day commemoration that year, and it was subsequently redone in marble following a design competition held in the summer of 1923, after the

Unknown Soldier had already been laid to rest at the site of the Tomb. The final form of the Tomb, as it remained until World War II (and as seen in figure 4.2), took shape only in 1934, when a marble candelabrum was placed at the head of the funerary stone.

A committee comprising army and city hall administrators selected the design, but virtually all four choices presented to them represented different versions of a traditional princely tombstone, as seen in churches from Curtea de Argeş to Putna. There were no designs that offered a more secular or modern representation of piety and honor, even as the Society for Heroes Graves (affiliated with the Heroes Cult) was trying to coordinate activities to render war monuments more monumental following modern criteria (e.g., obelisks) and looking less like traditional funerary markers. The Tomb of the Unknown Soldier ended up looking rather flat and simple, with the ten posts surrounding it and connecting the bronze chain around the Tomb as the most prominent three-dimensional feature from far away. This design ensured that most people who visited the Tomb came close enough to the stone to actually touch it. In photographs from the interwar period one can see groups of visiting students standing next to the Tomb as they read the inscription and listen to lectures. The Tomb communicated respect for the soldier who lay beneath the beautiful stone, as well as intimacy.

The design on the funerary stone was inspired by the heavily decorative Brâncoveanu Baroque style, with flowers and other stylized plants as the frame for the inscription at the stone's center. Above the inscription there was an angel, a reference to Orthodox religious traditions, and above the angel was the symbol of the Romanian crown—a vulture (or eagle) wearing the royal crown and covered by a shield that had symbols of all the new territories acquired by Romania after 1918, holding a scepter and a sword in its claws, as well as a cross in its beak. The inscription at the center of the funerary stone read: "Here sleeps happily under God the unknown soldier, who sacrificed his life for the unity of the Romanian people; on his bones rests the soil of unified Romania: 1916–1919." An eternal flame of remembrance burned permanently at the head of the funerary stone.

There was no question as to what vision of Romania this tombstone offered. It was a Romania defined by the royal crown, by its achievements in the war in terms of territorial acquisitions, and where the Romanian people, as a unified cohesive Orthodox Christian (and implicitly ethnically Romanian) whole dwelled. For those who didn't fit this description, there was virtually no room to reinterpret the Tomb, for the words were carefully chosen to have a clear, albeit metaphorical, message. But for Romanian parents and spouses who lost loved ones on the front, this stone and the inscription had the power both to evoke a sense of personal loss felt by families and also to connect it to the greatness of the heroism and sacrifices undertaken by these families on behalf of the country and nation.

The elaborate ceremonial of selecting the soldier to be buried in the Tomb was also carefully planned to reinforce the same nationalist vision. The Unknown Soldier was to be chosen from a group of first eight and eventually ten unknown soldiers, selected from places where "some of the toughest fighting" had taken place. The first eight locations were linked to the Walachian and Moldavian fronts, the site of most of the fighting during the war. At the last minute, three days before the first body was to be exhumed, the special military commission designated to deal with the ceremony decided to add two more locations: the town of Ciucea in Transylvania and Bessarabia's capital, Chișinău. Both places were presumably to symbolize the sacrifice of "Romanians under foreign rule." In each location, a school pupil, preferably a war orphan, was to select the body to be exhumed. The bodies were placed in specially designed identical coffins, and a local Orthodox priest performed a burial ceremony together with a *parastas* for the dead soldier. In each of the ten locales, the local population came in droves, bringing flowers and candles, to participate in the religious ceremony and *parastas*.[67] (See figure 4.3.)

The ten coffins traveled to Mărășești, symbolically chosen because of its already mythical position in the war narrative. At Mărășești work was under way for a large mausoleum, but a chapel already stood in place and the local community had been commemorating the battle on 6 August since 1919, so that a tradition was already locally established. At the Church of the Assumption in Mărășești, Amilcar Săndulescu, a young war orphan enrolled in a military school, chose one of the ten coffins, which was to be buried in Bucharest. After a religious sermon in the church overflowing with military personnel, schoolchildren, and townspeople, Săndulescu, whose young frame was barely visible above the ten coffins, went around them with the Minister of War several times, until he stopped in front of the fourth, laid his hand on it, and supposedly said spontaneously: "This is my father!" He then knelt and prayed out loud for the ten soldiers in the quiet church.[68]

The chosen coffin was placed in a special train that stopped in every train station from Mărășești to Bucharest, according to a well-publicized schedule. It gave a chance to each of these towns and villages to place flowers and wreaths next to the coffin, and thus participate in the reburial of this soldier. Brief Orthodox ceremonies were also held along the way. At North Station in Bucharest, thousands of people had come to see the train and have a viewing of the coffin, as it was transported slowly toward an open cart that took it to the Michael Voivode Orthodox Church. There, the coffin could be viewed for two days, before being taken to the Charles I Park. The trip to Bucharest was filmed and shown at many movie theaters across the country, displaying an impressive popular response to the ceremony. Sweeping shots of the people gathered along the way showed an unmistakable spontaneous show of emotion on the part of those who

Figure 4.3. The reburial of the Unknown Soldier, 1923.
Photo courtesy of the National Military Museum.

came to see the coffin. In small towns it looked like the entire population had come to view the coffin, with people hanging out of windows, on top of buildings, and up in trees to catch a glimpse of the Unknown Soldier.

The ceremonial was heavily dominated by the presence of the Orthodox Church and was structured around Orthodox traditions of burial and remembrance of the dead. Yet an important element was quite different. While local communities participated in these rituals, they were mainly observers or secondary participants. The choice of who would be exhumed, the look of the coffin and its preparation, the preparation of the body, and the transport were visibly controlled by the military establishment, with assistance from local priests and other administrative personnel. Lay people and the families of the dead soldiers had an opportunity to lay flowers, kneel, take part in the *parastas,* but they were not in charge of the ritual. The nation (ethnically Romanian and Orthodox Christian, to the implicit exclusion of Hungarians, Germans, Jews, Catholics, Uniates, and Protestants) had taken over the process.[69] The Tomb of the Unknown Soldier and the ceremonies undertaken for the burial were also to become models for future monuments and commemorative rituals. But the Bucharest officials quickly discovered that most communities continued to bury their loved ones in the same fashion they had done before this lavish ceremony, and that monuments erected by communities to commemorate their war dead continued to reflect local traditions and tastes more than Bucharest norms.

Mărăşeşti: The Church of the Nation

The 1923 ceremonies brought renewed attention to the Mărăşeşti field and the project that was underway there to erect a large mausoleum to host the bones of over five thousand recovered bodies from the major battle of the Romanian front. This project, coordinated by the National Orthodox Romanian Women's Society, had become almost an obsession for its leader, Alexandrina Cantacuzino. She had already established herself as a force to be reckoned with at the founding of the Heroes Cult society, when she made the initial and successful bid for overseeing fundraising and the architectural competition for the mausoleum.

Over the 1920s and 1930s her confrontations with the military establishment continued, especially since the cost (forty million lei) of the project chosen for the mausoleum far exceeded the funds collected by the National Orthodox Romanian Women's Society in its multiple campaigns. It is not clear why the Romanian government, having placed such emphasis from the beginning of the interwar period on the need to properly honor the war dead, did not also make clear provisions for funding such a monument. One possible explanation is that the government was faced with major financial problems in this area of expenditure. The first responsibility of the military was to locate, gather, and bury all of its soldiers who perished in the war, including those who had died on foreign soil. Establishing military cemeteries and offering proper burial to all the soldiers who were located on Romania's soil was also the responsibility of the military. Given the immense number of dead bodies and the size of the front, these two tasks were in fact extremely costly. The army ultimately had to count on local people to help with this work, both by gathering bones and by paying the cost of burying them and erecting military cemeteries. In addition, the government paid for the stupendous expenses involved in selecting and burying the Unknown Soldier. But it did not show the same magnanimity when it came to Mărăşeşti. It might also be that, given all the different requests for supporting local initiatives for monuments, the Bucharest authorities did not wish to privilege this one project at the expense of all others. But at the same time, both the 1923 ceremonies and many other documents support the notion that Mărăşeşti was regarded as a unique and special place in terms of remembering the war, to be treated with greater devotion and respect than other commemorative sites.

There is another possible explanation, having to do with the initial success of the National Orthodox Romanian Women's Society in securing control over the process of

building the monument and their profile as a women's organization. The military officials dealing with the military cemeteries and the Heroes Cult did not trust Cantacuzino and her organization enough to offer financial support without strings attached.
In addition, the National Orthodox Romanian Women's Society boasted of its great
connections in Orthodox communities throughout the country and its ability to
mobilize people for the purposes of fundraising. Given this image that the organization
presented to the military establishment in the early 1920s, and the subsequent lack of
success in raising sufficient funds, the National Orthodox Romanian Women's Society
looked rather like a fiscally unsound and even possibly irresponsible outfit. In fact, articles to this effect appeared in the press in the 1920s and 1930s, without any proof, however, of actual misdeeds.[70] Ultimately, it looked more likely that the National Orthodox
Romanian Women's Society had overestimated its powers of financial persuasion,
as well as economic well-being and public generosity in postwar Romania.

Whatever the reasons behind the discrepancy between the official signals regarding the importance of Mărășești, on the one hand, and the lack of government financial
support for the project, on the other hand, the building of the mausoleum dragged on
throughout the 1920s and 1930s. This was not for lack of effort. The National Orthodox Romanian Women's Society did everything from organizing charity balls and
cultural events in Bucharest and other cities, to selling bricks (donors would donate
the equivalent of a brick to be placed at the foundation of the monument), sending
around collection boxes at state schools and Orthodox churches.[71] The money trickled
in, but it didn't flow.

Several elements account for this lack of popular response, the most important
being the lack of tradition for fundraising on this scale. Asking people to give money
for something they were likely to never see was unprecedented in Romanian cultural
tradition. The Orthodox Church had encouraged philanthropic actions before, but
always inside or in the vicinity of the community that gave the money. The beneficia-
ries of such actions, moreover, were usually monks or nuns—essentially the Church
itself. If people accepted the abstract notion that giving to the Church would help them
achieve salvation, they were not yet invested (in terms of deep beliefs and actions) in
the abstract notion that giving to the nation was their duty and a way to honor the
war dead.

People also had limited resources. Romanians were, on average, poor, and generally preferred to give any surplus to causes they could follow directly and were personally invested in. Even the poor (for instance, war widows) were willing to give money
to monuments that were to be located in their communities, and where the names of
their loved ones would be inscribed for eternal remembrance. But giving money to a

monument in a town far away, which they might never see, and where nobody they knew was buried, made little sense to most people.

After the start of the Great Depression, both private and public financial resources for projects such as Mărășești diminished. It was only in the mid-1930s, when Charles II's projects of rebuilding Romanian defense resources helped in the partial recovery of the economy, that significant support for the monument resumed. By then the mothers and fathers of those who had been buried at Mărășești had grown old, and could no longer make the annual trip to the site on 6 August in the hope of seeing the monument. It was the children of the war dead who watched over the finishing of the Mausoleum.

The sight that awaited the massive delegations of military, clerical, lay adult, and schoolchildren participants at the official dedication of the Mărășești Mausoleum on 18 September 1938 was truly impressive. The monument stood in the middle of the field, away from any obstructions, dominating the entire landscape with its massive presence. Over seventy-three feet (twenty-two meters) tall and surrounded by six terraces that extended out for a length of over two hundred feet (sixty meters), the Mausoleum was topped by a traditional Orthodox cross (in the same Brâncovenesc style as the Unknown Soldier tombstone) that stood over eleven feet tall (3.37 meters).

The exterior design of the mausoleum itself recalled nothing from the Romanian Orthodox tradition, however, save for the cross. Instead, it combined a fortress-like surface and use of materials (especially stone) with a circular design that echoed a much older famous site in Romania, the Adamclisi memorial in Dobrodgea, one of the oldest and proudest monuments preserved from the brief Roman presence in the area. This design was in fact a compromise, reached after the initial design, a majestic and much larger structure, was abandoned due to lack of funds. Initially the Mausoleum was going to be a Church of the Nation [Biserica Neamului], as the architects of the winning design in the 1921 contest named it. The initial design was reminiscent much more of the Curtea de Argeș church where Charles I and Elisabeth were buried. The architects who had won the competition initially resisted any kind of money-saving compromises, of reducing the scale of the 150-foot structure (forty-five meters), by stating emphatically that "before being architects, we are Romanians, and anything that is done in this country, in the name of the Romanian people [neam], concerns us as much as any other Romanian."[72] Yet compromise they did, as the National Ortho-dox Romanian Women's Society found it ultimately impossible to raise the necessary forty million lei.[73] The final project cost around sixteen million lei,[74] raised over sixteen years of negotiations and hard fundraising efforts, and finally by cajoling the government to offer five million lei to finish the works.[75] (See figure 4.5.)

Figure 4.4. The Archangels Daniel (*left*) and Michael (*right*) inside the Mărăşeşti Mausoleum Chapel. Photo courtesy of the National Military Museum.

Eight heraldic signs, alternating with inscriptions that identified the most important battlefields of the war, framed the entrance to the Mausoleum. Most of these names were from the Regat, but a few, like Sibiu, recalled the Transylvanian front. Above the entrance a large inscription read "To the glory of the nation's heroes,"[76] which made use of the archaic and religious term *slava* (instead of the more modern sounding *gloria*) and the equally traditional and organic sounding term *neam* (rather than *naţie*). Both choices reflected a desire to identify the monument with an unmistakably ethnic Romanian Orthodox version of glorifying the nation, and an attempt to combine familiar images, words, and rituals with the new aggressively nationalist commemorative vocabulary of the Romanian state after World War I. (See p. vi.)

Above the entrance was also a bas-relief frieze, recalling the Adamclisi design again. The themes and specific style of the sculpture were unmistakably, however, of the times. The sculptors who had worked on it, Ion Jalea (1887–1983) and Corneliu Medrea (1888–1964),[77] were well known for their monumental art-deco modernist style, which resembled the work of sculptor Ivan Meštrović (1883–1962) in Yugoslavia. The bas-relief represented various aspects of the war effort, focusing primarily on types of warfare. Above the entrance the frieze depicted an angel or winged victory, a female figure that vaguely resembled Queen Marie. Gathered around this figure were soldiers, some of them presented in aggressive postures but generally standing majestically in defense of their country and nation, represented through smaller figures of children and women.

At the back of the frieze, invisible to most viewers, one can see the first public commemoration of the role women played in the war. Nurses caring for wounded soldiers are presented in one frame, which is rather unusual because of the presence of these women among the troops, and also because of the representation of soldiers in pain, somewhat emasculated by their suffering, to be brought back to their full strength by the women. But since this image was so difficult to view, its presence at the back of the frieze in fact rearticulated the near invisibility or marginalization of women as heroic figures in the war. Instead, a masculine image of heroism and self-sacrifice dominated the frieze.

Once inside, the visitor was quickly reminded of the religious and specifically Orthodox nature of the memorial, but not before reading the Founding Act of the Mausoleum, which has remained until today the only trace to commemorate not only the memory of the dead soldiers, but also that of the people who were most influential in building the monument, especially the leadership of the National Orthodox Romanian Women's Society.[78] On the lower level were situated all the crypts of the soldiers whose bones were gathered from the surrounding fields, most of them unknown. Lower grade officers were placed together with the soldiers.

But the Mausoleum also included an individual funerary marker that stood out, that of General Eremia Grigorescu (1863–1919), the one leader of the Romanian army fighting at Mărășești who was universally identified as the greatest hero of the battle. Though he died after the end of the war (21 July 1919), he was buried in the Mărășești cemetery, according to his wishes.[79] This unusual choice reflected Grigorescu's personal attachment to the troops, as well as the government's endorsement of such a move, for it took the approval of the army and a royal decree for the body to be reburied there.[80]

One other individual marker existed at Mărășești: the tomb of Ecaterina Teodoroiu (1894–1917), the second most famous woman connected to remembering World War I, after Queen Marie. Her story was in a way more spectacular (because it was unique) than that of any other soldier at Mărășești.[81] Not only was she a volunteer, but she fought at Mărășești after incurring a severe wound and before she could fully recover from it. After her death in battle she was posthumously awarded the grade of sub-lieutenant, becoming the first woman officer of the Romanian army.[82] Interestingly, though she died on the battlefield and was initially buried there, Teodoroiu's body was subsequently removed from Mărășești (1921) at the request of the people of

Târgu Jiu, her native city, in order to have her remains closer to the community that best loved her. The marker raised for her after the body was removed might suggest a tribute to women's heroism in the war, or at least an attempt to add a feminine aspect to the martial commemorations of the war. Instead, I see the interest of the army and many people in Teodoroiu as a means to highlight her exceptionalism as a woman soldier.[83] The commemorative discourse that developed around Teodoroiu in fact rendered gender significant only as a means to highlight her "natural" vulnerabilities in contrast to her valiant (implicitly manly) actions.

Based on these precedents, the Mausoleum therefore already contained a certain instability regarding the dead bodies buried there: bodies that had not been recovered from the Mărăşeşti battlefield could subsequently be buried there in connection to the battle (Grigorescu as well as the nine unknown soldiers who were not picked to lie in the Tomb of the Unknown Soldier), while others who were intimately connected to the battle could be removed. In both cases, the relationship between the site of the burial and the presence of the buried body suggested a selective interpretation of traditional Orthodox rituals about honoring the dead. If Teodoroiu was exhumed from Mărăşeşti in order to have those who most loved her care for her tomb, Grigorescu wished to be buried there based on his own notion of being close to the spirits of the community he was most fond of and on the acceptance of others around him that he would be well taken care of according to proper Orthodox customs there. The reburial of the nine unknown soldiers from other locales to Mărăşeşti followed a similar logic: their own families could not take care of them because they were unknown, and thus those who carried the brightest flame of the war's remembrance—the families, priests, and community around Mărăşeşti who annually remembered these soldiers in the 6 August commemorations—would be the best caretakers of those nine soldiers.

At the center of the Mausoleum, accessible only after viewing the crypts, was the Chapel of Glory, a round tall room, which served as the Orthodox chapel for religious services there. Unusual in its circular structure, the chapel included unmistakable elements of the Orthodox rite and art, such as the iconostasis, the icons, the candelabra, and the painted frescoes on the walls and cupola. Saints dear to the Romanian Orthodox population, most prominently the archangels Michael and Daniel, adorned the walls. In the context of the growth of a fascist group in Romania that used the symbol of the Archangel Michael to identify itself, the prominence of the same archangel in images stylistically similar to depictions in fascist propaganda seems an unlikely coincidence. Though for some the Archangel Michael might have been just a religious symbol of heroism and self-sacrifice, for the growing following of Corneliu Zelea-Codreanu (1899–1938) the same image represented a validation of their own self-perception as heirs of the Romanian army's great sacrifices in the war.[84] By contrast,

Figure 4.5. Drawing for the Mărășești Mausoleum. Photo courtesy of the National Military Museum.

for any Jewish families who stepped inside the Mausoleum to visit it or honor family members or co-religionists, the symbology of the Archangel Michael in the center of the monument did not arouse positive reactions. (See figure 4.4.)

But on the morning of 18 September 1938, all were welcomed as participants (if not central figures) in the inauguration of the monument. The ceremony centered on the presence of Charles II. For many, the recent loss of his mother, Queen Marie, offered another layer of sadness and imposed a sense of piety before the dead, bringing back into focus feelings of loss that had dominated the first commemorations in Mărășești. Over two decades had passed since the battle, and recurrent commemorations and pilgrimages to the site had helped alleviate for participants, families, and friends the intense sense of loss and the troublesome memories of the events. The commemorations had done what such traditional rituals were supposed to do: heal the memories of those left alive; help them mourn and eventually gain a peaceful perspective on the departure of their loved ones. However, the death of the queen, a figure so popular with most ethnic Romanians young and old, someone who had been actively involved in the Mărășești project and had personally visited it on several occasions, became an opportunity to step back into a mood of mourning and great sadness.

Indeed, the commemorations were sober. Generally speaking the ritual was the same as had been in years past, with a religious ceremony, a *parastas,* a military parade, speeches by Alexandrina Cantancuzino, veterans, representatives of the government and local authorities, and crowned by the presence of Charles II and his gesture of officially opening the door to the completed monument. What made the commemoration unusual was the sheer size of the crowds who participated. Not only army personnel, but civilians from all over the country and especially school students—the government had approved a 75 percent discount for tickets purchased to attend the ceremony, making it affordable for virtually anyone to take part—came to Mărăşeşti on that September morning. To those standing on the terraces above the fields, it seemed that the entire nation was there to properly honor those who had fallen for the country.

In these large crowds and the emotions of the moment, it was indeed rather easy to forget those who were implicitly excluded from the celebrations—the soldiers who had died for the other side, the civilians who had volunteered in hospitals and on the front but were only marginally remembered, or those whose religious or ethnic identity made them stand out from the assumed Orthodox ethnic Romanian norm. Anyone from these categories had the opportunity to come to Mărăşeşti. But their experience would have been to have their sense of invisibility and marginalization reinforced by the rituals, speeches, and the monument itself. Even as Charles II, and Cantacuzino herself, believed the Mausoleum would become a great symbol of Romanian heroism and help fortify the Romanian nation against its enemies, they failed to see that the same symbol added new dimensions to the tensions or outright antagonisms between different communities inside Romania.

Streamlining Monument Building: An Unsuccessful Project

Another dimension of the government's attempts to unify the collective remembrance of the war into one homogenous exalted representation of heroism resembling the Tomb of the Unknown Soldier and the Mărăşeşti Mausoleum was the creation of a Commission for Monuments in 1929 at the Ministry of Education, Culture, and the Arts, which had as its sole task examining any and all projects for monuments to be built in public spaces (from streets to churchyards). The Commission came about as a result of the realization by the government that war memorials were sprouting up everywhere in the country and looked significantly different from place to place. From the point of view of the army and the Heroes Cult, which had been entrusted with building military cemeteries and overseeing the building of monuments to commemorate war heroes, the diversity of such markers created aesthetically and ideologically unacceptable representations of the war. The government wanted to see unity and conformity in these monuments: each village should echo through its markers the same sentiments of pride and honor toward the war dead as the Tomb of the Unknown Soldier, for instance.

But, as we know from the preceding chapter, families and communities did not wait for the approval of the government and army to bury their dead and go about honoring their memory. In fact, for obvious reasons having to do with traditional burial practices, most of the memorials dedicated to World War I had already been built by 1929, when the Commission of Monuments came into existence. Across all religious denominations, people believed that the sooner a funerary marker was erected and the body was laid to rest, the sooner it would find peace in the afterlife. Even those who lacked resources for a truly monumental marker attempted their best to create a memorial for the same reason, so that, indeed, by 1929 the country was peppered with large and small, modest and pompous crosses, obelisks, stone soldiers, and other symbols marking the loss of lives in the war.

Those who wished, in the first five years after the war, to offer more than a traditional funerary monument in places away from the seat of state power found a general lack of good examples at the center. Already in the early 1920s some local secular authorities, such as the mayor, a local teacher, or a well-to-do urban dweller with roots in the village, attempted to distinguish themselves as civic leaders and true patriots by trying to elevate the monuments to the war dead to a new level of nationalist aesthetics.[85] One such teacher, Ion Nicolaescu, wrote a letter to the Ministry of Education in November 1922, stating:

> In our country many monuments were raised after the war to honor those who died for the country. None of them, however, have been signed by an artist. The one erected in the village of Mătău . . . , only through the great efforts of one teacher [the author refers to himself in the third person here], is signed by the sculptor D. Mătăuanu. . . . I consider it my duty, Mr. Minister of Arts, to ask you to take part in its inauguration, not to find any reward for all the work [this teacher] has undertaken for his village, a work of art, but to honor this art [form] with your presence, and to encourage other villages to raise more artistic monuments to honor those dead in battle.[86]

This enthusiastic local leader wished to set himself apart from others in terms of the success of his venture. He also wanted to establish a different (in his view, higher) standard of representing heroism based on aesthetic considerations separate from the religious folk-art of other monuments. For this teacher, honoring the dead was not just about the sincerity of the local effort, but also about the quality of the artistic representation employed, a quality that had to resonate with broader concepts of heroism and beauty rather than the local needs of the family of the deceased.

This document offers a revealing look at the self-representations of some local initiatives to lead the way in constructing an aesthetic vocabulary for nationalism and wartime heroism. To begin with, in this case, instead of the family of a dead soldier taking the initiative together with the local priest/rabbi/preacher, more often the case was that the local secular intellectual, the teacher, who initiated the commemorative effort. There was a clear attempt on his part to employ the authority of his official position to underline the significance of his actions, in terms of both leadership qualities and aesthetic vision. Nicolaescu set himself up as arbiter of "proper" aesthetic representations of heroism and sacrifice. It also appears from his description that his motivation and goals were linked not so much to sentiments of loss and pain as to emotions like pride and honor. Here we see an important shift away from the earliest monuments for the war dead, which bore the attributes of mourning and loss and aimed at remembering the dead in a more traditional religious aesthetic vocabulary, without references to the nation or heroism. Nicolaescu was articulating a nationalist discourse assuming that an authoritative version of his ideas of nationalist aesthetics already existed in Bucharest; in fact he was helping give that discourse new shape. Despite his stated intentions of pleading with higher authorities for sanctioning his initiative, *he* was in fact acting as the voice pushing officials at the Ministry of Education to deal with this question of just how to represent the heroic sacrifice of soldiers in the war in a unitary fashion. Central government institutions tried to keep up with and respond to local initiatives, but in the early 1920s they were not yet the leading voice in war commemorative markers.

The gap between local efforts and official commemorative goals was not lost on government in Bucharest. This realization came in part from repeated reports by, especially, representatives of the Heroes Cult. Already in 1919 one report suggested that the goal of the Heroes Cult should be to incorporate private initiatives into broader projects initiated by this organization.[87] Such concerns on the part of the Bucharest organization can be interpreted as a pragmatic, well-intentioned concern to eliminate the duplication of commemorative efforts: if a local community wished to put up its own memorial to the war dead, and the Heroes Cult intended to also raise a monument there, it would make more sense for them to work together. But this goal may be also viewed as an attempt to control the direction and content of commemorative efforts, recasting them from local traditions to mourn the dead into localized symbols of a broader discussion of patriotic sacrifice for the nation.

The success of the Heroes Cult in controlling the building of war memorials according to their own vision of heroism and patriotic sacrifice was at best limited. In the 1920s, the Heroes Cult was merely able to report on the new monuments being built, rather than selecting and controlling the choices of local initiatives.[88] A similar account from the Ministry of National Defense, reflecting the concerned reports of the Heroes Cult, emphasized that "in different places in the country, to commemorate our Heroes and historic deeds, various monuments are raised that lack in beauty and greatness; instead of reinforcing sentiments of piety and national uplifting, they diminish [such sentiments]."[89] What "beauty and greatness" would have to look like was unclear, but the small ornate wooden crosses erected in most rural communities did not conform to the aesthetic ideals developing in Bucharest.

By the late 1920s the government finally began reacting to the monument mania in the countryside in a more unified manner. Suddenly, the central government embarked upon an organized policy of regulating monument building, from subject and location to aesthetic choices. In 1929 it set up a Commission for Public Monuments within the Ministry of Education and Cults. Three artists and two regular employees of the Ministry sat on this body, which met occasionally, as requests for the approval of new monuments reached the Ministry.[90]

In March 1930 the Commission published a set of regulations for the building of any public monument. Most important was the requirement to send a request for such a project well in advance of commencing it. These requests were to include the blueprints for the monument, with specifications for the location, materials, and other building details. Article one stated that the attributes of the Commission were:

a. To examine and give its *approval* for commemorative projects from an aesthetic point of view, [and determine] . . . if they have a public character or are of national interest.
b. To examine and give its approval for any work that has an aesthetic character.
c. To make proposals for any problems relating to the aesthetics of public monuments in the entire country.[91]

This apparently simple description suggests that the attributes of the Commission were limited in terms of content and ideology. The words nationalism, glory, and heroism did not appear here. The only potential sign that the Commission did in fact have a nationalist agenda was the first point, which emphasized "national interest" as a criterion for evaluation, though it didn't explain this vague term. In reality, archival documents show that the Commission made decisions on the basis of complex readings of the projects, often *with* nationalist considerations in mind. The aesthetic quality of these monuments was to be intrinsically connected to the message they were to convey—pride in the heroic sacrifice of the soldiers, victory of the Romanian state, and the reinforcement of the military character of heroic nationalism, rather than any sentiments of loss and bereavement.

In one case, the Commission rejected a monument because it was "a cemetery monument, not a Heroes monument." The distinction was made even clearer further down, under recommendations for improvement: "Instead of the Madonna on a pedestal, which gives the impression of a funerary monument, [they] should place a Victory to symbolize war."[92] This comment is particularly striking because it signifies the rejection of one well-established form of commemoration, the funerary monument, which was in fact much more popular and resonated more intimately in many small communities, in favor of its normative replacement by a new visual vocabulary.

This vocabulary would be more secular and civic in orientation, embracing the neo-classical symbols already predominant since the nineteenth century in western Europe (winged Victory/Nike—a revival of the ancient Greek symbol), and it would focus more directly on the war, the violence and heroism in furtherance of a great ideal—the nation. After all, victory often stood in as a symbol for the victorious nation. The aesthetic ideals of the Commission were thus to be closely bound to a normative reading of "appropriate" representations of heroism and the nation attending a more secular nationalist discourse.

One has to ask, however: how successful were the attempts of this Commission to "tame" monument mania, to discipline the efforts of local private initiatives? The answer is mixed at best. To begin with, it is not clear how well these new rules were publicized. I have not seen any newspaper accounts, for instance, that reported on this issue. It is likely, though I have been unable to locate such evidence, that local law enforcement officials in most towns would have received copies of these regulations, and it is even possible that the regulations would have been posted in public areas for the local population. But how many of the smaller rural communities would have actually received these regulations and would have regarded them as official and non-negotiable? Furthermore, it is not clear what the mechanism of enforcement was, as the regulations did not stipulate any clear, severe punishments for those who didn't abide by them.

In addition, the Commission met infrequently and saw, at best, a small fraction of the projects for war monuments that were actually built. A document from 1936 indicates that in its first five years, the Commission examined "over 100 projects," rejecting at least 15 percent of those.[93] The total number of projects that were approved cannot possibly reflect the total number of war monuments that were actually built during the same period. The Heroes Cult approximated the number of crosses erected during the first fifteen years after the war at around 1,300. Even if the great majority of these monuments were built in the first decade after the war (and this is probable, if they were funerary monuments built by survivors in small communities), it is unlikely that only one hundred projects were developed between 1930 and 1935, since crosses were only one of several types of war commemorative monuments built through local initiatives.

The gross discrepancy between the total number of commemorative monuments and the number of projects presented before the Commission of Public Monuments suggests that the authority of this governmental body was rather ineffectual. Even as the central government tried in multiple ways to direct the representation of heroism in monuments, local communities and private initiatives ignored the regulations set up in 1930. Since these were initiatives publicized in the local context, often garnering the support of local authorities such as the mayor or police, and also had a direct impact on changing the physical and official commemorative landscape of the community where the monument was raised, one cannot dismiss these local attitudes as ignorant or unable to understand and follow the regulations set up by the central authorities. Vernacular voices all over the country were in fact making a choice not only to ignore a bureaucratic process, but also to assert their own interpretation of the war deaths in a fashion that reflected the sentiments of the local community.[94] This was a consistent attitude, which prompted a resentful response from the Commission: "Our task is not to acknowledge the completion of monuments, but to control the artistic qualities of these monuments while they are still on paper."[95]

But what of those who did make the choice to seek the approval of the Commission? The archival resources of the Commission reveal no clear type of monument or consistent attitude of deference toward the central government on the part of local initiatives. But there are some revealing cases for explaining at least *why* some communities sought approval from the central government, other than obeying state regulations.

In some cases, especially in territories acquired by Romania after World War I, requests by local ethnic Romanians indicated their desire to use such monuments to mark the reversal of ethnic power relations. The requests of such committees were aggressively nationalistic and indicated a wish to have their ethno-nationalist position endorsed by the central government. One such petition wanted to raise a cross to commemorate the "massacre of almost 100 Romanians" during the war. The cross would "serve as a pilgrimage place . . . to announce to passersby not only the great blood sacrifice of Romanians in this region. . . . But also the Romanian and Christian character of this city [Arad] on the western frontier."[96] The document, signed by the Orthodox Bishop of Arad, also implied that the only authentic form of Christianity in Romania had to be Orthodoxy. This exclusivist stance has to be understood in the context of the ethnic mix and recent history of Arad itself, an overwhelmingly Hungarian city in numbers and in civic culture. The bishop, not surprisingly, wanted to use aggressive nationalism in a twofold manner: negatively, to re-signify a public space with Romanian nationalist symbols (and claim it from the larger finite economy of civic spaces); and also positively, by inscribing the monument (and by extension broader public space) with specific religious meaning. The director of the Commission of Public Monuments responded cautiously to this request by allowing the bishop to start raising funds for such a cross, but requesting that the building be held off until the formal approval of the project's design was passed by the Commission.[97]

This example suggests that the process of building war memorials had gained an embattled quality in the decade and a half since the end of the war. As with struggles over education, where an ethno-Romanian version of national standards was established, and where ethnic Romanians pushed aggressively in multiethnic communities,[98] so in the realm of war monuments local communities were using nationalist discourses dominant in Bucharest to settle local xenophobic scores. In the case of the Arad Romanians, the government in Bucharest favored Christian Orthodox and monarchical representations of heroism in the war. But, in sending their proposals to the Commission for Public Monuments, these Romanian committees were not merely following regulations set up in Bucharest. They sought the approval of the central committee for their *own*, local goals and in the context of long-standing Hungarian–Romanian animosities in Arad itself. The aims of the Bucharest officials might have been served by such endeavors; yet the two efforts—the local and the central—were fellow travelers, rather than part of a unitary cultural practice of nationalism.

A more aggressive nationalist stance on the part of the Commission becomes apparent when looking at the proposals for monuments sent by German or Hungarian ethnics. In 1935 a group of citizens from the village of Jamul Mare, from a region with a large German population, wrote to ask for permission to place on a street, in the vicinity of the local Catholic church, a monument for local soldiers who died between 1914–1918, having fought against the Romanian state.[99] The committee had gone about this request in proper fashion, submitting all the necessary paperwork for approval. The initial response of the authorities was to approve the request with one provision: remove one symbol, the sword from the claws of the eagle atop the monument, probably as a way to eliminate any irredentist connotations. In the context of an ethnic German village, the sword itself could have generically symbolized an aggressive, anti-Romanian stance, but it might also have appeared too similar to two other non-Romanian nationalist symbols—the eagle on the coat of arms of post-Habsburg Austria, or the eagle of the seven tribes of Árpád, a Hungarian nationalist symbol.[100]

But a second hand-written opinion appears on top of the initial response, dated a few months later. It states in an emphatic and underlined script: "Public monuments, meaning [those placed] in squares and places that belong to the village, region, or the State, cannot be erected *without the approval of the Ministry of Cults and Arts* and can *have an inscription only in the official language of the State, in Romanian.*"[101] Nothing in the regulations of the Commission of Public Monuments indicated the need to use Romanian language for the inscriptions. The tone of the response suggests more of an outburst of nationalism, as if the inscription in German were a personal insult to the central authorities. It didn't matter to these authorities that the local population might have been largely or entirely German speakers and that all the dead in that village had

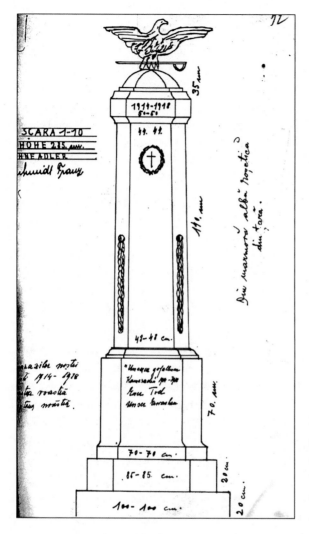

Figure 4.6. The project for a German-language obelisk from Jamul Mare village. Photo courtesy of the National State Archives, Bucharest.

been German. This reaction suggests, thus, that in matters of nationalist undertones, the Commission for Public Monuments was willing to tolerate strong Romanian statements but would not stand for any inkling of such attitudes among ethnic minorities. (See figure 4.6.)

We don't know how the local German community in this village reacted to the response of the Commission. But throughout Transylvania, there are many such monuments from the interwar period with the inscription in German. They are placed, however, predominantly in places of worship, inside churches, or in the graveyards of Catholic and Protestant churches.[102] Their presence indicates that, whatever the intentions of the central authorities, local communities built memorials either despite limitations imposed from Bucharest or by finding loopholes in these rules. After all, the Commission for Public Monuments did not have jurisdiction over the property of churches in most cases.[103] Those places were public, yet beyond the direct control of secular authorities. In some cases, this loophole served as a way to enable local communities to commemorate their war dead, even when the representations themselves were in fact not of a funerary, mournful nature, but rather more secular and even martial in style. (See figures 2.5 and 2.6.)

Though the Commission for Public Monuments generally failed to control the building of war monuments, it became a site for lodging grievances. In particular, disgruntled artists or local initiative committees might on occasion contact the Commission to complain about the quality of the monuments, or about the slowness with which a monument was being erected.[104] In these cases, the local actors were again selectively appealing to the central authorities, using them for personal or local purposes, rather than attempting to ingratiate themselves with the Bucharest officials along the lines of any broad national vision of what the war monuments might mean.

In one case from 1934, a sculptor from Bucharest wrote the Minister of Education with the request "not to approve the execution of a heroes' monument in the village of Comanu," because of the "uniform" and "ridiculous" look of monuments like the one planned there.[105] The polite, if self-serving, tone of the correspondence sent to the Bucharest officials in the early 1920s by people like Nicolaescu had been replaced by a more aggressive stance in which local actors demanded (rather than inviting) the interference of the state in local commemorative efforts. However, the arguments were still about the failure of the state to live up to its goals of honoring the dead heroes and the nation—in this case, through pointing out the unsatisfactory aesthetics of the models provided by the Bucharest officials.

The memo sent by this forgotten sculptor to the Ministry of Education criticized the standardization of monument building as going against any good taste and creativity. It ended by stating: "These monuments made in the same shape, with the same statuary clichés, have become banal, and no longer represent anything interesting from the point of view of artistic composition, nor as a document, but instead compromise the good name of the deceased sculptor."[106] The culprits in this process of "banalization" were the entrepreneurs who had purchased or "borrowed" the molds for the monuments and continued to produce them without any quality control. Incidentally, the sculptor whose work was supposedly being "bastardized" through serial reproduction was the same D. Mătăuanu who had been praised highly in the 1924 request discussed earlier in this section. In the early 1920s he had been held up by a local initiator as a great example of building more refined and inspiring monuments. By 1935, his talents were poorly represented through the serialization of monument building.

Struggles between the center and regional/local actors in controlling the shape and meaning of commemorative memorials came to a head in 1938. It was only at a point when democracy was losing ground and Charles II was assuming dictatorial powers that the government finally began to gain better control over commemorative war efforts.[107] Among the king's many initiatives to place public life more tightly in the hands of the authoritarian Front for National Rebirth was a new decree regarding Regulations for Public Monuments. Though minor by comparison with Romania's other great political, social, and economic problems of the day, this new law was dear to Charles II, as he had been personally invested in the public spectacle of national holidays and war commemorations.[108] The new regulations also reflected the growing concern among central authorities about their ineffectiveness in controlling the building of public monuments. In addition to the old regulations established in 1930, the new decree outlined in minute detail the exact responsibilities of all central and local authorities over authorizing, building, and maintaining public monuments. It also included new and substantial punitive measures of one to twenty days in jail and fines of 100 to 2,000 lei for project authors, contractors, and committee members who did not abide by the decisions of the government authorities.[109] This last feature was a particularly strong message, meant to curb disregard for the law.

The new regulations were also more inclusive in what they considered public monuments, to encompass not just statues and crosses, but also "wells, columns, and commemorative plaques." Finally, these rules spelled out more clearly the obligation of the local authorities "not to approve the execution or allow commencement of any buildings unless the projects had already received the approval of the Ministry."[110] This stipulation made local authorities more accountable to the official rules set up in Bucharest, rather than local enthusiasts and popular feelings. There is also evidence that the government made a greater effort to publicize the new regulations.[111]

Yet it is unclear what impact this decree had over the entire territory of Romania, as by 1938 many communities, especially villages, with limited economic and energy resources for such projects, had already built commemorative monuments. Most monument projects affected by the new law were civic ones in bigger towns and in Romania's large cities, where local officials and other nationalist enthusiasts with access to larger purses of public money wished to ingratiate themselves with Charles's dictatorship by building monuments to mark the twentieth anniversary of the end of the war and the king's own important role in it.

For the 1938–1940 period, the archives of the Ministry of Education show mostly grand monuments in large urban settings, such as the Monument of the Union built in Chişinău on the occasion of the twentieth anniversary of the union of Bessarabia with Romania.[112] Generally speaking, though, the amount of paperwork related to public monuments was much smaller in the last two years before World War II than in the previous two decades, suggesting a tapering down of monument building activity.

Between 1918 and 1940 the Romanian state attempted to capitalize on its enormous losses in the Great War in stone, word, and ritual, as a way to forge a sense of loyalty and pride toward the Romanian nation and, indirectly, the state itself. The strategy of turning tragedy into nationalist victory and attempting to profoundly reshape the public space and vocabulary of cultural production of rituals and markers that represented the community was common to all participants in the Great War, but contingent upon the specific traditions of the respective community where the commemorations took place. Thus, a "European" pattern can be discerned only at the level of state efforts. Yet, although some similar monuments sprouted everywhere in Europe, many more were quite dissimilar, and different rituals, values, and contestations of those monuments came to define the use of nationalist idioms. Great War commemorations might have looked similar at the highest official level, but they were in fact quite different, not only among different countries, but within individual states. The Romanian case offers ample evidence.

The attempt of the state to create a cohesive, unitary commemorative vocabulary of the war was successful to some degree, though it failed on many other accounts. While a new official holiday, Heroes Day, was established and became the most important moment for remembering the dead of the entire war, this day continued to compete with other holidays during the annual calendar of official holidays, and it was also molded into local interpretations among diverse communities—religiously and ethnically—of what this day meant. In particular, the religious identification of the war commemoration with a specific Orthodox Christian cult of the dead meant that Protestants, Catholics, Jews, and Muslims, had to invent new ways of remembering their dead in order to join these official commemorations, or were left out. In some cases, especially among the Jewish communities that aspired to gain citizenship, individual communities made special efforts to blend their own religious traditions with a respectful honoring of the war dead. Nonetheless, because of important differences along ethnic, religious, and regional lines, Heroes Day came to increasingly underscore not only commonalities among some citizens of Romania, but also important, presumably unbridgeable dissimilarities between that majority and a sizeable non-Orthodox minority, around 30 percent of the total population.

The attempt to unify and solidify the physical representation of heroism and patriotism in the Great War was also unevenly successful. Starting in May 1924, the

Tomb of the Unknown Soldier stood in the Charles I Park in Bucharest. It continued to adorn the esplanade of the Military Museum for the rest of the interwar period, frequently visited by veterans, schoolchildren, and politicians. The wider public came to recognize it as *the* official symbol of the sacrifices made in the war by average soldiers, but not everyone identified with this symbol. Furthermore, in an era of still uneven communication and with literacy remaining low in the countryside, knowledge about the Tomb remained partial. Most people in Romania continued to think about the losses in the war in connection to those close to them—family members, friends, and neighbors—rather than to the nation as an abstract greater whole.

Even those with war dead not officially commemorated managed to bury or at least honor these lost lives in keeping with traditions in their respective community. The annual recurrences of official commemorations thus only served to mark over and over again the gaps between what was close to the hearts of these communities and what was viewed as publicly acceptable. Counter-commemorations became a permanent feature of the global phenomenon of war commemorations.

During World War II and afterward, the state (especially the military establishment) learned from the difficulties presented by the Great War and attempted to better consolidate its grip over the commemorative vocabulary focused on the war dead. The next section follows the paths taken by state and local communities to negotiate new relationships in the dialogue (and often conflicts) regarding the proper way to honor and remember the war dead.

In response to your petition registered with the number 63.110/1941, which requests the approval to raise a monument in memory of your son fallen for the Fatherland in the battles around Odessa, we have the honor of letting you know that for the moment, the building of Monuments for Heroes is suspended, until new orders.

—Ministry of Education (1941)[1]

Mărășești will remain for eternity the symbol of the Romanian people's heroism, the great moral trait that today finds its brilliant illustration in the work full of enthusiasm undertaken by the proletariat in our fatherland, under the leadership of the Party, on the wide front of building socialism.

—"The Semi-Centenary of Mărășești and Oituz" (1968)[2]

WAR COMMEMORATIONS AND STATE PROPAGANDA UNDER DICTATORSHIP

From the Crusade against Bolshevism to Ceaușescu's Cult of Personality, 1940–1989

In the fall of 1941, Nicolae Gheorghe Dumitrescu, a self-described devoted citizen from the village of Punghina, wrote to the Minister of Education to request permission for building a memorial to his son. Dumitrescu was the father of a lieutenant who had died while fighting in the bloody campaigns around Odessa at the beginning of Romania's invasion of the Soviet Union on the side of the Nazis. The Ministry's response was polite but unequivocal. No such monuments were to be erected by families for the moment, until a new law for building commemorative markers was passed. Furthermore, the bodies of those who perished fighting in the war were under the authority of the Ministry of War, and their policy was crystal clear. All combatants would be buried with military honors at (or close to) the place where they had perished, in military cemeteries assembled by the army.[3] Families were instructed that they were not to put up any funerary markers that identified their departed ones as having perished in the war.

If in World War I the Romanian state was unprepared to deal with the massive deaths and their damaging psychological impact for the multitudes of families and communities directly affected by these losses, the regime of Ion Antonescu (1882–1946) in World War II began combat fully prepared to control the process of burying, mourning, and commemorating the soldiers who died in the war. Legislation passed initially by Charles II in 1938[4] and then revised slightly by the Antonescu government in 1941[5] was detailed and placed responsibility for war commemorations on the shoulders of the state, to the detriment of vernacular activities. Due to this legislation and the nature of the fighting, with the troops moving quickly through large swaths of territory and fighting predominantly on soil beyond the authority of the Romanian state,[6] most of those who perished fighting in the Romanian army, whether on the side of the Nazis (21 June 1941–23 August 1944) or on the side of the Soviets (23 August 1944–8 May 1945), had their earthly remains buried on foreign ground: in the East on Soviet soil, from Ukraine and Transnistria to deep into the Russian steppe, as far as Stalingrad; or in the West, from Hungary to the Tatra Mountains in Czechoslovakia. These conditions throughout World War II forced families and local communities into a secondary role in terms of constructing war commemorative discourses. The new regulations also placed these actors in the position of having to construct clandestine counter-memories to the official ones.

The presence of the Soviet armies as "liberators" starting in 1944 in Romania and other eastern European countries also insured that the memory of World War II would be shaped in keeping with the political goals of the Soviet Union. In the first postwar decade the role of the Soviets was overpowering, but by no means uniform. Statues to Soviet soldiers went up everywhere in the area, and 9 May became an official holiday in all of these countries, with parades and other rituals to demonstrate their loyalty to the Soviet Union. But behind this uniform façade there were important national and regional nuances. How various populations and armies had behaved during the war vis-à-vis the Soviets (and to some extent the Nazis) did make a difference in how commemorative discourses developed. This chapter traces the impact of the Soviets for how the Romanian state began to engage the memory of World War II, especially given the complicated history of its participation on both sides of the war and direct contribution to material and human destruction in the Soviet Union.

This chapter also identifies the shift in the official discourse about remembering World War II after 1965, when Nicolae Ceauşescu assumed the position of general secretary of the Romanian Communist Party (RCP) and launched Romania into a uniquely nationalist authoritarian rule. The Ceauşescu regime also marked a period of nationalist reassessment of the memory of World War I at the official level, reintroducing the symbols and commemorative rituals connected to the Great War for the generation that had grown up after the interwar period, as the second epigraph suggests.

Equally important is the issue of how the commemoration of atrocities committed by the Romanian armies and civilians during World War II against Jews, Roma, and Hungarians were increasingly minimized during the Communist period, so much so that by the end of that era ethnic Romanians (civilians and soldiers) appeared as victims of various "foreign" fascist influences and forces—the German Nazis and the Horthyst Hungarians most prominently—rather than perpetrators of their own horrendous Holocaust. At the same time, in the 1980s the Romanian state began for the first time to develop rituals and symbols for commemorating civilian victims of World War II. My analysis offers a synthesis of the perversely selective nature of these commemorations and markers, which suggest a policy of erasing public awareness of the atrocities committed by Romanians against their own Jewish and Hungarian co-citizens, while acknowledging with great pomp the atrocities committed by ethnic Hungarian citizens in Hungarian-ruled Transylvania against Jews and Romanians living there.

In order to paint a nuanced picture of the process by which this victimological discourse developed, I examine parallel and somewhat related areas of legal, educational, and cultural action through or under direct state control. The first site of analysis is the actions of the army under Antonescu's leadership during the war, and the important challenges for the Romanian authorities raised by the nature of the fighting and killing in World War II.

In looking at how commemorative discourses about World War II were reshaped after 1945, I turn to the war crime trials, which constituted a complex first moment of constructing the memory of wartime atrocities through individual voices that acted as witnesses under heavy oversight from the Soviet Union. This first staging of remembrances of guilt and victimization helped shape subsequent official, as well as individual, narratives about World War II. My focus then turns to how the army, as the most important state institution to control commemorations of the war dead, provided an important arena for contestation inside the state apparatus, especially as the Communist regime was seeking to gain legitimacy among the ranks of the military.

The state's effort to appeal to average citizens and shape war remembrance through educational texts, museum displays, film, and fictional writing demonstrates the obsession of the Communist Party with controlling every public manifestation linked to remembering World War II. Having made a date linked to World War II its national holiday, the Communist regime placed itself in a position of needing to constantly rearticulate the significance of the war for its own legitimacy. The commemorative discourse about World War II was a constant presence in the official propaganda, especially after 1965, as well as a site of remembrance periodically "refreshed" with new elements added to the narrative by the culturniks of the Communist regime.[7] Ultimately, this strategy worked against the interests of the Communist state, as my last two chapters argue. Still, the official commemorative discourses promoted aggressively by the Communist regime in word, image, and stone, proved to have a lasting impact in solidifying narratives of victimhood.

What emerges from this analysis is a picture of the state more directly involved than before 1945, and even obsessively interested in shaping remembrances of World War II. After 1965, this growing preoccupation also resulted in resurrecting the central meaning of World War I for the nationalist founding myths of Communist Romania. While Katherine Verdery developed a picture of the nationalist discourse promoted by the Communist regime in Romania under Ceaușescu in the realm of intellectual production, I turn to how the state and the Communist Party aimed to mobilize the citizenry around specific cultural processes linked to the world wars and the values of heroism and patriotic self-sacrifice.[8] Furthermore, I show that changes in the cult of the dead in the post-Communist period are clearly linked to commemorative discourses that took shape in the Communist period.[9] In this chapter, my focus will be on how, starting in 1938, Romanian authoritarian regimes asserted new levels of control over war commemorative practices. From this perspective that emphasizes continuities across World War II, Communist Romania appears as more effective than, though not radically different from, the interwar regime in its attempts to solidify the memory of the two world wars among the population of the country. Even as the Communists claimed to stand apart from the bourgeois nationalist regimes that had celebrated World War I or the fascist Antonescu regime, Ceaușescu's regime built upon the rituals and symbols used by these regimes.

Background to the Official Commemorative
Discourse in World War II

Romania's preparations for a future war commenced as soon as the ink dried on the paper that solidified its post–World War I borders. Having gained territory from two defeated powers, Hungary and Russia, and controlling a large area that contained populations bent on revisionism, over the interwar period Romania became an increasingly militarized state and society. Especially under Charles II, building up the military capabilities of the army became a growing preoccupation of the government.[10] However, for most of his reign the king worked to retain alliances with western Europe. It was only after Munich and in view of the Soviet threat on the eastern border that Charles finally began to turn more clearly toward a policy friendly to the Nazis.

Alongside Charles II, various organizations, especially the League of the Archangel Michael, boasted their own paramilitary units that focused on preparing the Romanian people for any imminent confrontation with revisionist claims. Though in some regards similar in their nationalist, militarizing, and anti-Bolshevik rhetoric, Charles II and Codreanu came to blows by 1938. The king resented the popularity of the legionaries and their open criticism of his liaison with a Jewish woman, Elena Lupescu (1895?–1977). Codreanu's legionaries became the focus of heavy official repression after several prominent Romanian politicians were assassinated. In 1938, despite his rising popularity, Codreanu was arrested and summarily executed under Charles's orders while purportedly trying to escape. The legionary movement was sent underground, but many of their anti-Semitic and radical nationalist ideas became part of Charles's official policies.

Charles's control over the state, however, was slipping away. Due to various internal and external push-pull factors, Romania became truncated after the Second Vienna Award in August 1940, losing northern Transylvania to its ally, Hungary, without a single official shot being fired.[11] Largely peaceful, the transfer of populations along the Romanian-Hungarian new border was marred by atrocities committed on both sides of the border by their armies and civilian populations.[12] This humiliating loss brought about a fascist coup d'état in Bucharest, which deposed Charles II and brought to power Ion Antonescu as regent and formal head of a fascist regime, with legionary Horia Sima (1907–1993) as shadow leader.

A full ten months before Romania officially entered the war, the country was thrown into the chaos of a virtual civil war between its rightwing fascist political forces, with the army at the top of the hierarchy, and with the Jewish, Roma, and other "undesirable" so-called foreigners as the main victims of this regime of violence. The legionary regime of thuggish state and street violence culminated with a pogrom of the Jewish communities in Bucharest in January 1941, when over 120 people were brutally killed and thousands of Jewish homes, businesses, and places of worship were vandalized or destroyed. Though personally favoring anti-Semitic measures, Antonescu disliked the disorganized violence of the legionaries and after two days sent out the army to quell the rebellion. Around 200 legionaries were killed, Sima fled to Germany, and the movement was sent underground again. However, Antonescu continued the anti-Semitic and xenophobic policies of the legionaries, especially after Romania's entry into the war.

On 21 June 1941 Romania formally entered the war: Antonescu sent troops over the Dniester River into Soviet territory alongside Hitler's armies, in a "crusade against Bolshevism." This action coincided with a new level of violence perpetrated against Romanian Jews, most prominently the rounding up and murder of over 10,000 Jews from Iași on 22–29 June 1941. Over the next three years Romania fought alongside the Nazis. The Germans welcomed among their ranks ethnic Germans from Romanian controlled parts of Transylvania, some of whom even joined the SS. Over 160,000 Romanian troops (out of 538,000 soldiers) died on the eastern front. The Romanian troops were part of the advancing forces toward Stalingrad, as well as controlling Transnistria, over which Romania assumed political jurisdiction, placing a Romanian governor to oversee the mostly military occupation of that region. The greatest atrocities committed by the Romanian army happened in this region, comfortably away from the eyes and ears of the civilian population in Romania proper. Between 280,000 and 380,000 Jews perished in the Romanian Holocaust, and over 11,000 of the 25,000 deported Roma also found their end in camps in Transnistria.[13]

After the defeat of the Axis forces at Stalingrad and Kursk, the Romanians began to reconsider their choice of fighting alongside Hitler. On 23 August 1944, young King Michael (1921–), together with a select group of high-ranking officers, effected a coup d'état, removing Antonescu and placing him in prison. The most important element of the coup was that Romania joined the Allies and overnight came to fight against the Nazis and on the side of the Soviets. Being able to save some face before the Allies was a costly matter, however. Starting in August, the Romanian troops came to bear the brunt of the fighting in areas where they helped the Soviet armies. The casualties incurred by the Romanians were tremendous, around 167,000 out of the total 538,000 (over 31 percent).

By the end of the war, over 300,000 (around 60 percent of the fighting Romanian forces) had perished on the front, and over 100,000 had been made prisoners by the Soviets. The Romanian army was largely decimated in the course of World War II in a way unimaginable to any civilian and political leaders before 1941. Most of these men (and some women) died on foreign soil.[14] The civilian casualties were likewise staggering, amounting to 469,000, the vast majority of whom were the victims of the Holocaust. With over 833,000 deaths in the war, Romania lost 4.5 percent of its prewar population, a percentage similar to other eastern European combatants and generally larger than in any western European countries, save for Germany. Only Russia, Lithuania, Latvia, Poland, and Yugoslavia saw significantly greater devastation on the continent, with percentages from 6.7 percent in Yugoslavia to 18.5 percent in Poland.[15]

The Memory of the Dead as Wartime Propaganda, 1940–1944

It is impossible to understand the extent of investment that the military establishment had in the memory of World War II without first analyzing its role in the commemorative process during the war. This role was also connected to the personal involvement of both Romanian dictators before 1944, Charles and Antonescu, who personally oversaw cultural policies linked to war commemorations. Starting with Charles II's military pageants and commemorative celebrations, Romanian citizens began to experience new levels of state nationalist propaganda aimed at mobilizing patriotic feelings and actions, as well as censorship against actions that dissented from the norms established by the state. This had become increasingly plain in schools and publications even before the war. The Ministry of Education drew up lists of books that offered weak patriotic models, to be removed from school library shelves, alongside lists of approved books that provided the right image of patriotism, courage, and knowledge. Among those viewed as great models were works by Dimitrie Gusti (1880–1955), Mihai Eminescu (1850–1889), Nichifor Crainic (1889–1972), Octavian Goga (1881–1938), and Mihail Sadoveanu (1880–1961).[16] Absent from these lists were any accounts of World War I that focused on the suffering of the soldiers on the front (e.g., Camil Petrescu's *Last Night of Love*) and any female models of self-sacrifice.

The short-lived legionary state (September 1940–January 1941) brought the concept of mobilization through ritual to new heights (or rather depths), in terms of both the extent of the public spectacles organized by the state and the violence of their ideology and racist exclusionary actions. The legionaries established a clearer norm than any previous regime that only Orthodox religious symbols and rituals would be accepted as public manifestations of Romanianness. Catholics, Protestants, and especially Jews had to bow to this stricture by abstaining from any public display of their own symbols and also by participating as members of the public in state-organized ceremonies.

Despite the growing violence against them, many Jewish communities in Romania continued to express their loyalty toward the state in matters of honoring the war dead. On 27 May 1941, a month before the horrible pogrom in Iași, the Jewish community in that town had "the great honor of requesting that [the mayor of Iași] honor with his presence the solemn occasion of [commemorating Heroes Day]."[17] The mayor's office responded by sending a representative. One might revel in this spirit of ecumenical mutual appreciation in the common pursuit of honoring the nation's war dead, were it not for the horrible shadow of the 29 June pogrom, which casts great doubt on the Romanian authorities' good intentions in the summer of 1941 toward their non-ethnic Romanian co-nationals. The gesture of the Jewish community (and the response of the mayor's office) was in fact a well-established tradition in that town, having started immediately after the war and the beginning of the official celebrations on Heroes Day. But the significance of this gesture in the tense context of the moment seems different: while the Jewish community tried desperately to remind the government about their patriotism and dedication to the ideal of Greater Romania, local state authorities responded through a small gesture of recognition, rendered insignificant in view of subsequent violence perpetrated with the endorsement of the same authorities.

The Charles II dictatorship, the short-lived legionary regime, and the authoritarian wartime Antonescu government chose to control public mobilization and patriotic propaganda also through silences. Death was no longer the purview of families and communities, but rather of the state. Violence perpetrated against "undesirables" remained a non-item in the heavily censored press and other news media. There was no publicity about the murders of innocent Jewish civilians by Iron Guard thugs or the massacre of thousands of civilian Jews in the streets of Iași and in the sealed trains that made their way from Iași to Târgu Frumos via different Moldavian towns during the week of 22–29 June 1941. Those who had witnessed such horrors became the only voice through which the dead could still reach the living. The bodies of these victims were whisked away, buried in Jewish cemeteries in common graves, the public mention of their murder a taboo.[18]

In the meantime, as Antonescu's regime was entering Bessarabia and rounding up Jews there and over the river Bug into Transnistria, the army was also losing great numbers of soldiers and saw the need to bolster military morale through special celebrations. At Antonescu's direct order sent on 23 October 1941, "the whole Romanian population who has sons or relatives who fell for their country in Transnistria should"—on following Sunday, 26 October 1941—"decorate with flowers all heroes' monuments in their villages and cities," and the officials should organize religious and secular celebrations.[19] With one to two days of preparation before the official commemoration, one can only imagine the kind of scrambling mayors, priests, teachers, and the local law enforcement agencies had to do.

By the same token, it is not difficult to consider the conflicted reactions such commemorations encountered among Romania's citizens. Four months into the war the Romanian troops had made impressive advances into Soviet territory alongside their Nazi allies, but the campaign had been exceedingly bloody, with high casualties among soldiers and civilians. While the soldiers were being praised for their patriotism, many of their victims, most of them innocent Jews who had been murdered on the orders of the military for their "Bolshevik" activities against the Romanian armies, remained forgotten.

As the front moved eastward, more military cemeteries sprang up throughout Soviet territory. The army was faithfully following the regulations established before the war in 1938 and revised in 1941, to identify and bury all soldiers as soon as they died, preferably in groups, and organized in proper fashion in military cemeteries, taking into consideration the religious and national identity of individual combatants (keeping them separate according to religion and citizenship). On the matter of taking care of all fallen combatants, "irrespective of religious or ethnic origin," regulations were plain. "The graves of those fighting for belligerent states—allies or enemies—will enjoy the same regime as the graves of our nationals under the condition of reciprocity." Among those to be buried in military cemeteries were also "nurses and any other persons who died fulfilling an important service [to the country] under direct orders or as a volunteer . . . , including those who fell placing themselves benevolently in the service of the Fatherland." This rule also included interned civilians and prisoners of war.[20] Regulations also included directions about the funerary markers to be used, though Orthodox Christian symbols, the cross or troika, were the only options offered.[21] (See figure 5.1.)

These regulations seemed more inclusive in their spirit of treating all combatants and civilians involved in the war with the same honors, compared to the attitude prevalent after World War I, when the Heroes Cult had rejected the notion that civilian actions might be considered heroic and thus worthy of the same respect as soldiers' sacrifices. Many more people previously excluded, especially women, could now lay claim to heroism in the service of the country. This more gender-inclusive policy had to do with the larger numbers of female volunteers in the medical services and women's entry in the public service sectors. In addition, the nationalist ideologization of women's role as the guardians of the nation's future also provided ways for integrating women's social roles into a broader definition of self-sacrifice on the altar of the nation.[22] The official policies regarding proper burial and in particular what it meant to honor those who had fallen heroically for their country presented a more inclusive and potentially non-martial view of heroism and self-sacrifice.

The reality on the ground was different, however. How officers kept track of the dead, and how they accounted for civilians dying in the vicinity or midst of combat, especially when such combat included violence against civilians, contravened all

Figure 5.1. Burial in military cemetery on the eastern front (1941).
Photo courtesy of the National Military Museum.

these rules for honoring the dead. Officers scrupulously filed the forms requested by the army after identifying dead soldiers from their own fighting units, and the army kept good records of the military cemeteries they built on Soviet soil, no matter how fast the blitzkrieg moved in the first year and a half.[23] In November 1941 the army had already requested a report about the status of military cemeteries, which was duly submitted by a team of officers at the beginning of December, noting the thirty-four such cemeteries, all well marked and in good condition.[24] The same cannot be said for the hundreds of thousands of civilian victims who were killed by the Romanian army. Still, no representative of the army was ever reprimanded, even in writing, for having such an exclusionary interpretation of the regulations established by the Romanian state.

During the first two years of war, Antonescu's regime also made preparations to build war memorials in Bucharest, starting with a new military cemetery to be placed close to the Bellu military cemetery.[25] A more ambitious project, which remained unfulfilled, was to demolish one of the Jewish cemeteries in Bucharest and place in that space a grandiose monument in a style Nazi architect Albert Speer (1905–1981) would have been proud of. The desecration of spaces that had non-ethnically Romanian connotation was endorsed in other cases as well. Valeriu Voineag, an Orthodox priest serving in Braşov, initiated such an action during a visit by high officials from

Bucharest. After noting that one of the prominent markers visible on the nearby Tâmpa mountain was the antiquated pedestal where once stood the statue of Árpád (c. 845–c. 907), one of the leaders of the Magyar tribes who had arrived in Transylvania in the tenth century, Voineag suggested taking it down and replacing it with a "Cross of Romanian Justice."[26] Voineag found enthusiastic supporters, and in July 1943, in the midst of a war that Romania was losing with great human casualties, the Romanian state approved the creation of a committee to raise funds for such a monument.[27]

By the end of 1943 the Antonescu government began to loosen its tight grip on more localized commemorations. The Ministry of Education finally wrote the still hopeful father of Captain Dumitrescu N. Gheorghe from the village of Punghina, to let him know that his project for a commemorative cross had been approved.[28] Others who lost sons and loved ones on the eastern front received favorable responses.[29]

Some, however, went ahead in contravention of the official policies. A striking example is the cemetery dedicated to the war dead on the eastern front in the small Romanian village of Sântimbru, located a few miles north of Alba Iulia, in the heart of Transylvania. The village is quite isolated; it didn't have a paved road leading to it even in the late 1990s. But it was close to a major urban center. In 1943, the families of those who perished fighting in World War II and whose bodies were never returned decided to erect a military cemetery in honor of those men. Representatives of the army and local politicians attended its dedication in June. We don't know why these local state officials came to support a commemorative event that openly contravened official policy. It is not clear that the local community was aware of these regulations, but the officers and local administrators knew them. Yet local documents from Sântimbru show the willingness of local officials to go along with the monument. This example reflects the kind of continued selective implementation of the official regulations on the part of remote rural communities, as well as the double role on the part of local officials, of misrepresenting the state while embodying its institutional authority.[30]

In another case, even in the midst of the new, volatile political conditions erupting after 23 August 1944, the Ministry of Education called on a local committee to "send the plans for the Monument and a representation of the surroundings to the Superior Commission for Public Monuments," appending the regulations passed in 1942 and apparently still enforced in December 1944.[31] In the midst of a political storm, the cultural bureaucrats of the central state apparatus were still preoccupied with directing local war commemorations. This example suggests that there was at least a continued intention on the part of state bureaucracy throughout the war to control the commemorative processes linked to the war.

From the Antonescu Dictatorship to the Communist Takeover: Forging Narratives of Victimhood

By May 1945, it was becoming apparent that the Soviets were fully in charge of Romania's fortune, as the western Allies had largely turned their attention to the fate of Germany, Austria, Hungary, and Czechoslovakia, while Soviet troops and advisers had come to dominate the affairs of the government headed by General Constantin Sănătescu (1885–1947), with King Michael as the formal head of state. The official discourse about war commemorations came to be connected directly to the Communists' political struggle for legitimacy in Romania, with the Soviet advisers watching closely in the wings and sometimes acting directly to protect their interests. The story of what happened in Romania was in fact similar to how the Poles, Czechs, Hungarians, Bulgarians, Albanians, East Germans, and Yugoslavs began to engage with official commemorations of World War II.[32] Yet in each of these cases, as in Romania, the circumstances of that country's participation in the war and experiences of its army and political leadership played a role in generating slightly different commemorations, even when the rituals and representations seem to be similar. The politicization of the war's remembrance was also similar in western Europe, where politicians sought to (re)legitimate their role in the postwar world order by referencing specific experiences and angles of the war.[33]

Soon after the Petru Groza (1884–1958) government came to power in March 1945, Law no. 312 of 21 April 1945, for tracking down and sanctioning war criminals, provided the first institutional framework for defining war victims and perpetrators.[34] This law became the starting point for creating Peoples Tribunals similar to those established in other Soviet occupied eastern European states. These Tribunals worked to purge the political and military hierarchies of any perpetrators of war crimes and also clear the ground for the establishment of a new elite, dominated (if not entirely comprised of) Moscow loyalists. Much as in Czechoslovakia, Poland, and Hungary, in Romania these trials also became an occasion for settling personal scores and getting rid of inconvenient political enemies. They were also the first occasion for creating a public record of wartime violence and constructing an official narrative about what witnesses and victims remembered of those actions. They were the first frameworks for postwar public memory work.

As others have noted, these trials fell short of rendering legitimate and transparent verdicts.[35] To begin with, the Communist authorities heavily orchestrated them with the assistance of the Soviet Union (though less so than apologists for the war criminals have claimed). Evidence against the accused sometimes proved inconclusive or was tampered with. Here the Soviet Union proved an obstacle against the Tribunals, as

Moscow authorities delayed in sending the necessary documents, which were mostly in their hands. For instance, much of the paperwork that demonstrated the specific involvement of Romanian military and civilian authorities in Transnistria was in the Ukraine and Moscow. However, the Soviets offered little assistance in locating and actually producing these documents for the rushed trials.[36]

In addition, many of those who were accused in the trials held in Bucharest (citizens of wartime Romania) and Cluj (citizens of wartime Hungary) were judged in absentia. Around 1,300 people were prosecuted and 668 sentenced. Of these, among the first 185 to be tried, only 51 of the accused were actually in custody during the trials.[37] The less than 30 percent reflects the general ratio of presence among the accused at the trials. This meant that, for many of those who came before the tribunals as victims or witnesses, the trials brought little closure. On the contrary, given the politicized and heavy-handed manner of the Peoples Tribunals, I suspect that fear, rather than any sense of satisfaction from having acted as witnesses on behalf of truth or justice, dominated the experience of those called to testify in these trials. In the similar case of Jedwabne, Poland, a Peoples Tribunal helped create a document that served as the explosive starting point for reconsidering that atrocity's history and memory over half a century after the trial. Jan Gross's book reveals the kind of unease witnesses had about that record. They were neither relieved about having a public record of their recollections, nor eager to resurrect those memories when the émigré historian came inquiring in the 1990s.[38] Through their experience of recollecting their painful memories of the war in public, victims were victimized once again, rather than seeing retribution for their suffering.

The trials themselves were publicized heavily in the official media, with large front-page pictures of the accused and official transcripts from the interrogations by the public prosecutors and reports on the radio. Thus, even if they didn't offer emotional closure for victims and witnesses, these trials became an important component of the emerging Communist regime's attempt to create a public image of strength and legitimacy in its work to wipe out any traces of the wartime fascist regime. As such, the trials became the foundation of the official remembrance of the war, but also the basis for counter-memories that were created in the shadow of this official discourse.

Three important elements stand out in the way the trials shaped official war commemorations. To begin with, the pro-Nazi factions in Hungarian-controlled Transylvania were pursued more aggressively than their Romanian counterparts. This unevenness made it clear from the beginning for the Hungarian and German minorities in Transylvania that they wouldn't be treated in the same way as ethnic Romanians; nationalist suspicion of their wartime collaboration would hang over these two ethnic minorities after Transylvania came under Romanian rule again. For instance, atrocities committed by Hungarians against Romanians at the beginning of the retrocession of northern Transylvania in August–September 1940 were fully publicized and heavily prosecuted. Yet atrocities committed by ethnic Romanians against Hungarians during the same period of chaos were summarily swept under the rug of public forgetting. Looking at the number of sentences passed in Cluj versus in Bucharest (481 versus 187), a great discrepancy was already visible in the treatment of war criminals along ethnic and regional lines. By 1946 the Communist government was sending the signal that Romanian citizens had been victims of foreign-minded leadership, while depicting ethnic Hungarians and Germans as Horthy's "willing executioners," aiding and abetting the fascist government against the Jewish and Romanian innocent civilian victims.[39]

In addition to this ethnocentric aspect of the official discourse about the war, two other elements were important in constructing public remembering and forgetting. The Holocaust, though acknowledged repeatedly in many of the trials, was never defined as genocide—the systematic killing of Jewish people under a blanket racist policy of "purification." A sentence passed against one unambiguous case of racist mass murder of Jews stated: "Jews also had to be exterminated as a diversion aimed at distracting the attention from the huge numbers of victims of the war, victims that fell in sacrifice to the interests of the bankers and industrialists . . . a sacrifice aimed at giving satisfaction to the bestial instincts of plunder and destruction long fomented in the propaganda of racial hatred."[40] The nature of the explanation and indictment was strictly speaking correct, but the context in which it placed the racist actions of employees of the Romanian state described this violence as covering up for other excesses, rather than an end in itself. Somehow, in their urge to bend over backward and explain the war's aims in terms of capitalist imperialist interests, the Peoples Tribunals used language similar to that of the Antonescu anti-Semitic regime in describing the threats to the nation posed by "bankers and industrialists," a euphemism for the "Jewish international conspiracy."

The extent of the Holocaust, the participation of elite figures and average people in these atrocities, and the gruesome details of these violent actions were not subject to much public discussion. Between 1945 and 1948, during the time of these trials, the commemoration of the Iaşi pogroms was publicized widely only once, in an article on page five of *Universul,* one of the three most popular newspapers of the time.[41] Commemorations that took place every year in the Jewish Cemetery in Iaşi were reported in the Jewish press, but awareness of these events and participation in them was limited to the Jewish community and low-ranking Party officials. Only on the occasion of the tenth anniversary of the pogroms did the press offer more details about the massacres, with an article on page 2 of *Universul,* "Ten Years since the Massacres of Iaşi." The word "pogrom" was not used, and the narrative, while impressing upon readers the grue-some and gratuitous forms of violence, also left no room for identifying the perpetra-tors as anything other than foreigners: "The Hitlerist officers and soldiers, using all the hooligans in the city, were the patrons of this mass killing."[42] The term "Hitlerist," while presumably applicable to Romanian officers and soldiers to denote their Nazi leanings, was in fact a term that obfuscated the citizenship of these individuals, plac-ing emphasis instead on their foreign loyalty. A reference to them as "Antonescian" would have been just as correct in emphasizing their fascist loyalties and citizenship. But Antonescu had dropped from the picture of the pogroms.

This systematic attempt to depict the horrors of World War II as actions by foreign agents or people with foreign loyalties was reflected in how the war crimes trials were conducted and commemorations staged. On the opposite side of these fascist or "Hitlerist" influences stood the friendly brotherhood of the Soviet people, who had presumably liberated the Romanian nation from the shackles of this corrupt and generally foreign influence. The bargain was plain: in order to bury or forget the true extent of the corruption and guilt of the past, Romanian people had to embrace Soviet brotherhood and thus become expunged from any compromising links with these foreign influences.

Inside the army, changes were also underway regarding the institutional set-up and specific ideological guidelines for remembering the war dead. Between 1944 and 1948, with new leadership emerging and the Soviet military watching closely, the "Queen Marie Establishment," as the Heroes Cult had been renamed during the war, became a problem for the Romanian military authorities. The institution had taken over burial and commemorative actions regarding military personnel and retained their deeply religious Orthodox aspects. Heroes Day was organized in each garrison, town, and village where there were active members of the Establishment just as before, on Ascension Day. Military personnel had been buried with the same respect, as the regulations indicated, regardless of their religious and ethnic background. Crosses had been placed at their heads, as regulations indicated. This meant, however, that by 1948 there were military cemeteries peppered throughout Romania, with Christian symbols at the head of Soviet soldiers and officers. Equally offensive to the Soviet observers was the fact that these soldiers were buried often in the vicinity of, if not next to, German or Romanian soldiers who had fought on the eastern front against the Soviets. This was in fact nothing new; a similar procedure had governed the burial of military personnel in World War I. But in the increasingly polarized ideology of the Cold War, the sight of such funerary markers disturbed Soviet observers.

As a result, during the late 1940s, many of the military cemeteries created in 1944–1945 were subject to repeated inspections by Romanian and Soviet army and

Party representatives, and many of the graves and other commemorative markers for the Soviet soldiers were moved to locations separated from the rest of the combatants.[43] A great deal of effort and expense went into this endeavor, and archival records show evidence of frustration and even outright resentment on the part of the Romanian officers, who saw themselves and their own military heroes marginalized and denigrated at the expense of this ideologically driven activity.[44]

In addition, the Ministry of Defense offered a redefinition of heroism along ideological lines:

> Heroes are those who fought and sacrificed their lives on the battlefield to defend their country, as well as those who fought and suffered for democracy, freedom, justice, equality, etc. Emphasis will be placed and examples will be given from among the heroes who fought and bled on the western front, against fascism. Those who fell on the eastern front were victims of dictatorial regimes.[45]

With this one sweeping gesture, official silence descended upon the deaths of over 30 percent of the fighting Romanian forces in the war, something that the established military rank and file found unacceptable. However, for members of the infamous Tudor Vladimirescu Division, Soviet POWs who had been "reeducated" and brought into Romania starting in 1944 as Moscow loyalists, this order opened the way for a rise to prominence.[46]

The new definition of heroism also opened the door for possibly revisiting the silence that was falling over the Holocaust. In 1946, at a ceremony commemorating Heroes Day, the chief rabbi of the Bucharest Jewish community, Alexandru Şafran (1910–2006), defined heroism to include "anyone who left his or her life in this war, not only those who fell fighting against the Hitlerist army, but also those who fell during the first campaigns of this war, *those killed in concentration camps.*"[47] Though such language might strike the reader as expressing solidarity with the soldiers trying to keep alive the memory of the soldiers fighting on the eastern front, that was not the case. One of the results of silencing references to the eastern campaigns at the request of Soviet advisers was to also silence commemorations of the Holocaust, and Şafran attempted to bring it back into broad commemorative discourses. Alas, he and subsequent leaders of the Jewish community in Romania had to remain satisfied with the low-key, strictly intra-Jewish future commemorations of these horrors.

By 1950 the monuments and cemeteries dedicated to the Soviet army had been completely redone, and annual commemorative events took place on 9 May in all military units and at military cemeteries where there were Soviet soldiers. The Romanian army went along with all this, but reports of disobedience continued to be recorded for the entire period. At one commemoration, officers who had received the Michael the

Brave decoration and the Soviet Victory medal refused to wear the latter next to their Michael the Brave one, offering as a justification the specific directions governing the Michael the Brave decoration: "no other decoration can be worn next to it."[48] But given the fact that among army rank and file the Michael the Brave decoration was broadly associated with fighting on the eastern front, while the Victory medal rewarded action on the western front, this act represented a form of political anti-Soviet protest. Even such small gestures signaled to the political and military leadership that the heavy-handed Soviet propaganda about the heroism of the war dead was not going down easily or effectively with the Romanian army.

From Moscow Loyalists to Romanian Nationalists, 1953–1965: The Role of the Army in Commemorative Sites

The period of thaw experienced by eastern Europe after Stalin's death has been the subject of much scholarship and debate. But what was real rather than palliative thaw? How far was "liberalization" manipulated by Nikita Khrushchev (1894–1971) to use eastern European resources for Soviet goals? And how much was nationalism a true sentiment of the national leaders in eastern Europe rather than a tool for personal empowerment or Soviet goals? In Romania's case, Vladimir Tismăneanu has documented the lack of internal liberalization in the Politburo after 1953, and the ideological straitjacketing of all cultural affairs.[49] However, the military had avenues for contesting these pressures from above, along with the external mythologies of liberation and salvation through war commemorative activities.

Attempts at stalinizing the military and official memorializing of World War II inside the army only lasted while they were forcefully enforced by the presence of Soviet advisers. Wherever those advisers were not present, and especially after the Soviet troops were finally pulled out in 1959, the care of Soviet cemeteries, the pomp of 9 May commemorations, and the representation of the Soviet–Romanian brotherhood in the official landscape of cultural celebrations were reduced to a nod rather than a full embrace. The grandiose monument that marked Victory Square in Bucharest (one of the two most important sites of official commemorations and parades throughout the 1960s) was eventually moved to its current location, fifteen minutes by car from its original place, but tucked away at the edge of Herăstrău Park, the tall column that had supported it erased from the landscape. The monument that had looked imposing thirty feet above the sidewalk now looked heavy and out of place at eye level among the graves of Soviet soldiers. (See figure 5.2a,b.)

As the Romanian army attempted to distance itself from the Soviet Union, the Department for Propaganda and Education at the Ministry of Defense, headed by

Figure 5.2a,b. The Statue of the Soviet Soldier, Bucharest, in its initial (Victory Square, 1966) and current (Herăstrău neighborhood, 2008) location. Photo 5.2a courtesy of the National Military Museum; photo 5.2b Maria Bucur.

Nicolae Ceaușescu, began work on new markers for the Romanian heroes in World War II and more nationalist war commemorations. In a report from 1952 about commemorations of 9 May around the country, an official from Sibiu remarked that he had taken a personal initiative to honor the Romanian soldiers, and not only the Soviet ones, by placing flowers at the local military cemeteries. The Bucharest office responded positively to this initiative, which five years earlier would have been unthinkable: in addition to supporting the Sibiu official and suggesting a similar, broader directive for all other commemorations, the report also signaled that "not placing crosses at the heads of the Romanian soldiers' graves is a great political mistake."[50] Religious symbols were once again endorsed by the regime, which is surprising considering the atheist ideology. Yet, in this case, the crosses have to be understood as a nationalist symbol and in particular a bow to the religious sensibilities of senior military officers and their families.

In addition, by the late 1950s the Department for Propaganda and Education began work on war monuments to Romanian soldiers. Until 1957, with the exception of military cemeteries, there was no central monument dedicated to the Romanian army in World War II. That year, through a decision by the Council of Ministers, the square in front of the old military academy in Bucharest was designated as the future place for such a monument. The location was significant for a few reasons. To begin with, it was in a part of Bucharest that had been renovated under Charles II and remained one of the fashionable places in central Bucharest. The monument's location was also close to several monuments commemorating the Great War, most prominently a statue for the medical personnel, with a central allegorical female figure modeled after Queen Marie. The location of the new monument was connected most directly with the function of the building behind it. The military academy (renamed for Ştefan Gheorghiu) had become a training ground for Party apparatchiks and a citadel of the Party elite.

By the same token, this location was far from the usual itinerary of commemorative parades. The spatial setting of the square offered a nice vista for a large gathering, but the relative narrowness of the streets surrounding it made it practically impossible to incorporate the new monument into any future great parades. Practically speaking, on important national holidays a separate wreath-laying ceremony for the Romanian heroes would be held in the future at this monument, at once visible for many Romanians and centrally located, while less visible for the Soviet observers who would still be able to enjoy their separate commemoration. (See figure 5.3.)

Another important monument dedicated to Romanian heroes was in the works in Liberty Park, which had been the Charles I Park before the war. Around the same time that the Ministry of National Defense was working to articulate a nationalist commemorative discourse regarding World War II, its Propaganda and Education

Figure 5.3. Monument to the Romanian Soldiers in World War II in front of Military Academy, Bucharest, 9 May 1959. Photo courtesy of the National Military Museum.

Department was also working with the Party Central Committee to erect a memorial to Party heroes. Creating a legitimizing genealogy of the Communist regime had been on the agenda of all of the post-1948 eastern European states, under the approving yet watchful eye of the Soviet Union. The Soviets had their own rituals that their eastern European satellites could emulate; in some cases, most prominently Bulgaria, the indigenous Communist parties followed the Soviet model. After the death of Georgi Dimitrov (1882–1949), the Bulgarian leadership built a mausoleum to the much feared and internationally known Communist leader in a prominent central location in Sofia, close to religious sites (almost across from the Russian Orthodox Church, for instance), but creating its own space for future commemorations, which could be used both to appease the Soviet authorities and to create a Bulgarian *sui generis* official memory of the Communist Party's pre-war and postwar history.[51]

The Romanian leadership also opted for a mausoleum. Their choice of location, however, was rather different from the ones in Moscow and Sofia. The monument was to be built in a location far from the main downtown hub in Bucharest, and the location was to link the memorial to a well-recognized symbol, preserving the power of the place, but erasing (or so the regime hoped) the meanings of the past and replacing them with new symbolism. The mausoleum of the Communist heroes would be situated in the space where the Military Museum had stood before being destroyed in World War II, and right above the platform where the Tomb of the Unknown Soldier was located. For the purpose of erecting this memorial, the Tomb of the Unknown Soldier was to be moved to Mărășești.

It is impossible to reconstruct fully the thinking behind this decision. If the Communist Party leadership was already moving on a path of nationalist rhetoric, why remove a nationalist monument that seemed to have no anti-Soviet symbology from a site that was not centrally located in Bucharest? If the Department of Propaganda and Education Section the army was already aware of some of the nationalist grumbling among its officers about the direction of commemorating World War II, why remove from its original place a symbol that was so dear to the military? The only explanation I can offer points toward nationalist compromises in the complex ensemble of commemorative projects during that same two- to three-year period. The mythology of the pre-war Communist Party's activities was linked in part to the anti-war stance of the Communists between 1916 and 1918 and to clashes with the army in December 1918. In part, the Party's narrative about the 1920s was linked to the work the Communists had done illegally under a regime forged during World War I. The heroes who were to be buried in the new mausoleum were intimately linked to this story, and it would have been rather difficult and even contradictory to display a narrative of heroic resistance to imperialism next to a monument that celebrated the patriotism of the soldiers who had fought in the same war.

That the Tomb of the Unknown Soldier was moved and not destroyed speaks in fact to the careful negotiations taking place among Romanian Communist leaders to retain the loyalty of the army and not upset the Soviet Union, while erecting the Communists' own version of the glorious past of the Romanian nation. In fact, by building the monument to the Romanian soldiers who fought in the anti-fascist struggle in World War II at the same time that the Tomb of the Unknown Soldier was being moved to Mărășești also indicates that the new World War II monument in Bucharest might have been in part a compensatory measure for the important symbolic loss felt by the army. In addition, the Communist leadership began rebuilding a military museum in Bucharest, another nod to the army that their self-identity as the protectors of Romania would be publicly acknowledged. In fact, by the 1980s the army became an extremely nationalist, even xenophobic public institution, openly professing animosity toward the Hungarian minorities and celebrating Antonescu as a patriotic leader. Although after 1989 the army complained about the relocation of the Tomb of the Unknown Soldier as an injustice they had suffered at the hands of the evil Communist regime, the reality of how that decision was reached, and the extent to which the army leadership went along with it willingly, reveals a more complicated situation. I would venture to say that the army had some bargaining power and went along with the compromise in part to secure other gains, such as the new military museum. Nicolae Ceauşescu was at the center of this negotiation between the army and the Party.

Another measure of this nationalist perspective on the remembrance of World War II that attempted to appease the military's view of its heroism on the eastern front is illustrated by the building of a military cemetery in Sinaia for the Romanian war dead separately from the Soviet one. In the late 1940s, a military cemetery for the Soviet soldiers was erected alongside the most heavily used national highway in Prahova Valley, which connects Bucharest with Braşov and the rest of Central Europe via Transylvania. The cemetery was placed across from an Orthodox church and cemetery, and a few miles away from the military cemetery for the dead in World War I discussed in chapter 2. The place where the military cemetery to Soviet soldiers fallen in World War II went up was not the site of a major battle, but all the Soviet soldiers who were buried there had died in the summer of 1944 on Romanian soil. Therefore, selecting this site had less to do with army regulations about where to bury soldiers (close to where they had died) and more with visibility to foreign visitors.

In the early 1950s, the military began to consider erecting a military cemetery next to the Soviet one, to honor the Romanian soldiers who perished in World War II.[52] The cemetery was eventually built on an adjacent plot, with markers that identified the Romanian soldiers as having died in years between 1941 and 1945. The Romanian army audaciously chose to honor its dead who had fallen fighting against the Soviet soldiers commemorated right next door. Though the two cemeteries were adjacent, Romanians tended to visit the Romanian one and Soviet delegations their own. Still, considering the close attention paid by the Soviet authorities to how monuments to their soldiers were treated and the strong words used in the late 1940s against any type of acknowledgement of the Romanian troops' fighting on the eastern front as heroic, this was a bold move of insubordination on the part of the army in the face of the Communist leadership.

New Commemorations: World War II as Founding Event of the Communist Regime

In addition to erecting these new monuments in the late 1950s, the Communist regime was also generating a number of commemorative anniversaries meant to replace or supplant old national holidays. The day celebrating the monarchy, 10 May, was conveniently replaced by 9 May, the day on which the Soviet armies were said to have brought World War II to an end in Europe. The first of May also became another holiday celebrating international Communism, and over time completely eclipsed 9 May in terms of parades and popular participation. By the 1960s 9 May became an ossified form of paying homage to the Allies in World War II, less visible than the extravagant parades and cultural events scheduled for 1 May.

The Romanian national holiday was set on 23 August, the day on which King Michael had effected the palace coup against Antonescu. However, the figure of the king vanished from official commemorations, replaced by the actions of the Communist Party. The story became one of the anti-fascist struggle by the Communist forces, erasing from public memory any vilification of Antonescu as well. In the mid-1950s 23 August became a national holiday, marked by massive parades organized across the country by military and Party organizations, with mass participation from among the civilian population. It was a day off from work, but most people had to report for duty in the parades, as did many schoolchildren, even though it was in the middle of summer vacation. Marx, Engels, Lenin, Stalin (until 1953), and various subsequent Soviet leaders were featured prominently among the emblematic pictures in these parades; but the role of the Soviet Union itself was played down more and more over time, bringing into focus instead the role of the RCP and army. Though not an ideal situation, this still allowed the military to construct a more self-promoting image than had been the case in the late 1940s, when they had been constrained to depict themselves as junior partners to the Soviet liberating forces. These commemorations focused on the heroism of armed resistance (whether military or by partisans), where the image of the enemy combined representations of capitalists and fascists. Though women were not missing from the ranks of the Party at that time, the Communist elite and military made no effort to render a more gender-inclusive image of this resistance. The face of Romanian anti-fascist resistance remained decidedly masculine, even when a woman, Ana Pauker (1893–1960), was the shadow leader of the Party.[53]

One additional holiday, Armed Forces Day, set on 25 October, was inaugurated in the 1950s as the date on which the Romanian armies "had liberated the last spot of Romanian soil" in World War II.[54] In the early 1950s this was primarily an intramural date of commemoration and celebration for the army. In keeping with the Soviet directives that only the war in the West, fought on the side of the Soviets, was to be commemorated as heroic, the Romanian army proceeded to construct a nationalist mythology that focused on their sacrifices and heroism. Armed Forces Day was to be commemorated by laying wreaths at sites connected to battles fought between 23 August and 25 October 1944, which were primarily located in Transylvania, where the army had seen massive casualties as the first line of fire on the side of the Soviets. This factual basis offered a platform for preserving an anti-Hungarian nationalist discourse in the army. The battles to liberate Transylvania were fought against Hungarian and German forces, even when this element was not stated directly. Equally important for the army was the exclusive focus on its own sacrifices, which were not to be placed in the larger context of the Soviet Union's role, as was the case with 9 May, for instance. It was also important that this date came almost two weeks before 7 November, the National Day of the USSR, so that it offered a nationalist compensatory ceremony before the obligatory genuflections all Communist states were forced to make before their Soviet "protectors." Finally, this new commemorative date also included the opportunity for war veterans to participate directly in public remembrance of their experiences in the war. This was a new element, as in the late 1940s any such focus on individual experiences had been taboo.

Remembering the War in Word and Images: The Growing Nationalist Discourse in State Education and Culture, 1953–1965

The Communist regime in Romania had the same obsessive compulsion to control the ideological content of all education and culture as most other Communist bloc countries during this period, and this had a direct impact on how war remembrances were shaped. Communist propaganda in cultural activities and education was two-pronged: for the generations who had lived through the war it offered a "corrective" version of those memories that would silence any incorrect versions; and for the generations growing up after the war, it tried to shape their loyalty toward the Communist regime and distance them from counter-memories to which they might have been exposed at home. The silences present in these official discourses are as important to mark as their overt statements. A brief examination of the nature of these cultural products—textbooks and museums, in particular—will illuminate the specific perspectives from which I view the role of propaganda in shaping war commemorations.[55]

The Communist regimes made no secret of their indoctrinating goals with regard to education, both in the classroom and more widely in public arenas such as museum exhibits. In particular, given the intimate and complex relationship between the assumption of power by the Communists and the events of World War II, it comes as no surprise that the Party kept close watch over the ways in which historians, educators, museum curators, and other representatives of the Party in cultural affairs would construct their narratives of the war.[56] Given the extent of the war losses, it was also clear that such endeavors had to confront the personal experiences of those who had lived through the war under different circumstances, and who often harbored different memories of the behavior of the Communists and the Soviet armies than what the Party aimed to convey.

Textbooks in particular have to be seen as attempting not just to construct a narrative of the war, but also to erase from public discussion (and eventually awareness) any inconvenient events and remembrances. Silencing was an essential component of this process, and the rote style of learning that pervaded the teaching of history from elementary schools all the way through university education reinforced this unambiguous direction of education as propaganda. What textbooks did *not* say forms a part of how they aimed to train both knowledge and willful forgetting. Indirectly, history textbooks during this period also devalued individual, personal memories, asking students (and their teachers) to read and memorize, in other words incorporate as official memory and knowledge, the narratives published by the Institute of the History of the Party. Publicly uttered personal recollections, if they diverged from these narratives, would be at best folly and misinterpretation of the "dialectical materialism" offered in these textbooks. At worst they would be outright heresy, liable to severe punishment, including imprisonment.

The best guide for the Party propaganda of the 1950s is the publications of the Institute for the History of the Party affiliated with the Central Committee. School textbooks, museum displays, films, literature, and other forms of cultural production had to take their cue from these publications. The Central Committee also had a network of censors employed at publishing houses and in other cultural institutions, who oversaw the implementation of these directives. Reading through *Lessons to Assist Those Who Study the History of the Romanian Workers' Party,* one has a sense of the direction of the official narrative about World War II. The period 22 June 1941–23 August 1944 is described as a prelude to the insurrection led by the RCP on 23 August 1944. The text describes Romania's entry in the war as a plot by enemies of the Romanian nation:

> Throwing Romania into the anti-Soviet war was prepared by the entire anti-national policy of the exploiting classes. . . . The wide masses of our working people/nation [*poporul muncitor*] rejected this odious war, foreign to their interests, directed against the first socialist state in the world, in which the most arduous wishes of working people for a better life had found expression.[57]

The Romanian people were thus cast as victims of their own political leadership, innocent of atrocities committed in the war. While paying allegiance to the Soviets as the liberators of Romania, the Romanian Communist regime attempted to swiftly cast itself as the embodiment of the wishes of the Romanian nation. Two-thirds of the chapter dedicated to the 1941–1944 period focused in fact on the activities of the RCP and other allies in opposing the war effort. The actions on the front were barely mentioned, while the economic impact of the war on workers and peasants received much attention. Carefully picked examples were meant to convey a sense of thorough chaos in Romania during the war, both in cities and in the countryside, and of great hardship for all working people and especially those active in partisan activities, the Communists.

One brief phrase reminds one that it was not only ethnic Romanians who suffered: "The policy of oppressing national minorities worsened, leading to the extermination of tens of thousands of people through starvation and massacres."[58] This is the most explicit reference to the Holocaust in the entire discussion of the war, if one is to take "extermination" to mean an expressly racist policy. But of course, the lack of detail, and use of the impersonal third person obfuscated rather than illuminated the tragedy of the Jewish people in Romania during the war. Equally important is the lack of direct link between this tragedy and the actions of the Romanian army. An impersonal "they"—meaning the "bourgeois-landed aristocracy," the "military-fascist dictatorship," the "imperialist forces of Germany," or any other entity that was an enemy of the Romanian working people—was held responsible. This narrative rendered impossible any correlation between guilt for the massive deaths of civilians in the war and the Romanian people themselves.

The textbook gives greater attention to the purported activities of the Communist Party around and after 23 August (almost seventy pages, compared to the thirty pages focusing on the previous three years of the war). While reminding readers of the support of the Soviet armies, the textbook offers greater detail about the conditions in which the army fought and the heroic actions that made the Romanian troops worthy of recognition and praise: "participating in the anti-Hitlerist war, the Romanian troops, filled with the sense of justice toward the cause for which they were fighting, covered themselves in glory."[59] By contrast, the number of civilians killed in the war is never fully recounted, and the largest number ever mentioned is the "tens of thousands" of minorities killed during the war. In the 1950s, after the war crimes trials, the Romanian regime was aware that those deaths were in the hundreds of thousands, surpassing in fact the number of soldiers who died on the front. But such casualties would have raised questions about guilt and responsibilities, as well as diminishing the mythology the Communist Party was erecting about being first among the victims of the "militarist-fascist dictatorship" of the war. Thus silence about the Holocaust and atrocities against the Hungarian minorities, especially in the summer and fall of 1944, pervaded official narratives about the war. This silence instructed victims, perpetrators, and witnesses to forget these atrocities.

The narrative about the war aimed to also destroy any positive identification with the monarchy and the parties of the interwar period. King Michael, the most important actor of the 23 August coup, was described as Antonescu's loyal supporter at the beginning of the war; his role in the coup was recast as a "treasonous agreement" with the Nazi leadership to allow the Germans safe retreat from Romania.[60] This narrative about the king was carefully cast against the awareness that the young monarch had been quite popular during his brief rule, and that many people had viewed his forced abdication in December 1947 as the final act in the illegitimate, forceful Communist takeover. To state that Michael stood by Antonescu in 1941 could not be contested, even though the actions of a nineteen-year-old man could scarcely be considered a fully mature political attitude. The accusation that he had been a collaborator of the Nazis at the end of the war, though outrageous, could not be openly questioned, being so dear to the Party's mythology of anti-fascist struggle. This line suggested how Michael should be represented in cultural and educational settings—both minimized and vilified in his role in the war. But for the generation who had lived through the war, such a caricature would only reinforce the profound lack of trust toward official propaganda. Even for the Jewish population, who were aware of the role Queen Helen (1896–1982), Michael's mother, played in trying to alleviate their tragedy, this two-dimensional figure of the king did not fit with their own memories of the war.[61]

Similarly, Iuliu Maniu (1873–1953), the leader of the National Peasant Party, and Gheorghe Brătianu (1898–1953), the leader of the National Liberal Party, the two most important parties in interwar Romania, who had remained broadly popular during the war and after, were also vilified. Maniu's support for the war at the beginning was refashioned as a partnership with the fascist-military dictatorship and his subsequent actions to help Romania switch sides deemed insincere. The two leaders were identified as allies of the imperialist forces that had brought ruin to the Romanian people. To those who had followed these two parties as simple voters, the Communist Party wanted to render apparent that they had been fooled, and that it was the RCP itself who catered to their needs and interests.

History museums followed these general propaganda lines faithfully. During the Communist period the institution of the history museum grew throughout the country, to the point that every county and medium size city boasted its own history museum. This was remarkable, considering the small number of such institutions before the Communist period.[62] Most of these museums were made to reflect the visual narrative initiated in the Museum for the History of the Communist Party in both spatial organization and choice of artifacts. It is not clear how the average person responded to the new museums, but we know that pupils and groups of workers were brought to these museums for compulsory visits. In the late 1990s, the archives and displays of the history museums I visited in Bucharest, Sibiu, Cluj, Braşov, Satu Mare, Focşani, and Iaşi still had visual traces of those visits in the form of black and white photographs of pioneers in awe inside the exhibition rooms, and workers listening closely to curators.

Even if we can't evaluate the impact of the museums on their visitors, it is still possible to examine the exhibits in terms of their intentions. Like most other museums of history created in eastern Europe during the Communist period, the Romanian examples generally privileged political and institutional stories over cultural and social ones, and generally made no effort to present personalized, witness-based memorial narratives about the past. Still, as the literature on history museums has generally observed, the nature of these exhibits always carries evocative elements, even when the intention is to just illustrate facts. For instance, for the population with personal recollections of the war, photographs used in the World War II exhibits had the potential of bringing back flashes of vivid personal emotions and images.

The museum that structured future curatorial choices in representing World War II was the Museum for the History of the Communist Party. Its exhibit offered plentiful displays about the partisan work of the Communist Party, marginalizing in word and images the actions of any other anti-fascist groups. The actions of the Romanian army on the eastern front were completely ignored, while lavish displays showed the Romanian troops entering Bucharest to liberate it, and then fighting in Transylvania and beyond Romania's western borders to help win the war for the Allies. The king, Maniu, and Brătianu were nowhere pictured, and images of Antonescu appeared sparsely. Images of atrocities committed by ethnic Romanians against minorities were absent. Even as an imagology of the Holocaust was taking root in Poland and East Germany, in Romania the photos of the death trains and of the emaciated bodies of the survivors of the death camps were never included among the iconic photographs connected to the war. The largest photo displayed in the section dedicated to the war was full wall image of healthy, happy Romanian soldiers marching under the Triumphal Arch in Bucharest to liberate it.

If size and prominence in the room are an indication of a specific message to be imprinted upon the retina of museum visitors, then this photograph seems to have been the single most important symbol: the Romanian army, not the Soviets, had liberated Bucharest (and by extension Romania). Though another image of Romania's liberation dominated the western media, of Ana Pauker atop a tank entering Bucharest,[63] Gheorghe Gheorghiu-Dej, the Communist leader until 1965, did not favor it (the notion of a female Jewish leader of Romanian Communism offended the sensibilities of many Romanians). More palatable was the image of healthy ethnic Romanian young men, embraced by the population at large. For many visitors in the 1950s, this image was a personalized one—many of the inhabitants of the capital had come out in August 1944 to welcome these soldiers back—some of them brothers, husbands, fathers, and sons. The image was evocative of emotional memories for people of that generation.

The sight of the Triumphal Arch was another familiar and evocative element in the commemorative landscape of Bucharest. The Arch, framing the soldiers' victorious return, suggested connections with World War I. This monument offered a link with the narrative about the struggle of the Romanian soldiers in 1916–1918 to liberate Romania. Thus, even as the propaganda of the Communist Party identified World War I as a conflict among imperialist forces, it used celebratory commemorative symbols of that war to frame the struggle of the Romanian army in World War II as patriotic, fighting on behalf of liberating the country. Along the lines that the war crimes trials and the historical narratives had done, the visual representations in these history museums reverberated with the same sense of patriotism, self-sacrifice, and innocence with regard to any war crimes. There were no images that paired Romanian soldiers with representation of the horrors of the Holocaust. Instead, the civilian atrocities of the war were cast on the shoulders of others—the Nazis, the Hungarians—and away from areas that had been under Romanian occupation during the war.

Literary and Film Representations of the War

The Communist regime controlled the public cultural discourse around commemorations of World War II just as closely in literature and film. An explanation is required here, to clarify my shift in treating literature and movies not as expressions of individual remembrances of the war, those of the writer/director, but rather of the official discourse. The reason for this shift is simple. Publishing books and producing and showing movies were exclusive prerogatives of the one-party state. Therefore, though initially an expression of individual ideas, their actual circulation in public represented a more complicated act of political propaganda. Whether overt or veiled, censorship loomed wide over the publication of books and the making of movies, and both authors/directors and their publics were aware of it. The Party was everywhere in that sense, so one cannot speak of unmediated individual memorializing of the war in the sphere of publishing and film production. Furthermore, though samizdat literature circulated in other eastern European countries, the phenomenon was insignificant in Romania.

Cultural propaganda through word and image in these two forms of entertainment was near and dear to the Communist Party and closely monitored by ideological apparatchiks.[64] In the first decade of Communist rule film screenplays were discussed at Politburo meetings, at a time when the Party was also dealing with nationalization, eliminating political enemies of the state, and collectivization. The enormous amount of energy (human and material) spent in the field of censorship underscores the centrality of cultural propaganda of this new regime. Before Stalin's death, the subject of

the war remained generally taboo in popular literature and film. "Proletcultist" literature sought instead to imitate (and in many cases just translate) worthy models from
the Soviet panoply of socialist realist propaganda, from Maxim Gorky (1868–1936) to
Fyodor Gladkov (1883–1958).

A few exceptions should be noted—the memoirs of survivors of the Transnistrian
camps and the Iași pogrom.[65] In the late 1940s, Marius Mîrcu (1909–2008) and a handful of other survivors of the anti-Semitic policies during the war were able to publish
testimonials about these horrible events; but these books were quickly swept off the
shelves of bookstores and libraries, to remain buried in the "S" (secret) files until 1989.
Just as was the case with Șafran's unsuccessful attempts to bring wider public attention to the horrors of the Holocaust, these books remained in a limbo—published yet
not widely public, available only to those who had managed to buy them after their
initial release. During the Communist period these books remained inside the Jewish
communities about which they spoke, but invisible to the rest of the population.

It was in the mid-1950s that literary and film critics identify a rebirth (with some
atrocious mutations) of Romanian "authentic" writing and film making, with sufficient esthetic qualities to qualify them as art, rather than political pamphleteering.
The extent to which this new crop of cultural creation was essentially or only partially
compromised by its socialist realist components has been the subject of much debate
since 1989, unresolved, in my opinion.[66] But this literature was read avidly, and the
public went to see the new movies in droves. Irrespective of its quality, this cultural
production presented an important force in enabling the official discourse about
remembering the war.

Among the books focusing on World War II that came out during this first
decade of demi-thaw (in Romanian the more critical term is the "obsessive decade"
[*obsedantul deceniu*]),[67] two books stand out: one that has been largely forgotten—
Laurențiu Fulga's unfinished trilogy, *The Heroic;* and another one that remained popular throughout the Communist period—Titus Popovici's (1930–1994) *The Stranger.*[68]
Fulga had his literary debut in 1937 in the avant-garde publication *Bilete de papagal*
and later served in the war, where he was severely injured (there was even an obituary
published in the press announcing his death) and taken prisoner by the Soviets. He
returned to Romania as part of the Tudor Vladimirescu Division of Romanian POWs
who had joined the Communist Party, and in 1956 published the first volume of his
Heroic trilogy, *People without Glory.*

The book constitutes the first attempt at openly depicting life on the eastern
front among Romanian troops at the point when the tide of the war was about to
turn against the Axis. Over seven hundred pages long, the autobiographical novel
depicts a brief moment in the long war, so it is not a narrative of the war so much as

a series of frescoes, some absurdly two-dimensional in their pro-Soviet depictions. Other sections of the book are much more directly memorialistic in trying to recreate descriptions of the physical sensations of freezing cold weather and hunger, as well as fear and trauma. These descriptions are profoundly poetic and moving in painting the existential angst of many different types of soldiers in the midst of total war, along generational, class, and educational divisions. The narrative moves slowly back and forth, and there is not much to the plot. But there are moments of great evocative intensity in the author's description of the numbing madness experienced by soldiers in the midst of battle:

> Before his clouded eyes, in a single second, commenced to appear like a congress of spirits the entire avalanche of known and unknown people who had perished in the war. Endless columns of shadows darkened the skies. Up from the dead climbed those fallen at Țiganca and before Odessa, those burned alive in the fires of Chișinău, and those crushed by tanks on the Hills of Tsarina. Those who had perished next to the walls of Kharkov and those drowned in the marshes of Sivaș appeared next. Together they met those sacrificed at the crossing of the Pruth and those who had frozen during the last days on the Don.[69]

Though the death of those in the anti-Soviet campaign was not glorified in this text, it was at least a subject of remembrance, and at times of empathetic compassion ("sacrificed"), something unprecedented to that point. Such compassion extended only to simple soldiers, rather than officers, generally depicted as "class enemies." Yet the human typologies presented in the book, including the sympathetic portrait of the main character, Ștefan Corbu, allowed both veterans and younger generations to imagine the individual drama of those soldiers as human beings, not just as two-dimensional clichés of misguided troops. Likewise, war itself is presented as a complex human tragedy and not simply the struggle between imperialist forces and the glorious Soviet army. Fulga depicts the suffering of soldiers as a complicated and self-contradictory combination of guilt, solidarity, idealism, and demoralization, with graphic details of the violence in which soldiers had engaged. Though the heroism of those who became part of the Tudor Vladimirescu Division is depicted in unambiguous clichés, the overall picture of the book avoids a simplistic equation of victimization with heroism. The book was not reprinted after its initial publication, and the author saw some recognition only in the late 1960s, generally without reference to this autobiographical war novel.[70] This representation of the war was not to the taste of the regime.

By contrast, *The Stranger,* published in 1955, launched Titus Popovici's career and became a popular book, reissued in 1979, and also the subject of a popular movie.[71] The book is not autobiographical, as the author was born in 1930 and had been too young to participate in any activities akin to those described in the novel, which takes place in the summer of 1944, on the eve of the arrival of the Soviet troops in Romania. Why then include it in a section about official remembrances of the war? I decided to analyze it in this section because the novel is painstakingly (though by no means accurately) constructed as a historical novel, and its aim seems to be to connect the subjective individual fate and memories of simple people to the larger forces of history taking place around them. It was also a first in openly tackling the tense ethnic relations in Transylvania during the war, emphasizing the atrocities committed by both Romanians and Hungarians, while also reminding readers of the policies of the Antonescu regime.

While Fulga's novel returned obsessively to the maddening and dehumanizing conditions of the front, *The Stranger* created a complex plot, where characters intersected, influenced each other, then parted ways, making the novel a much more compelling read in terms of action and character development. It also placed the existential struggle of an adolescent, Andrei Sabin, at the center of the novel, rendering him sympathetic with the young generation coming of age in the mid-1950s. By presenting the action in the novel through the eyes of this young character, *The Stranger* made itself an important player in how the post-memory of the war emerged among the first generation growing up without a direct memory of the war's atrocities. However, in terms of readability, like the struggle of the adolescent it depicts, the novel suffers from lack of depth and maturity in terms of building psychological profiles, falling easily (though not always) into clichés. I suspect, however, that this kind of easy recognition of various human types—the introspective budding intellectual, the materialist lawyer, the courageous worker, the maternal mother, the drunken brutal peasant, etc.—made the book a success especially with younger readers.

What makes *The Stranger* a departure in depictions of the war is the subject of interethnic relations in Transylvania between 1940 and 1944. We read about massacres suffered by civilian Romanians at the hands of Hungarians in the fall of 1940; the names Ip and Treznea[72] come up in the narrative; and there is a vivid description of a massacre suffered by inhabitants of a Hungarian village at the hands of the Maniu guards[73] at the end of the war. These atrocities had been the subject of trials by Peoples Tribunals in the 1940s, but not of broad dissemination since then, as the Communist regime aimed to deal with Romanian–Hungarian animosities by not talking about them. Likewise, the anti-Semitic attitudes of the officials and Romanian population also receive some attention. The most horrendous atrocities committed against Jews are, however, depicted as the actions of German troops or deviant legionaries. The notion that the average Romanian population itself was engaged in anti-Semitic attitudes on a daily basis is never made plain. The Holocaust appears again as something marginal and foreign, rather than an integral policy of the Romanian wartime government. However, there is a clear attempt to deal with questions of guilt and responsibility for atrocities committed during the war, especially in Transylvania. Though somewhat cut and dried in their engagement with these questions, the book's characters still manage to bring different angles into the picture of how violence took place, from questions of historical precedence in Romanian–Hungarian relations to tensions over property, ideological radicalization on the right, and even gender-specific tensions (in the form of lust). The perpetrators are generally not monstrous strangers, but neighbors of those being victimized. This, more than anything else, makes *The Stranger's* depiction of wartime violence among civilians unprecedented.

The novel launched Popovici as a prominent writer. It has continued to be read and appreciated by many up to today, even though literary critics have argued harshly about his "noxious" influence over Romanian readers. The frequency of references to this novel (and the eponymous movie, whose screenplay he also wrote) and to Popovici in general, in both Romanian and international publications about postwar literature, reflect the popularity of this particular depiction of the war both with those growing up in the 1950s and with subsequent generations.[74]

In film a more Romanian-centric view of the war experience was also becoming visible during this period. The film industry had a hard time getting restarted after the war, and only in 1949 did the first postwar full feature film have its premiere.[75] Film was also completely subjugated to the ideological propaganda preoccupations of the regime, so the first movies reflected an obsessive focus on the joys of collectivization and building a modern economy out of a pre-modern agrarian society. Then, in 1959, *Life Doesn't Forgive* came out and established new artistic and thematic directions for Romanian postwar film, offering also the first individual psychological profile on film of a man caught in the web of his traumatic war memories. In a recent history of Romanian cinema, this movie is compared to *Hiroshima, Mon Amour* (1959) and *Last Year at Marienbad* (1961) in terms of narrative structure. Using frequent flashbacks and creative editing techniques, the movie makes the subjective, irrational way in which the mind forgets and remembers the focus of its aesthetic vision.

Life Doesn't Forgive examines the fragmented memory of a war veteran who had fought at the bloody Mărășești battle (1917), where his best friend died. The death of this friend is clouded by trauma, and the veteran is pushed to remembering it by the inquisitive questioning of his dead friend's son. A commemorative parade produces the kind of memory trigger psychologists often talk about in the case of trauma, and the veteran slowly begins to recall the events, arriving at the horrible realization that he had been ordered to kill his friend. Aside from the facile portraiture of the war profiteers and upper class society as profoundly corrupt, following the well established

Marxist clichés of the time, the movie offers the first attempt in Romanian cinematography to deal with the memory of the war from the soldier/veteran's individual perspective. It depicts the horrors of the war with great intuition in terms of psychological theories of trauma, and of loss and recovery of memory in vogue at that time.

The movie also focuses on forgetting and forgiving as distinct issues, proposing that forgiveness can only take place after recovering and working through traumatic memories. The movie also suggests that "shame" and "heroism" in terms of wartime violence are ultimately a matter of perspective, rather than fact. This notion in itself was explosive at the time, as it opened up the way for World War II veterans to assert personal interpretations of *their* wartime experiences. Finally, the film also indirectly presents a call out to the viewers who are younger to ask themselves and their parents about their wartime (World War II) experiences. In fact, as both directors (who also wrote the screenplay) were in their mid-twenties when the movie came out, *Life Doesn't Forgive* represents an example of post-memory engagement with the need to keep alive certain memories, albeit traumatic, of the war. The focus on World War I might have been part of the directors' personal relation with the memory of that war, but it was more likely a way to deal with wartime memory without getting too close to the concrete and politically volatile issues of how World War II was to be remembered.

The aesthetic of the movie, its convoluted narrative that mixes temporal planes—present, past, and future—in a way that confounds any attempt at a linear reading of the film, made it hard to criticize from a strict ideological perspective, especially given the nod to class struggle given by the directors. But ultimately the movie did prove too controversial in its insistence on the inability to separate guilt from heroism; it had a limited release and was generally ignored by movie critics of that time. Therefore, its impact was far less on the national scale than that of later movies depicting the experience of the two world wars. However, in the 1980s the movie was being shown at art movie houses and gained a reputation as an important film.

The popular novel *The Stranger* premiered as a movie in 1964 and met with more acclaim than *Life Doesn't Forgive,* attracting a sizeable audience. The screenplay was signed by Popovici and faithfully followed the action and the dialogue in the novel (reduced, however, from the six hundred pages of the book). The movie featured a superb cast of young actors, who subsequently became superstars of Romanian theater, film, and television, in great part due to their work in this project.[76] The film reinforced the youthful gaze toward the wartime experience through the eyes of its young actors, suggesting as forcefully as the novel the moral morass of Romanian society during the war and the work of the RCP to clear the way for a different path after the war. The performance of the outstanding cast turned this propagandistic vision into an entertaining and even emotional experience for the viewers.

These two movies aside, most of Romanian film between 1949 and 1970 did not focus on the two world wars in feature, documentary, or television series. In the rest of eastern Europe, the war was the subject of some filmmaking, but, with the exception of the Soviet Union, there was not a continuous preoccupation with shaping its memory through film. Some Polish (*Kanal*), Czech (*Closely Watched Trains*), and Hungarian (*Mephisto*) productions created notable representations of the experience of war for the civilian population, but most directors stayed away from dealing with the complexities of the war in terms of the front and especially relations with the Soviet Union.[77] In Romania, the standard fare was much closer to social-realist topics of building Communism in the countryside and the city, or light comedies, echoing the style established by the longer Soviet film tradition. It was during Ceauşescu's years at the helm of the Romanian state that both world wars were more thoroughly integrated into the mythology of Romanian Communist nationalism that the dictator wove with the aid of an army of culturniks.

The Paroxysm of Romanian Nationalist Commemorations of the World Wars, 1965–1989

The shift toward an overtly nationalist discourse about World War II, to the detriment of one under domineering Soviet guidance, became accentuated after 1965, when Ceauşescu became general secretary of the RCP. Contrary to views that this was a new course, I would argue it was just a continuation of a vision Ceauşescu had been finessing since the 1950s.[78] The new constellation of Soviet–eastern European relations also allowed for a more openly nationalist course, provided that such a direction was not anti-Soviet, as the Hungarian fifty-sixers learned at a heavy price. But it was already apparent from Ceauşescu's early years in power that historical discourse and commemorations of wartime heroism were central to his desire to construct a glorious image of himself as great leader of his people.

In 1967 Ceauşescu ordered the Ministry of Defense to organize the festivities for the fiftieth anniversary of the Mărăşeşti Battle. Since 1948 the battle had been commemorated through small ceremonies organized by the army, with the added detail of having the Tomb of the Unknown Soldier incorporated into the ceremony in the mid-1950s. What we see in 1967 is a switch in the commemorative discourse about World War I on the part of the Communist regime, folding this event and its living memory, through veterans, into the emerging discourse about the Romanian nation and its victimized-heroic profile throughout history. The festivities planned for 1967 prefigured the extravagant montages of film, dance, military parade, sports demonstrations, and theatrical performance that came to dominate all major public holidays in the late 1970s and 1980s. Reading through the detailed script of the festivities, it becomes apparent that every aspect of this jubilee was carefully connected to specific symbolic meanings of the battle that were to become a new orthodoxy in terms of correctly "remembering" the war and representing it in the future.

The battle was constructed within a longer nationalist framework of great historical figures who had struggled for Romanian independence, placing emphasis on the actions of a few common folk heroes who were to be identified as both correct in terms of class pedigree (the "proletariat"), and also as ethnically Romanian in a rather ostensible fashion. Ecaterina Teodoroiu, the "virgin from Jiu," was resurrected as a symbol of the battle alongside generals Eremia Grigorescu and Ion Dragalina (1860–1916), who had been relegated to marginality in the 1940s and '50s. Several other figures made their debut as important heroes of the battle: Captain Grigore Ignat (1889–1917), Maria Zaharia (1908–1917), and Captain Constantin Muşat (1890–1917).[79] The presence of two female figures, Teodoroiu and Zaharia, was at best tokenism. Both were presented in imagery that rendered them exceptional, in other words atypical for women's behavior during the war. These female figures served to make women visible, but also render them marginal in the wider image of the battle.

The two generals, having been part of the Romanian social elites, were depicted as class enemies in the late 1940s and 1950s, and now saw a full "rehabilitation" by the officials as leading heroes of the war. Others, like Averescu, were not viewed so positively and remained marginal to the official war commemorations. But those who more fittingly embodied the Communist-nationalist heroic ideals of the day were the simple peasants like Maria Zaharia, a volunteer scout, poor teachers like Ecaterina Teodoroiu, or lower officers who lost their lives in the midst of their troops, like Grigore Ignat. By using basic facts about their actions on the battlefield and weaving around them mythical stories of heroism, the Communist regime resurrected the narrative of World War I as an important moment in the construction of the Romanian nation. This new direction was part of an attempt by the Communist regime to cast itself as independent by comparison with other Communist regimes that were merely following the Soviet party line.[80]

The Mărăşeşti semi-centenary represents an important moment in the construction of the official war commemorative discourse of the Ceauşescu Communist regime on several levels. It represented a re-institutionalization of the memory of World War I as a struggle for national survival and the fulfillment of legitimate political goals. Though *Life Doesn't Forgive,* for instance, had offered a view of the war from the point of view of a traumatized veteran, there had not been anything on the scale of the jubilee held on 12 August 1967 to suggest the centrality of World War I for the history of contemporary Romania. The script of the celebration made nationalism unambiguously central:

Voice-over: The stone of the monument is the memory of history. The stone and time. . . .

(On the soundtrack: Lion Cubs) [in Romanian, "Pui de lei," a famous nationalist anthem published in 1891].

Voice-over: Bring your ear next to this stone and you will hear the sound of age-old struggles, inscribed with the letters from the eternal fire, since the days of Decebal and Trajan. . . . On these fields the heroes from Mărășești sacrificed their lives, but the decisiveness of their struggle started at the same time as our millenary breath.[81]

The script connected the battle of 1917 with the purported birth of the Romanian people out of the synthesis of endogenous Dacians and occupying Romans. This nationalist line about the "birth" of the Romanian language and people had been popular since the nineteenth century, but was silenced during the first decade of Communist rule. As the regime was becoming more overtly nationalist, this theory came back in fashion and has remained so ever since. What strikes the reader now, and no doubt seemed at odds with any view of history as change, was the notion that soldiers at Mărășești fought for the same ideals as the Dacians in the second century AD.

This script also inaugurated the notion that there is such a thing as uninterrupted memory, the memory of stone ("bring your ear next to this stone"), what Pierre Nora might identify as a *lieu de memoir,* a kind of voice of immemorial times, carrying over to the present the testimony of long-dead ancestors. This notion, no matter how absurd in terms of facts, did represent a poetics of identity construction that was meaningful to average Romanians, for whom a religious cult of the dead continued unabated under the officially atheistic Communist regime.

The Mărășești jubilee reintroduced another important aspect of official war commemorations: around two hundred veterans were invited to participate in the official delegation, alongside members of the Central Committee, Ceaușescu himself, and foreign representatives of all the accredited diplomatic missions in Bucharest, including a delegation of French veterans who had fought alongside the Romanians in 1917.[82] Veterans were placed front and center in these commemorations, as living memory of the wartime heroic sacrifices of the Romanian army, honored by the state, and no doubt proud to have their role in the war recognized again, after years of marginalization. Yet the veterans were to be seen and not heard, and thus remained objects of symbolic attention in official commemorations, rather than active participants. In addition to these two hundred veterans, fifty thousand others were given decorations for their role in the war. It is not clear whether the decorations were purely symbolic or carried any remunerative value.[83] But the total number represented a powerful statement about the Romanian state's recognition of virtually all surviving veterans, regardless of their social position during the war—peasant, worker, or bourgeois. Still, people serving in the Austro-Hungarian army were not honored, and thus the jubilee came to reinforce the Romanian exclusivist notion of heroism and sacrifice associated with World War I.

Over the years of Ceaușescu's rule, Mărășești became a regular site of pilgrimage for young pioneers, much as it had been in the interwar period. I remember making a trip to the remote mausoleum in the 1970s during my elementary school years, soon after I had become a pioneer.[84] Many people of my generation have similar recollections. As more people became able to purchase cars during the short period of consumer-oriented socialist economy (roughly, the mid-1960s until the late 1970s), Mărășești became visible to a new generation of Romanians and saw a growing number of visitors.

Another date linked to World War I made a comeback during the same period. In 1968 the Communist regime decided to commemorate 1 December with the same panache as the Mărășești commemoration. Historians and museum curators were encouraged to prepare books of documents and exhibits to reinstate that date as another important moment in the "fulfillment of age-old aspirations" of the Romanian people.[85] Old and new heroes of the Transylvanian Romanian nationalist movement were resurrected, and with the exception of the few remaining taboos, the representation of 1 December resembled a great deal the official discourse from the interwar period. The written and visual (in permanent museum exhibits) narrative of World War I came to end on 1 December, with that date symbolizing the apotheosis of the "will of the people." The Versailles peace negotiations and the role of the monarchy and Brătianu government were deemed irrelevant and officially ignored. Instead, the war seemed to have ended with the mass rally in Alba Iulia. Such a view served a Romanian ethno-nationalist view of the war, which was to Ceaușescu's liking and was heartily approved by the leadership of the Party.

One important trend during the Ceaușescu years was the increasing obsession of the regime with proper celebratory spectacles. After his visit to North Korea in 1971, when Ceaușescu witnessed to his great delight the power of a totalitarian regime in manipulating hundreds of thousands of people into displaying adulatory messages, the Romanian dictator tried to implement that vision at home. Within a few years, 24 January, 26 January (Ceaușescu's birthday), 1 May, 23 August, and 1 December all became moments at which the Romanian leader wanted to see the entire nation on display, genuflecting before him through marching, song, and other kinds of performances.

By the beginning of the 1980s, 23 August in particular had become a closely monitored nation-wide affair. Having television at his disposal, Ceaușescu could in fact view the festivities organized throughout the country live, from either the official balcony overlooking the Bucharest parades or from the comfort of his residence. Hundreds of thousands of people marched every year, and Party members in particular were obligated to be present on that date, officially a day of rest. People came to dread this holiday, as it typically meant interrupting or shortening one's summer vacation and was generally felt to be an inconvenient, pointless, and humiliating exercise. From the official balcony, the parades on 23 August were meant to look like a river of love and loyalty flowing under the gaze of the loving leader, much as Leni Riefenstahl's images displayed the smiling Aryan marches under Hitler's eyes. Viewing those images from the distance of two decades of post-Communism, one is in fact struck by the grandeur of the spectacle.

Yet beneath this veneer of moving crowds were the real thoughts and feelings of those made to wake up at the break of dawn for months in advance, repeating the same routine over and over like automatons, and made to listen to speeches that were to arouse and threaten them into performing perfectly. My parents and those of most of my friends went to these parades, and we were brought up to ridicule and despise them. There was no satisfaction or sense of pride in their participating in these events. On the contrary, plenty of derision and some of the worst language I remember hearing uttered in my home were reserved for Ceaușescu and the Party on the occasion of these important holidays and parades. I grew up imagining that living in a free country meant that one did *not* participate in parades, but rather took the national day off as an opportunity to rest. This vision was echoed in oral history interviews I did in 1998 and 1999, and in many other informal discussions. Many people were surprised I wanted to revisit the issue of the 23 August parades, these being something so reviled as to provoke instant disgust rather than intellectual interest for anyone old enough to remember them personally.

It appears that the more omnipresent and outlandish these parades became, the less people who were forced to take part in them (and nobody volunteered repeatedly for them, even those who were opportunistically hoping to climb up the Party ladder) identified in any way with the symbolism of the celebrations. What 23 August stood for was quickly lost in the fog of nationalist rhetoric that tied Decebal and Trajan to Ceaușescu, rendering World War II a bump on the road to the glorious regime of the current "Golden Era." Even members of the army, prominently featured in the parades, did not find their specific experience or remembrance of the war represented in these performances. By 1989, most people dreaded the 23 August parades and the holiday that occasioned them. There is no other explanation for why the Romanian regime was in a hurry to get rid of this date as its national holiday after the fall of the Communist regime. In addition to the complete falsification of all the facts regarding the actual change of political regime, the RCP had succeeded in demonizing this date in the eyes of several generations of Romanians, who even today have a hard time thinking of it as an important and positive moment in the history of modern Romania.[86]

Anti-Hungarian Victimology: Re-Articulating the Memory of World War II in Transylvania

Ceauşescu's brand of nationalism had other specific consequences for official war com-memorations, especially with regard to questions of guilt and victimization among the civilian population in World War II. Ceauşescu was passionately anti-Hungarian. In the 1980s, this sentiment reached a paroxysmal state, as the president embarked upon a campaign to reveal the horrors of the Horthy regime. Several factors account for the intensification of anti-Hungarian activities. The most prominent internal factor came from the army. In the early 1980s the division in charge of wartime monuments noti-fied Ceauşescu that a large number of monuments with a "fascist-Horthyist" character existed all over Transylvania and posed a threat to the Romanian state.[87] Externally, a history of Transylvania published by the Hungarian Academy of Sciences sent the Romanian historical establishment into a decade-long fit, generating a great deal of nationalist posturing back and forth across the border between the two countries' academic establishments.[88]

As a result, the state took a number of commemorative and anti-commemorative actions. To begin with, all county offices of the National Patrimony Office were to sur-vey every single war memorial on their territory, according to a list of items that went from physical description (size, material, and placement) to analyses of the content and recommendations for future action. The result of this survey undertaken between 1983 and 1989 is the fullest register of wartime monuments. Unfortunately, the results were sent to the Museum for the History of the RCP, which was vandalized in the days after the 21 December 1989 flight of the Ceauşescus, and the papers disappeared. However, some of the county offices of the National Patrimony Office still have some of these surveys, and I was fortunate enough to see the full records of the Satu Mare and Sibiu counties, both interesting and illustrative of the nationalist policies of the Ceauşescu regime, as Satu Mare has a sizeable Hungarian population, while Sibiu still had a sizeable German population in the 1980s.[89]

As one reads through the hundreds of files compiled by these two offices, several important elements become apparent. In the 1980s Romania was filled with public symbols commemorating the two world wars, most of the interwar ones still intact. In addition, though a large number of markers in Transylvania had been destroyed by Romanians and Hungarians during World War II, and then again by the Romanians as they swept through northern Transylvania in the fall of 1944, one could find plenty of memorials constructed during the war and afterward, all the way up to the 1980s. These markers were semi-private and semi-public in their character, especially those put up by ethnic minorities, and I will return to their description and significance in the following chapter. The important issue here is that such monuments could be built at all at a time when Romanian ethno-nationalism was on the rise, and when Ceaușescu was gaining the reputation of being a totalitarian dictator, fully in charge of cultural discourse in Romania.

The markers and surveys themselves suggest, however, that the cultural production of official discourses was done partly at the local and regional level, and that the voice of the Party and state was far from monolithic. That the very existence of monuments dedicated to ethnic Germans fighting on the eastern front, with death dates ranging from 1943 to 1949, was possible in German villages suggests that local Party organizations were either unaware of these monuments or went along with them. Both scenarios are likely. In some rural areas the Party leadership was ethnically Romanian, hated and distrusted by the local majority population (Hungarians or Germans) on both ideological and ethnic grounds. In places like that, memorials were built inside places of worship, visible to the local community but invisible to the officials, similarly to the interwar period. In other areas, where ethnic Hungarians or Germans dominated the local Party leadership, they often harbored intense loyalty toward their ethnic group and likely went along with such memorials.

The surveys themselves are a good indication of how localized commemorative policies were even in the most all-encompassing of Communist dictatorships in eastern Europe, as Ceaușescu's regime is described in the scholarly literature. The survey conducted in Satu Mare contained negative evaluations of Hungarian monuments on almost each page, identifying them as "fascist-Horthyist" markers and recommending they be demolished and replaced with adequate expressions of Romanian sacrifices during the war. The survey done in Sibiu had virtually no such recommendations. The descriptions are much drier, and one has the sense that the person doing the survey was either too lazy to go into any detail or intentionally feigning disinterest in order to protect questionable monuments from being destroyed. Whatever the reasons, the data and tone of the two surveys are quite different, even though the materials present on site were comparable. This suggests that, in their attempt to create a unified commemorative discourse, the Party leadership in Bucharest was dependent on local representatives, who interpreted their responsibilities in different ways. This relationship is reminiscent of the double role state authorities played during the interwar period with regard to commemorative activities. The difference is in the claims to complete knowledge and control that the RCP made about its regime of power, which previous regimes did not assert.

To examine the results of these surveys, I visited some of the controversial sites slated for destruction. The results didn't surprise me: in rural areas, in 1999 and 2000 most monuments were still there. This is not to say that the Romanian state had not in fact destroyed Hungarian monuments erected between 1940 and 1944.[90] But in many places, monuments honoring the Hungarian soldiers fighting on the side of the Axis in World War II went up during the years of Communist rule and are still there. The same could be said for many German villages where people served in either the Romanian or German armies and where civilians were deported to Siberia. These traces suggest that, even though on the most visible level—television, other mass media, parades, state museums, and education—the Communist state was able to construct a consistent ethno-nationalist commemorative discourse about World War II, there is ample evidence of important variations in the implementation of these policies at the local level, especially in rural areas.

The campaign of reshaping the official commemorations of World War II included bringing greater visibility to the atrocities suffered by Jews and Romanians in Transylvania. This is possibly the most perverse aspect of selective official commemoration of World War II in Communist Romania. While the Romanian Holocaust had been safely hidden away from general view with plaques and memorials situated inside synagogues and Jewish cemeteries, in the 1980s the Communist regime began an enterprise of placing more visible markers that commemorated the victims of the Holocaust in Transylvania. The most prominent was a statue placed in a public square in the town of Dej, depicting a group of civilians—a young mother, a child, and an elderly man—who represent the thousands of deportees taken to the death camps in the spring of 1944. Other markers included a large menorah-like bas-relief facing the street on the fence of the Jewish cemetery in Sighet (figure 7.4), the birthplace of Elie Wiesel (1928–).

In addition to these sculptural commemorative markers, photographs of the horrors of the Holocaust also appeared in books and newspapers, acquainting new generations with images that had become iconic in the West.[91] The important interpretive twist given to these images was that they focused exclusively on the dead in Transylvania, re-enforcing the silence regarding the Holocaust of the Jews in Moldavia, Bessarabia, and Transnistria. The anti-Hungarian aspect of this selective remembering was obvious and manipulative: the Holocaust on the Romanian territory was to be remembered exclusively as an evil done by the Hungarian administration and population.[92] Ethnic Romanians could continue to consider themselves as innocent bystanders in the process.

In addition to this revisionist campaign in stone, image, and word, the Romanian Communist regime also proceeded to raise prominent monuments to Romanian civilian populations murdered during the process of retrocession of northern Transylvania in the fall of 1940 and later on, during the four years of Hungarian rule. The most widely known are the monuments built in Ip and Treznea, two small villages

Figure 5.4.
Treznea monument.
Photo Maria Bucur.

in the ethnically mixed Satu Mare County, which are today predominantly (Ip) or exclusively (Treznea) Romanian. In September 1940, in both villages, a number of the local Romanian and Jewish villagers were murdered by what appears to have been a motley crew of locals and strangers, ethnic Hungarians wearing uniforms of the Hungarian army and carrying guns issued to regular soldiers. The number of people killed, the circumstances in which they were killed, as well as the motivation behind these killings have remained disputed ever since. But the truth was that, at least in the village of Treznea, a sizeable fraction of the population was killed (over eighty out of two thousand), and thus the event had undisputed local repercussions for the Romanian population. The Romanian nationalist version of these events, that the murders were the result of official Budapest policy, suited the RCP in its attempt to construct an image of victimization of the Romanian civilians during World War II. With the help of court poet Adrian Păunescu (1943–), as well as several military officers turned historians, the regime agreed to place two prominent monuments in Ip and Treznea, both dedicated by high officials from Bucharest. (See figure 5.4.)

In addition to the monuments and subsequent annual commemorations, the regime also began to circulate and prominently display images of deported Romanians in sealed trains. By introducing these images at the same time that images of the death trains to Auschwitz were becoming familiar among the Romanian public, the RCP carefully manipulated visual symbols that came to define the Hungarian wartime administration of northern Transylvania. One could easily surmise that the ethnic Romanians under Hungarian rule were slated for the same fate as the Jews of northern Transylvania. Such juxtapositions both minimized the meaning of the Holocaust and also greatly exaggerated the reality of the Hungarian abuses against ethnic Romanians. For instance, even according to the most maximalist nationalist assessments of murders committed by the advancing troops, fewer than six hundred Romanians were killed during the period of Hungarian takeover. That hardly compares with the hundreds of thousands of Jews deported to the death camps. (See figure 5.5.)

Figure 5.5. Photo of Romanian deportees (1940), used frequently in museum exhibits and propaganda books. Photo from Ion Ardelean et al., *Teroarea Horthysto-fascistă în nord-vestul României: septembrie 1940–octombrie 1944.*

These efforts to distort the historical record and to present a specifically ethnonationalist version of memorializing World War II in Transylvania included other attempts to silence wartime remembrances. Romanians on the other side of the border, those who were left under Romanian administration, had not always behaved as good hosts to people trying to escape from northern Transylvania. During the months when the Romanian army was making its way back through the area (August–October 1944), plenty of comparable atrocities were committed by the Romanians against Hungarian civilians. But there was no public accounting for these events. Instead, because the silence about such matters served the image of the Romanian people as victims of abuses by others—Hungarians Horthyists and German Nazis—in the 1980s the Romanian Communist regime successfully thwarted official commemorations of World War II even at the local level in some areas. Yet Hungarian and German memorials in many of the villages inhabited by these ethnic minorities continued to exist, allowing for continued counter-memories aimed at preserving some alternative counter-truths to the official propaganda.

Literature and the Consolidation of a Victimist
Commemorative Discourse

Aspects of this nationalist victimist discourse made their way into literature as well. In the 1960s and '70s censorship became less obvious, in the sense that many authors internalized it, or that critics who acted as censors were sometimes willing to allow some creative license and liberties regarding criticisms vis-à-vis the Party.[93] Alongside memoirs by veterans, most of which nostalgically looked back at a time of youth and decried the death of loved comrades, a few novels by younger authors appeared that focused on the memory of the war. *Sweet as the Honey Is the Fatherland's Bullet* (1970) was a novel penned by the young writer Petru Popescu (1954–), which explored the coming of age of a young college graduate in his months of obligatory military service. The book is written from the point of view of this young man, alternating among three planes: the daily reality of the military service; his passionate love affair with a mysterious woman; and meetings with his uncle, a World War II veteran, who spends all of his time reminiscing about the war with other veterans. The book portrays life in Communist Romania as lacking direction even in terms of eroticism, and empty of any authentic morality. By contrast, the sections on the memories of World War II veterans vacillate between intense admiration for those men and disgust for the regime disrespecting them.

But the book also reflects the post-memory of Popescu's generation, born after the war. Popescu's writing shows he had done some research into the historiography of World War II and was fairly up to date on the trends in some of the scholarship abroad. His references to American historiography on the war are generally accurate, and his critiques are those of a careful reader. When it comes to actual remembrances of the war, his character is generally ready to listen without questioning to his elders, the veterans. We learn about the mistreatment of the veterans by the Communist regime, which had not offered them proper honors and had dismissed some of them summarily even though, in their own words, they had served Romania and not a political regime.

Popescu's sympathetic tone toward the veterans and their remembrances, which contrasts greatly with the cynical representation of other authority figures, reflects a "fellow travelers" attitude. The old men and the young character are all disenchanted with life around them, and they are to be viewed as victims of the regime. Because of this tacit partnership, Popescu's main character, who has a degree in history, never inquires, as a good historian should, about the actions of those generals and other officers during the war against civilians. There are no confrontations with the veterans as perpetrators. Through this omission, Popescu allows veterans to posture as victims of the Communist regime, something rather comfortable for most people in Romania to identify with.

The most remarkable embodiment of that attitude on the part of a scholar of wartime remembrance appears in the ending of the novel. In the final ten pages Popescu sends the main character on a drunken peregrination through sites in downtown Bucharest, including an old synagogue. The Jewish community is depicted from a distance, as strange, exotic, ghost-like appearances, with whom the character doesn't interact. His one point of focus is two inscriptions, reproduced in detail in the text, both engraved on war memorials. One is to the Jewish soldiers who fought in the 1877–1878 war and the other to World War I. The character's reaction to these plaques reveals the profound ignorance of his generation about the ethnic aspects of both world wars: "The two wars [were] romantic and popular even with the [ethnic] minorities, I searched fruitlessly a plaque for the last war, this last war had been a political war, the Jews were no longer in the army."[94] "Popular" and "romantic" are hardly accurate descriptions of the War of Independence and World War I, and placing those words in the mouth of this young character suggests the author's intent in showing the generational reinterpretation of those events in the light of the last war, which they saw as greatly humiliating and nonsensical. But of course the notion that the minorities in general had volunteered for the war is also an illustration of the profound misrepresentation both of what motivated people to fight, and of who in fact fought in those wars. Jews had important practical reasons for service in World War I, having to do with gaining political rights. But Popescu and his main character seem unaware (or conveniently ignorant) about the anti-Semitism prevalent in Romanian politics in the modern period.

Even more naïve is the notion that a plaque to Jews fighting in World War II could have been placed alongside the other two. In fact, commemorative plaques for the Shoah did exist; but they remained largely invisible to the non-Jewish public. This straight representation of the main character's naïveté is disturbing, insofar as it completely avoids naming the Holocaust. Anyone reading the novel and knowing anything about the anti-Semitic policies of the Antonescu regime would find the expectation that Jews might have served in World War II as regular army personnel completely naïve. So for the discerning reader, this stance reinforces the notion that the official discourse about World War II, including professional historical training, avoided placing the Holocaust in a central place. Yet for the unknowing reader, this contrived scene does nothing to bring about an honest recounting of other kinds of victimization besides those of the old Romanian officers at the hand of the Communist regime. Even in briefly bringing up the fate of the Jews in World War II, the book avoids discussing the role of the Romanian army officers as perpetrators.

Sweet as the Honey went on to become a bestseller and has remained one of the top ten "best books in Romanian" for many readers until today. What is one to make of it, especially given the openly critical stance of the main character toward contemporary Communist Romania? Was this one of those novels published without the awareness of the censors, a sort of underground novel that had to be tolerated because of its great success (the book sold over thirty thousand copies in the first printing)? In fact, as the author himself conceded, such a book and others like it could not have been published without the implicit approval of the RCP. They were ultimately viewed not as a threat, but rather as a form of escapism and appeasement during a period of apparent, but never full or even true, liberalization.[95] After all, the author of the book was allowed to also travel abroad to Germany on a scholarship and later to the United States. Subversive opponents of the Communist regime were generally not treated this way. This is why such a book can be regarded not only as the expression of the author's ideas and personal view of the memory of the war, but also as a perspective implicitly endorsed by the Party and thus part of the larger picture of how the Communist regime wished to frame remembering World War II.

A book similarly endorsed by the regime, though touted for a long time as a great "alternative" novel, was *The Delirium*, by Marin Preda (1922–1980); the book was published in 1975 in several hundreds of thousands of copies. At the time, Preda had already made a great mark on Romanian literature with his cycle of novels centered on the Moromete peasant family, the first volume of which had won the highest literary prize offered by the Romanian Communist regime in 1956. By 1975 Preda had become a celebrated writer who was named director of the prominent Romanian Book publishing house (1970) and a member of the Romanian Academy (1974). A great deal of controversy has developed around *The Delirium*, as some critics, such as Victor Eşkenasy, have considered it a "book on command," written by Preda with the implicit endorsement of the RCP and with the specific agenda of rehabilitating Antonescu's wartime administration, while others have viewed the book as another one of the Preda's outstanding novels.[96] Given Preda's prominent official positions at the time, it is impossible to imagine his book having been published without at least the implicit endorsement of the regime. Even if there was no overt censorship and Preda was his own publisher (the book came out with Romanian Book), the writer was fully aware of the direct consequences of publishing a book with strong political overtones, as *The Delirium* was, and there is no indication that he felt he was placing his career on the line for this novel.

The novel itself takes place during World War II and offers a historical reconstruction of the period, with the fictional Moromete characters at the center, but placing them in settings easily recognizable as real events and places. In particular, Preda uses his literary license to improvise "might have been" conversations between Charles II and Antonescu, Zelea Codreanu and his private legionary advisers, and other historic figures. Most prominent among them is, however, Antonescu, to whom Preda yields the floor on numerous occasions, constructing extended monologues purportedly uttered by the military leader. Antonescu appears unequivocally as a man of honor, fundamentally loyal to his country and unafraid to stand up for his beliefs—patriotic and courageous, a great role model for younger officers. The violence of the legionaries is counter-posed to his calm and levelheaded personality, and we never hear Antonescu speak his mind on the Jewish question.

This is where *The Delirium* reaches from literary novel into revisionist history, and specifically revisionist remembrance. Preda was of the generation that came of age in 1940. He did not serve in the army, but spent the war in Bucharest, while his brother Nilă died fighting in the army. For Preda, writing about the impression "the people" had of Antonescu and reconstructing the atmosphere of those years had a strong personal evocative element. Whether he remembered Antonescu in the way he described the dictator, or whether this was work done "on command," is irrelevant. More important is the skill with which the author constructed a view of the dictator that the wartime generation still recognized. *The Delirium* re-legitimated that positive memory of Antonescu as truthful, with repeated phrases such as "the population [has a] millenary instinct that always helps it guess the truth correctly, in the same way that it knows to be born and die without asking questions."[97] Its publication in the mid-1970s can be said to have refamiliarized a new postwar generation with the thorny political and personal questions of World War II, introducing a persuasive scenario of Antonescu as hero and a model of patriotic self-control, rather than the perpetrator of the Romanian Holocaust. The impact of this novel cannot be overstated, as it made its way both onto the shelves of many an average Romanian, as well as into their stories about the joy of reading good historical fiction during the 1970s and 1980s.[98]

Between 1940 and 1989, Romania underwent enormous political change, largely shaped by the experiences of World War II. How to remember it became an obsessive preoccupation for the regime in its early years, who tried to use the war as a legitimizing tool while fully aware that commemorations needed to be subjugated to directives from Moscow. Even so, accents of nationalism were present from the beginning, at least inside the army.

With the stabilization of the Communist regime and especially after the death of Stalin, a new official version developed, marginalizing the contribution of the Soviet Union and instead placing emphasis on the role of the Romanian army on the side of the anti-fascist coalition. Along with this shift there emerged a new openness to publicly remembering the deaths of those who fought on the eastern front. However, the victims of that campaign did not fare as well as the perpetrators. The Holocaust remained an occulted subject during this period, generally depicted as having taken place outside of Romania, executed by the Hungarian and German fascist regimes, leaving the Romanian army out of the picture. There were new attempts to memorialize civilian victims of World War II in official public settings, but only in Transylvania, where both Romanian and Jewish victims of the Hungarian wartime regime were to be commemorated.

The rehabilitation of the memory of World War I was also an important element of the new official nationalism of the Ceauşescu regime, aimed at re-legitimating the notion of patriotic heroism on the battlefield, regardless of the political regime under which the soldier fought, as well as the interpretation that World War I had been a "people's" war. Veterans' testimonies and even women's contributions were reintroduced as important elements in reconstructing the memory and meaning of that war.

The most unexpected development in the last decade, however, was the rehabilitation of Antonescu as a wartime patriot. Though sentenced and executed in 1946, Antonescu's role in the war was slowly minimized and his crimes merely schematically presented in public representations, from textbooks to popular history magazines and museums. The documentary film of his execution was hidden from public knowledge. The Communist regime at best avoided dealing with him until the mid-1970s, and at worst nourished the myths that circulated around him. Then, when Preda's very popular book came out in 1975 with a thoroughly revisionist view of the dictator, the regime's stance became more and more suspect. Increasingly positive images of Antonescu as heroic patriotic officer fighting for his country circulated in other literary, film, and museum representations of the war.

Another overarching context came to define how the regime depicted the memory of both world wars. Ceauşescu's cult of personality began to take over all areas of state-sponsored cultural production. If the actions and memories of Great War veterans were reintroduced in the 1960s into official commemorations of the war, by the 1980s any individual actions of greater or lesser figures in Romanian history had to be subsumed to the larger narrative of Ceauşescu's "Golden Age." Mărăşeşti had been a step toward the Golden Age; so had 1 December 1918, and likewise 23 August 1944. People came to resent being made to participate in public activities, commemorative parades, and variety shows that became empty, ludicrous façades for celebrating "Romania's most beloved son." By December 1989, Ceauşescu's festivals of the working people and endless parades were universally viewed as forms of social control and disregarded as shams.

The following chapter will turn the tables, examining the extent to which these commemorative discourses promoted by the state through various cultural artifacts and actions found resonance among the population. As I have argued elsewhere in the book, this relationship was complex, and while resistance against the official discourse developed, there is also evidence of various forms of compliance and even outright support. Showing the depth of the complicated and sometimes self-contradictory blend of these different engagements with the Communist regime's official commemorations of the two world wars is the most important argument of chapter 6.

Do not forget, my son, all that happened. You will live;
you have to live, to recount, to write, to tell your children,
your grandchildren, everyone. Do not forget.

—Leo Schaddach[1]

We live in unique times, we don't know how to recognize them,
we mistake them for an everyday existence, and we live through
them in banality. During the other war [World War I] it was
different, I think. We had a healthy opposition toward the enemy—
today . . . the opposition is weak. I would volunteer for the front,
maybe there life is dynamic, in the proximity of death; here, I'm
just lying around. I need to bury myself in work; I have to.

—Alice Voinescu (1942)[2]

EVERYONE A VICTIM

Forging the Mythology of Anti-Communism Counter-Memory

If the official narratives about World War II were unwilling to engage in any dialogue with the voices that dissented from the ideological flavor of the day—whether pro-Soviet or ultra-nationalist Romanian—personal memories developed in divergent ways and tended to generate many counter-memories of the war. This chapter explores some of the salient dimensions of these counter-memories. They cannot be incorporated into any linear narrative, as they tended to come from different angles of experience, witness, and political positioning. However, they all had one thing in common. Those whose memories were unaccounted for in the official commemorations of World War II created counter-myths of the war's memory, positing recollections of their own personal experiences as the truthful version of what had happened, in contradistinction to the official version. Concealed from public discussion and confrontation, these counter-memories evolved into undisputed family- and community-nourished myths that self-identified as opposition against the corrupt Communist dictatorship, to be prized and never questioned, because of their intrinsic moral value in opposing the Communist regime.

Out of this dialectical relationship between official commemorative discourses and counter-memories grew parallel stories about the victimization of Jews in Transnistria and Transylvania, of Romanians and Germans in Siberia (the Donbas, Komi, and other labor camps), of Hungarians in Transylvania, and of the heroic resistance of hajduk-like figures in the mountains at the end of the war, some of them ardent supporters of the Iron Guard. This resistance to Communist dictatorship through counter-memory was by no means exclusively (or even dominantly) democratic. It was, instead, community based, invoking values that were anti-Communist, ranging from religious beliefs in the importance of self-sacrifice and the need to remember to xenophobia and anti-Semitism.

Most personal memories recorded on paper or through spoken word in the familial and communal context between 1945 and 1989 were not made public in Romania during that period. Those who wrote journals or memoirs hid them at great risk or managed to have them smuggled abroad. Therefore, these written manuscripts were viewed by few people in Romania itself. The number of written autobiographical testimonies from this period is rather small. Some were translated and published by various diasporas—Romanian, Hungarian, Jewish, or German.[3] Others were destroyed. Some of them will be the subjects of my discussion in the subsequent chapter, as they entered a broader public discourse after 1989, when most of these manuscripts were finally published in Romania itself. But at this point I take materials recorded during the Communist period as evidence for the subterranean counter-memory developing beyond the control of the state.

In addition to these sparse memory traces, I use oral testimonies gathered in the two decades since the end of the Communist regime. These oral histories have all the problems that other such research has come up against: the passage of time; the mythologizing of counter-memories I mentioned above; the fear of speaking out, especially among respondents participating in oral histories in the first decade after 1989; and age.[4] Yet the accumulation of hundreds of life stories provides the historian with leitmotifs that are significant precisely because of their prevalence, rather than any factual truthfulness. These oral histories speak more strongly to questions of myth-making than to questions of accurate remembrance of wartime experiences, especially as it is quite easy to see the factual unreliability of some of the testimonies.

Periodizing the War in Personal Remembrances: 1940–1953

One important issue that confronts anyone attempting to conduct life histories with World War II survivors is periodization. In my interviews with veterans and civilians, I found that people started their story of what they did or where they were at the beginning of the war at different points in time. Though most people, whether educated or not, were somewhat aware of what was happening beyond Romania's borders in September 1939, they did not speak about the war at that point as something that involved Romania. Only the Second Vienna Award made the war and Romania's alliance with the Axis real. For those in Transylvania, the Second Vienna Award seemed to be the beginning of hostilities. One veteran and legionary supporter remarked that, upon hearing about the Vienna Award, he felt "the earth open up before my very eyes."[5] For Hungarians, the moment was tinged with pride and vengeance, but also troubled memories of violence, suffered and also inflicted by members of their communities and the victorious Hungarian army. For Romanians, humiliation and a sense of victimization prevailed: "It was a disaster in Cluj. Romanian people were walking down the street crying: 'What's going to become of us. . . .'"[6] Romanian civilians remembered this moment as the beginning, while veterans might or might not. Those in northern Transylvania who had to vacate the area with the troops remembered it as a humiliating loss, something that could not be equated in the mind of a soldier with "war." Those who were incorporated into the army at that point do remember, however, that they had to leave their families behind to go fight to free up Transylvania. For some Jews in northern Transylvania, ironically, this moment was viewed with some relief; many believed, to their subsequent peril, that the Hungarian administration would be more tolerant than the Romanian one had been during the interwar period.[7]

For people living in the rest of Romania, what marked the beginning of the war depended on whether they were Jewish or not. The anti-Semitic legislation inaugurated in 1938 and subsequently augmented with Nuremberg-like levels of exclusion and ghettoization already represented a kind of civil war for Jews.[8] The rest of the population either looked the other way or tried to profit in some fashion from new job opportunities, if they weren't outright applauding the righteousness of these measures.[9] But most Romanian Jews, like others in Europe at that time, were trying to survive and negotiate the tough measures by living with them.

The inauguration of the Legionary National State on 9 September 1940 did bring, however, a new level of militarization to Romanian society and a brand of racist ideology that made it plain that Romanians were thenceforth engaged in a war to purify their nation of all the "undesirables" identified by Sima and Antonescu. Yet most ethnic Romanians did not mark this event as the beginning of the war, though it signaled to Jewish Romanians that their situation was becoming more precarious and their existence fundamentally threatened.[10]

For those living in Bucharest, the legionary rebellion in January 1941 represented a bloody civil war between the army and the Iron Guard, with the Jewish population as the victims. Writer Mihail Sebastian (1907–1945) was unsure about the nature of the conflict on 21 January, asking himself: "Revolution? Coup d'état?"—only to refer to the violence a few days later as "battlefields" (27 January) and subsequently as a "pogrom" (4 February).[11] Ethnic Romanians viewed this event mostly with indifference in terms of the violence perpetrated against their Jewish co-nationals, preoccupied instead with the civil war between the legionaries and the army: "Great events are taking place. . . . I suffer to see Romanians fighting against Romanians, spilling Romanian blood when the enemy is in the country and at the border, and those around me don't understand."[12]

The official entry into the war was marked in all journals and most people could recall the day. But the sense of enthusiasm for fighting a just war to recover Bessarabia and northern Transylvania, as the official discourses justified entry in the war, was missing from personal recollections: "The manifestation in front of the palace [supporting the declaration of war was] *very weak*. Few and anemic. When I heard the amplification on the radio I smiled and recognized the Italian system. . . . Maybe many of us felt painfully that we were making common cause with the aggressors, were liars, and guilty. . . . This is an immoral war."[13]

What is missing in virtually all ethnic Romanians' remembrance of that first week of war was the Iaşi pogrom, which was kept quiet and remained a non-event for those who didn't lose loved ones or didn't see the incidents.[14] In other words, most Romanians did not identify it as a national event or tragedy. For the Jewish population, however, given the all too recent memory of the January 1941 pogroms, what happened on 29–30 June in Iaşi only reinforced their sense of impending doom. On 1 July, Sebastian recorded: "The inability to speak or write. A sort of deaf terror, suppressed. You barely dare to look beyond this passing hour, beyond this day that hasn't ended yet."[15] The juxtaposition between ethnic Romanians' lack of acknowledgement of this event as personally resonant and the intense self-identification of Jews with this tragedy underscores the caesuras that run deeply through Romanian society in personal remembrances of the war.

As the battleground extended farther and farther to the east, the reality of the war changed drastically for the military, diverging from the civilian experience. Correspondence with the front was greatly curtailed, so that many heard about the death of their loved ones with great delay. With newspapers reporting censored facts about the front, most civilians learned to read between the lines. The Jewish reality was terror about the deaths in Transnistria and the ghettos in Bessarabia and Bukovina, combined with the humiliations legislated by the Romanian authorities on a daily basis. In addition, Jews who went into the forced labor service to avoid being deported began to manifest a sense of guilt for being alive: "I was thinking last night, when I was returning the shovel, that there are millions of people like me, making the exact same gestures, all over the world. I come back, to sleep, eat, forget. But where do they return? Those from the prisoner camps? Those from internment camps? Those in my detachment are in an inexplicable good mood. . . . We are an amazing people, after all."[16]

For ethnic Romanian civilians in Romania proper, the war was rather uneventful, punctuated at times by Allied bombings. If Bucharest, Brașov, and the Prahova Valley, the site of most Romanian oil fields, saw repeated bombings, the rest of the country was relatively unscathed by the war. Social services from education to healthcare were disrupted, but ethnic Romanians were able to continue working and living much the same as before the war: "Life is taking its normal course. You'd have the impression we're not at war, if people weren't dressed so shabbily: missing hats, women without stockings, which give the city [Bucharest] a provincial look. . . . Life seems like a dream—ugly, without excitement, confused."[17] The greatest disruptions came in the form of news from the front about the death of loved ones, who couldn't be retrieved and be given proper burial.[18]

For Jews in northern Transylvania, the spring of 1944 brought about the doom of most of their communities. The intensification of the Final Solution meant that, in Hungarian-ruled territories, most Jews were brought into ghettos and eventually sent on death trains to extermination camps. By August, when Romanian and Soviet troops arrived in northern Transylvania, most Jews were gone. The end of the war for these communities was in the gas chambers of the Nazi camps.

For other civilians living in wartime Romania, however, the experience of occupation, violence, and serious privations of the sort Jews had experienced since 1939 began only in 1944. As German troops retreated and the Soviet army advanced, Romania suddenly found itself in the midst of a chaotic battlefield, instead of comfortably behind the lines. Allied bombing intensified in the spring and summer of 1944. With the Soviet entry into Romanian territory in July, the civilian population was engulfed in total war. The "liberation" by Soviet troops signaled the beginning of the war in rural communities.

The end of the war was an equally subjective moment in personal recollections of those years. Many of those keeping journals at the time or writing later about the period strongly identified the end of the war with personal experiences in their lives, sometimes separate from the official end of hostilities. Those who survived the death camps in Transnistria or the Third Reich viewed the end of the war through the lens of their liberation from these places of doom. Even for them, however, the date and experience of liberation varied from place to place. The camps in Transnistria were closed down before those in Poland, and thus survivors from there returned home earlier. The Soviets, upon their arrival on Romanian territories, sent some unfortunate survivors to labor camps as far away as Siberia.

As the Soviets and Romanian troops advanced through Transylvania, Hungarian civilians saw their own largely peaceful wartime years disrupted. The vengeance of the Romanian troops, followed by that of the Soviets, brought about destruction in these communities. The official date on which these violent events are said to have ended is 25 October 1944. However, both civilians and soldiers continued to experience the reality of the war long after that. Soldiers continued to fight beyond the western borders of Romania all the way to Czechoslovakia, and many were demobilized only after the official end of the war in Europe, on 9 May 1945. Their war ended when they were able to finally return home to Romania.

Some civilians and demobilized soldiers began to experience a new reality of war, however, as soon as the new Romanian administration and its Soviet allies took over. In January 1945 the Soviets demanded retribution from the Germans, and the Romanian state complied. Over seventy thousand German civilians were deported, men and women, mostly ages eighteen to forty-five, but on occasion much younger. For these people, the experience of World War II blended with their deportation and ended when they returned home, some as late as 1953.[19]

Finally, as the new regime was taking shape, bands of demobilized military men (those deemed unreliable by Soviet advisers in 1944), as well as younger men and a few women who had been part of the Iron Guard or other rightist paramilitary groups, such as the Black Coats [*Sumanele negre*], took to the mountains and organized themselves into anti-Communist brigades. Those with battlefield experience viewed these actions as the continuation of their "crusade against Bolshevism." For younger participants this was the beginning of their wartime activities. For these individuals, the war extended into the late 1940s and 1950s.[20] For the most audacious and resourceful, their wartime activities extended into the 1960s.

Thus, from an individual, subjective perspective, one can speak about the beginning of the war in 1940 and the end of the war in 1953, or even later.[21] This periodization extends far beyond the official 1941–1944 span for Romania and might appear too elastic to represent the war as an event defined by a generally recognizable set of circumstances. One might ask, why not extend the war back to the return of Charles II in 1930, or forward into the Cold War all the way to 1989? The change of the borders experienced by Romania marks 4 September 1940 as the beginning of a wartime regime in areas that were no longer under Romanian rule. And though the official end date for war hostilities was 25 October 1944 for Romania and 9 May 1945 for the whole of Europe, the experience of wartime violence, privation, and insecurity extended into the following years, from the point of view of both the military and especially of civilians. Those who were deported in 1944–1945 did not even know the war had ended until their release. Those who experienced combat and violence after that official end date linked their privations and strife to the war. Their choice to do so represents an important consideration in analyzing the nature and, especially, the meaning of the actions taken either by anti-Communist "crusaders" or by Romanian officials in deporting ethnic minorities or social "undesirables."

The most important consideration in rethinking the periodization of World War II, however, pertains to how historians interpret the meaning of specific actions and words. Periodizing the war strictly from June 1941 to October 1944 allows one to easily avoid discussing the important anti-Semitic policies and pogroms experienced by Jews in Romania between the fall of 1940 and summer of 1941. It also excludes the violence that took place in northern Transylvania in the fall of 1940. Not extending the war beyond 1944 places the experiences of violence between November 1944 and the 1950s into a context that is circumscribed to Cold War politics. But the Cold War on the ground was not a mere projection of the Soviet desire for power and control in Romania. There were realities within Romania connected to the World War II experience that better explain the violent actions taken after October 1944 and their meaning for those caught in them.

The effects of the current official periodization in curtailing a fuller understanding of the experience and memory of the war include isolating the Holocaust in Transnistria from that in northern Transylvania, and separating the violence of anti-Communist partisans after 1944, which had different, generally more destructive consequences, from their actions before August 1944. Survivors of wartime violence and witnesses have not considered their subjective experiences outside their immediate context, the wider historical one. A broader periodization would help mediate the meaning of such experiences within this larger context. Therefore, in recounting and analyzing the different kinds of personal remembrances, I hope to also bring about a reconceptualization of the *when* and not merely the *what* signified by living through and remembering wartime violence in Communist Romania.

Communism and Counter-Memory as the Great Equalizers: Heroes=Victims

The literature on victims and perpetrators during World War II is by now vast, but it largely focuses on Germany.[22] Only recently has this historiography begun to grow in the eastern European context, especially in discussing Polish-German-Jewish relations.[23] But the nature of the discussion in my context is different from that in most of the books that have come out on the topic. The periodization of the war differed, and the roles of those who were victims and victimizers shifted several times, especially in the case of Poland and the Baltics, with two occupation regimes during the war. In addition, these roles became even more complicated during the early years of Soviet occupation and Communist rule. People experienced intense violence at the hands of various regimes during this period. Therefore, the layering of contexts was more complicated in the Communist bloc than in the rest of Europe. This is another reason I want to reiterate the need for a different periodization of the war.

The angle I wish to follow in this discussion is to trace how individuals who lived through these events themselves portrayed their experiences: where did they place themselves and their community on the spectrum of victim-hero-perpetrator? And how do various representations of these roles compare to each other, especially when speaking about similar events from different experiential vantage points? In the interest of simplifying a complicated set of actors, I want to divide personal recollections into those of soldiers and those of civilians. Soldiers fell into three categories: those who fought only on the eastern front and returned without being taken prisoner; those who were taken prisoner by the Soviets; and those who fought on both the eastern and western fronts. The experience of the soldiers who served only on the western front was easily incorporated into official commemorations of the war, and did not generate significantly different counter-memories from the other categories of soldiers. Civilians fell into four categories, in order of their approximate size: ethnic Romanians, living either in Romania or Hungarian-ruled northern Transylvania; Hungarians; Germans; and Jews.

We Fought Bravely for Our Country: Soldiers' Narratives of Heroism and Victimization

Among soldiers who fought on the eastern front without being taken prisoner, few wrote memoirs during the Communist period and none published them. These memoirs and journals remained hidden. One can assume that some family and friends would have seen the manuscripts, or would have at least heard part of the narratives put on paper in these secret writings. My discussion, therefore, is perforce speculative, as there is no way to reconstruct the actual reception or modes of communication of these counter-narratives during the Communist period. The reason for the secrecy of such memoirs is simple. As mentioned in the previous chapter, the Soviets made it plain to their postwar Romanian partners that soldiers fighting on the eastern front were to be regarded as misguided at best and criminal at worst. There was no room for commemorating their deaths and suffering in any public fashion in the first decade after the end of the war.

And so, to protect their families and themselves, these soldiers hid away their recollections of the eastern front. Mihai Bălaj, who had ample reason during the Communist period not to make his journal visible to the authorities, was such an author. In 1951, after having served for over two decades as a teacher and later school inspector in Satu Mare County in Transylvania, he lost his job and was denied the request to work as a teacher for the next ten years. If his service as a teacher and on the eastern front under the previous "bourgeois" regime placed him in the category of undesirable class enemy, one can only imagine what a journal kept during 1942–1943, while serving on the Soviet front, would have meant for Bălaj. Yet, even though the journal was kept secret, Bălaj's attitude toward his wife, as expressed in the journal itself, suggests that he shared at least some of the contents with her, and maybe others.[24]

His narrative is heroic, focusing on the bravery of his comrades and the ability of his unit to withstand battlefield privations and fight against the Soviets.[25] There are recurrent references to the church or the Romanian identity of some of the local population in Transnistria, giving the impression that a peaceful relationship existed between the Romanian army and civilians under their occupation.[26] But he also makes comments about women in the Soviet army that suggest his tacit acceptance, if not endorsement, of rape of the enemy's women as normal: "We receive photos of some officer girls found among the dead Russian officers. 'If these had fallen into our claws, then yes!'"[27] The author had no qualms about regarding women among enemy troops as lesser beings, worthy of sexual abuse.

For Bălaj, fighting in the war had a just goal: he was from northern Transylvania and wanted to see that region retroceded to Romania. As he pondered the great numbers of casualties, Bălaj stated that these losses "demand an adequate reward," meaning regaining the territories lost in 1940.[28] His personal reason for wanting those territories back is described, however, in terms of paying proper homage to the dead and keeping their memory alive: "I simply cannot understand especially this: not being able to go to see the grave of my father."[29]

The journal takes a more demoralized tone around the battle of Stalingrad, and by 14 February 1943, Bălaj looks upon the Romanian army less as a brave force fighting for a just cause, and more as a victim of the German and Soviet struggle: "I see with sadness how the flower of our army has perished, and how our deadly enemy, Hungary, through cunning, has known how to preserve their army nearly intact."[30] He depicts the Germans at this point as treacherous and inefficient in battle: "The cities [under occupation] . . . were centers for partying for the Germans. . . . We had to fight in the most difficult sectors. And often we had to reconquer excellent positions we had ceded to the Germans, which they subsequently lost."[31] His return to Romania after seven hundred days on the front placed Bălaj in Hațeg at the end of the war, and we are unable to peer any further into his mind and soul, as he abruptly ended the journal.

A few other elements are important to note in terms of the soldiers' impressions of the war and their ways of narrating the events. There are few references to the Nazis in the journal; they appear either to award medals, in the sky in their airplanes, or rarely in the midst of battle in person. It is fair to say that Bălaj did not have a prolonged experience of fighting side by side with the German army, and that his impressions of these allies were fragmentary.

Likewise, he had little to say about the Soviet army. There are just a handful of qualitative references to the enemy, mentioning how civilians, churches, and other buildings suffered during the retreat or advance of Soviet forces. Otherwise, the vilification of the Russians, as found in official wartime propaganda, is entirely missing. The only truly passionate words of hatred were reserved for the Hungarians. Bălaj almost never referred to the Soviets as "Bolsheviks," but rather in ethnic terms. There are only two references in the journal to the ideology of the Soviet state—a brief one about atheism and another about the abolition of private property. But he differentiated between the state and the people he encountered, all of whom he identified by ethnicity—Moldavians, Romanians, Russians, Uzbeks, Tadjiks, and Kazakhs.

Bălaj's journal represents a good example of how soldiers who were not taken prisoner by the Soviets experienced and wrote about the war. The remembrances they wove out of these impressions had a rather distant view of the Germans, whom they resented, especially when the Axis started to lose ground to the Soviets. The frustrations of these soldiers about losing the war were often taken out on their Hungarian allies, whom they resented doubly for not having as many losses in the war and also for having won northern Transylvania with the stroke of a pen.[32]

These were generally not the soldiers who told horror stories about the violence perpetrated by the Soviet army on their advance toward Romania. These soldiers were also not likely to have witnessed the Holocaust violence in Transnistria. Those like Bălaj, who traveled by train through the areas where the most horrible crimes were committed, saw the region as a landscape and were not part of the forces stationed there as either witnesses to or participants in these atrocities.

For other memoirs of this period, however, participation in or witnessing the Holocaust seems more plausible, though in several cases it is difficult to place individuals at the site of a crime, since many atrocities were not fully documented. An example is the writing of Stanciu Stroia, another Transylvanian who ardently wished to see his native region returned to Romania.[33] He served on the eastern front as an officer and a medical doctor of infectious diseases in the Oceacov district in Transnistria, where he visited regional clinics to oversee the treatment of typhus. Stroia had little to say about his residence in Oceacov in 1942, focusing in particular in describing how he served the local population as a doctor and the respect he gained there for being able to identify one case of liver cancer.[34]

Two important aspects of life in the Oceacov district are absent from Stroia's memoir: first, the Romanian army was under direct order from Bucharest not to treat any cases of typhus found among ethnic minorities during that time (meaning specifically Ukrainians, Jews, Russians, and Roma), concentrating instead on the Romanian army and ethnic Romanians in the area;[35] and second, the Oceacov district was an area where Roma were deported during that period to a camp where many perished.[36] If Stroia was so involved in medical treatment and traveled so widely (something he acknowledged) in the area, it is hard to imagine he was unaware of the atrocities committed under his eyes. One can be sure that he was aware of the order from Bucharest. Did he follow it? We know, from his silence, that at least he didn't oppose it, even though it contravened the Hippocratic Oath, and Stroia was otherwise proud of his work as a doctor. In memoirs such as his, suspicion lingers over the text with regard to the participation in or at least witnessing by Romanian soldiers and officers of atrocities committed against Jews, Roma, and other innocent civilian populations. If not perpetrators, these men were at least the kind of bystanders whose innocence has been greatly questioned in German and more recently Polish historiography.[37]

Along with their role of perpetrators of violence during the war, people like Stroia and Bălaj also became victims of the Communist regime. Bălaj was denied work in his profession and was condemned to poverty and intellectual humiliation until his later years. Stroia fared much worse, spending years in the Aiud political prison, where he suffered tremendously. Their personal remembrance of fighting on the eastern front was thus framed by both the public denial of their sacrifices for a worthy goal (regaining northern Transylvania), as well as suffering under the Communist regime. As they shaped their counter-memories vis-à-vis official lies, these soldiers easily avoided talking about any guilt regarding atrocities they may have witnessed or participated in. Official narratives about the war had already cordoned off the subject of the Holocaust, and there was no need to account for those crimes. These men wished they could pass on to their families that they had fought bravely and were publicly forgotten and subsequently punished for their patriotic behavior. They managed to paint themselves as both heroes and victims, with the Communist regime cast as their victimizer.

Such counter-memories had to remain secret, for they were anathema to the Communist regime's desire to paint itself as a legitimate representative of the Romanian nation. Yet official narratives did affect counter-memories. Those who felt victimized by the Communists denied some central tenets of the official narrative, but in doing so, they constructed a counter-mythology as flimsy in its evidentiary basis as the myth they were contesting. Counter-memories insisted on the brutality of the Soviet army on Romanian ground during the war as a way to contest the positive images in the official propaganda; yet personal memoirs of people such as Bălaj did not support these claims. Counter-memoirs also used silences in the official narrative, especially about atrocities on the eastern front, to avoid dealing with uncomfortable questions of guilt. In his description of a survivor from Auschwitz, Stroia avoided dealing with a full picture of that individual's cruelty in Aiud. He described this man as "the most repulsive individual I ever met in prison, despicable in every aspect, a former executioner at Auschwitz [who] had been a prisoner. . . . No hint of remorse was present in his voice when he recounted his deeds."[38] That Stroia, as a doctor and a person interested in the psychological effects of life in a detention camp, never stopped to wonder what life in Auschwitz might have done to the humanity of its inmates, reveals his convenient avoidance of questions about guilt in relation to the Holocaust.

∽

Soldiers who were taken prisoners by the Soviets had a different experience of the front and the enemy, as well as a different self-identification with notions of heroism and victimhood in the war. The memoir of a low-ranking officer, Alexandru Teodorescu-Schei, written in 1959, recounts his days fighting in Transnistria and beyond and his eventual capture by the Russians. For this soldier, the war lasted from 1941 to 1949, when he finally made it back home from his forced exile in Siberia. For Teodorescu-Schei, writing from the distance of a decade after his return, the memory of the war seems both fresh and also somewhat distant, insofar as he contemplates with emotional dispassion the actions of his comrades and the enemy. Even though he acknowledges from the outset that he distrusts the Russians, stating that they had taken Bessarabia illegitimately in 1940, he is also critical of the Romanian state and army in their handling of the entry into the war, without guarantees and without a clear objective. He dismisses the "crusade against Bolshevism" as outright propaganda.[39]

Later on, as he spends some time with Russian civilians in various villages under Romanian occupation, he has the opportunity to hear various complaints about the plight of the Ukrainian peasants during collectivization and their fear of Stalin.

He develops a more nuanced relationship with these people, empathetic (though not trusting) toward their poverty and hospitality, distinguishing them from their government and army.[40]

His view of the Germans is as distant as that of many other lower-ranking officers, and he also doesn't spend much time discussing the enemy until he becomes prisoner. One important difference between this memoir and the journal kept by Bălaj or Stroia's memoir is Teodorescu-Schei's direct reference to the plight of civilians, in particular the Jewish population in Romania proper and in Transnistria, during his passage through those areas. He traverses Iași a couple of days after the horrible pogrom of June 1941 and remarks:

> They say that in this old city there had been an uprising, provoked by the Jews, when the prefect was Col. Căptaru. Such a reaction on their part would have been possible, when they were persecuted, but I personally didn't see any traces of such an uprising. They insisted there had been one. It was quiet.[41]

This fragment attests to the inability, even on the part of someone who was on the lookout for the horrible crimes committed in Iași a few days earlier, to witness their effects. The author is unable to imagine other reasons for the quiet, such as fear and death itself. We are made to know as readers what kinds of rumors were spread in the army to account for any possible information the soldiers would have picked up on the street. These rumors suggest that the army was both allowing and even spreading information about the pogrom to its soldiers going to the front, so that those arriving in Bessarabia and Transnistria in June–July 1941 would have had some information (or misinformation) about violence perpetrated against civilian Jews in Romania.

As he passes through Bessarabia, the author also witnesses the aftermath of a pogrom, which both sickens him and also provokes a defensive reaction:

> You could see the traces of the SS special troops. . . . I saw unimaginable scenes. Gathered in one room, dozens of Jews, men, women, and children, had been massacred, probably with one grenade. . . . What barbarity! The only hopeful thought I had was that Romanians do not do such things. Even the government itself had declared that the Jewish problem belongs to the country that has sovereignty over a territory, and our soldiers, though incited against the Jews . . . did not act ferociously. . . . On our way we would meet many frightened, lost Jews, living permanently in fear, but no Romanian soldier ever touched them.[42]

This passage is rather troubling to the reader aware of the extent of violence perpetrated by ethnic Romanians against Jews in Transnistria and Bessarabia. Is the author trying to conceal something he knows in 1959, or in 1998, when the book was published? Or is it possible that he simply did not see any such violence and thus didn't want to even consider it was possible for the Romanian army to have done such things? Following the general route Teodorescu-Schei took, it is possible that he in fact did not go through areas where there were Romanian-perpetrated pogroms. It is also likely that the army continued to have a policy of hiding these actions from the rank and file who were not selected to participate in such activities. That the author believed the pogroms in Bessarabia were the work of SS troops and not Romanians suggests again that the Romanian army used such a story to cover for some of its own atrocities. It was easier for the Romanians to think of the Germans as barbarians than to consider their own comrades in that way.

Teodorescu-Schei also offers a rare glimpse into wartime sexual power relations and, in particular, women's vulnerabilities. The author narrates encounters with Russian women in rural areas where he was stationed. He casually describes how the local population welcomed the Romanian soldiers and sought their protection, presumably against the oppressive Soviet regime. He goes on to describe how one woman took him in and became his lover, taking care of his needs. Teodorescu-Schei describes this relationship as consensual: "My walks with her were energizing. We got along a bit in German, a bit in Russian; the most important thing was that we were able to communicate our desire to be closer. . . . She always smiled. For me this was stimulating and relaxing."[43] He goes on to brag about his honorable position toward other women, who, according to the author, tried to throw themselves at him: "Russian women seem made to be attracted to men of other nationalities."[44] He describes them as having repulsive morals and himself as upholding a greater code of honor: "I revolted. This woman was provoking in me a moral conflict with my own conscience. . . . You couldn't trust her. Despite the strong attraction I felt toward her, I forbade her with all my authority to come to me any longer."[45]

This portrayal of erotic liaisons by military personnel with women in zones of occupation reveals the fundamental lack of self-reflexivity that soldiers had in regard to their own coercive powers vis-à-vis civilian populations in these areas, especially single women. It never occurs to Teodorescu-Schei that the woman got involved with him to protect herself against other abuses; that her erotic appeal was the only resource she could leverage in an otherwise uneven power relation. She did make a choice to act this way, but she was not a fully free individual, as Teodorescu-Schei portrays her. His blindness on this matter is not surprising.[46] He wants to remember this relationship as a bright spot in his dreary days on the front. It is difficult to generalize based on one memoir, but this example reminds us of the silences regarding the gender-specific forms of victimization during the war, which most memoirs do not address, and scholars since then have not attended to.

Teodorescu-Schei's memoir of the prisoner camp seems nuanced by comparison with his considerations regarding the Holocaust. He sees the Soviets as less inclined to physical barbarity than the Germans, especially in matters ideological. He was among the thousands of officers the Soviet army hoped to retrain and group into the Romanian Tudor Vladimirescu Division, which subsequently fought alongside the Soviets and remained completely loyal to their ideology. The author recounts his rejection of this idea, despite his left-wing sympathies; he sees the Soviet strategy as a form of imperialism. Still, Teodorescu-Schei acknowledges that nobody forced him to join the Tudor Vladimirescu Division; he actually had free choice in the matter. He suffers a great deal in his more than six years of incarceration, especially from hunger and cold. Still, he never states outright that these two aspects of his detention were part of a policy of extermination.

Teodorescu-Schei's narrative undeniably presents the author as both a hero and victim, but never as a perpetrator. He faithfully follows army orders, thus remaining a tool of the state. Yet he never witnesses, much less participates in, any atrocities committed by Romanians and, to boot, he is someone who chooses not to join the Soviet-controlled Romanian troops. As such, he presents himself as both loyal and brave in standing aside from political opportunism. In the end, his counter-narrative of the war is one of tragic victimization, as the author and many like him were never openly rewarded by the Romanian state during the Communist period for their service in World War II simply because they didn't openly go along with the Soviet propaganda. He was the type of tragic counter-hero depicted in *Sweet as the Honey*.

Among the few unofficial public forms of remembering soldiers who died fighting against the Soviet Union, or as Soviet POWs, were grave markers and other memorials, mostly plaques, placed by family and close-knit communities, especially in the countryside. These markers appeared in Romanian, German, and Hungarian communities alike, and identified as relevant dates years ranging from 1941 to 1949, thus including the eastern and the western front as well as deportations after 1944. In the village of Apa in Satu Mare County, in 1948 the Romanian community placed a small monument next to the Orthodox church to commemorate "the heroes from Apa, who fell on the battlefield in the two world wars, bringing their supreme sacrifice to fulfill national unification." The dates for World War II were 1940/1941–1945, and listed on the plaque were soldiers who had fallen both on the eastern and western front.[47] This forthrightly contravened the directive of the RCP demanding that those fallen in the east would not be commemorated as heroes.

Likewise, in the village of Ciumești, also in Satu Mare County, in the 1950s the local Catholic population, ethnic Hungarians and Germans, placed a large black cross with the inscription: "In memory of the victims of war from Ciumești, their bodies

Figure 6.1. Monument raised in Romanian village through local initiative (1945). Photo courtesy of the National Military Museum.

rest on foreign soil, their souls live among us. God give them eternal rest: 1914–1918; 1939–1945."[48] This monument is even more remarkable than the previous one in that it identified the death of the soldiers from the village "on foreign soil," which would have meant fighting on the eastern front until 1943 or being deported by the Soviets. It also identifies the beginning of the war in 1939, suggesting indirectly that men from this village had volunteered for the German army before the Romanian state had entered the war. This monument, a symbolic funerary cross to make up for the absence of the dead bodies, was erected at a point when the Communist regime was starting to openly embrace ethno-nationalism. Yet the monument continued to stand there throughout the Communist period. It allowed the local population to identify their war dead, who had fought on the side of the Axis, as victims.

The Orthodox (Romanian) and Catholic (Hungarian and German) memorials discussed here, as well as most others erected in the years after World War II by their local communities, identified 1945 as the end of the war. I suspect this was a bow to convention. For some who died "on foreign soil" as deportees or POWs, the date of their death was unknown. Not having received certificates of death or the bodies, their families had to imagine when the person could have died. (See figure 6.1.)

The monuments identified here were raised throughout the Communist period, some right after the war, most likely as funerary monuments at a point when families were still in deep mourning. Others, however, were put up as late as the 1980s and had a different function at the local level. Without any documents to attest to intentions, one has to speculate. For the Romanians, considering the location of these latter monuments, inside or around the local Orthodox church, it is likely these monuments were built with the support of (or at least without protests from) the local priest and government authorities. Some monuments have a design found in official military cemeteries, a segment from Constantin Brâncuşi's Endless Column, a reference to a much more famous World War I monument, which was also becoming branded at that time in the official nationalist discourse as archetypically Romanian. Any such monuments, mass produced in cement, were available only upon request from state suppliers.

There are other examples suggesting that local communities followed the commemorative parameters established in Bucharest when these were suitable to local interests. One such case is a Romanian monument built in 1960 with money from the Romanian diaspora in the United States, clearly identifying the source of funding, and placed in a very prominent location, on the side of a well-traveled European road.[49] The remarkable appearance of such a monument can only be understood in the larger context of how the Romanian Communist regime dealt with the Romanian diaspora. Emigration to the United States was nearly impossible in the early years after the Communist assumption of power. There had been emigration from that area before the war and right after, especially by those who feared a Communist takeover. The Romanian diaspora was not a large, unified community, but rather a dispersed collection of peasants who had gone to America in search of work as migrants, but ended up staying; Jews who had made it out before World War II; members of the Iron Guard who left the country after the 1941 rebellion; and people who happened to be studying and working abroad at the beginning of the war, who never returned.[50] The Communist regime kept tabs on these communities, but did not wish for them to have contact with Romanians in the home country, lest the outside world find out about the real conditions in which people lived under Communism. Therefore, allowing such a monument to be erected and leaving it standing for the rest of the Communist period seems rather out of character with the regime's strict anti-foreigner regulations.

Just as surprising are the monuments that were raised during the war by the Hungarian population and remained extant during the Communist period. To be sure, the Romanian armies and some local populations vandalized and destroyed many more of the monuments Hungarians erected between 1941 and 1944.[51] Still, some were left standing. Such monuments represented precious relics of a better time and, as with most other such monuments, markers of the Hungarians' victimization during the war and afterward. One such memorial, built in 1941–1942 and still standing in the courtyard of the local Hungarian Protestant church in the 1980s, had the following inscription: "Any creature is like the grass, and all of its brilliance like a wildflower. The grass dries, the flower falls, when the Lord's wind blows over His creation. In truth, a people are like the grass; the grass dries, the flower falls, but God's word remains unto the ages. Isaiah 40: 6, 78."[52] This biblical quote, though set in stone before some of the greatest losses on the eastern front of the Axis powers, seemed suitable as a site of mournful memory for the families of those who perished in the war.

These monuments suggest several important elements about the counter-memories celebrated in word and in stone among rural communities that had lost soldiers fighting on the eastern front. Whether Romanian, Hungarian, or German, these populations had an opportunity to erect markers to those about whom it was officially forbidden to speak as heroes. At the local level, whether with the support of the local authorities or due to their silence about such contraventions, markers appeared both in open places (the main road or the courtyard of the local church) and also more concealed ones (inside places of worship). For the locals this provided an opportunity to honor the memory of their dead and construct counter-memories of the war for younger populations. Such commemorative discourses were framed, by the nature of these monuments, as a form of survival and opposition against the Communist propaganda. They were narratives of heroism and persecution, casting the Soviets and, at times, the Romanians as the victimizers.

∽

Those who also fought on the western front constructed different narratives of their wartime years. Some had been part of the POW group Teodorescu-Schei described. Out of opportunism, if we are to believe Teodorescu-Schei, or out of a change in conviction, they joined the Tudor Vladimirescu Division and fought alongside the Soviets after having fought against them. In officially endorsed narratives, like the one penned by Laurențiu Fulga in *The Heroic,* participating on the eastern front could be presented as a mistake, something that could be forgiven (and that would be promptly forgotten in official commemorations) due to the participant's fighting alongside the Allies in the second half of the war.

In fact, striking among the many personal memoirs that surfaced after 1989 is the absence of any autobiographical recounting of participating on the eastern front, being taken prisoner and joining the Tudor Vladimirescu Division, and subsequently fighting on the other side of the war. Some of these voices were incorporated in official remembrances of World War II, but with important silences in the middle, about fighting on the eastern front and also their POW period. Therefore, one can assume that another version of these stories, one uncensored by the Communist regime, circulated in some form of counter-memory. Such narratives that account for the entire experience of the war have not surfaced, and even those who acknowledge being part of these experiences separate the eastern and western front experiences into two narratives, as though they were two different wars.[53] It seems that the personal memories of these soldiers could not be crafted into coherent narratives of victimization and heroism. These silences also added to the fragmented image of the war in the realm of personal remembrances of the war.

The subterranean narratives constructed by surviving soldiers and the families of those who perished combined elements of self-serving mythologizing with escapism, if not outright denial of any wrongdoing. Virtually no memoirs or journals I have viewed from among those written during the Communist period ever spoke of violent actions undertaken by these soldiers who were carrying guns and who certainly both witnessed and participated in a great deal of violence. These autobiographical writings are quicker to point out boredom and to focus on the landscape and people in the area than to offer any self-examination on the author's part.[54] In most of these narratives the author emerges as a tragic figure, someone made to obey orders to defend his country and then denied any recognition for his sacrifices. Soldiers fighting on the eastern front are quintessentially both victims and heroes.

But who are the victimizers, the perpetrators of death and destruction? Generally, they are the distant and cold Germans, or the uneducated and rough Russians. On occasion, among the German and Hungarian minorities in Transylvania, they are the vengeful Romanians returning to northern Transylvania in 1944. These remembrances also make little reference to abuses by their own superiors, who are more often than not portrayed loyally as victims of the Germans and Soviets, alongside their troops. Thus, even though the first part of the counter-myth of heroism rejected the official narratives about the war, this second part, defining the perpetrators, fits to some extent in the official narratives of the war, at least with regard to the image of the Germans.

Civilians' Narratives of Victimization

If the soldiers' memories of the fighting on the two fronts were quite different and could not be constructed into a cohesive narrative, the memories of the different categories of civilians are even more fragmented and contradictory. Ethnic Romanians, the largest group of civilians, generally lived through the war in relative peace. Those who moved to Romania after the retrocession of northern Transylvania encountered material and logistical difficulties; but the vast majority of Romanians in northern Transylvania remained in place during the war. Those living in the rest of the country experienced some bombings between 1941 and 1944, especially in the oil-producing Prahova Valley. Ploieşti, Bucharest, and Braşov were bombed, but even these cities were spared great destruction. In the countryside life went on even more uninterrupted, save for the occasional tragic news that another son, husband, or father had perished far away on the eastern front.

Compared with the much harsher regime of German occupation during World War I, the presence of the Germans in Romania during World War II was more visible among politicians and social elites than in the average population. Romanians began to see death and destruction only beginning in the summer of 1944, when the Soviets entered the country and the Germans, together with the Hungarian authorities from northern Transylvania, began to retreat. The front began to move through the entire territory of Romania, and a great deal of destruction took place during those short months (July–October 1944). This is where Romania presents a dissimilar case compared to German-occupied Poland, Czechoslovakia, and Yugoslavia, and one more similar to Hungary.[55]

Ethnic Romanian civilians did not generally see themselves as anything other than victims, because of their own powerless position before advancing armies of various sorts, or under their own political elites. In this regard there was division, based on specific local experiences, over identifying culprits for the suffering of civilians. In his wartime journal, Ioan Hudiţă, who had been a prominent actor in the National Peasant Party, had "only harsh words" for Antonescu.[56] Alice Voinescu, however, believed in the integrity of the dictator, while pointing a finger at Mihai Antonescu as the corrupt influence during the war: "If, God forbid, the Marshal would disappear and we'd be left in the hands of this moral void [Mihai Antonescu], poor us! Even the Marshal deserves to be forgiven for his policies, because he is convinced he is doing the right thing, but the other [Mihai Antonescu], Lord, have mercy on us and all people!"[57]

The Germans are generally identified, however, as the culprits for Romania's loss of northern Transylvania, and as selfish allies, cold and greedy.[58] Voinescu sees the loss of Transylvania as more broadly connected to the greedy policies of the Germans, Italians, and Russians, with the Hungarians playing a secondary role: "I curse forever Hitler, Mussolini, and Stalin, from all my being, and I wish for the collapse of their work and the dispersing of their people, which are not fit to be part of the world of culture. The Germans and Italians are the shame of civilized humanity. . . . For the Hungarians I wish that one day they will know the weight of the German boot and the claws of the facetious macaronis [*macaronari*]."[59]

For those who supported the Iron Guard before August 1940, Charles II appeared as a corrupt leader and a culprit for Romania's weakness in 1940. Some of these radical right-wingers came to look critically upon Antonescu as well, especially in the brief period between the crushing of the legionary rebellion in January 1941 and Romania's entry into the war in June. One such proud legionnaire stated clearly that he "was against General [*sic*] Antonescu's attitude and against the German troops that had occupied the country."[60] Overall, legionaries tended to be divided over support for or vilification of the Germans, especially as the war progressed and the losses of the Romanian army increased manyfold.[61]

For those from Transylvania, the loss of their native region to Hungary appears more of a Hungarian plot than the machinations of the Axis powers.[62] For these populations, the presence of the Germans was never as close as that of the Hungarian authorities. Some had traumatic memories of the days after the retrocession of northern Transylvania, but those were generally isolated incidents. Still, these examples were amplified by their retelling during the war and accounts in the papers and court trials after 1945. Many who did not suffer personally still invoked them as factual and exemplary of how Romanians were victimized by Hungarians during war.[63] However, in interviews I conducted in Treznea, the village where around eighty-six ethnic Romanians and five Jews were killed by a motley crew of Hungarians on 9 September 1940, I found that the people who had witnessed those events or were personally victimized by them had a more differentiated discourse about the wartime years. They were careful to separate that incident at the beginning of the war from life in the next four years. They did not wish to take the massacre of 9 September 1940 as exemplary of Romanian-Hungarian relations in the village and region before or during the war.[64]

Ethnic Romanians were subjected to deportation during the period of Soviet occupation of Bukovina and Bessarabia at the beginning of the war (1940–1941).[65] At the end of the war, more deportations took place, this time in all regions of the country, when the Soviet army was sweeping through the country and trying to clear the ground for the postwar regime, eliminating those who might be deemed class enemies or who could fall under the broad category of fascist collaborators. At the end of the war many such "undesirables" were also incarcerated or deported internally, especially to the Bărăgan region.[66] For them the war was marked especially by their experience of victimization and violence at the hands of the Communists (Soviet or Romanian). The stories of these deportees constituted a special type of counter-narrative for several reasons. Their deportation took them from the normal context of civilian life in a harsh and sudden fashion, comparable to the anti-Jewish pogroms at the beginning of the war and the later deportations to death camps. These deportations and incarcerations were kept hidden and remained a taboo subject throughout the Communist period; information about these experiences was scarce and tinged with great fear, as well as with the contours of an anti-Communist martyrology. Upon their return, many who survived the deportations understood that forgetting was important in order to assure their social and psychological reintegration into normal existence.[67] The survivors of these experiences were less willing to talk about them than others. This trend was present everywhere in eastern Europe, in areas from the Baltics through Poland, Czechoslovakia, and Bulgaria.[68] In these Communist bloc countries (or former countries, in the case of Estonia, Latvia, and Lithuania), deportations were also the subject of a great deal of rumor, but survivors were not particularly willing to talk about these issues even with their families. The counter-narratives of these experiences became part of public discussion only in the post-Communist period.

The anti-Communist resistance fighters were another category of ethnic Romanian civilians whose wartime experiences were memorialized as part of a counter-narrative only in close circles. In addition to demobilized or fleeing soldiers who took to the forests and mountains after the Soviets entered Romania in 1944, a number of civilians engaged in anti-Communist resistance against the Soviets and their Romanian allies. These individuals went into hiding for various reasons, sometimes at odds with each other, but ended up being considered as part of the same great tradition of tragic heroism. Some of them supported interwar parliamentary democratic parties, such as the National Peasant Party, which hoped for a postwar regime that would not be subservient to the Soviets. Others were outright supporters of the Iron Guard. Finally, some were peasants who had heard about collectivization and did not wish to lose their land to the Communists.[69] These people represented a heterogeneous group of traveling fellows. They were mostly young, though some were in their forties when they went into hiding. Most of these groups were rural or had close rural roots, and they tended to stay close to the areas they were familiar with. They were both men and women, the latter often joining the groups together with their husbands, brothers, or lovers, but on occasion because of their own personal convictions.[70]

The experiences of these groups were known only to their families and in the regions where these pockets of anti-Communist resistance took place, as well as to the Securitate secret police. Stories about these groups did circulate, but they were the stuff of legend, and few knew the details beyond those directly involved in the events: "In Transylvania there were nests, places where the poor brigands in the mountains . . . hid for a week or two to erase their traces when the Securitate came around our area. In our village there were some people sentenced for hiding the so-called partisans."[71] In other words, there was no full counter-memory narrative available, only a fragmentary mythology of these rebels, who were deemed tragic heroes and on occasion victims of betrayal by people they knew and, more importantly, victims of the Securitate. A full description of their activities became available, however, after 1989; that is when the heroic narrative of anti-Communist resistance was also fully forged. But during the Communist period there was nothing in Romania to the extent of, for instance, the counter-memories of tragic heroism that the Home Army was able to forge in Poland before it was wiped out.[72]

Among the many variations in how ethnic Romanian civilians identified themselves as victims and defined their victimizers, there was a general silence over the fate of the Jews who lived among them. Most people, including politicians, did not identify with the policies of the state, even when they expressed open admiration and loyalty toward Antonescu, and thus separated themselves from whatever responsibility could be placed on the shoulders of the government with regard to the fate of the Jews in World War II. Most Romanians are silent altogether with regard to what was happening to Jews in January 1941, June 1941, or for the rest of the war, when they were either sent off to death camps, herded into ghettos, or humiliated in public places and in public ways. In this regard, Alice Voinescu's memoirs are singular in their acknowledgement of the open forms of anti-Semitism she was witnessing around her:

> Ică [Mihai Antonescu] must be sadistic and lacking imagination, otherwise he wouldn't order the massacring of Jews and pillaging of their homes. If he realized even a little bit what a terrible perversion of our souls he's provoking, he wouldn't be so proud. . . . We call ourselves Christians and the priests call us to kill! I am profoundly disgusted.[73]

After volunteering in a hospital for a while, she extends her disgust also to soldiers, some of whom she depicts as "poisoned" by the racist anti-democratic propaganda they were exposed to in the army.[74] Her account seems to confirm the suspicion raised by Teodorescu-Schei regarding the rumors spread by the army in order to avoid confronting the responsibility of the Romanian military in anti-Semitic violence.

In Transylvania, where some civilian Romanians were subject to violence both at the beginning of the war and at the end, and where Romanians and Jews often lived in adjoining communities, there was also a lack of empathy for the suffering of these neighbors. In Treznea, for instance, the narratives villagers tell about the events of World War II include descriptions of the massacre at the beginning of the war, but almost never any acknowledgement of the deportation of the Jewish population from that village in the spring of 1944. In interviews I conducted with people who had been old enough to remember that period, only one respondent brought up the victimization of the Jews at the end of the war as something tragic in the history of the village.[75] There seemed to be little solidarity between the Romanians of Treznea and their Jewish neighbors in terms of their parallel and even shared experiences of violence during the war.[76]

There are gaping silences about another category of civilians who suffered specific forms of violence during the war: women. The frequent incidence of rape and sexual liaisons defined by profound power inequalities between men (as armed soldiers) and women (as vulnerable civilians) during World War II is well known and documented in the scholarship, and a number of recent studies have shed more light on the specific experiences of women on the eastern front, in/from Poland, Ukraine, Yugoslavia, and the Baltics.[77] In the Romanian context, there has been virtually no open discussion of these issues. Even in the context of framing civilians' victimization at the hand of the Soviets, the subject of rapes by Soviet soldiers came up informally, but it was not a frequent topic and neither women nor male observers of the civilian experiences at the end of the war were willing to write or talk about them. This is not surprising, as women of this society did not have a tradition of discussing such issues in a public context or even in the intimacy of their home. Insights into these gender-specific memories of victimhood became publicly articulated and acknowledged only after 1989.

༄

For ethnic Hungarian civilians living in Romania after 1945, the memories of World War II were forged into a different tragic story of heroism and victimization. They had seen their dream of rejoining their fatherland come true in 1940, and then crushed again in 1944. The end of this experience threw them again into the position of a tolerated minority, though the autonomous Hungarian region established between 1952 and 1968 did offer more self-rule for that period. Starting in 1968, however, the increasingly aggressive anti-Hungarian measures of the Communist regime rendered Hungarian voices marginal in public representations of the past. This predicament, in which Hungarians identified a recurrence of their social marginalization as a people and culture as they had experienced it after 1919, made the experience of 1940–1944 even more of a precious counter-memory to be nourished as a bright period in an otherwise unhappy story of rule by unfriendly governments. The Hungarian stories of wartime victimization and heroism were tied closely to the ways in which these communities sought to preserve their ethnic and community ties under Communism. Their counter-memories of the war could not be publicized in word, but the markers many of them managed to erect during the Communist period were precious sites of remembrance, combining ethnic and religious identity into one binding mix. Missing from the counter-memories, just as with civilian Romanians, were acknowledgements about the nature of Hungary's participation in the war, and their role as perpetrators against both Romanian civilians at the beginning of the war and, especially, Jews at the end of the war. In this regard, the Romanian and Hungarian civilians opted for similar strategies of remembrance and forgetting.

༄

A similar dynamic is true for German civilians. This community differed from ethnic Hungarians insofar as they had never laid claim to a homeland inside Romania and did not experience a return to primacy in World War II, followed by a loss of that homeland at the end of the war. Germans in Transylvania had benefited from autonomy and special economic and political privileges before World War I, which were subsequently denied. The memory of their fallen heroes in World War I had already been cast as a counter-memory to the ethno-nationalist official discourse emanating from Bucharest.

Romania's alliance with Nazi Germany at the beginning of the war afforded Germans the possibility of regaining some of their autonomy and social standing. Some in the community volunteered to participate in the war in the German, rather than the Romanian, army.[78] The civilians sometimes benefited from special treatment during the war and generally suffered little, like the civilian Romanians and Hungarians. The end of the war, however, brought a wave of vengefulness against the entire German population, regardless of their actual actions during the war. In early 1945, under direct supervision of the Soviet armies, the Romanian government started to round up most Germans, civilians and demobilized soldiers, from teenagers to the elderly, to send them off to labor camps deep into Siberia or in Bărăgan.

This experience of violent victimization brought civilian Germans closer to the experience of the ethnic Romanians during that same period. But these experiences remained equally concealed from non-Germans upon the deportees' return and also hidden in the intimacy of the family inside the German communities themselves. After the war the Romanian government had to some degree prosecuted participation at the front on the side of the Nazis as well as civilian collaboration, so the role of Germans as "willing executioners" became part of the official narrative of the war soon after its end. Combined with their experiences of deportation, these official narratives generated silences among Germans about their activities during the war, generally structured again in the context of their victimization at the war's end.[79] In their counter-memories, Germans also saw themselves as primarily victims of the war, and in some of the more audacious markers placed in German communities during the Communist period, also as its heroes.

It is virtually impossible to consider this claim to both victimization and tragic heroism as anything other than preposterous in the context of Germans inside Germany proper. Yet in Romania ethnic Germans saw themselves not as part of the Third Reich, but rather as Germans who were joining their brothers on the front. Their experiences at the end of the war helped these people substitute tough critical questions about loyalty toward the Nazis with narratives of innocent suffering at the hands of the brutal Soviet and Romanian authorities who deported innocent Germans to Siberia.[80]

Their case bears similarities to Germans in Lithuania, Poland, and Czechoslovakia. Yet the different institutional integration of these populations into the institutions of the Third Reich did also have direct consequences for how various German minorities both experienced and narrated their memories of the war after 1945.

∾

The Jewish populations deported to Transnistria from Romanian-controlled territories or to Poland from Hungarian-controlled ones managed to communicate during and immediately after the war stories of unspeakable terror suffered in these death camps. The literature on these narratives has been discussed elsewhere, and I want to insist here especially on how these recollections became situated in the broader landscape of counter-memories vis-à-vis official narratives of the war.[81]

Forgetting (whether willful or traumatic) and holding only fragmentary memories of the horrors suffered in the camps was reflected in many of the personal narratives of Jewish victims. But a call to remember and bear witness was also part of many of those narratives: "Do not forget, my son, all that happened. You will live; you have to live, to recount, to write, to tell your children, your grandchildren, everyone."[82] An emphasis on rescuing and constructing truthful narratives about the Holocaust was present already during the war, more emphatically than in texts written by other ethnic groups, who often pondered the need to construct counter-memories after the war's end.

It was not possible to speak about those experiences during the war, however, outside the confines of the Jewish community itself. Fear of repercussions in states (both Hungary and Romania) that had legislated anti-Semitism as an official public policy drove most Jews to speak very little to those who were not Jewish about their experiences in the extermination camps. The horrors were often so hard to imagine, even for those predisposed to believe the survivors, that speaking to a wider audience did not seem wise.

At the end of the war, before the war crimes trials that made the subject of anti-civilian atrocities during the war an open subject of discussion, a handful of eyewitness accounts of the Iași 1941 pogrom and the death camps in Transnistria were published in Romania.[83] These attempts to inform the wider population about the anti-Semitic actions of the Romanian state during World War II remained, however, without much echo. It is unclear, first of all, how much these books circulated or were read. Ethnic Romanians writing journals or memoirs of the war during the Communist period did not reference these books. Teodorescu-Schei, for instance, writing in the 1950s, refers to rumors about the Iași pogrom as he had heard them before going to Iași in July 1941, but he doesn't mention any subsequent accounts that would have corrected those misrepresentations of the pogrom as having been a Jewish "rebellion."

The war crimes trials in Bucharest and Cluj in the mid-1940s constructed at least a partial view of the camps and deportations for the wider population. For ethnic Romanians, Hungarians, and Germans, the story of the Jewish Holocaust became tied to the official narratives of the war, to be treated with inconsideration by victims whose suffering went unacknowledged. For those who had been active supporters or at least untroubled bystanders of the anti-Semitic policies during the war, the apparently singular, special attention Jews, as victims, were receiving at the end of the war seemed both an uncomfortable reminder of their passive role in the oppression of this group, and also an affront when non-Jews considered the silences regarding their own suffering during the war.

The persistent anti-Semitism of many Romanians and their identification of the Communist regime with a Judeo-Bolshevik plot (much like the żydokomuna among Poles) likewise pushed Jews into public silence and subterranean counter-memories of their wartime experiences. In addition, the departure of many Jews from Romania meant a dwindling of the survivors and a loss of the central role they had initially played in remembering the Holocaust. Some of these survivors subsequently published their memoirs or war journals in Hebrew, English, or French, but these individual narratives got around only among small circles inside Romania itself.[84] These memories have been recovered mostly after 1989.

The memory of wartime experiences that Holocaust survivors articulated under Communism identifies Jewish civilians as victims of the Romanian regime's anti-Semitic legislation and actions. The difference between these narratives and those of other populations who also identified themselves as mere victims is that Jews saw the coming of their plight even before the beginning of the war. There was a continuum between the policies of the Romanian state during peacetime and at war in terms of how Jews were treated, and thus the perpetrators were squarely identified as the Romanian state and its "willing executioners," rather than the conditions of war, or the Nazis alone.

For the Hungarian Jews of northern Transylvania, the story is even more tragic. In 1940 many chose to stay in that area because they had faith, based on their memories of pre-1918 Austria-Hungary, that they would be treated better than under the Romanian interwar administration.[85] The narratives of these Hungarian loyalists focused on their betrayal by the Hungarian authorities at the end of the war, and thus in a sense a double victimization, given their hopes and expectations at the outset.

In the larger context of how ethnic Romanians, Hungarians, and Germans generally refused to confront questions of responsibility for wartime atrocities, it is not surprising that the Jewish narratives of their horrendous experiences remained confined to the Jewish communities. In the 1980s, when the Ceaușescu regime began to use the story of the plight of the Transylvanian Jews as a way to vilify the Hungarian state, some of the personal narratives of Holocaust survivors became public. But they appeared in a context of already strong ethno-nationalism with anti-Semitic undertones, including a positive view of the Antonescu regime among many Romanians, as well as a tacit rehabilitation of Antonescu's image by the Romanian Communist regime.

Where Have All the Perpetrators Gone?

Compared to France and Germany, in Romania individual counter-memories of World War II were never incorporated into any public discussion and remained both fragmented and subject to their own myth-making. In the same way that individuals came to see themselves as oppressed by the Communist regime and living as subjects and victims of that regime, they also projected it over their memories of the war. The state had confronted the question of guilt at the end of the war, but the auspices of those war crime trials were defined by their affiliation with the much-hated Soviet occupation and lost legitimacy among most people. Even those supposedly vindicated by the rulings of the Peoples Tribunals were left with little sense of justice having been handed out, especially when the guilty were absent, or when real charges were replaced with trumped-up political ones.

Fragmented and threatened by persecution, people in general tried to preserve their cultural identity by resisting, in small informal ways, the encroachment of the Communist propaganda. For the first postwar generation, preserving concealed counter-memories of the war was an important aspect of their desire not to become completely "brainwashed" by the Communists. Yet these counter-narratives also avoided important questions of guilt and collaborationism with the wartime fascist authoritarian state in the case of atrocities committed against civilians. By contrast, multiple strands of stories of heroism and victimization were constructed and passed down to the postwar generations as precious kernels of truth. These stories remained unreconciled with each other, and also with the historical record of the war, until after 1989. One might conclude that these counter-memories were a result of the perverted ways in which the Communist regimes controlled information and historical discourse for ideological propaganda purposes. That is partly true. But in avoiding questions of responsibility during the war, local communities did their own part in suggesting models of cultural identity that focused on victimhood rather than the need for accountability in individual actions for all people, not just "they"—the unnamed henchmen of the Communist regime.

The results of how these disparate stories of victimization isolated intimately known communities from any responsibility for political acts and violence have become more apparent after 1989, when a flood of memoirs about the war finally appeared in Romania. These memoirs have led to debates that rage until today, replicating many of these parallel stories of the various ethnic communities, now competing for public attention, moral capital (the greatest victims would have the moral upper hand in the post-Communist world), and material retribution. In this regard, the Romanian case is comparable to the Polish, Czech, Bulgarian, Hungarian, and Yugoslav ones. In all these cases the fragmentation of remembrances about World War II is far greater than in western Europe, where even the memoirs of self-avowed perpetrators from World War II have been acknowledged as important, alongside those of their victims.[86] My last chapter turns toward these legacies of the Communist period for the last two decades.

THE DILEMMAS OF POST-MEMORY
IN POST-COMMUNIST ROMANIA

The fall of the Ceauşescu regime in 1989 opened up the floodgates of memory. In the following decade, the most important debates in politics and culture were about authenticity, rebirth, traditions, and truths that needed to be uttered and heard in order to restore moral order in a Romanian society deeply corrupted by the Communist regime.[3] These debates were more existential than political, just as in all other eastern European societies in the first post-Communist decade. Adam Michnik's call that "gray is beautiful" did not hold much water with masses of people who wanted palpable, unquestionable truths, rather than tolerant wisdom.[4] Politically, it was obvious from the beginning that a clean slate was not to be. Romania lived through a difficult transition of Communists turned social democrats and liberals overnight, with people who had lived in the Communist prisons of the 1940s and 1950s as the only "untainted" leaders.[5]

Overall, people didn't look to the political scene for signs of moral restoration; there was little faith in political processes in post-Communist Romania.[6] Instead, with the exception of figures like Corneliu Coposu (1914–1995), who was regarded as a rare moral compass in politics, most people looked toward intellectuals and especially those who had suffered under Communism as heroic victims situated above the corruption and moral morass of the late Communist period. But Romania had no Václav Havel (1936–), nor did it have a Solidarity movement. Dissent in Romania had meant far lesser things, and most people were unaware of even significant dissident actions, such as the 1977 miners' strikes in the Jiu Valley, or the responses of writer Paul Goma (1935–) to those events and his expulsion to France.[7]

Romanians started to search for signs of subterranean truths and authentic forms of resistance that had to be hidden because of the particularly harsh nature of the Ceauşescu regime, with its insidious Securitate.[8] The phrase "resistance through culture" became a mantra of the intelligentsia who had lived in the Communist "velvet prison" and wished to paint themselves as victims of the regime.[9] The counter-memories and counter-myths forged during the Communist period became a source for creating new narratives about courage, opposition, and sacrifice. The flood of memoirs and other autobiographical writings, from journals and correspondence to fictionalized accounts of personal histories that appeared in the next decade and a half, show the unprecedented desire to speak out, as well as the thirst to read such accounts.

Not only cultural elites, but also a host of other people who had been kept silent during the Communist period, from veterans of World War II to victims of the Holocaust, brought out into the open their memoirs, some written during the Communist years, others in the early 1990s. Families of those who had passed away during the Communist period as victims of that regime also wanted to honor the memory of their dead in word, by bringing to light evidence about their sacrifices and suffering. Writers and their public alike wanted to read about misery, victimization, and the heroism of living with some dignity through the years of oppression. People were more interested in speaking out their pain or reading about suffering as a confirmation of the evil nature of the Communist regime, and less interested in finding out who were the perpetrators of the suffering that had taken place over the past half century. Ceauşescu's rushed execution was a preview of how questions of guilt were addressed in courts of law, signifying wider problems in Romanian society in the next decade.[10]

This cavalcade of stories of victimization during the first post-Communist decade has given way in the last few years to questions about guilt. Two presidential commissions, one inquiring into the culpability of the Romanian state for events of the

Holocaust (2003) and a second dealing with the "crimes of Communism" (2006), have introduced into public discussion questions of collaborationism, state and individual responsibilities for war crimes, crimes against humanity, and genocide. Remembering World War II and the Holocaust has gained new prominence in the Romanian political and cultural discourse.

Yet political debates about guilt and moral responsibility have not had an important echo in how the population at large, individually and collectively, commemorates the wartime violence of the twentieth century. In fact, remembrances of World War II, the Holocaust, and the years of Communist terror have remained either isolated from each other or in competition for media attention and other cultural resources. The government of democratic Romania, now a member of the European Union, is staging new commemorations that ask citizens to consider more comprehensively the history of violence in the middle of the twentieth century. Yet many people are still turning away from the state and insisting on their own forms of remembering, continuing to focus selectively on suffering and oppression of those who perished in the 1940–1953 period, unable to look globally and with empathy toward *all* the victims and perpetrators of violence during that period. The neatness of a Western-centric narrative of World War II, the Holocaust, and the postwar (Cold War) period is not yet possible in Romania, as it is not possible in other post-Communist countries. The sanitized post–Cold War victorious neoliberal narrative is easier to construct officially in Brussels or Bucharest than to enact successfully through locally based cultural commemorations in communities that are still finding their voices, insisting that their dead have never properly been honored. This chapter brings up to date these debates, which remain unresolved.

This blend of searching for absolute truths, for collective forms of rebirth or salvation with a focus on individualism, and attempting to render audible a multitude of individual voices as precious sources of this absolute truth, represents an important if poorly understood element of the post-Communist transition everywhere in Europe. Some observers (for instance Michnik) have insisted in defining the desire for absolute truths as undemocratic, while ignoring the second important aspect—the assertive individualism—of the transition.[11] Other observers have identified this second trend as proof of pro-liberal sensibilities, by not paying enough attention to the first, collective element of this paradoxical blend.[12] Both of these partial views ultimately suggest that the reality on the ground in the post-Communist European states was ill suited for utilizing paradigms and labels that fit western Europe. Examining the cultural phenomena explored in this chapter, in addition to more traditional forms of civic/political action such as voting and poll-taking, is an essential step toward taking in a more comprehensive picture of these complicated realities. This chapter suggests that the attribute "post"-Communist is still important for understanding the new members or members-to-be of the EU. In fact, the Communist and World War II periods still serve as powerful referents for people in the former eastern European Communist countries.

War Commemorations and Legitimizing the Post-Communist Regime

The decade following the collapse of Communism witnessed the publication of thousands of memoirs, many of them relating to World War II and others focusing on the early years of the Communist regime. A small but steadily growing set of memoirs recounting the events of the Holocaust and of anti-Semitism in pre-war and wartime Romania also appeared. Hundreds of monuments and other public forms of remembering (especially street and institution renaming) also sprang up all over the country. Museums were opened up, exhibitions refurbished, and new commemorations inaugurated in every ethnic community that had lost soldiers and civilians during World War II. Filmmakers, now able to pursue a more independent agenda, turned again toward World War I and World War II as sites of cultural production, rendering the memory of these two moments in the history of twentieth-century Romania visible and relevant for a new generation of people.

Most of the new or renewed forms of remembering were taking place simultaneously at the local and highest levels of government, as neo-Communist president Ion Iliescu (1930–) attempted to gain legitimacy among the populace. One of the first changes legislated by his Front for National Salvation in 1990 was to change the national day.[13] The speed of this change suggests that the Iliescu government considered 23 August illegitimate and did not wish to have its own self-celebration spoiled by having the national holiday on that date. Given the lack of protest from war veterans to diehard monarchists, it seems 23 August was at least not too dear to people's hearts. The immediacy of the change also suggests the government believed in the symbolic importance of an appropriate national holiday, which indirectly points to interpreting the obsession of the Ceaușescu regime with nationalist celebrations as a partial success. If Iliescu's government believed the population would be roused by a better choice of a national holiday, then, despite its failure to turn 23 August into a popular celebration, the Communist regime at least instilled the legitimacy of such a national holiday. The fact that the post-Communist national day also ended up being a date linked to war was not a coincidence.

Equally illuminating in showing the continuing salience of commemorating the world wars for the new government were the discussions over what the new national day might become. Several dates were suggested along the way. Among them were

22 December, the day in 1989 when Ceaușescu fled Bucharest in a de-facto abdication from power; 17 December, the day in 1989 when protests in Timișoara started unraveling the regime; 10 May, the old day celebrating Romania's declaration of independence in 1877; and 1 December, the day of the mass gathering at Alba Iulia in 1918, which had become an important official cultural commemorative marker during the interwar period and again after 1968. A few interesting aspects emerge here in terms of the commemorative imagination of policy makers in early 1990. Their gaze focused on two kinds of legitimating moments in Romanian history: either the December 1989 events, which would then link the new government exclusively with post-Communism and the very recent past; or events that hailed back eighty years or more, linking the legitimacy of the post-Communist state to the formation of the first Romanian independent state, or Greater Romania. This second vision, tied to the more distant past and suggesting the rebirth of an older democratic legacy, won in the end. The national holiday became and has remained 1 December.

The first of December was a compromise, as some people wanted to opt for 17 December and others for 22 December, while another faction looked toward springtime (10 May) as a more fitting season for a national holiday. The Romanian elites and population did not register 1 December itself as a problematic holiday; they just had various personal preferences. The uncontroversial discussions about 1 December suggest that the ethno-nationalist discourse about that date, first constructed in the interwar period and then reintroduced and amplified during the Ceaușescu years, had become normalized for ethnic Romanians.[14] It would be impossible to determine whether state actions or personal sentiments played a greater role in generating this ethno-nationalist predisposition. But the same kind of ethnically contentious elements that had been present since 1918 still remained. Hungarians especially saw 1 December not as a day of rejoicing, but rather as a painful reminder of the loss of the status and rights they had enjoyed in Austria-Hungary.[15]

After 1 December became the national holiday, people all over Romania grumbled over the choice. They have continued to do so since then, but for reasons having to do with the seasonal choice or with current politics.[16] It is usually too cold to have an outdoor celebration that lasts a whole day; it is more expensive and constraining to organize indoor events; the weather is unpredictable and often snow or sleet make the festivities difficult to stage for most people; and having a day off so they can shovel snow or stay inside seems like an unappealing way to celebrate. In the late 1990s, when I was conducting interviews with people of various generations on this topic, most compared 1 December unfavorably to 4 July, stating that they "wished 1 December were more like your Fourth of July."[17] With the United States Embassy throwing a great Fourth of July party every year since 1990, most people in Romania have become familiar with the hotdogs, hamburgers, and fireworks routine of a Fourth of July barbeque.[18] In fact, the Romanian state has tried to put on a similar show, but fireworks do not work as well in snow, and neither do outdoor barbeques. What ethnic Romanians, even in Transylvania, have not been as willing to consider, however, is the possibility that this holiday is in fact a way to rake Hungary over the coals, a choice to resist ethnic reconciliation at point in Romania's history when such reconciliation was much needed.

The first of December has not been the only means by which remembering World War I has become more present in the calendar of Romanian holidays. Heroes Day has also made a comeback. Starting in 1995, the Romanian state decreed that Ascension Day would again become the day on which all war heroes should be commemorated.[19] In addition, the army was adamant about returning the Tomb of the Unknown Soldier back to Bucharest.[20] Their combined actions to move the Tomb and revive Heroes Day, restoring both to their interwar-era place in the panoply of nationalist symbols and holidays, was a means to rehabilitate the image of the army as a Romanian institution with deep roots. The army represented itself as having been oppressed by the Communists in its attempts to honor the heroes of the country, but, as chapter 5 has shown, the army had in fact been able to exert its own voice in constructing and maintaining the memory of the wartime dead.

Reframing Wartime Memory in Community and Individual Discourses

The first of December and Heroes Day offered new opportunities for politicians to perform their patriotic roles in public view. In no time, these days became media festivities, staged in front of and for the sake of cameras, featured on the evening news and in all the newspapers.[21] Some groups, especially war veterans, came to appreciate these celebrations as the delayed honors they had not received for many years; they have continued to participate in them in significant numbers, even as many are passing away.[22] But the population at large has not been as quick to respond to the official commemorations, especially of Heroes Day, which falls on a Thursday and is neither a school nor a business holiday, so that most people are not free to celebrate. (See figure 7.2.)

There are a few notable exceptions to this. In the countryside, the Ascension remained an important religious holiday throughout the Communist period, and Orthodox believers continued to informally celebrate that day also as Heroes Day. This continuity shows that the policies of the interwar Romanian state *did* have a long-term impact on how people have come to remember their war dead. The date itself gained legitimacy in terms of honoring the war, at least among Orthodox Romanians. However, it is not apparent people in the countryside have performed such rituals of remembrance in the way intended by the interwar regime. It is more fitting to say that Orthodox believers incorporated the war dead as part of their larger ensemble of ancestor worship. Katherine Verdery's work on the return of the cult of the dead and the reburials of prominent historical figures in Romania, and more broadly eastern Europe, was an important analysis that resonated with my own findings. The book drew attention to the ways in which, despite modernization, urbanization, and secularization, the Communist regime did not manage to suppress the kinds of traditional practices and beliefs associated with the cult of the dead.[23] My own analysis connects the post-Communist developments with important Communist and pre-Communist antecedents.

From the 1940s onward, the lists of those who died in World War I were augmented by those who died on both fronts and as deportees during World War II and after, and who became part of the living memory of dead ancestors in each village, remembered alongside mothers, fathers, children, and spouses who had died over the years. The one specific way in which the war dead were separated from the rest was generally in their absence from the local cemetery. If families laid flowers, lit candles, and left food for the soul of the dearly departed on the individual graves of those they were remembering through such rituals, for those who had died far away and whose bodies had not been retrieved, the marker (a cross, a plaque, some other inscription) served as a substitute for a grave, reminding the village every year of the unusual and, from a religious point of view, tragic way in which these souls had perished, unable to find peace.

Thus, the revival of Heroes Day was not as much a comeback as it was a public re-acknowledgment of a practice that had continued in the countryside among Orthodox Romanians since the interwar period. In interviews I conducted in Transylvania, from Satu Mare County to Baia Mare and beyond into Maramureş, people in the countryside spoke of these rituals as being the way things had always been done.[24] They were unaware of when Heroes Day had originated and viewed it as a part of their traditional cult of the dead.

Of course, life in the countryside permits performing such rituals mid-week, as most people are still engaged in agricultural work that doesn't fit in the forty-hour workweek of industrialized economies. The rituals performed in small churches by a handful of women, with the assistance of a local priest if one is available, remained, however, generally invisible to the Communist elites between 1945 and 1989; they have remained so to most politicians and the media since then. On Heroes Day one may view on the evening news, as I did a few years ago in 2005, sequences from a

Figure 7.1. Heroes Day commemoration in Liberty Park, 2005. Photo Maria Bucur.

government-organized ceremony at the Tomb of the Unknown Soldier in Bucharest, with politicians from most political parties laying wreaths, with the military in attendance, overseeing the ceremony, and with Orthodox and Catholic priests officiating a brief *Te Deum* in memory of the soldiers commemorated symbolically there (figure 7.1). Veterans were present, as were a handful of schoolchildren whose teachers had been coaxed into taking part. The "wider" public was a handful of grandparents and their small grandchildren playing at the playground in the vicinity, and stopping for thirty minutes to watch the spectacle from the side.[25] Plainclothes security men milling around kept most of this public away from a close look. The entire ceremony seemed like a publicity stunt, performed by politicians for the media, with the army, clergy, students, and veterans as a backdrop. Both in the flesh and on TV the commemoration lacked any personal resonance with the specific sacrifices being commemorated.[26]

Invisible from the bright lights of television cameras, however, women elsewhere in the countryside were performing their ritual of ancestor remembrance on the same day, thinking of God, the dead, and their community as the only important audiences for these rituals.[27] The gendered nature of this memory work has continued unchallenged in the twentieth century, undisturbed by changing marriage and residence patterns, or by the forced secularization of Romanian culture at the official

Figure 7.2. Heroes Day/Ascension at the Pantelimon Church in Voluntari (2008). Photo Maria Bucur.

level during the Communist regime. The state and mass media have been unable to make an effective connection between officially sponsored commemorations and what happens at the local level, among people who are still crying for their dead, and who are truly invested in preserving alive the memory of the soldiers who perished in the two world wars—not so much as heroes, but as sons of their communities. During the Communist period, local observances remained public for those in the immediate communities who wished to see a visible continuation of these rituals of remembrance. They were not an open form of resistance to specific ideologies—nationalist or Communist—but rather a more subdued form of resistance to the encroachment of modern ways of thinking about death and the importance of keeping alive the memory of the dearly departed. It is the same phenomenon that Katherine Verdery outlined in *The Political Lives of Dead Bodies*.

Yet a new grassroots movement in urban areas is attempting to reconnect with the "authentic" spirit of Heroes Day. In Bucharest, in particular, there has been a growing movement among university students to reinstate religion in the classroom and Orthodoxy in particular as the single denomination, represented visually everywhere through icons. The opening of an Orthodox chapel on the premises of the university provoked a great deal of debate a few years ago. It is within this context of proselytizing within the university that Orthodox students began to organize Heroes

Day commemorations, placing expensive posters all over the halls of the university and calling their fellow students to prayer on Ascension.[28] There is no doubt about the sincerity of these young people in their attempt to return to a more authentic way of living as Romanians after fifty years of official atheism. Yet their approach to Orthodoxy has been intolerant of other religions and of the idea that a secular state institution is not a place for religious proselytizing. Heroes Day has become thus a means to justify Orthodox exclusivism, because the commemorative day is defined by the Orthodox calendar. These Orthodox students are performing the same uncritical (and intolerant) role as enthusiastic young ethnic Romanian intellectuals were in the early 1920s, when Heroes Day was initially celebrated.

∞

Film has again become a medium for individual representations of the two world wars, with a wide public impact, especially for younger generations.[29] The end of the Communist regime brought about liberalization in filmmaking from ideological censorship. But that actually meant the virtual death of film production in Romania in the first decade after 1989. State funding was slashed, and many filmmakers found themselves unemployed.[30] However, a few directors made the transition largely unscathed, because of their solid reputation with funding agencies and with the public. Sergiu Nicolaescu (1930–) was the most prominent among them.[31] During the Communist period he had made the largest number of historical films and had become an icon of World War II movies, taking roles in some of them as well, playing alternatively either German SS officers or great Romanian patriots.[32] Two of his post-Communist films stand out as being revisionist and for preserving some of the nationalist ideas of the Communist period.[33] *The Beginning of the Truth—the Mirror* (1993) positioned itself from the title as historical truth-telling in the same presumptuous way that came to characterize Nicolaescu's public presence throughout the post-Communist period. One critic has ironically noted that "the beginning of the truth" implies the end of the lie; one has to wonder whether Nicolaescu was trying to be honest and self-reflexive in indirectly acknowledging his own contributions to that lie as a director of World War II action movies during the Communist period.[34] More likely, the title stands as a purported unveiling of truths about Romania in World War II that could not be uttered before, especially regarding Antonescu. Nicolaescu painted himself more as someone finally able to live out his full potential as an artist, who had been censored before, and less as a collaborator of the Communist regime. He made his more personal stake in this movie plainly visible, both in his depiction of Antonescu and in interviews he gave about the movie: "I hope I was objective; though, in many instances, the spiritual links I have with the King were confronted by the respect the dramatic destiny of the Marshal inspired in me."[35]

Based on research in the archives and access to documentary films that had not been made public (most prominently the execution of Antonescu), Nicolaescu portrayed the Romanian wartime dictator as a tragic figure, a victim of both the Germans and the Soviets. The movie contained much that was unprecedented—full depictions of Iuliu Maniu, King Michael, Lucrețiu Pătrășcanu (1900–1954), and other leading politicians, whose presence in wartime and immediate postwar politics had not been the subject of public history since the late 1940s. The main plot of the movie, Romania's tragic victimization at the hands of the Germans and Soviets, was, however, not a new narrative. Neither was Antonescu's public rehabilitation as a tragic hero a new "truth," since the novel *The Delirium* had appeared in 1977 and had already been available to two generations of fans of its author, Marin Preda.

Instead, *The Mirror* is a work of re-solidifying the myth of Romania's victimization in World War II for the generations that were coming of age in the post-Communist period. The movie, though not particularly "good" in terms of filmmaking aesthetics, has been shown again and again on Romanian television since then, without much in the way of critical commentary on the portrayal of Romania during World War II. Regardless of the movie's qualities, it has remained popular with viewers, old and young alike, who have been unconvinced by criticisms of the movie as having an agenda to rehabilitate Antonescu.[36] The image of the dictator as a heroic victim echoes comfortably the image of the war that was constructed in the counter-memory discourses of the Communist period.[37]

Nicolaescu attempted to also depict World War I along more a more "truthful" narrative line with *The Death Triangle* (1999).[38] In this case, with the help of the radical right-wing politician and ex–court poet of the Communist regime, Corneliu Vadim Tudor (1949–), who co-wrote the screenplay, Nicolaescu wished to revisit the nationalist mythologizing of the war as it had been constructed after 1918, together with a pro-Averescu view of the Romanian army and politics. The movie also became a vehicle for Nicolaescu's penchant for pyrotechnics and action montages. *The Death Triangle* brought to the screen fictionalized representations of King Ferdinand and Queen Marie, both of them making their first appearance in such a movie, as they had been taboo subjects before 1989. Nicolaescu offered the perspective of the discontented Averescu, especially as expressed in his wartime memoir published in 1937, as an objective and admirable one. We have, therefore, a historical dramatization of part of World War I viewed from a memorialistic perspective, where historical narrative is based on a war journal of a military leader. The narrative focuses on the tragic losses of valiant heroes, from average soldiers fighting in the front lines to Averescu's own tragedy of not being able to lead his troops effectively due to the inability of politicians to reconcile their differences. Soldiers are rendered as heroes and victims of the enemy within, the political elites.

⌇

Movies presented avenues for remembering the two world wars in somewhat revisionist ways, while incorporating both official Communist commemorative clichés and counter-memory discourse leitmotifs shaped in the shadow of the official Communist ones. Other new memorial traces amplified this combined trajectory of change and persistence. Even more problematic in the rush to re-signify remembrances of the world wars and soldiers' sacrifices have been local volunteer activities to mark streets and other public spaces (squares, buildings, institutions) with names that recalled heroes of those wars. This effort was a double one—of erasure, removing names that had become odious to those proposing the change, and of inscription and re-signification. This process was by definition discursive and engaged all people in the community, from local politicians and administrators to everyone who happened to live on a street with a name deemed necessary for change. While in some cases the initiative came from politically invested organizations, rather than the neighborhood to be affected by the change, it was impossible to go about the process of renaming without engaging at least some of the people who lived there to support such initiatives. That meant engaging in discussions about the inappropriateness of a previous name, such as that of a Communist Party leader. In such cases, it was certainly easy for most people to agree with the need to change the name. These discussions focused more importantly on possible new names to use, and here the variety of existing commemorative discourses—official, local, individual—about the meaning of the past and in particular World War II revealed their impact on how people understood the notion of properly remembering the war.

The streets considered for change sometimes had obviously questionable names, but other cases were more ambiguous. For instance, one prominent boulevard in Bucharest had been renamed for Ana Ipătescu (1805–1855) during the Communist period, as a means to honor one of the few female leaders in the 1848 revolutionary uprisings.[39] Soon after 1990 that street was renamed for Lascăr Catargi (1823–1899), its namesake in pre-Communist times, even though the 1848 heroine was not associated with Communism in any other way than through the renaming of that particular street from Catargi to Ipătescu under the Communist regime.[40] There were also many public spaces with names such as "liberty" (e.g., Liberty Park) and "victory" (e.g., Victory Square), which initially had meant the liberty brought by the Soviets and the victory of the Communist forces in Romania. But subsequent generations came to view these names as innocuous, having no direct referent to the initial connotation, except in rare cases where their parents and grandparents would remind them that their street used to have a different name, maybe connected to the monarchy, or with some interwar nationalist symbol. In these cases, it was more difficult to rationalize the need for change for younger generations, without a whole history lesson about what had been there before.[41]

Where new street names were considered, the committee formed to propose this change—sometimes appointed by the local administration, other times formed from the grass roots—had at least one idea for the new name, but arguments over what would be legitimate varied. To begin with, many streets had had another name before. If some felt the Communist name to be illegitimate, then one argument was that the street should regain its pre-Communist period name. But that name was not always one the local population wanted to revive, especially in Transylvania, where many of the names of important streets in the large cities had been renamed during the war by the Hungarian administration. In those cases, the gaze went back to the interwar period, or in a more pointed nationalist revisionist trend, to the Romanian heroism and sacrifices in World War II.

A related development was to redefine what was public and what was private. Would a church placed on a busy road have the right to place any commemorative monument it wished on its property, or would the publicness of such a marker make it subject to state oversight and legitimate public debate? Undoubtedly, such efforts were meant to be for public viewing, but in some cases debates ensued over who had the right to make such changes, in view of the ownership of a particular establishment, building, space (garden, green space, sidewalk) or even square. Streets, however, fell easily within the purview of city government, and thus were subject to scrutiny by mayors and city councils in regularized fashion. For a number of commemorative efforts, there was legal uncertainty regarding how public and private property was defined. It took over a decade after the fall of Communism for a functioning, clear definition of private property to be set into law.[42]

Therefore, in the early 1990s, decisions about public monuments and markers were locally negotiated and contested, and the national government or courts rarely became involved in these discussions. The most contentious of the suggested changes in many urban locales was naming a street or square, usually in a central location, for Marshal Antonescu. In Oradea, a boulevard was renamed Antonescu.[43] In Tîrgu Mureş, a statue of Antonescu was to be erected in the green dividing space of a central street, in front of a military garrison, and in Slobozia a statue was placed in the courtyard of a factory.[44] In Bucharest, in front of a church Antonescu had built during

World War II, a commemorative plaque received a prominent location. These attempts to rehabilitate the wartime dictator took place all over the country, soon after the fall of Communism. Those who initiated the name changes and markers were sometimes local politicians (the mayor, members of the city council), and at other times local notables, such as officers from the local military unit or managers of factories.

In virtually all of these instances the change occurred swiftly, without much debate in the local press or at city hall, even though informal discussions in the affected neighborhoods did take place and the press reported these events. Protests over these street changes and proposed statues (some were only partially erected, for instance in Tîrgu Mureş) came only after permits for the project had been granted and work was under way to commemorate Antonescu. Challenges generally came from outside the immediate community, especially from the Jewish diaspora, while the Romanian media and public intellectuals offered very few critical comments.[45] One exception was historian Andrei Pippidi, who wrote on several occasions about the serious historical and political-ethical problems posed by renamed streets and statues.[46] Pressure from abroad, as Romania was trying to create an international image of a democratic state, finally had some impact, and in the next decade some of these public commemorations of Antonescu disappeared. But some continued to stand even after the protests.[47] Even in the early 2000s, when I last visited the National Military Museum, a large bust of Antonescu adorned the hallway in front of director's office (figure 7.3), dominating the entire space. For anyone waiting to see this chief administrator who is an officer of the Romanian army, now part of NATO, such a permanent, proud reminder of Romania's participation in World War II under the leadership of a fascist dictator is an uncomfortable testimony to the continuing subterranean counter-memories of the war.

❧

Even if street names were only temporarily changed and statues to Antonescu had to be moved to more "discreet" locations, other forms of rehabilitating the dictator and a Romanian-exclusivist version of wartime heroism have lasted, from the filmic revisionism recounted above to a multitude of other, individual attempts. With the explosion in the publishing business, after 1989 veterans of the battles on the eastern front who had written memoirs or journals during and after World War II were finally able to publish them. These books have come out with prestigious publishers capable of wide distribution, such as "All" in Bucharest, as well as with tiny ones, such as the "National Association of War Veterans, the Baia Mare organization."[48] Some of these wartime memory traces have found a wide audience, while others have remained relatively unknown. Overall, hundreds of titles telling individual stories about the war in the East appeared in the first decade after 1989 and continued to appear in the

Figure 7.3. Bust of Ion Antonescu inside the National Military Museum (1994). Photo courtesy of the National Military Museum.

next decade. This ongoing interest in the stories told by veterans of the eastern front suggests that many people were eager to read such accounts, or to have stories they heard at home, their subterranean counter-memories, confirmed. While a few of these memoirs maintain some distance from the claims of the Antonescu regime that it was fighting for a legitimate or even sacred cause on the eastern front, the vast majority of memoirs written by Romanian veterans exhibit sympathy toward Antonescu, if not outright veneration. One such veteran reminisced in 2001: "We have never lived [as well] under any other regime as under Antonescu."[49]

A parallel story could be told about the large Hungarian and small German ethnic communities. These groups were able to reconnect more directly and publicly with stories about their experiences, especially through foreign publications, though some titles in German and Hungarian did appear in Romania itself, with new privately owned publications sprouting among these populations as well.[50] However, since they were not published in Romanian, these books remained rather limited in their reach. Many Romanians in Transylvania still speak Hungarian, but it is a declining proportion, and these books were not sold widely.

The literature connected to the experience of Jews during World War II also began to reappear during this period, but here the effort was more to finally educate ethnic Romanians, Hungarians, and Germans about the reality of the horrors Jews lived through, rather than a community-based attempt to commemorate one's own dead. After all, most of the Jewish communities on the Romanian territory had disappeared by 1989, initially due to the Holocaust and subsequently to emigration to Israel. The Hasefer publishing house made the most enduring and extensive efforts to restore this kind of Judaica, but other smaller publishing houses also made such memoirs and journals available.

The most publicized recollection of Romanian anti-Semitism during World War II was Mihail Sebastian's *Journal,* which appeared in 1996. This publication generated a great deal of discussion about pre-war anti-Semitism, as well as the activities of some of the most prominent Romanian intellectuals that served to silence and humiliate Romanian Jews during World War II. The debate started from a profound divergence in how public intellectuals chose to read the journal. Historians such as Leon Volovici, Zigu Ornea, and Victor Neumann, who had already written important texts about the radical right and anti-Semitism in Romania in the 1930s, approached Sebastian's journal as a rich source providing incontrovertible evidence about the profound anti-Semitic sentiments of such intellectuals as Mircea Eliade (1907–1986) in the privacy of their dinner parties and salons where Sebastian was a disregarded and pained witness. This approach rubbed against the visceral, cult-like regard of many Romanian intellectuals for Nae Ionescu (1890–1940), Eliade, Constantin Noica (1909–1987) and other figures depicted critically in Sebastian's journal.[51]

Some of the most prominent public intellectuals of the day, such as Gabriel Liiceanu (the director of the prestigious publishing house that brought Sebastian's journal to print, as well as a scholar of the controversial German philosopher Martin Heidegger), reacted to the publication of the book in a defensively empathetic manner. In a speech before the Jewish community in Bucharest, Liiceanu identified Sebastian as his "brother," meaning by such an association that Liiceanu himself had suffered under the Communist regime, and even after 1989, from similar forms of persecution as Sebastian documented in his journal. The speech amounted to both an exaggeration of Liiceanu's own privations (e.g., he had been able to travel abroad multiple times during the Communist regime at a time when most Romanians had no hope of ever securing a passport), and a minimizing of the Holocaust and of the persecution of the Jews as being something comparable to what Romanian people experienced under Communism.[52] In this talk Liiceanu also blended, as many others in the post-Communist period have done, two registers of knowledge and authority: on the one hand, Liiceanu remembered in public his own personal suffering, rendering it authoritative knowledge by way of sharing strong, authentic, first-hand emotions he had been unable to utter before 1989; on the other hand, Liiceanu took a blend of Sebastian's recollections and Liiceanu's own readings on the Holocaust and World War II, including the history of the Romanian intelligentsia, and made himself an arbiter of that complicated story, rendering it meaningful not through its own context, but rather through Liiceanu's personal memories of the Communist period. It was as if living under Communism made someone, especially an intellectual (the operative category of self-identification here), uniquely able to understand the plight of the entire Jewish population in the Holocaust.

The speech became the subject of an extended polemic that touched more widely on the comparability of the Holocaust with the violence suffered by people in Romania after 1945, in which writers, philosophers, journalists, political scientists, and on occasion historians participated. The ongoing conversation exposed the rawness, the emotional intensity that Sebastian's book had awakened in many people. These debates also revealed an understanding of the Holocaust and World War II that bore the marks of the counter-myths of victimization and heroism constructed in the 1945–1989 period. In a sophisticated philosophical discussion in which he deconstructed notions such as "incomparable" and "unique" as associated with the Holocaust, Andrei Cornea concluded that Liiceanu's attempt to empathize with Sebastian, and to compare the Communist regime with Antonescu's in terms of victimization, was a valiant attempt at dialogue, rather than minimizing. Yet Cornea himself avoided the most important question that looms over the Sebastian journal and criticisms of Liiceanu himself: Who were the perpetrators? By the late 1990s, when these debates were taking place in the Romanian press, a rich literature on the question of perpetrators had developed in German, English, and French.[53] Cornea, Liiceanu, and others had access to this literature, yet they preferred an angle of empathy toward Sebastian, unaccompanied by any critical questions about culpability. In a more sophisticated language, with well-articulated arguments and beautifully penned turns of phrase, these intellectuals have performed the same avoidance of discussing guilt and have reproduced the discourse of victimization as heroic resistance of the Communist period. Liiceanu never apologized for his speech and continues to be a prominent public figure, with a TV show, who is much admired in many intellectual circles in Romania.[54]

ᴄᴧᴈ

Over the past few years, remembering the war and the Holocaust has gained a new dimension: restitution. The cultural work of remembering one's victimization at the hands of others has been augmented by the possibility of regaining lost property and goods through new legislation about the retrocession of illegitimately expropriated goods, which covers the wartime and Communist periods.[55] This legislation received its first impetus from the Uniate Church, which had been trying since 1989 to reclaim property the Communist regime had taken away from it in 1948, when that church was declared illegal.[56] More recently, the royal family has gained back some of its extensive real estate, from the Peleș Castle to large properties throughout the country.[57] Since 2007, Jews whose property was illegally seized during the war and ethnic Hungarians who similarly lost property in the 1944–1948 period have also been making claims for return of their properties. If these claims are to be treated in the same way under the retrocession law, then the claim to victimhood of all these categories of civilians will in fact be elevated to the same level of legal legitimacy. That raises provocative questions about claims and victim status for populations elsewhere in Europe—for instance, Germans in post-1945 Sudetenland and divided Germany. Locally, however, such claims have been treated as lacking the same legitimacy as the claims of the Uniate Church and ethnic Romanians. Some Romanian authorities have shown less sympathy to claims by victims of the Holocaust and ethnic Hungarians. Speaking in 2006 about retrocession claims leveled by ethnic Hungarians against the Romanian state with regard to buildings in Cluj, a spokesman for the mayor's office stated: "The [ethnic] minorities' churches have worked very cleverly until now, and acted on the sly, without much noise in the press, so that the majority of these activities have gone unnoticed, until one day we woke up to see that we no longer own the downtown areas in our cities!"[58] This critical statement presumes that cities in Transylvania belong to the Romanian state or the Romanian people, and that the prior ownership of buildings by private Hungarian citizens or religious institutions does not have the same claim to legitimacy represented by the collective "our" in thinking about public spaces in Transylvania.

Constructing a Genealogy of Moral Valor: The Sighet Memorial

The question of how World War II and the Holocaust could and *should* be remembered in both informal and official commemorations became complicated by another phenomenon. Romania's Communist experience had been plagued by two important particularities that weighed heavily on the shoulders of most Romanians after 1989:

the number of people who joined the Communist Party, and especially the number of people who agreed to collaborate with the regime's system of policing, was larger in terms of percentages than in any other Communist bloc country; and Romania could not boast of a Solidarity or any other remarkable narrative of dissent.[59] These two issues (whether true or just subjectively constructed as oppressive realities) became obsessive subjects of discussion in Romanian politics and the media early in the 1990s. They seemed to denote a lack of moral fiber among Romanians.

The reaction of some Romanians against this image of self-doubt and demoralization was to discover (or construct) models of courage and opposition that one could look toward as a genealogy of integrity and moral valor for the post-Communist period. The most spectacular site for constructing such links became the movements of anti-Communist resistance of the mid-1940s to the 1950s. The new discourse of anti-Communist bravery grew out of a series of projects, all looking to find heroes and uncover the extent of victimization of Romanians in the early years of Communist rule. The Sighet Memorial, the most prominent among the initiatives to bring out the truth about Communist prisons in the late 1940s and early 1950s, established a museum, a multi-year research project, as well as publications linked to it. The Civic Academy, an NGO turned political organization, which ran the initial actions linked to the Sighet Memorial, was dedicated exclusively to bringing out the tragic stories of the prominent intellectuals and politicians who were imprisoned and died there.[60]

These actions were so singularly focused on the prison and on the intellectual and political idols of the initiators, that the Civic Academy failed to notice obvious ways in which Sighet was not the site of one single type of oppression. Before the prison was used by the Communist regime to imprison "bourgeois class enemies," the large Jewish population of Sighet, which numbered among its inhabitants one Elie Wiesel, had suffered a great deal during World War II. A few streets over from the Sighet Prison a memorial dedicated to the victims of the Holocaust stood at the entrance to the large Jewish cemetery. (See figure 7.4.) The synagogue of the tiny surviving Jewish community in Sighet was also located a few blocs from the prison, and it too had tales of horror to tell within its walls.

In the first few years of the Civic Academy's annual pilgrimages to Sighet, where international conferences were held every summer and many foreign politicians and intellectuals were invited (e.g., Stephane Courtois, Thomas Blanton, and Pierre Hassner), the program went to great lengths to be hospitable to its guests and featured many cultural events.[61] Visiting the Jewish sites mentioned above was never a part of the extracurricular activities, nor was the plight of the victims of the Holocaust in the spring of 1944 a theme covered by conferences and occasional exhibits.[62] The leaders of the Civic Academy see themselves as simply pursuing one single important issue

Figure 7.4. The Holocaust memorial in the Sighet Jewish cemetery. Photo courtesy of the National Military Museum.

in Romania's complex past. While that is self-evident, the question remains whether one could seriously consider separating the pre-August 1944 years neatly from the post-1944 ones as distinct historical periods. As I suggested above, periodization is subjectively meaningful, and in terms of understanding the complexities of these years, thinking across the 1944 divide would enable us to better understand what "war" meant for people subjectively and individually, and also how various moments of aggression and disruption between 1940 and 1953 were related to each other. Ultimately, in a place like Sighet, where the fate of the local population was shaped by successive authoritarian regimes, one cannot hope to represent the meaning of these past tragic events by making reference to only one of the regimes. At best, such an attitude is short-sighted. At worst, it is exclusionary and thus counterproductive to understanding in all its complexities the divided and complicated meaning of the 1940–1953 years for the people who lived through that period.

The publication of many memoirs, interviews, and television programs about the heroes of the anti-Communist resistance worked even more to separate these issues and enable a failure to examine the 1940–1944 period. Lucia Hossu Longin's television series *The Memorial of Pain,* which focused on the broad victimization of Romanians under Communism and the heroism of anti-Communist resistance fighters, greatly impacted a whole generation of young people coming of age in the mid-1990s, through rendering vivid images of suffering and injustice associated with men and women who could have been their own grandparents.[63] One viewer recently commented: "I don't get fired up on themes of Romanian history or patriotism. On the contrary, I actually think it is more appropriate to speak of Romania and Romanians only through the prism of sarcasm. . . . But I think I had forgotten or never clearly knew that, if today I live in normalcy, it is because of them above all. . . . Thanks to the political prisoners."[64] Shown on TV for over a year and recently released on DVD, the documentary fundamentally influenced how victimization and resistance under Communism were to be viewed, placing the recollections of the documentary's simple heroes at center stage in this narrative. Missing from it, as from the Sighet Memorial projects, were references to the perpetrators of violence and their victims during World War II, before the Communists' arrival to power.

Coming to Terms with Guilt and Responsibility

The issue of guilt and responsibility for the atrocities committed during World War II finally came to the fore of policy making in 2000, when President Iliescu visited Washington. At that time, Romania was trying to present itself as a democratic state that embraced the same values as NATO and EU members, partly in hope of gaining admission into the EU. One of Iliescu's stops in Washington was the Holocaust Museum, and on that occasion he began to contemplate a commission (the Wiesel Commission) that would formally present a historical account of the Holocaust in Romania.

This new governmental attitude led to passing legislation that made it illegal to "erect or maintain in public places . . . statues, statuary ensembles, [and] commemorative plaques that make reference to persons guilty of infractions against peace and humanity."[65] Emergency Order no. 31/2002 also included provisions regarding naming public places and organizations after such persons, which in more concrete terms meant that the names of anyone convicted of war crimes, such as Ion Antonescu, would be prohibited from being used in any public commemorations and representations of World War II. The twenty-five streets that at that time were named after Antonescu had to be renamed, and the existing statues to the dictator removed.

How some average people reacted to both the new government regulations and these attempts to confront tough questions of culpability about the war becomes visible through Internet archives. Reactions to the creation of the Wiesel Commission and its findings among journalists, public intellectuals, and readers ranged from factual reporting to contestations or minimizing of the Holocaust and aspersions on the Commission as an American-Israeli plot. Whether they supported Iliescu or opposed him, many viewed his actions in creating the Commission as cowering before foreign pressure, rather than acting, regardless of his intentions and of foreign pressure, to actually rectify misperceptions in Romania about the Holocaust.[66]

In 2004 the Wiesel Commission presented its findings in Washington, Jerusalem, and Bucharest.[67] Its *Final Report* was made available on the Internet site of the Romanian Ministry of Foreign Affairs and also published as a book. Its findings were not startling for anyone who studies the Holocaust, but it was in fact the first official acknowledgment of the Romanian state that it bore responsibility for the victimization of the Jews in World War II. The report also contains important analyses of how the Holocaust had been minimized or denied during the Communist period and since, offering a harsh picture of the kind of victimology I have described in this book.

The presentations of the *Final Report* in Romania placed emphasis on officially acknowledging these atrocities and on future actions to better educate the Romanian people. Three important official steps were taken. First, the Holocaust would be recognized as an important historical event in official commemorations, and both the international date of Holocaust commemoration and the official date of the beginning of the 1941 Iași pogrom would be marked in schools and other official educational and cultural institutions. Second, an institute for the study of the Holocaust would be founded, complementing the regional centers for Jewish studies in Bucharest, Cluj, Iași, and Timișoara. Finally, the Ministry of Education would have to introduce the Holocaust as an important topic in secondary school curricula.

These recommendations blended classroom education for younger generations and historical research with commemorative elements, which were meant to make the past alive, to bring back into memory the horrific events of the Iași pogrom and Holocaust. By and large, however, this latter attempt has not been successful, for it has meant obligatory genuflections in parliament or at the graves of the pogrom victims rather than heartfelt participatory community events, much as in the early years of the Communist regime. These are not events widely publicized or attended. While the Jewish community participates broadly, the rest of the population in Romania doesn't share in these remembrances.

Counter-memories of victimization among others in Romania have in fact become an obstacle even in educating younger generations, those born after the fall of Communism, about the perpetrators of violence during World War II and their victims. The recommendation to teach optional courses on the Holocaust in secondary school has resulted in the creation of several such courses. The Ministry of Education, together with various foundations, has organized workshops for training teachers, providing them with the necessary teaching materials. While a broad majority of teachers have opted out, some brave souls have taken the opportunity to heart and offered such courses. Yet in one recent case, parents of the students asked to take this class revolted against the teacher, asking him to remove the course from the curriculum.[68]

Likewise, Emergency Order 13/2002 has had some supporters but also many foes among the broad public, from the inception and until today. In 2007, the pedestal of the Antonescu statute erected in the 1990s still stood in a very prominent location in Bucharest, by the Orthodox church built during World War II with the dictator's support. The pedestal still bore a plaque reading, "This holy abode, begun in these times of great decisions and great national pride for our country, is erected as permanent witness of the holy commitment that our church has always had to our nation and country. From the Founding Act, Marshal of Romania Ion Antonescu, 28 June 1943."[69] In a discussion about the continued presence of the plaque, people reacted with mostly mild to aggressive messages of support for rehabilitating the dictator: "Antonescu . . . deserves our respect for his remarkable military character . . . [as] he never used absolute power for selfish reasons. He deserves a statue and proper information about the black spots in his biography."[70] Only a few comments had anything critical to say about Antonescu.

Yet the same category of supporters of rehabilitating Antonescu as a great patriot used Emergency Order 13/2002 to suggest the need to bring down statues and other commemorative public markers for Hungarians who had been convicted of war crimes by the Peoples Tribunals in Romania after World War II. The case of Albert Wass (1908–1998) is a relevant one, similar to the work of rehabilitating prominent World War II Romanian intellectuals with radical right-wing leanings. After 1989 Wass, a talented writer and promoter of recreating pre-Trianon Hungary, became a cult figure among some Hungarians in Transylvania. Statues were raised to Wass and schools were named after him, even though the Peoples Tribunals had convicted him of war crimes in 1946. Based on this conviction, after Emergency Order 31/2002 was passed, the markers were all removed. Some among the Hungarian community have loudly protested against these actions, as Wass's conviction is clouded in controversy: he had fled to the United States at that point, and the U.S. government refused to extradite him due to lack of evidence. Yet several observers have shown that, at the very least, Wass was a radical right-wing nationalist, with fascist sympathies in his writings.[71]

Overall, localized efforts at rehabilitating such controversial figures in the name of patriotism and heroism during World War II continue in the face of legislative efforts by the Romanian government to condemn any kind of commemorations that celebrate perpetrators of war crimes. The democratization of education and even the best of intentions in moving past memories of victimization have not necessarily led to widening the spectrum of how older and younger generations see themselves connected to the events of World War II. The state has been only partially effective in raising the issue of responsibility beyond a symbolic level in parliament. Many ethnic Romanians in fact continue to view Jews in Romania as other than Romanians, just as some ethnic Hungarians look away from questions of guilt about the Holocaust vis-à-vis the Jewish population in Transylvania.

The debate over Liviu Librescu (1930–2007) is illustrative regarding the selective understanding of Jewish and Romanian identity through the prism of selective remembrances of World War II. On 18 April 2007, Romanian President Traian Băsescu (1951–) signed an order conferring the Star of Romania, the highest decoration offered by the Romanian state, to Librescu, who had died four days before in the massacre on the campus of Virginia Tech by turning himself into a human shield to save his students. As much a topic of media attention and Internet blogging in Romania as the tragic events surrounding his death was Librescu's own identity, in particular his Jewishness. Born in interwar Romania and a Holocaust survivor, Librescu returned to Romania and did not wish to leave the country until 1979—and then only after experiencing repeated frustrations at work and in society due to anti-Semitism. He lived in Israel for six years and then immigrated to the United States. Librescu, who had a Romanianized last name he never chose to change and a first name many in Romania would identify as ethnically Romanian, also taught his children Romanian at home, along with Hebrew and English. Like many other émigrés who longed for their home country, he also returned to Bucharest on several occasions after 1989 to see old friends and family, those with whom he had spent most of his life.

Librescu's movie-like life story brought renewed attention to the topic of the memory of the Holocaust in Romania and to questions of whether Jews from Romania are in fact Romanians or Jews born in Romania. Some of the most sympathetic messages of condolences and admiration toward Librescu's work and sacrifice contained strange statements of almost unconscious anti-Semitism, such as "I believe this professor was more Romanian than Jewish, otherwise I can't explain his courage."[72] Librescu's representation in the media and especially in Internet blogs consistently identified him as a Jew rather than a Romanian, as if such an identity would be hard to fathom. Many expressed sincere admiration for him and confessed to having cried when they read about his life. Especially for younger people, the experience of Romanian Jews during

World War II was rendered more real through the media focus on Librescu's tragic death. Yet even some who admired him felt it difficult to imagine Librescu as a hero in his actions, given the fact that he was Jewish. For some, his bravery and sacrifice were hard to comprehend as an attribute of a Jew, while for others it was difficult to equate his identity as victim of the Holocaust with the courage he displayed at Virginia Tech.

Librescu's case has opened up new avenues for discussing responsibility, victimhood, and courage in connection to World War II (usually used as a backdrop) and the Communist and post-Communist periods. Participants in various discussions about Librescu's identity often veered into explorations of what it would mean to be courageous as a citizen or politician either during the Communist period or since then.[73] Yet the events of the Holocaust, much better known today than they were twenty years ago, generally did not become a reference point in terms of what it means to survive as an oppressed individual or to suffer in fear of losing one's life. Instead, the referent was the Communist period. This suggests that for many people in Romania understanding the legacy of the Communist period has remained the more urgent moral matter. The violence of World War II has been rendered significant through the perspective of the post–World War II years. Post-memory has not worked diachronically, but rather in emotional and highly subjective, personalized ways. The emotional connection to particular references regarding victimization and heroic resistance has served for many as a center of gravity around which the meaning of other forms of violence during the twentieth century is articulated. As illogical as this seems from a strictly historical perspective, it is against this powerful emotive reality that education and public discussions by political and intellectual elites have had to struggle.

Post-Memory and Post-Communism

An important question to ponder for the two decades since the fall of Communism is: What kind of personal attachment, if any, do generations that came of age toward the end of the Communist period and since then have to the remembrances of the 1940–1953 period, as it was described in the previous chapter? The answer cannot be a comprehensive one, but tentatively it can be said that younger generations are still emotionally invested in specific personal narratives about those years, through the prism of the Communist years.

My approach to this issue of intergenerational remembrance builds on Marianne Hirsch's study, *Family Frames: Photography, Narrative, and Postmemory.* For over a decade now Hirsch has provoked historians, literary critics, artists, and a wide array of readers to broaden the concept of collective memory and to engage with different forms of constructing narratives about the past among generations after World

War II.[74] My own working definition of "post-memory" builds on Marianne Hirsch's: I see post-memory as the attempt by generations born after a particular event/series of events to reconstruct a picture/image of those events, based in part on recovered artifacts (words, images, objects) collected by witnesses of those events, and in part on narratives learned by these younger generations from those who were contemporaries of the events recounted. While this process of learning and self-identification might be dismissed as simply history, the term post-memory signals a specific emotional investment of those collecting and re-narrating the events. As Hirsch and others have observed about the Holocaust, and my own research has revealed, these younger generations sometimes live with renewed traumas, with intense emotional distress about the violence suffered by their parents or grandparents in the events these younger people are "remembering." They are first and foremost subjectively and emotionally invested in these events, they identify with them, even though they did not witness them. They also claim a unique kind of knowledge about these events, often identifying themselves as both witnesses (or the voices of witnesses now dead) and also experts in the history of the events narrated. This particularly complex mix of intellectual and personal affective link with the past makes post-memory a unique phenomenon of some, though not all, of the descendants born one or two generations after a particular event—in the case of my study, World War II to the beginning of the Communist regime.

Post-memory has been linked in analyses of remembering the Holocaust to questions of trauma that can be produced even when the person "witnessing" an event was never there, but in fact only learned about it subsequently and appropriated the persona of the victim in those circumstances. Romania and the other Communist countries of eastern Europe presented a context in which the wartime generation passed down its subterranean identification with victimhood to the generations born after 1940, which came of age under Communism. This first generation of children born after 1940 were themselves brought up on already solidified myths of resistance and oppression at the hands of the Communists, spun by their grandparents, and they themselves came to identify with the pain, the humiliations, and the victimhood of these elders.

How these memories have been transmitted to the post-1989 generations and appropriated by them in a way that shapes their sense of self is best illustrated in a collection fittingly entitled *Memory Exercises,* published in 1999 by the Civic Academy Foundation, the organization already discussed in this chapter in connection with the Sighet Memorial. Over one hundred young people aged eleven to eighteen responded to the question "What do I know about the years of Communism?" with tales of their grandparents and great-grandparents, describing various forms of oppression under

Communism and, on occasion, forms of courageous opposition these children take to be important moral lessons for the present. Many stories deal with episodes related to World War II, especially for those who had family in Bukovina and Bessarabia in 1940. The narratives told are similar to those of younger generations in the Baltics.[75] While they recount with horror and in great detail the arrival of the Soviets in 1940, they ignore the rest of the war and start the stories again in 1944:

> The repression started immediately after the act of reunion [of Bukovina with the Soviet Union, as part of Ukraine] in 1940. . . . The tragedy of 1 April 1941 shook up our entire region. It was a spring day; the crowds dressed in their Sunday best were slowly making their way toward the frontier. "And then that horrible massacre followed, where entire rows of people were gunned down. This was a true Katyn in daylight, wrote V. Levitschi, our own Katyn, the Romanians." . . . Then on 11 August 1944 another painful strike fell on our villagers. Again 16 people were mobilized in the forced labor units.[76]

The narrative presented by this eighteen-year-old girl about her grandparents and the fate of their village during World War II and afterward is undoubtedly how she heard things at home. She profoundly identifies with their fate, and orients her sense of victimization exclusively around the Soviet regime that deported tens of thousands of people from Bukovina during World War II and into the late 1940s. For her, the fate of Bukovina is synonymous with the fate of the Bukovinian Romanians, and she never looks beyond the localized ethnic group she is part of. What happened to the Ukrainians and Jews of Bukovina between 1940 and the late 1940s is of no consequence to her, even though she is aware of the suffering of other ethnic groups, as indicated by her reference to Katyn.

Another important facet of the seventy autobiographical texts published in this exercise at post-memory pertains to gender aspects of remembering and constructing narratives of heroism and victimization during the war. Over forty of the respondents, a majority of those selected for publication, are female. If one is to search this collection for any female models of morality, resistance to Communism, bravery, or even victimization, they are few and far between. In the case quoted above, the entire family of the young woman had been deported. Even though it was a family event, she remembers it as her grandfather's plight, as if, somehow, his suffering was both greater than and at the same time emblematic for that of his wife. This is not an unusual case, and it speaks to the assumptions of the generation that grew up in the 1980s and 1990s about what is historically representative about average people's lives, and who can speak for whom. Not unlike their predecessors, these young women have learned to think of themselves and their kin through the stories narrated about their male ancestors, even when they are narrated and remembered through female relatives.

I found a narrative of similar selective post-memory of victimization in a book published by a Romanian émigré to the United States after 1989. Though living in an environment replete with information about World War II and the Holocaust, in editing the autobiographical notes of his grandfather, Stanciu Stroia, Dan Duşleag preferred to focus his attention solely on the "Red Holocaust."[77] For this admiring grandchild of a man who suffered in Communist prisons, Stroia's experiences after World War II were the most important events of his life that needed to be recounted in detail. Duşleag grew up in Romania in the 1970s and '80s listening to these stories about his grandfather's life and profoundly identifying with them, wishing to become the voice of his deceased grandfather for the next generation.[78] In publishing his grandfather's memoirs, Duşleag wished to be both witness to events he felt he could faithfully represent and also a dispassionate storyteller to provide impartial historical contextualization for the next generation and especially unknowing American audiences. Having grown up in Communist Romania, Duşleag counted himself among the "educated consumers[s] of government-censored media, with an enhanced ability to read between the lines, to discern the truth."[79] Alas, this is a wishful self-representation of knowledge and objectivity, rather than a fact.

The trouble with his book, as with many post-memory exercises by those who grew up in the decades after 1989, is that it glosses over the period of World War II. A grandfather who served as an officer on the eastern front in Transnistria, in a region where there were Roma camps, and who traveled widely in the entire province during that period, could not have been completely oblivious to the atrocities happening there. It is possible the grandfather himself did not wish to talk about these issues. But why would the grandchild not ask questions about those years? The generation of the 1980s in West Germany had the courage to turn toward their parents and grandparents and to ask uncomfortable questions about their wartime years.[80] In the Romanian case, ancestor worship has been more the norm. In a country that was defined by polarities for so long, the notion that victims can also be perpetrators is not yet a possibility many want to contemplate.

A European Memory of War; or, Where To in the Memory Debates?

In the years preceding accession to the EU, the Romanian government took the initiative of beginning to celebrate Europe Day, both as a dress rehearsal for their accession and also as proof of their commitment to the idea of Europe as represented through the EU and Europe Day. The date selected for this commemoration is 9 May, which had served during the 1940s and early '50s to celebrate the Soviet liberation of eastern Europe from fascism. It had been a great deal easier for bureaucrats in Brussels to identify this day as Europe Day, and to speak about anti-fascism and thankfulness to the Soviet Army, as they had less problematic remembrances of the Soviets at the end of the war. For most western Europeans, the end of the war meant freedom and democracy. De-Nazification was, if incomplete, an uncontroversial issue in terms of how it proceeded and its ultimate goals. But that was not the case for many of the countries hoping to join the EU in the early 2000s, Romania included. From Riga to Bucharest, 9 May was a painful reminder of Soviet occupation and imperialism. For many it wasn't even the end of the war, but the shift to a conflict between the occupied countries and the Soviet imperialist aims in the area.

In the past year a discussion has emerged about the possibility for constructing a European Memory of World War II.[81] Many participants in this conversation have expressed concerns that citizenship in the European Union cannot become fully universal in terms of values, rights, and responsibilities without some consensus about the meaning and legacies of World War II for the generations that grew up in the postwar period. This discussion makes a great deal of sense in terms of the initial goals of the Common Market, as expressed by Robert Schumann in 1950.[82] The founding of the European Common Market was in fact directly linked to the memories of horror and destruction of the 1940s and to the desire not to repeat such actions again. In order not to repeat them, most agreed that a vigilant commemoration of those horrors was in order.

Yet this recent discourse has avoided dealing with the consequences of World War II for the other side of Europe. In fact, until the present, a triumphalist post–Cold War mood has continued in terms of the normative lines of discussing World War II and its legacies in Europe. The western European periodization and debates about victims and perpetrators, as well as forgotten voices (most recently, in discussions about colonial troops) have dominated, and they have had a more direct impact on how a European Memory of World War II would become embodied in cultural commemorative practices that are EU-wide. A perfect example is 9 May.

But for people in Romania, Estonia, Latvia, Lithuania, Poland, the Czech Republic, Slovakia, Hungary, Slovenia, and Bulgaria, these matters are far more complicated. Politicians have followed their own interests in trying to secure greater benefits for their post-Communist investment-hungry countries, meanwhile painting themselves good patriots. They celebrate Europe Day on 9 May, but they have also contributed to victimist partial remembrances of World War II in their own countries. The post-Communist states have not successfully become institutions that can combine moral leadership in commemorating the wars of the twentieth century with representing the complex memories of their citizens in a multilayered fashion.

In the meantime, many parents and grandparents are continuing to present to younger generations counter-memories that contradict the official narratives presented on TV, in politicized commemorations, and in history courses. These counter-narratives are a more integral part of public discourse than had been the case under the Communist period, as the media pays attention to them. Yet it is not clear that people look to government officials to truly represent their own emotional investment in such counter-narratives. On the contrary, with other public outlets for communicating about the past, many people look away from official commemorations for how they wish to remember the events of World War II. The contradictory, unreconciled counter-memories of victimization continue in the post-Communist generation, as fresh now as they were forty years ago. This is a reality with which the EU and intellectuals dreaming of one European Memory of World War II have to come to terms. The shadow of the Communist period is still overwhelmingly present over remembrances of the war; the post-Communist transition period is not over. Nor does it point toward an unquestionable embrace of democratic principles of citizenship, of responsibility and tolerance, especially given the way in which many people are still avoiding questions of responsibility for wartime atrocities, preferring instead to focus on heroic victimhood.

Notes

Preface

1. John Bodnar, *Remaking America: Public Memory, Commemoration, and Patriotism in the Twentieth Century* (Princeton, N.J.: Princeton University Press, 1992); John Gillis, ed., *Commemorations: The Politics of National Identity* (Princeton, N.J.: Princeton University Press, 1996); Jay Winter and Emmanuel Sivan, eds., *War and Remembrance in the Twentieth Century* (Cambridge: Cambridge University Press, 1999); Jay Winter, *Sites of Memory, Sites of Mourning: The Great War in European Cultural History* (Cambridge: Cambridge University Press, 1995); Catherine Merridale, *Night of Stone: Death and Memory in Twentieth-Century Russia* (New York: Viking, 2001); Nina Tumarkin, *The Living and the Dead: The Rise and Fall of the Cult of World War II in Russia* (New York: Basic Books, 1994); Gaines M. Foster, *Ghosts of the Confederacy: Defeat, the Lost Cause, and the Emergence of the New South, 1865 to 1913* (New York: Oxford University Press, 1987); Robert Moeller, *War Stories: The Search for a Usable Past in the Federal Republic of Germany* (Berkeley: University of California Press, 2003); Vieda Skultans, *The Testimony of Lives: Narrative and Memory in Post-Soviet Latvia* (London: Routledge, 1998); Rubie Watson, ed., *Memory, History, and Opposition under State Socialism* (Santa Fe, N.M.: School of American Research Press, 1994).

2. Winter, *Sites of Memory.*

3. Paul Connerton, *How Societies Remember* (Cambridge: Cambridge University Press, 1989).

4. Katherine Verdery, *The Political Lives of Dead Bodies: Reburial and Postsocialist Change* (New York: Columbia University Press, 1999).

5. Gail Kligman, *The Wedding of the Dead: Ritual, Poetics, and Popular Culture in Transylvania* (Berkeley: University of California Press, 1988).

6. Bruce Lincoln, *Death, War, and Sacrifice: Studies in Ideology and Practice* (Chicago: University of Chicago Press, 1991); Mircea Eliade, *De la Zalmoxis la Genghis-Han: Studii comparative despre religiile și folclorul Daciei și Europei Orientale,* trans. Maria and Cezar Ivănescu (Bucharest: Humanitas, 1995); Simion Florea Marian, *Înmormântarea la români: Studiu etnografic* (Bucharest: Editura Grai și Suflet, Cultura Națională, 1995); Loring M. Danforth, *The Death Rituals of Rural Greece* (Princeton, N.J.: Princeton University Press, 1982); Ștefan Dorondel, *Moartea și apa. Ritualuri funerare, simbolism acvatic și structura lumii de dincolo în imaginarul țărănesc* (Bucharest: Paideia, 2004).

7. See also Thomas C. Wolfe, "Past as Present, Myth, or History? Discourses of Time and the Great Fatherland War," in Claudio Fogu, W. Kansteiner, and R. Lebow, eds., *The Politics of Memory in Postwar Europe* (Durham, N.C.: Duke University Press, 2006), 249–283.

8. Patrice Dabrowski, *Commemorations and the Shaping of Modern Poland* (Bloomington: Indiana University Press, 2004); Jan Gross, *Neighbors: The Destruction of the Jewish Community in Jedwabne, Poland* (New York: Penguin, 2002); Jan Gross, Tony Judt, and Istvan Deák, eds., *The Politics of Retribution in Europe: World War II and its Aftermath* (Princeton, N.J.: Princeton University Press, 2000); Christoph Mick, "The Dead and the Living: War Veterans and Memorial Culture in East Galicia," paper presented at the conference "Sacrifice and Regeneration: The Legacy of the Great War in Interwar Eastern Europe," Southampton, UK, September 2007.

9. Maria Bucur and Nancy Wingfield, eds., *Staging the Past: The Politics of Commemoration in Habsburg Central Europe, 1848 to the Present* (West Lafayette, Ind.: Purdue University Press, 2001); Katherine R. Jolluck, *Exile and Identity: Polish Women in the Soviet Union during World War II* (Pittsburgh, Pa.: University of Pittsburgh Press, 2002); Nancy M. Wingfield and Maria Bucur, eds., *Gender and War in Twentieth-Century Eastern Europe* (Bloomington: Indiana University Press, 2006); Nancy Wingfield, *Flag Wars and Stone Saints: How the Bohemian Lands Became Czech* (Cambridge, Mass.: Harvard University Press, 2007); Wolfgang Höepken, "War, Memory and Education in a Fragmented Society: The Case of Yugoslavia," *East European Politics and Societies* 13, no. 1 (1999): 190–227; Maria Todorova, "The Mausoleum of Georgi Dimitrov as Lieu de Mémoire," *Journal of Modern History* 78, no. 2 (June 2005): 374–411; Snezhana Dimitrova, "'The Experienced War' and Bulgarian Modernization in the Inter-War Years," *Rethinking History* 6, no. 1 (April 2002): 15–34; Maria Todorova, ed., *Balkan Identities: Nation and Memory* (New York: New York University Press, 2004); Stef Jansen, "The Violence of Memories: Local Narratives of the Past after Ethnic Cleansing in Croatia," *Rethinking History* 6, no. 1 (April 2002): 77–93.

10. Jan Gross, "Introduction," in Gross, Judt, and Deak, eds., *Politics of Retribution,* 23.

11. Peter Kenez, *Hungary from the Nazis to the Soviets: The Establishment of the Communist Regime in Hungary, 1944–1948* (Cambridge: Cambridge University Press, 2006). On the issue of periodization in his book, see also Holly Case, "Suspending the Axe," http://www.h-net .org/reviews/showrev.php?id=13689 (accessed 2 January 2009); Tony Judt, *Postwar: A History of Europe since 1945* (New York: Penguin, 2005).

12. On the exceptionalism of the Romanian "frozen" Stalinist model, see Vladimir Tismăneanu, *Stalinism for All Seasons: A Political History of Romanian Communism* (Berkeley: University of California Press, 2003); for a critical view of the totalitarian paradigm, see Slavoj Žižek, *Did Somebody Say Totalitarianism?* (London: Verso, 2001); David Crowley and Susan E. Reid, "Style and Socialism: Modernity and Material Culture in Post-War Eastern Europe," in Susan E. Reid and David Crowley, eds., *Style and Socialism: Modernity and Material Culture in Post-War Eastern Europe* (Oxford: Berg, 2000), 1–24; Domenico Losurdo, "Towards a Critique of the Category of Totalitarianism," *Historical Materialism* 12, no. 2 (2004): 25–55.

13. David Kideckel, *The Solitude of Collectivism: Romanian Villagers to the Revolution and Beyond* (Ithaca, N.Y.: Cornell University Press, 1993); Dorin Dobrincu, ed., *Țărănimea și puterea: Procesul de colectivizare a agriculturii în România (1949–1962)* (Iași: Polirom, 2005);

Katherine Verdery, *Transylvanian Villagers: Three Centuries of Political, Economic, and Ethnic Change* (Berkeley: University of California Press, 1983).

14. There are a few examples, such as Constantin Rădulescu-Zoner and Beatrice Marinescu, *Bucureștii în anii primului război mondial, 1914–1918* (Bucharest: Editura Albatros, 1993), of historians actually using some of these autobiographical writings, but they do not offer a nuanced engagement with this specific genre of historical evidence.

15. I am fully aware that "censorship" often takes place in societies that do not live under authoritarian governments, and in fact, there is clear evidence of direct government interference in the 1938–1944 period in Romania as well. But, while the government controlled some publishing houses and newspapers, others existed that were privately owned, and people could seek them out to make their voices heard. During the Communist regime in Romania all publishing was directly controlled by the state, from publishing houses to access to ink, paper, printing presses, and sales. It is this obvious lack of choice on the part of authors in a market controlled by the state that leads me to consider all published work during the Communist period in Romania as either explicitly or at least implicitly collaborationist with the government.

16. This project, largely sponsored by the Aspera Foundation, consisted of working with a group of fifteen students in sociology from Transylvania University and with Ștefan Ungureanu, my local faculty collaborator for the project, and first training them in oral history techniques, including selecting subjects for their interviews and helping them design questionnaires. Subsequently, the students recorded interviews that were discussed among the group. The students used these discussions to improve their subsequent interviews and prepare for follow-up interviews.

17. Marian, *Înmormântarea.*

18. For an excellent discussion on this topic, see Daniel J. Cohen and Roy Rosenzweig, "Web of Lies? Historical Knowledge on the Internet," *First Monday* 10, no. 12 (December 2005), available at http://firstmonday.org/issues/issue10_12/cohen/index.html (accessed 2 January 2009).

Introduction

1. Claus Leggewie, "Equally Criminal? Totalitarian Experience and European Memory," first published in *Transit: Europäische Revue,* submitted to *Eurozine* on 1 June 2006, available at http://www.eurozine.com/articles/2006-06-01-leggewie-en.html (accessed 2 January 2009).

2. "European Histories: Towards a Grand Narrative?" http://www.eurozine.com/comp/focalpoints/eurohistories.html (accessed 6 February 2009).

3. As seen, for instance, in Leggewie, "Equally Criminal?"; Adam Phillips, "The Forgetting Museum," first published in *Index on Censorship* 34, no. 2 (2005), available at http://www.eurozine.com/articles/2005-06-24-phillips-en.html?filename=article/2005-06-24-phillips-en (accessed 2 January 2009); Timothy Snyder, "Balancing the Books," *Index on Censorship* 34, no. 2 (2005), also in *Eurozine,* available at http://www.eurozine.com/articles/2005-05-03-snyder-en.html (accessed 2 January 2009).

4. See, for instance Lev Gudkov, "The Fetters of Victory: How the War Provides

Russia with its Identity," posted on *Eurozine* on 3 May 2005, available at http://www.eurozine
.com/articles/2005-05-03-gudkov-en.html (accessed 2 January 2009); and Adam Krzeminski,
"As Many Wars as Nations," published initially in *Polytika* and referenced in the *Eurozine*
exchange, available in English at http://www.signandsight.com/features/96.html (accessed
2 January 2009).

5. There are important examples of how this trend is changing in both research and
writing. Jeremy King, Padraic Kenny, Mark Pittaway, Maureen Healey, and Holly Case, for
instance, have offered important examples of how incorporating the social and the local into
research about wider social and political processes helps in rethinking the larger narratives
that have prevailed in the historiography of eastern Europe, best exemplified in the work of
Peter Sugar.

6. I am using here this contrasting distinction as developed conceptually by John Bodnar
in *Remaking America*.

7. For a recent set of critical essays about this perspective, see Sorin Antohi, Balázs Trenc-
sényi, and Péter Apor, eds., *Narratives Unbound: Historical Studies in Post-Communist Eastern
Europe* (New York: Central European University Press, 2007). A classic analysis highly critical
of the modernist impulses of states created since the nineteenth century is James C. Scott,
Seeing Like a State: How Certain Schemes to Improve the Human Condition Have Failed (New
Haven: Yale University Press, 1998).

8. Jeremy King, "The Nationalization of East Central Europe: Ethnicism, Ethnicity, and
Beyond," in Bucur and Wingfield, eds., *Staging the Past,* 112–152; Rogers Brubaker et al.,
Nationalist Politics and Everyday Ethnicity in a Transylvanian Town (Princeton, N.J.: Princeton
University Press, 2006).

9. One of the most obvious such lacunae is the lack of interest in gender analysis, despite
opportunities to do so, especially in the past twenty years. For a discussion of the state of
gender analysis in eastern European historiography, see Maria Bucur "An Archipelago of
Stories: Gender History in Eastern Europe," *American Historical Review* 113, no. 5 (December
2008): 1375–1389.

10. Is there such a thing as "non-local" community, a colleague of mine asked? My response
is yes, people can certainly identify themselves with non-local communities, for instance
religiously. By using the apparently redundant "local communities" I am trying to draw attention to the quality of spatial proximity and potential intimacy that defines these particular
communities. The intimacy cannot be assumed; as I show below, intense conflicts can emerge
within local communities because of spatial proximity.

11. See, for instance, Dabrowski, *Commemorations;* Bucur and Wingfield, eds., *Staging the
Past;* Wingfield, *Flag Wars;* and various contributions by Nikolai Vukov, Nancy Wingfield,
Petra Svoljšak, Christoph Mick, Eva Fisli, Franz Horváth, Melissa Bokovoy, Mark Cornwall,
and Martin Zückert at the conference "Sacrifice and Regeneration: The Legacy of the Great
War in Interwar Eastern Europe," Southampton, UK, September 2007.

12. See Irina Livezeanu, *Cultural Politics in Greater Romania: Regionalism, Nation Building,
and Ethnic Struggle, 1918–1930* (Ithaca, N.Y.: Cornell University Press, 1995).

13. See, for instance, Gérard Emilien et al., *Memory: Neuropsychological, Imaging, and
Psychopharmacological Perspectives* (Hove, UK, New York: Psychology Press, 2004); Raymond P. Kesner and Joe L. Martinez, Jr., eds., *Neurobiology of Learning and Memory,* 2nd ed.

(Amsterdam: Academic Press, 2007); Naoyuki Osaka, Robert H. Logie, and Mark D'Esposito, eds., *The Cognitive Neuroscience of Working Memory* (Oxford: Oxford University Press, 2007).

14. Petri Hautaniemi, Helena Jerman, and Sharon MacDonald, eds., *Anthropological Perspectives on Social Memory* (Münster: Lit, 2006); Donna Coch, Kurt W. Fischer, and Geraldine Dawson, eds., *Human Behavior, Learning, and the Developing Brain: Typical Development* (New York: Guilford Press, 2007); R. Reed Hunt and James B. Worthen, eds., *Distinctiveness and Memory* (Oxford, New York: Oxford University Press, 2006); Eric Jensen, *Teaching with the Brain in Mind,* 2nd rev. ed. (Alexandria, Va.: Association for Supervision and Curriculum Development, 2005).

15. Herbert S. Terrace and Janet Metcalfe, eds., *The Missing Link in Cognition: Origins of Self-Reflective Consciousness* (Oxford: Oxford University Press, 2005).

16. The concept became an important site of research and debate in memory studies in the United States after the translation of Maurice Halbwachs' important study, *Les cadres sociaux de la mémoire* (Paris: Presses Universitaires de France, 1952). The English translation appeared as *On Collective Memory* (Chicago: University of Chicago Press, 1992). Since then, a great number of studies have employed this concept as well as contested it. See, for instance, John Gillis, ed., *Commemorations: The Politics of National Identity* (Princeton, N.J.: Princeton University Press, 1996), and more recently Fogu, Kansteiner, and Lebow, eds., *Politics of Memory;* and Jeffrey K. Olick, *The Politics of Regret: On Collective Memory and Historical Responsibility* (New York: Routledge, 2007). For a critical approach to the concept, see Jay Winter, *Remembering War: The Great War and Historical Memory in the Twentieth Century* (New Haven, Conn.: Yale University Press, 2006); and Noa Gedi and Yigal Elam, "Collective Memory: What is it?" *History and Memory* 8, no. 1 (1996): 30–50. A good recent overview of the literature on collective memory is to be found in Wulf Kansteiner, "Finding Meaning in Memory: A Methodological Critique of Collective Memory Studies," *History and Theory* 41 (May 2002): 179–197.

17. James Fentress and Chris Wickham, *Social Memory* (Oxford: Blackwell, 1992).

18. In their persuasively argued essay, "Beyond 'Identity,'" Frederick Cooper and Rogers Brubaker argue against the usefulness of the term "identity." Their critique focuses on the fuzziness of the term, which renders "identity" confusing rather than enlightening in analyzing social and political processes. As an alternative, they suggest the use of process-oriented words—"identification," "categorization," or "self-understanding—as well as notions that connote the desire for belonging in how people understand themselves—"commonality," "connectedness," and "groupness." Though I subscribe entirely to the notion that self-understanding is constructed socially, and I use these terms suggested by the two authors, I think that "identity" as a term invoked by historical actors themselves is in fact a useful cultural concept. I take such self-representations as important sites for historical analysis, to be viewed critically, but at the same time understood based on how they were deployed by those actors themselves, rather than on the basis of analytical usefulness in the social sciences. See Rogers Brubaker and Frederick Cooper, "Beyond 'Identity,'" *Theory and Society* 29, no. 1 (2000): 1–47.

19. James Zull, *The Art of Changing the Brain: Enriching Teaching by Exploring the Biology of Learning* (Sterling, Va.: Stylus, 2002); Kevin Falvey, "Memory and Knowledge of Content," in Susana Nuccetelli, ed., *New Essays on Semantic Externalism and Self-Knowledge* (Cambridge, Mass.: MIT Press, 2003), 219–240.

20. Bessel A. van der Kolk, Alexander C. McFarlane, and Lars Weisaeth, eds., *Traumatic Stress: The Effects of Overwhelming Experience on Mind, Body and Society* (New York: Guilford Press, 1996); J. Douglas Bremner and Charles R. Marmar, eds., *Trauma, Memory and Dissociation* (Washington, D.C.: APA Press, 1998). On the debates over "false" versus "true" recovered traumatic memory, see Martin Gardner, "The False Memory Syndrome," *Skeptical Inquirer* (Summer 1993): 370–375; Elizabeth Loftus, "The Reality of Repressed Memories," *American Psychologist* 48 (May 1993): 518–537; and John F. Kihlstrom, "The Trauma-Memory Argument," *Consciousness and Cognition* 4, no. 1 (March 1995): 63–67.

21. Pierre Nora, for instance, distinguished clearly, if simplistically, between the process of constructing historical knowledge and the act of remembering. For a critical discussion of Nora, see Kansteiner, "Finding Meaning."

22. Marianne Hirsch, *Family Frames: Photography, Narrative, and Postmemory* (Cambridge, Mass.: Harvard University Press, 1997); Fogu, Kansteiner, and Lebow, eds., *Politics of Memory*; James Young, *At Memory's Edge: After-Images of the Holocaust in Contemporary Art and Architecture* (New Haven, Conn.: Yale University Press, 2000); Jay Winter and Emmanuel Sivan, "Setting the Framework," in Jay Winter and Emmanuel Sivan, eds., *War and Remembrance*, 6–39.

23. Joan Scott, "The Evidence of Experience," *Critical Inquiry* 17 (Summer 1991): 773–797.

24. Halbwachs, *On Collective Memory*.

25. Joan Scott has taken up the issue of representativeness on a number of occasions, most powerfully in the recent book *Parité! Sexual Equality and the Crisis of French Universalism* (Chicago: University of Chicago Press, 2005).

26. My comments relate exclusively to the European front. There has been a great deal more attention paid to the "comfort women" in East Asia during World War II. A few historians have uncovered, however, valuable sites for examining this particular angle of the wartime experience: Jolluck, *Exile and Identity*, and "The Nation's Pain and Women's Shame: Polish Women and Wartime Violence," in Wingfield and Bucur, eds., *Gender and War*, 193–219; Elizabeth D. Heineman, "The Hour of the Woman: Memories of Germany's 'Crisis Years' and West German National Identity," *American Historical Review* 101, no. 2 (1996): 354–395; Claudia Opitz, "Von Frauen im Krieg zum Krieg gegen Frauen: Krieg, Gewalt und Geschlechterbeziehungen aus historischer Sicht," *L'homme: Europäische Zeitschrift für feministische Geschichts-wissenschaft* 3 (1992): 31–44; Lisa A. Kirschenbaum, "'The Alienated Body': Gender Identity and the Memory of the Siege of Leningrad," in Wingfield and Bucur, eds., *Gender and War*, 220–234.

27. For parallel attitudes in Poland see Jolluck, *Exile and Identity*; Anamaria Orla-Bukowska, "New Threads on an Old Loom: National Memory and Social Identity in Postwar and Post-Communist Poland," in Fogu, Kansteiner, and Lebow, eds., *Politics of Memory*, 177–209.

28. Anna Livia, *Queerly Phrased: Language, Gender, and Sexuality* (New York: Oxford University Press, 1997); Deborah Cameron, *The Myth of Mars and Venus* (Oxford: Oxford University Press, 2007); Mary Bucholtz, A. C. Liang, and Laurel A. Sutton, eds., *Reinventing Identities: The Gendered Self in Discourse* (New York: Oxford University Press, 1999); Deborah Cameron and Don Kulick, eds., *The Language and Sexuality Reader* (London, New York: Routledge, 2006); Deborah Tannen, *Gender and Discourse* (New York: Oxford University Press, 1994).

29. Maria Bucur, "Women's Stories as Sites of Memory: Remembering Romania's World Wars," in Wingfield and Bucur, eds., *Gender and War*, 171–192.

30. See, for instance, *Exerciții de memorie: Biblioteca Sighet* (Bucharest: Academia Civică, 1999). The volume contains sixty-five short memory exercises, in which young men (twenty) and women (forty-five) discuss their memories of growing up under Communism and post-Communism and invoke narratives of suffering and sacrifice in their communities. Most narratives focus on family members, and the heroes are predominantly male, even for women narrators.

31. Kligman, *Wedding of the Dead*.

32. For a recent articulation of this view of successful indoctrination, see Richard Ned Lebow, "The Memory of Politics in Postwar Europe," in Fogu, Kansteiner, and Lebow, eds., *Politics of Memory*, 14.

33. Antony Polonsky and Joanna Michlick, eds., *The Neighbors Respond: The Controversy over the Jedwabne Massacre in Poland* (Princeton, N.J.: Princeton University Press, 2004); Antony Polonsky, ed., *"My Brother's Keeper": Recent Polish Debates on the Holocaust* (London: Routledge, 1989); Gross, *Neighbors*.

1. Death and Ritual

1. Louis-Vincent Thomas, "La mort: un objet anthropologique," in M. Mafessoli and C. Rivière, eds., *Une anthropologie des turbulences: Hommage à Georges Balandier* (Paris: Berg International Editeurs, 1985), 171.

2. Marian, *Înmormântarea*, 79 (emphasis mine).

3. Ibid., 254.

4. Ibid.

5. In the Orthodox religious calendar and tradition, every Saturday is in principle a day on which the dead are to be specifically commemorated through special liturgies. For Catholics, too, there are holidays throughout the year when the names of the dead are to be remembered in the liturgy, and Judaic practice also reserves specific parts of the religious service, as well as days of the religious calendar, when the dead are to be remembered.

6. Winter, *Sites of Memory*, 5.

7. For details on the earlier periods that represent the background to my discussion here, see Toader Nicoară, *Transilvania la începuturlie timpurilor moderne (1680–1800): Societate rurală și mentalități colective* (Cluj: Presa universitară clujeană, 1997), esp. chapter 5; and Ştefan Lemny, *Sensibilitate și istorie în secolul XVIII românesc* (Bucharest: Editura Meridiane, 1990).

8. The anthropological and historical literature on the topic of the cult of the dead is too vast to cite here comprehensively, but some early and more recent titles include: Bertram S. Puckle, *Funeral Customs: Their Origin and Development* (London: T. Werner Laurie, 1926); Philippe Ariès, *Western Attitudes Toward Death: From the Middle Ages to the Present*, trans. Patricia M. Ranum (Baltimore, Md.: Johns Hopkins University Press, 1975); Danforth, *Death Rituals*; Donald Kyle, *Spectacles of Death in Ancient Rome* (New York: Routledge, 1998); Nancy Isenberg and Andrew Burstein, eds., *Mortal Remains: Death in Early America* (Philadelphia: University of Pennsylvania Press, 2003); Magdalena Midgley, *The Monumental Cemeteries*

of Prehistoric Europe (Stroud: Tempus, 2005); Matsunami Kodo, *International Handbook of Funeral Customs* (Westport, Conn.: Greenwood Press, 1998); Brain de Vries, ed., *End of Life Issues: Interdisciplinary and Multidimensional Perspectives* (New York: Springer, 1999); Antonius C. G. M. Robben, ed., *Death, Mourning and Burial: A Cross-Cultural Reader* (Malden, Mass.: Blackwell, 2004); Glennys Howarth and Peter C. Jupp, eds., *The Changing Face of Death: Historical Accounts of Death and Disposal* (New York: St. Martin's Press, 1997); Sarah Tarlow, *Bereavement and Commemoration: An Archaeology of Mortality* (Oxford: Blackwell, 1999); Hille Haker, Susan Ross, and Marie-Therese Wacker, eds., *Women's Voices in World Religions* (London: SCM Press, 2006); Valerie A. Kivelson and Robert H. Greene, eds., *Orthodox Russia: Belief and Practice under the Tsars* (University Park: Pennsylvania State University Press, 2003); Karen Farrington, *Historical Atlas of Religions* (New York: Checkmark Books, 2002).

9. Louis-Vincent, "La mort," 171.

10. Nicoară, *Transilvania*, 17–28.

11. On urbanization in these areas, see Peter Hanák, *The Garden and the Workshop*, new ed. (Princeton, N.J.: Princeton University Press, 1999); Gábor Gyáni, "Uses and Misuses of Public Space in Budapest, 1873–1914," in Thomas Bender and Carl Schorske, eds., *Budapest and New York: Studies in Metropolitan Transformation, 1870–1930* (New York: Russell Sage Foundation, 1994); Larry Wolff, "Dynastic Conservatism and Poetic Violence in Fin-de-Siècle Cracow: The Habsburg Matrix of Polish Modernism," *American Historical Review* 106, no. 3 (June 2001): 735–764; Livezeanu, *Cultural Politics;* John Lukács, *Budapest 1900: A Historical Portrait of a City and Its Culture* (New York: Grove, 1994); Hillel Kieval, *The Making of Czech Jewry: National Conflict and Jewish Society in Bohemia, 1870–1918* (New York: Oxford University Press, 1988); Nathan Wood, "Becoming Metropolitan: Cracow's Popular Press and the Representation of Modern Urban Life, 1900–1915" (PhD diss., Indiana University, 2004).

12. My definition of eastern Europe encompasses the Russian empire lands in Europe, Austria-Hungary, and the (post-)Ottoman lands in the Balkans.

13. On these general developments, see Keith Hitchins, *The Rumanians, 1774–1866* (Oxford: Clarendon, 1996); and *Rumania, 1866–1947* (Oxford: Clarendon, 1994); Nicoară, *Transilvania,* esp. 15–17. The division among Christian denominations in Transylvania in 1850 was as follows: 31.5 percent Greek-Catholic (all Romanian); 31 percent Orthodox (virtually all Romanian); 14 percent Calvinists (all Hungarian); 10.6 percent Catholics (mostly Hungarian); 9.6 percent Lutherans (all German); and 2.2 percent Unitarians (all Hungarian); see Krista Zach, "Toleranța religioasă și construirea stereotipurilor într-o regiune multiculturală: 'Biserici populare' în Transilvania," in Asociația de Studii Transilvane Heidelberg, eds., *Transilvania și sașii ardeleni în istoriografie* (Sibiu: Editura hora și Arbeitskreis für Siebenbürgische Landeskunde e. V. Heidelberg, 2001), 83. There are no similar statistics for the Jewish communities in Transylvania during the same period. For the Romanian state, the percentage of Orthodox believers was even higher, counting almost 90 percent of the total population, with a smattering of Catholics, Protestants, Muslims, and a more sizeable Jewish population.

14. Dorondel, *Moartea și apa. Ritualuri.*

15. Corina Turc, "Nation et confession dans l'opinion des représentants de l'Église orthodoxe et gréco-catholique en Transylvanie (dans la seconde moitié du XIXe siècle)," in Maria Crăciun and Ovidiu Ghitta, eds., *Ethnicity and Religion in Central and Eastern Europe* (Cluj:

Cluj University Press, 1995), 292–301; Nicolae Bocşan, Ion Lumperdean, Ioan-Aurel Pop, eds., *Etnie şi confesiune în Transilvania (sec. XIII–XIX)* (Oradea: Fundaţia "Cele Trei Crişuri," 1994).

16. Stella Hryniuk, *Peasants with Promise: Ukrainians in Southeastern Galicia 1880–1900* (Edmonton: University of Alberta, 1991), 23–24.

17. During this period, when Transylvania was part of the Hungarian Crown, Hungarians were overall a majority population in that larger territory, but constituted a minority, albeit sizable, in Transylvania proper. These demographic contexts are very significant for the kinds of commemorative and other nationalist debates that took place in Transylvania after 1918. See Peter Hanák, Peter F. Sugar, and Tibor Frank, eds., *History of Hungary* (Bloomington: Indiana University Press, 1994).

18. Victor Neuman, *Istoria Evreilor din Romania* (Timişoara: Editura Amarcord, 1996); Ezra Mendelsohn, *The Jews of East Central Europe between the World Wars* (Bloomington: Indiana University Press, 1983).

19. See Crăciun and Ghitta, eds., *Ethnicity and Religion.*

20. On the early history of the puritanical religious services and rituals among Calvinists (the larger denomination of Protestants in Transylvania), see Graeme Murdock, *Calvinism on the Frontier, 1600–1660: International Calvinism and the Reformed Church in Hungary and Transylvania* (Oxford: Clarendon, 2000), esp. 153–170; on tensions between Protestants and Catholics in nineteenth-century Hungary (including Transylvania), see *History of the Protestant Church in Hungary, from the Beginning of the Reformation to 1850; with Special Reference to Transylvania,* trans. Rev. J. Craig (London: J. Nisbet and Co., 1854).

21. Tunde Zentai, "The Sign-Language of Hungarian Graveyards," *Folklore* 90, no. 2 (1979): 131–140.

22. For several brief mentions of the significance of the Day of the Dead for German Catholics, see Smaranda Vultur, ed., *Germanii din Banat prin povestirile lor* (Bucharest: Paideia, 2000). For instance, the Archbishop of Banat, Msgr. Sebastian Kräuter, mentions visiting his village rarely, but most often "in November, when we think about our dead ones," 89.

23. See Marian, *Înmormântarea;* for a twentieth-century personal account, see Adrian Ciubotaru, "România mea catholică," available at http://adrian.filozofie.ro/romania-mea-catolica/ (published 23 November 2007; accessed 4 January 2009).

24. Many Jews migrated to Transylvania to escape the pogroms in the Russian empire.

25. See Neuman, *Istoria Evreilor;* I. Kara-Schwartz, *Mărturii din veacuri: Din istoria evreilor în România* (Bacău, 1947); M. A. Halevy, *Comunităţile evreieşti din Iaşi şi Bucureşti pînă la 1821* (N.p.: Institutul de istorie evreo-română, 1931); Moshe Carmilly-Weinberger, *Istoria evreilor din Transilvania* (Bucharest: Editura enciclopedică, 1994).

26. Michael Stanislawski, *Murder in Lemberg: Politics, Religion, and Violence in Modern Jewish History* (Princeton, N.J.: Princeton University Press, 2007); Yisraèl Bartal, *The Jews of Eastern Europe, 1772–1881* (Philadelphia: University of Pennsylvania Press, 2005); Gotthold Rhode, *Juden in Ostmitteleuropa von der Emanzipation bis zum Ersten Weltkrieg* (Marburg/Lahn: J. G. Herder-Institut, 1989); Michael Riff, *The Face of Survival: Jewish Life in Eastern Europe Past and Present* (London: V. Mitchell, 1992); Mendelsohn, *Jews of East Central Europe.*

27. Samuel C. Heilman, *When a Jew Dies: The Ethnography of a Bereaved Son* (Berkeley: University of California Press, 2001) and Maurice Lamm, *The Jewish Way in Death and*

Mourning (New York: Jonathan David, 2000). For the Romanian context, see Iulius Barasch, "Evreii din Moldova şi Valachia: Studiu istorico-social," in Lya Benjamin, ed., *Evreii din România în texte istoriografice: Antologie* (Bucharest: Hasefer, 2002), 42 [originally published as "Etwas über die gegenwärtigen Verhältnisse der Juden in den beiden Donaufürstenhümern (Moldau-Walachei)," *Jahrbuch für Israeliten* (Vienna: 1854)]; and Ana-Maria Caloianu, *Istoria comunităţii evreieşti din Alba Iulia* (Bucharest: Hasefer, 2006), 256–257.

28. Some of the oldest recorded examples in this area were the chevra kadisha in Oradea/ Nagyvárad, established in 1753; see Téreza Mózes, *Evreii din Oradea* (Bucharest: Hasefer, 1997), 36–38. In the city of Arad/Árad, the chevra kadisha was established in 1835; see "Statutele Confreriei Sacre (Hevra Kadisa) din Arad, 1835, februarie 9–1838, februarie, Arad," in Ladislau Gyémánt and Lya Benjamin, eds., *Izvoare şi mărturii referitoare la evreii din Romania*, vol. 3, part 2 (Bucharest: Hasefer, 1999), 82.

29. See Barasch, "Evreii"; on Jewish holidays as celebrated in Romania during the twentieth century, see Smaranda Vultur, ed., *Memoria salvată: Evreii din Banat, ieri şi azi* (Iaşi: Polirom, 2002); and Ayşę Gürsan-Salzmann and Laurence Salzmann, *The Last Jews of Rădăuţi* (New York: Dial Press, 1983), 116–129.

30. Daniel Unowsky, *The Pomp and Politics of Patriotism: Imperial Celebrations in Habsburg Austria, 1848–1916* (West Lafayette, Ind.: Purdue University Press, 2005).

31. Crăciun and Ghitta, eds., *Ethnicity and Religion.*

32. Robert P. Geraci and Michael Khodarkovsky, eds., *Of Religion and Empire: Missions, Conversion, and Tolerance in Tsarist Russia* (Ithaca, N.Y.: Cornell University Press, 2001).

33. William Oldson, *A Providential Anti-Semitism: Nationalism and Policy in Nineteenth Century Romania* (Philadelphia: American Philosophical Society, 1991); Neuman, *Istoria Evreilor;* Leon Volovici, *Ideologia naţionalistă şi "problema evreiască" în România anilor '30* (Bucharest: Humanitas, 1995).

34. Keith Hitchins, *Rumania, 1866–1947* (Oxford: Clarendon, 1994).

35. Ibid., 12–13.

36. Ibid., chapter 3.

37. Philip G. Eidelberg, *The Great Rumanian Peasant Revolt of 1907* (Leiden: Brill, 1974); Constantin Corbu, *Răscoala ţăranilor de la 1888* (Bucharest: Editura ştiinţifică şi enciclopedică, 1978).

38. Henry Roberts, *Rumania: Political Problems of an Agrarian State* (New Haven, Conn.: Yale University Press, 1951); David Mitrany, *The Land and the Peasant in Rumania: The War and Agrarian Reform, 1917–21* (New York: Greenwood Press [1968]).

39. Oldson, *Providential Anti-Semitism;* Neuman, *Istoria Evreilor.*

40. I want to thank Victor Neumann for help in identifying this figure. Estimates for that period range between 200,000 and 250,000. My choice of using the larger number is based on the fact that, due to the harsh anti-Semitic policies in Romania regarding citizenship for its Jewish inhabitants, the total Jewish population was systematically underrepresented in all statistics.

41. Carol Iancu, *Jews in Romania, 1866–1919: From Exclusion to Emancipation* (Boulder, Colo.: East European Monographs, 1996); Ileana Popovici, *Evreii din România în secolul XX, 1900–1920: Fast şi nefast într-un răstimp istoric; Documente şi mărturii* (Bucharest: Hasefer, 2003). This pattern was similar to that in neighboring Austria-Hungary. See Mária Kovács,

Liberal Professions and Illiberal Politics: Hungary from the Habsburgs to the Holocaust (Washington, D.C.: Wilson Center Press, 1994); Heiko Haumann, *A History of East European Jews* (Budapest: Central European University Press, 2002); Mendelsohn, *Jews of East Central Europe.*

42. Neuman, *Istoria Evreilor.*

43. After World War I women gained more civil rights through the Civil Code of 1932, but they were only granted education-based limited voting rights (in municipal elections) in 1929, and had to wait until the Communist takeover for full political rights. But the Communist regime handed them voting rights when political enfranchisement had become virtually meaningless, as all elections were manipulated by the Communist Party. See Paraschiva Câncea, *Mişcarea pentru emanciparea femeii în România* (Bucharest: Editura politică, 1976); Ghizela Cosma, *Femeile şi politica în România: Evoluţia dreptului de vot în perioada interbelică* (Cluj-Napoca: Presa universitară clujeană, 2002); Ştefania Mihăilescu, *Emanciparea femeii române: Studiu şi antologie de texte. Vol. II (1919–1948)* (Bucharest: Editura ecumenică, 2005); Maria Bucur, "Calypso Botez: Gender Difference and the Limits of Pluralism in Interwar Romania," *Jahrbücher für Geschichte und Kultur Südosteuropas* 3 (2001): 63–78.

44. Constantin Iordachi, "From the 'Right of the Natives' to 'Constitutional Nationalism': The Making of Romanian Citizenship, 1817–1919" (PhD diss., Central European University, 2003). The thesis is coming out in book format as *The Making of Nation-State Citizenship in Southeastern Europe: The Case of Romania, 1817–1919* (forthcoming with the CEU Press, Book Series: Pasts Incorporated CEU Studies in the Humanities); Maria Bucur, "Between Liberal and Republican Citizenship: Romanian Feminists and Nationalism, 1880–1918," *Aspasia* 1 (2007): 84–102.

45. Bucur, "Between Liberal and Republican Citizenship."

46. Carmen Tănăsoiu, *Iconografia regelui Carol I* (Timişoara: Editura Amarcord, 1999).

47. On Queen Victoria, see David Cannadine, "The Context, Performance and Meaning of Ritual: The British Monarchy and the 'Invention of Tradition,' c. 1820–1977," in Eric Hobsbawm and Terence Ranger, eds., *The Invention of Tradition* (Cambridge: Cambridge University Press, 1992), 101–164; on responses, see Unowsky, *Pomp and Politics of Patriotism.*

48. Grigore Ionescu, *Istoria arhitecturii în România,* vols. 1–2 (Bucharest: Editura Academiei R.S.R., 1963–1964); Mihai Haret, *Castelul Peleş: Monografie istorică, geografică, turistică, pitorească, descriptivă a Castelelor Regale din Sinaia cu împrejurimile lor* (Bucharest: Cartea Românească, 1924).

49. My estimates are based on a compilation published in Communist Romania in 1983, at the height of the Ceauşescu regime's obsession with proper commemorative memorials for Romania's glorious nationalist past. Though such slants are a reason to be concerned about the reliability and completeness of this compilation (especially since the Communists themselves tore down some important monuments, something I'll return to in subsequent chapters), my own travels through some of the areas covered by the compilation enabled me to verify the reliability of those descriptions. Therefore, I feel comfortable offering these estimates as close to the historical facts. The volume is Col. Dr. Florian Tucă and Mircea Cociu, *Monumente ale anilor de luptă şi jertfă* (Bucharest: Editura militară, 1983).

50. The Michael the Brave statue was erected in 1874, while the Heliade Rădulescu one was built in 1879, bearing the commemorative personal message: "To Ion Heliade Rădulescu, the

grateful Romanians, 1802–1872." See Tucă and Cociu, *Monumente,* 79–81 (Michael the Brave) and 88 (Ion Heliade Rădulescu).

51. Nancy Wingfield, "Statues of Emperor Joseph II as Sites of German Identity," in Bucur and Wingfield, eds., *Staging the Past,* 178–208; Dabrowski, *Commemorations;* Unowsky, *Pomp and Politics of Patriotism.*

52. Tănăsoiu, *Iconografia regelui Carol I.*

53. David Jeffreys, ed., *Views of Ancient Egypt since Napoleon Bonaparte: Imperialism, Colonialism and Modern Appropriations* (Oxford: Berg, 2006); Todd B. Porterfield, *The Allure of Empire: Art in the Service of French Imperialism, 1798–1836* (Princeton, N.J.: Princeton University Press, 1998).

54. Ibid.; Malte Fuhrmann, *Der Traum vom deutschen Orient: Zwei deutsche Kolonien im Osmanischen Reich 1851–1918* (Frankfurt am Main: Campus, 2006); Ian Baucom, *Out of Place: Englishness, Empire, and the Locations of Identity* (Princeton, N.J.: Princeton University Press, 1999).

55. On the history of art and architecture in this area, see I. D. Ştefănescu, *Iconografia artei bizantine și a picturii feudale românești* (Bucharest: Editura meridiane, 1973); Corina Nicolescu, *Moştenirea artei bizantine în România* (Bucharest: Editura meridiane, 1971); G. Ionescu, *Istoria Arhitecturii;* I. D. Ştefănescu, *Arta feudală în Ţările Române: Pictura murală și icoanele de la origini pînă în secolul al XIX-lea* (Timişoara: Editura Mitropoliei Banatului, 1981); Gheorghe Sasarman, ed., *Gîndirea estetică în arhitectura românească: a doua jumătate a secolului XIX și prima jumătate a secolului XX* (Bucharest: Editura meridiane, 1983).

56. For an indepth discussion of these influences on Romanian art and architecture, see Carmen Popescu, *Le style national roumain: Construire une nation à travers l'architecture, 1881–1945* (Rennes: Presses universitaires de Rennes, 2004); Shona Kallestrup, *Art and Design in Romania 1866–1927: Local and International Aspects of the Search for National Expression* (Boulder, Colo.: Eastern European Monographs, 2006).

57. Some scholars identify the trend starting in the 1880s of using such western European symbols and the overall style in building most of the massive public building projects (such as the Palace of the National Bank, the Palace of Justice, etc.) with the influence of especially French architects and engineers, such as A. Galleron and P. Gottereau. See, for instance, Georgică Mitrache, *Tradiție și modernism în arhitectura românească* (Bucharest: Editura universitară Ion Mincu, 2002), 60. Though these individuals undoubtedly played a major role, they were in fact commissioned to introduce these western European styles at the request of Romanians who wished to encourage this style. The role of the financial backers and commissioners in such endeavors cannot be viewed as secondary to the artistic symbols and style that emerged in the final products. See C. Popescu, *Le style national roumain.*

58. There is virtually no difference in terminology and visual representation between vultures and eagles in Romanian language and iconography. But eagles (in Romanian, the proper but rarely used term is *acvilă*) are very rare birds in Romania, while vultures are much more common, so that most people use the term *vultur* to mean either an eagle (such as the Carpathian eagle, a regional species) or the ugly vultures that devour carcasses of dead animals.

59. The Walachian vulture is to be found on the pedestal of the statue of Michael the Brave, erected in 1874 in Bucharest, to commemorate the brief union of Walachia, Moldavia, and Transylvania under this ruler at the beginning of the seventeenth century.

60. C. Popescu, *Le style national roumain;* Florentin Popescu, *Ctitorii brâncovenești,* 2nd rev. ed. (Târgoviște: Editura Bibliotheca, 2004); Cristian Moisescu, *Arhitectura epocii lui Matei Basarab* (Bucharest: Editura meridiane, 2002).

61. The terminology employed on this marker, *"neatîrnare"* rather than *"independență,"* is also an important inflection, as it represents a less foreign-sounding option, which at that time was used more frequently. Over the twentieth century *"independență"* came to be the preferred term.

62. Initially identified as the Charles I Bridge, it was subsequently renamed the Saligny Bridge to honor the architect who built it. During the Communist period it was renamed the Cernavodă Bridge, after the town nearby. Today it is known by any of these three names, though the Romanian railroad corporation uses Cernavodă in its official schedules, while acknowledging its initial name.

63. Symbology of this sort acted as a central component of political action from the very beginning of his rule. The Star of Romania remains the highest decoration to be offered to any person, military or civilian, for exceptional services brought to the state, and only a small number of people have received it.

64. Ion Safta, Rotaru Jipa, Tiberiu Velter, and Floricel Marinescu, *Decorații românești de război, 1860–1947* (Bucharest: Editura Universitaria, 1993).

65. Of princely background, daughter of Hermann and Marie of Wied, Elisabeth met Charles I in Berlin in 1861 and was married to him in 1869. Elisabeth, Queen of Romania, *From Memory's Shrine: The Reminiscences of Carmen Sylva,* trans. Edith Hopkirk (Philadelphia: J. B. Lippincott, 1911).

66. Safta et al., *Decorații,* 102.

67. *Pametnitsi na bălgaro-ruskata i bălgaro-săvetskata druzhba v Plovdivski okrăg* (Plovdiv, 1980); M. Raichev, *Muzei, starini i pametnitsi v Bulgaria* (Sofia: Nauka i izkustvo, 1981); for recent analyses, see Maria Todorova, "Creating a National Hero: Vasil Levski in Bulgarian Public Memory," in Sabrina P. Ramet, James R. Felak, and Herbert J. Ellison, eds., *Nations and Nationalisms in East-Central Europe, 1806–1948: A Festschrift for Peter Sugar* (Bloomington, Ind.: Slavica, 2002), 159–181.

68. Snezhana Dimitrova and Elena Tacheva, eds., *Рицари и Мироворци на Балканите. Походи, Преселения н Поксонничетво* (Blagoevgrad, Bulgaria: Neofit Riilski University, 2001); Melissa Bokovoy, "Scattered Graves, Ordered Cemeteries: Commemorating Serbia's Wars of National Liberation, 1912–1918," in Bucur and Wingfield, eds., *Staging the Past,* 236–254.

69. *The Other Balkan Wars: A 1913 Carnegie Endowment Inquiry in Retrospect* (Washington, D.C.: Carnegie Endowment for International Peace, 1993).

70. Bokovoy, "Scattered Graves."

71. Though the relationship between the state and its subjects was not as distant and top-down in states such as Great Britain (at least in the metropole), France, and the United States, for instance, or even in some Latin American states, this description does fit the post-Ottoman states in the Balkans that tried to create European-style monarchies, including by means of installing a European (non-indigenous) monarch, as was the case in Greece, Bulgaria, and Romania. Even in the Habsburg and Russian empires, much older states with a wider reach and policies implemented throughout their territories, in the peripheral

areas under discussion here—Bessarabia and Transylvania—and in particular in the area of cultural policy, these states were weakly represented.

72. Luminiţa Murgescu, *Între "bunul creştin" şi "bravul român." Rolul şcolii primare în construirea identităţii naţionale româneşti (1831–1878)* (Iaşi: Editura A '92, 1999); Charles Jelavich, *South-Slav Nationalism: Textbooks and Yugoslav Union before 1914* (Columbus: Ohio University Press, 1994).

73. *Istoria învăţământului din Romania, Vol. 2 (1821–1918)* (Bucharest: Editura didactică şi pedagogică, 1993); Murgescu, *Între "bunul creştin,"* 38.

74. Unowsky, *Pomp and Politics of Patriotism;* see also Bucur and Wingfield, eds., *Staging the Past.*

75. On nationalism in Austria-Hungary, see Robert Kann, *The Multinational Empire: Nationalism and National Reform in the Habsburg Monarchy, 1848–1918,* 2 vols. (New York: Columbia University Press, 1950); Jeremy King, *Budweisers into Czechs and Germans: A Local History of Bohemian Politics, 1848–1948* (Princeton, N.J.: Princeton University Press, 2002); Unowsky, *Pomp and Politics of Patriotism;* Bucur and Wingfield, eds., *Staging the Past.*

76. Unowsky, *Pomp and Politics of Patriotism;* Daniel Unowsky, "Reasserting Empire: Habsburg Imperial Celebrations after the Revolutions of 1848–1849," in Bucur and Wingfield, eds., *Staging the Past,* 13–45.

77. Unowsky, *Pomp and Politics of Patriotism,* esp. chapter 5.

78. Liviu Maior, "Contribuţii la istoria raportului biserică-putere în Transilvania (1867–1918)," in Nicolae Bocşan, Nicolae Edroiu, and Vasile Vesa, eds., *Convergenţe europene: Istorie şi societate în epoca modernă* (Cluj-Napoca: Editura Dacia, 1993), 174–182.

79. Magda Teter, *Jews and Heretics in Catholic Poland: A Beleaguered Church in the Post-Reformation Era* (Cambridge: Cambridge University Press, 2006).

80. Maior, "Contribuţii," and Crăciun and Ghitta, eds., *Ethnicity and Religion.*

81. Brian Porter, *When Nationalism Began to Hate: Imagining Modern Politics in Nineteenth-Century Poland* (New York: Oxford University Press, 2000); Andrzej Walicki, *Philosophy and Romantic Nationalism: The Case of Poland* (Oxford: Clarendon Press, 1982).

82. Dabrowski, *Commemorations;* Keely Stauter-Halstead, "Rural Myth and the Modern Nation: Peasant Commemorations of Polish National Holidays, 1879–1910," in Bucur and Wingfield, eds., *Staging the Past,* 153–177.

83. Alice Freifeld, "The Cult of March 15: Sustaining the Hungarian Myth of Revolution, 1849–1999," in Bucur and Wingfield, eds., *Staging the Past,* 255–285; King, "Nationalization"; Brubaker et al., *Nationalist Politics.*

84. Steven Beller, "Kraus's Firework: State Consciousness Raising in the 1908 Jubilee Parade in Vienna and the Problem of Austrian Identity," in Bucur and Wingfield, eds., *Staging the Past,* 46–71.

85. Ibid.; István Deák, *Beyond Nationalism: A Social and Political History of the Habsburg Officer Corps, 1848–1918* (New York: Columbia University Press, 1990).

86. Deák, *Beyond Nationalism.*

87. Beller, "Kraus's Firework"; Lawrence Cole, "Patriotic Celebrations in Late-Nineteenth- and Early-Twentieth-Century Tirol," in Bucur and Wingfield, eds., *Staging the Past,* 75–111.

88. Brubaker et al., *Nationalist Politics.*

89. Freifeld, "Cult of March 15."

90. Livezeanu, *Cultural Politics;* Ion Nistor, *Românii și rutenii din Bucovina* (Iași: Do-MinoR, 2001 [1915]); Andrei Corbea-Hoisie, *La Bucovine: Éléments d'histoire politique et culturelle* (Paris: Institut d'études slaves, 2004); Paul Robert Magocsi, *The Roots of Ukrainian Nationalism: Galicia as Ukraine's Piedmont* (Toronto: University of Toronto Press, 2002). Bukovina has continued to be treated as a backwater in much of the historiography on Ukraine. In Timothy Snyder's *The Reconstruction of Nations: Poland, Ukraine, Lithuania, Belarus, 1569–1999* (New Haven, Conn.: Yale University Press, 2003), it doesn't appear in the discussion of Austrian-ruled Ukraine.

91. See Bucur and Wingfield, eds., *Staging the Past.*

92. Urban areas saw more direct clashes, as Jeremy King aptly shows in his *Budweisers.* But for the rural populations, even those living close to these foci of antagonism, life remained more peaceful.

93. For the Hungarians, the Battle of Mohács was the main event whose importance was validated through such a commemoration; see Eva Fisli, "Hungarian Remembrance of the Great War in Mohács," paper presented at the conference "Sacrifice and Regeneration," Southampton, UK, September 2007; for commemorations of 1848–1849, see Freifeld, "Cult of March 15."

94. Wolff, "Dynastic Conservatism"; Wood, "Becoming Metropolitan"; Unowsky, *Pomp and Politics of Patriotism,* 88–94.

95. Mark von Hagen, Jane Burbank, and Anatolyi Remnev, eds., *Russian Empire: Space, People, Power, 1700–1930* (Bloomington: Indiana University Press, 2007); Austin Jersild, *Orientalism and Empire: North Caucasus Mountain Peoples and the Georgian Frontier, 1845–1917* (Montreal: McGill-Queen's University Press, 2002); Valerie Kivelson, *Cartographies of Tsardom: The Land and its Meanings in Seventeenth-Century Russia* (Ithaca, N.Y.: Cornell University Press, 2006); Karen Barkey and Mark von Hagen, eds., *After Empire: Multiethnic Societies and Nation-building; The Soviet Union and the Russian, Ottoman, and Habsburg Empires* (Boulder, Colo.: Westview Press, 1997); Daniel Brower, *Russia's Orient: Imperial Borderlands and Peoples, 1700–1917* (Bloomington: Indiana University Press, 1997).

96. Merridale, *Night of Stone,* 22.

97. Larry Wolff, *The Enlightenment and the Orthodox World* (Athens: Institute for Neohellenic Research, National Hellenic Research Foundation, 2001); Barbara Jelavich, *Russia's Balkan Entanglements, 1806–1914* (Cambridge: Cambridge University Press, 1991).

98. Vlad Georgescu, *Political Ideas and the Enlightenment in the Romanian Principalities, 1750–1831* (Boulder, Colo.: East European Quarterly, 1971); Hitchins, *The Rumanians;* Frederick Kellogg, *The Road to Romanian Independence* (West Lafayette, Ind.: Purdue University Press, 1995); Kivelson, *Cartographies;* Richard Clogg, *A Concise History of Greece,* 2nd ed. (Cambridge: Cambridge University Press, 2002); B. Jelavich, *Russia's Balkan Entanglements.*

99. This was a view disputed by the Patriarch of Constantinople and the Ottoman Sultan. Yet the millet system did place the Patriarch of Constantinople among employees of the Ottoman state, and therefore wholly dependent upon the goodwill of the sultan. Since the eighteenth century, Russian rulers had challenged the notion that the Patriarch of Constantinople could indeed play such an autonomous and effective role on behalf of the Orthodox population/millet.

100. Merridale, *Night of Stone,* 26–29.

101. Ibid., 27–28.

102. Ibid., chapter 2.

103. Ibid., 62–63.

104. Gillis, ed., *Commemorations;* Hobsbawm and Ranger, eds., *Invention of Tradition;* Pierre Nora, gen. ed., *Realms of Memory: Rethinking the French Past* (New York: Columbia University Press, 1996); Winter, *Sites of Memory;* Winter and Sivan, eds., *War and Remembrance.*

105. Hobsbawm and Ranger, eds., *Invention of Tradition.*

106. Bernard Cohn, "Representing Authority in Victorian India," in Hobsbawm and Ranger, eds., *Invention of Tradition,* 165–210; Anne McClintock, *Imperial Leather: Race, Gender, and Sexuality in the Colonial Contest* (New York: Routledge, 1995).

107. Terence Ranger, "The Invention of Tradition in Colonial Africa," in Hobsbawm and Ranger, eds., *Invention of Tradition,* 211–262; Graham Johnson, *Social Democratic Politics in Britain, 1881–1911* (Lewiston, N.Y.: E. Mellen Press, 2002).

108. Benedict Anderson, *Imagined Communities: Reflections on the Origin and Spread of Nationalism* (London: Verso, 1983); Anthony D. Smith, *Myths and Memories of the Nation* (Oxford: Oxford University Press, 1999); Ernest Gellner, *Encounters with Nationalism* (Oxford: Blackwell, 1994).

109. Here I am conveniently *not* counting the vast colonial populations of Britain overseas, which would have dwarfed the white populations in the British Isles proper. My assessment is based on looking toward the British Isles and not India and the African territories.

110. This is the assumption that underlies Jay Winter's analysis in *Sites of Memory,* which, in view of the important differences between these better studied cases and the eastern European examples presented here, appears more relevant for the French and British cases than for "modern Europe" as a whole. See Winter, *Sites of Memory,* 80.

111. Susan Grayzel, *Women's Identities at War: Gender, Motherhood, and Politics in Britain and France during the First World War* (Chapel Hill: University of North Carolina Press, 1999); Nicoletta F. Gullace, *The Blood of our Sons: Men, Women, and the Renegotiation of British Citizenship during the Great War* (New York: Palgrave Macmillian, 2002); David Silbey, *The British Working Class and Enthusiasm for War, 1914–1916* (London, New York: Frank Cass, 2005).

112. For an excellent comparative analysis of the failures of these three empires before and during World War I, see Aviel Roshwald, *Ethnic Nationalism and the Fall of Empires: Central Europe, Russia, and the Middle East, 1914–1923* (London, New York: Routledge, 2001).

113. The Romanian and Hungarian nationalist historiographies have made a great deal out of the nationalist movement among the educated elites of these areas. While the Hungarians were relatively more educated than the Romanians (for institutional reasons highlighted in this chapter), most people among these ethnic groups were still illiterate and lived in small rural communities that lacked adequate connections to urban areas to enable such penetration of nationalist ideology and cultural practices.

114. Unowsky, *Pomp and Politics of Patriotism;* Beller, "Kraus's Firework"; Cole, "Patriotic Celebrations."

115. C. Jelavich, *South-Slav Nationalism;* Eleni Bastea, *The Creation of Modern Athens: Planning the Myth* (New York: Cambridge University Press, 1999); Todorova, ed., *Balkan Identities;* John R. Lampe and Mark Mazower, eds., *Ideologies and National Identities: The*

Case of Twentieth-Century Southeastern Europe (Budapest, New York: Central European University Press, 2004).

116. Such arguments were fodder for a scholarly and political feud between Romanians and Hungarians over Transylvania, whose legitimate authority both ethnic groups have claimed emphatically and uncompromisingly over the past two and a half centuries. One such work is Dardu Nicolaescu-Plopşor and Wanda Wolski, *Elemente de demografie şi ritual funerar la populaţiile vechi din România* (Bucharest: Editura Academiei Republicii Socialiste România, 1975). Though possibly suspicious in its conclusions, as they focus on the ethnic dimension of these burial rituals, the research is still reliable in its descriptive content. Much of it deals with details of material culture and is quite nuanced both in drawing definitive conclusions and in stating the inability to do so, due to insufficient evidence.

117. Ibid., 212–217.

118. Eve Levin, *Sex and Society in the World of the Orthodox Slavs, 900–1700* (Ithaca, N.Y.: Cornell University Press, 1989); Haker, Ross, and Wacker, eds., *Women's Voices;* Kivelson and Greene, eds., *Orthodox Russia;* on sati practices, see Lata Mani, *Contentious Traditions: The Debate on Sati in Colonial India* (San Francisco: University of California Press, 1998).

119. Catherine Merridale expresses the same sense of frustration in *Night of Stone,* yet she also chooses to embrace the challenge of piecing together at least a partial picture of the traces present from the late nineteenth century onward. See Merridale, *Night of Stone,* 23–24.

120. Ibid., 31–32; Vuk Karadžić, *Narodne srpske poslovice i druge različne, kao i one u običaj uzete riječi* (Cetinje: U Narodnoj štampariji, 1836) and *Songs of the Serbian People: From the Collections of Vuk Karadzic* (Pittsburgh, Pa.: University of Pittsburgh Press, 1997); Edith Durham, *The Burden of the Balkans* (London: E. Arnold, 1905); Rebecca West, *Black Lamb and Grey Falcon: A Journey through Yugoslavia* (New York: Penguin, 1994).

121. See, for instance, El. Sevastos, *Călătorii prin Ţara Românească* (Iaşi, 1888); T. T. Burada, *Datinele poporului român la înmormântări* (Iaşi, 1882); R. H. Kaindl and Al. Manstyrski, *Die Rutenen in der Bukowina,* vol. 2 (Cernowitz: Theil, 1890); D. Stănescu, "Obiceiuri religioase," *Biserica ortodoxă română* 9 (1885): 330; Vasile Alecsandri, *Poezii populare ale românilor* (Bucharest, 1866); A. Lambrior, "Obiceiuri şi credinţe la români: Înmormântările," *Convorbiri literare* 9 (1875): 151.

122. Simion Fl. Marian, *[Trilogia vieţii,] I: Nunta la români* (Bucharest: Tipografia Carol Göbl, 1890); *II: Naşterea la români* (Bucharest: Tipografia Carol Göbl, 1892); *III: Înmormântarea la români* (Bucharest: Tipografia Carol Göbl, 1892). The books were reprinted in 1995, with the same title, by the Grai şi Suflet—Cultura Naţională publishing house. It is this reprinted edition that I use here.

123. See, for instance, Marian, *Înmormântarea,* 32, where he cites Ovid to suggest that there are continuities between Roman practices of closing the eyes of the dead person and those of "our ancestors."

124. Ibid., 7; see also the rest of chapter 1, "Signs of Death."

125. The incantations used prevalently religious symbols and Christian language in defining sin, evil, and redemption, but also incorporated pagan elements in the mix.

126. Marian, *Înmormântarea,* 6.

127. Ibid., 19.

128. Ibid., 36.

129. Ibid.

130. In Romanian, though the generic third person plural is masculine, and passive voice often makes it impossible to discern the gender of the actor in a specific action, there are plural and singular third person forms to indicate actions performed exclusively by women.

131. "Iar cum le-au cumpărat, îndata se apucă mai multe femei, care se află de faţă, de croiesc şi cos veştmintele trebuincioase şi apoi se îmbracă peste schimburi cu veştmintele mai sus amintite." Marian, Înmormântarea, 47 and 48 respectively for this quote.

132. Kligman, Wedding of the Dead; and Dorondel, Moartea şi apa. Ritualuri, esp. chapter 6.

133. Marian, Înmormântarea, 45; italics mine for emphasis of the vague passive voice, which points implicitly to women's work.

134. Ibid., 79. Italics mine.

135. Ibid. A similar distant role seems prevalent in other rural settings where the Orthodox Christian communities lived.

136. Bette Denich, "Sex and Power in the Balkans," in M. Rosaldo and L. Lamphere, eds., Woman, Culture, and Society (Stanford, Calif.: Stanford University Press, 1974), 243–262; Anna Caraveli-Chaves, "Bridge between Worlds: The Greek Women's Lament as Communicative Event," Journal of American Folklore 93 (1980): 129–157; Danforth, Death Rituals; Merridale, Night of Stone, 41; for a comparison further afield, see Nadia Seremetakis, The Last Word: Women, Death, and Divination in Inner Mani (Chicago: University of Chicago Press, 1991).

137. This meal for the deceased has been more elaborate in some areas (such as Walachia) than others (such as the Greek Islands, where the name for this offering was makario, meaning "that which is blessed"), but the meaning, both evocative of taking communion (the meal often includes a special sweet bread and wine that have been blessed by the priest) and also more generally symbolic of keeping the memory of the dead person alive, is similar. The participants in this ritual are to say "may God forgive him/her" upon receiving the food. This is said to help release the soul of the dead person. See Danforth, Death Rituals, 43.

138. Marian, Înmormântarea, 221.

139. Kligman, Wedding of the Dead; Aurora Liiceanu, Nici alb, nici negru: Radiografia unui sat românesc, 1948–1998 (Bucharest: Nemira, 2000); Aurora Liiceanu, Valurile, smintelile, păcatele: Psihologiile românilor de azi (Bucharest: Nemira, 1998); Claude Karnoouh, Rituri şi discursuri versificate la ţăranii maramureşeni: A trăi şi a supravieţui în România comunistă (Cluj: Editura Dacia, 1998); Valentina Marinescu, Muncile casnice în satul românesc actual: Studii de caz (Iaşi: Polirom, 2002).

140. Câncea, Mişcarea; Bucur, "Calypso Botez"; Michel Ciocâlteau, Les Régimes matrimoniaux dans le projet de code civil roumain (Paris: Rousseau et Cie, 1936); in the Habsburg ruled territories, women gained more civil rights, including the right to administer their dowry, in the nineteenth century, but these rights were not protected as well in the rural backwaters of Transylvania as they were in urban areas.

141. Anamaria Iuga, "Rolul femeilor în constituirea identităţii maramureşene," in Ghizela Cosma, Enikő Magyari-Vincze, Ovidiu Pecican, eds., Prezenţe feminine: Studii despre femei în România (Cluj-Napoca: Editura Fundaţiei DESIRE, 2002), 347–374.

142. Sabrina P. Ramet, ed., Gender Politics in the Western Balkans: Women and Society in Yugoslavia and the Yugoslav Successor States (University Park: Pennsylvania State University

Press, 1999); Anelia Kassabova-Dincheva, *Migration und Familie: Familienforschung und Politik (Am Beispiel Bulgariens)* (Sofia: Variant 2000, 2002).

143. Crăciun and Ghitta, eds., *Ethnicity and Religion;* David Ransel and Bozena Shallcross, eds., *Polish Encounters, Russian Identity* (Bloomington: Indiana University Press, 2005); Gyula Kornis, *Education in Hungary* (New York: Teachers College, Columbia University, 1932); Mihály Bucsay, *A protestantizmus története Magyarországon, 1521–1945* (Budapest: Gondolat, 1985); D. A. Kerr, ed., *Religion, State and Ethnic Groups* (New York: New York University Press, 1992).

144. Rochelle L. Millen, *Women, Birth, and Death in Jewish Law and Practice* (Hanover, N.H.: Brandeis University Press, 2004); Judith R. Baskin, ed., *Jewish Women in Historical Perspective,* 2nd ed. (Detroit, Mich.: Wayne State University Press, 1998); Anita Diamant, *Saying Kaddish: How to Comfort the Dying, Bury the Dead, and Mourn as a Jew* (New York: Schocken Books, 1998); Leona Anderson and Pamela Dickey Young, eds., *Women and Religious Traditions* (New York: Oxford University Press, 2004).

145. My translation of the term comes from the better-known Russian case. In Romanian, the word *troiţă* means both this type of three-pronged cross and also a type of sled pulled by three horses. The term in Romanian comes also from Slavonic.

146. A *waqf* is a charitable and religious trust in Islamic societies. Peter Sugar, *Southeastern Europe under Ottoman Rule, 1354–1804* (Seattle: University of Washington Press, 1977); Nicoară Beldiceanu, *Le monde ottoman des Balkans (1402–1566): Institutions, société, économie* (London: Variorum Reprints, 1976); L. Carl Brown, ed., *Imperial Legacy: The Ottoman Imprint on the Balkans and the Middle East* (New York: Columbia University Press, 1996); Bokovoy, "Scattered Graves."

147. Marian, *Înmormântarea.*

148. Ştefănescu, *Arta feudală.*

149. Dabrowski, *Commemorations;* Stauter-Halstead, "Rural Myth"; Lemny, *Sensibilitate.*

2. Mourning, Burying, and Remembering the War Dead

1. *Cultul eroilor noştri* 3, no. 3 (July 1922): 9.

2. Constantin Kiriţescu, *Istoria războiului pentru întregirea României, 1916–1919,* 2 vols., 3rd rev. ed. (Bucharest: Editura ştiinţifică şi enciclopedică, 1989); Ion Mamina, *Regalitatea în România: 1866–1947: Instituţia monarhică, Familia regală, domniile, contribuţii la dezvoltarea instituţiilor culturale, monumentele de for public, cronologie* (Bucharest: Compania, 2004); Dumitru Ogăşanu, *Legitimitatea Marii Uniri: 1 Decembrie 1918* (Oradea: Editura Universităţii din Oradea, 2002).

3. The figures are based on Department of Defense statistics, as cited at www.infoplease .com/ipa/A0004617.html (accessed 5 January 2009). Most calculations of the war casualties look at the combatants as divided into the two fighting camps—the Allies and the Central Powers. But in terms of the experience and memorialization of actual deaths and violent events on the ground, dividing the participation and casualties between the eastern versus western fronts also makes sense. There are difficulties in doing so with any precision, as Germany, Great Britain, and Italy fought on both of these fronts. For my calculations here I counted Italy as fighting in the west, Germany divided equally between east and west,

and Great Britain as fighting overwhelmingly (8 million out of 8.9) in the west. This is by no means an exact division, but it helps give a good approximation of the ratios between participation and losses in the eastern versus western fronts. I counted Austria-Hungary's figures only toward the eastern front.

4. H. P. Willmott, *World War I* (London: Dorling Kindersley, 2003), 307. Estimates for East versus West were calculated along the lines described in footnote 4.

5. Jay Winter, *The Experience of World War I* (New York: Oxford University Press, 1995), 207.

6. This obvious disparity can be observed in both academic and more popular tracts. See Willmott, *World War I* and Winter, *Experience of World War I*.

7. Nicolae Petrescu-Comnene, *The Great War and the Romanians: Notes and Documents on World War 1* (Iaşi: Centre for Romanian Studies, 2000); the Mărăşeşti battle had around 72,000 casualties on the two sides (around 350,000 Romanian soldiers died in the war).

8. Willmott, *World War I*, 307.

9. Kiriţescu, *Istoria războiului*.

10. Hunt Tooley, *The Western Front: Battleground and Home Front in the First World War* (New York: Palgrave, 2003).

11. Susan Grayzel, *Women and the First World War* (London, New York: Longman, 2002); Maria Bucur, "Between the Mother of the Wounded and the Virgin from Jiu: Romanian Women and the Gender of Heroism during the Great War," *Journal of Women's History* 12, no. 2 (Summer 2000): 30–56; Maureen Healy, *Vienna and the Fall of the Habsburg Empire: Total War and Everyday Life in World War I* (New York, Cambridge: Cambridge University Press, 2004).

12. Richard Stites, *The Women's Liberation Movement in Russia: Feminism, Nihilism, and Bolshevism, 1860–1930*, new rev. ed. (Princeton, N.J.: Princeton University Press, 1991); Barbara Alpern Engel, *Women in Russia, 1700–2000* (Cambridge, New York: Cambridge University Press, 2004); Marceline Hutton, *Russian and West European Women, 1860–1939: Dreams, Struggles, and Nightmares* (Lanham, Md.: Rowman & Littlefield, 2001); Natalia Pushkareva, *Women in Russian History: From the Tenth to the Twentieth Century* (Stroud: Sutton, 1999).

13. Bucur, "Between the Mother of the Wounded."

14. On this issue in other Balkan states, see Jovana Knižević, "War, Occupation, and Liberation: Women's Sacrifice and the First World War in Yugoslavia," paper presented at the conference "Sacrifice and Regeneration," Southampton, UK, September 2007.

15. Nicolae Russu Ardeleanu, *Prizonier în ţara ta* (Botoşani, 1918); Ecaterina Raicoveanu (Fulmen), *Jurnalul unei surori de caritate, 1916–1918* (Brăila, 1920).

16. Bucur, "Between the Mother of the Wounded"; Healy, *Vienna and the Fall of the Habsburg Empire*.

17. Bucur, "Between the Mother of the Wounded"; Bucur, "Calypso Botez"; Maria Bucur, "Romania: War, Occupation, Liberation," in Aviel Roshwald and Richard Stites, eds., *European Culture in the Great War: The Arts, Entertainment, and Propaganda* (Cambridge: Cambridge University Press, 1999), 243–266.

18. Kligman, *Wedding of the Dead*, 152–157.

19. Marian, *Înmormântarea*, 270; this belief is of course found in other cultures without an Orthodox Christian presence.

20. Melissa Bokovoy, "Kosovo Maiden(s): Serbian Women Commemorate the Wars of National Liberation, 1912–1918," in Wingfield and Bucur, eds., *Gender and War,* 157–171.

21. Hew Strachan, *The First World War* (Oxford: Oxford University Press, 2001).

22. Antoine Prost, *Les anciens combattants et la société française: 1914–1939* ([Paris]: Presses de la Fondation nationale des sciences politiques, 1977); Jay Winter and Antoine Prost, *The Great War in History: Debates and Controversies, 1914 to the Present* (New York: Cambridge University Press, 2005).

23. Cassian R. Munteanu, "Înmormântarea," *Cultul eroilor noştri* 2, no. 1 (1921): 8–13. In the Romanian original, the word priest [*preot*] could be a reference either to a Roman Catholic priest, probably of Hungarian ethnicity, or to a protestant minister. Since Protestant denominations were vary rare among ethnic Romanians, the term "minister" with this religious connotation hadn't yet entered the vocabulary of most Romanians in 1921.

24. "Dintr-un sat de munte (Stoeneşti-Muscel)," *Cultul eroilor noştri* 2, no. 1 (1921): 27.

25. "Acte de pietate naţională: Readucerea osemintelor de eroi după front," *Cultul eroilor noştri* 3, no. 1 (1922): 13–14.

26. "Pentru eroii căzuţi pe valea Oltului," *Cultul eroilor noştri* 2, no. 2 (1921): 64, mentions that in the villages of Brezoi, Muereasca, Bujoreni, and Jiblea, which had seen a great deal of fighting during the war, local committees had come together to gather the remains of all soldiers, Romanians and others, fighting on both sides of the war, into a common cemetery. A similar action is described in "Pilda unui călugar," *Cultul eroilor noştri* 2, no. 3 (1921): 15.

27. "Procesiuni de eroi în munţi," *Cultul eroilor noştri* 2, no. 4 (1921): 9.

28. "Înmormântarea a 225 eroi la Câineni-Grebleşti (Argeş)," *Cultul eroilor noştri* 2, no. 3 (1921): 16.

29. *Cultul eroilor noştri* 3, no. 3 (July 1922): 9. Two similar letters, from a Jewish couple expressing thanks for the return of the remains of their two sons and from the wife of an officer, appear on the same page of the publication.

30. More on the Heroes Cult in chapter 4.

31. Ofelia Văduva, *Steps Towards the Sacred* (Bucharest: Editura Fundaţiei Culturale Române, 1999).

32. On the inclusion of the *parastas* in these commemorations, see *Cultul eroilor noştri* 2 (September 1920): 14.

33. In Romanian literally the "elders," it is a holiday in the spring commemorating all saints in the Orthodox calendar. See George Lungulescu, "Sărbătoarea Moşilor: Cea mai veche sărbatoare eroică a românismului," *Cultul eroilor noştri* 5, nos. 9–12 (1924): 17–19; and Angela Doina Ivaş, "Cultul strămoşilor la români" (PhD diss., Babeş-Bolyai University, Cluj, 1993), especially chapter 4.

34. On Jewish commemorations (Hassidic and Sephardic ones were separate, and performed in their respective cemeteries), see *Cultul eroilor noştri* 2 (September 1920): 14.

35. Ibid.

36. More on the development of this official holiday in chapter 4.

37. First introduced in 1582, the Gregorian calendar had become the international civilian calendar by 1919. Still, some Orthodox Christian communities refused to shift to it.

38. "O comemorare pentru eroii israeliţi," *Cultul eroilor noştri* 3, no. 6 (September 1922): 14.

39. R., "Un erou musulman mort pentru România," *Cultul eroilor noştri* 2, no. 3 (1922): 28.

40. See multiple documents in NSA, Zalău County, MOA Zalău, dos. 96/1932.

41. Ibid.

42. Ibid., 99.

43. Letter sent by the school administrator of Jugani village, in Roman County, on 24 June 1924, in NSA, Bucharest, MEA, dos. 213/1924. The quote is from a memorandum added by an administrator of the ministry at the end of the letter (signature indecipherable), in response to the entire correspondence. In describing the Catholics' intentions as connected to "unifying themselves with their Hungarian brothers," the local official wanted to render the impression that the Catholics were non-Romanians, even when they were in fact ethnically Romanian. In the region of Roman, the identification of ethnicity with confession among Catholics is complicated, for some of the ethnic Romanians and Hungarians (Csángó/Ciangăi) lived in mixed communities in that area. Thus, the Catholic Romanians were already brothers with their Catholic Hungarian neighbors, religiously speaking, and in some cases even through intermarriage. The comment in this document, however, relates more to the fear of Hungarian revisionism, a constant obsession for many at the Ministry of Education in Bucharest.

44. State schools, however, were obligated to organize commemorative celebrations, and did so everywhere.

45. "Pământul sacru," *Cultul eroilor noștri* 2, no. 1 (1921): 13.

46. HCA, dos. 4.

47. HCA, dos. 250.

48. Daniel Sherman, "Bodies and Names: The Emergence of Commemoration in Interwar France," *American Historical Review* 103, no. 2 (April 1998): 443–466; Thomas Laqueur, "Memory and Naming in the Great War," in Gillis, ed., *Commemorations,* 150–167.

49. On this issue, see also Popovici, *Evreii.*

50. See also *Cultul eroilor noștri* 2 (September 1920): 14.

51. Captain Gheorghe Popa, "Trădătorul," *Cultul eroilor noștri* 3, no. 1 (1922): 4–5.

52. Ministerul de Război, *Statutul Societății "Mormintele eroilor căzuți în război"* (Bucharest: Editura Răsăritul, 1921); and *Instrucțiunile asupra aplicării legei cinstirei memoriei Eroilor căzuți și a statutului societății "Mormintele Eroilor căzuți în război"* (Bucharest: Editura Răsăritul,1921), 3. See also Valeria Bălescu, *Soldatul Necunoscut* (Bucharest: Editura militară, 2005), 39.

53. HCA, dos. 9.

54. The ethnic geography of Transylvania has changed to some extent, but at the beginning of the interwar period Hungarians were in a large minority in the region, second only to ethnic Romanians. Though spread throughout the region, both groups tended to have "strongholds." For the Hungarians, in addition to the urban areas (if we are to count acculturated Jews among those who considered themselves Hungarians), Hungarians also lived in large concentrations in Arad and Cluj/Koloszvár and in the Székelyland region, including the towns of Odorheiu Secuiesc/Székelyudvarhely, Sfântu Gheorghe/Sepsiszentgyörgy, Covasna/Kovászna, Târgu Mureș/Marosvásárhely. Romanians lived in the Maramureș region, in the rural areas on the Transylvanian plain, along the Criș rivers, the Făgăraș region, and the mountainous regions of the Southern Carpathians.

55. NSA, Bucharest, MEA, AD, dos. 61/1935, 44.

56. NSA, Bucharest, MEA, AD, dos. 60/1935, 3.

57. Nicolae Basilescu, *La Roumanie dans la guerre et dans la paix* (Paris: F. Alcan, 1919).

58. Alon Rachamimov, *POWs and the Great War: Captivity on the Eastern Front* (Oxford, New York: Berg, 2002); Maureen Healy, *Vienna and the Fall of the Habsburg Empire;* King, *Budweisers.*

59. See Franz Horváth, "The Divided War Memory of the Transylvanian Hungarians," paper presented at the conference "Sacrifice and Regeneration," Southampton, UK, September 2007.

60. The Commission for Public Monuments has a large archive that exemplifies this attitude. See, for instance, NSA, Bucharest, MEA, DA, dos. 57/1936. On recent reflections about these monuments, see Andrei Pippidi, *Despre statui și morminte: Pentru o teorie a istoriei simbolice* (Iași: Polirom, 2000); for a more recent discussion on similar topics, see Alexandra Bădicioiu, "Statuile României străjuiesc iluzia trecutului glorios," *Cotidianul* (22 July 2005), available at http://host2.cotidianul.ro/index.php?id=44&art=1355 (accessed 5 January 2009).

61. Bokovoy, "Kosovo Maiden(s)."

62. Mick, "The Dead and the Living."

3. Remembering the Great War through Autobiographical Narratives

1. Take Ionescu, "Iubite prieten," in Vasile Th. Cancicov, *Impresiuni și păreri personale din timpul războiului României: Jurnal zilnic, 13 august 1916–31 decembrie 1918,* 2 vols. (Bucharest: Atelierele societății "Universul," 1921), vol. 1, vi.

2. Jeana Col. Fodoreanu, *Femeia-Soldat* (Bucharest, 1928), 9.

3. Unfortunately, this development has not found its scholarly audience yet. The now-classic study by Paul Fussell, *The Great War and Modern Memory,* 25th anniversary ed. (New York: Oxford University Press, 2000), doesn't have a counterpart for eastern Europe. His lack of interest in the eastern European perspective has not been critiqued through any solid recounting of the developments in the literary world in the East. The volume edited by Richard Stites and Aviel Roshwald, *Culture and the Great War,* does offer, however, some partial, country-based considerations on this topic.

4. See Bucur, "Romania," in Roshwald and Stites, eds., *European Culture,* 243–266; Bucur, "Women's Stories." This marginalization is even greater when it comes to non-Romanian (and especially non-Romanian language) writings produced by Hungarians, Germans, and Jews after World War I.

5. Michael Sheringham, *French Autobiography: Devices and Desires; Rousseau to Perec* (Oxford: Oxford University Press, 1993); Jane Gary Harris, *Autobiographical Statements in Twentieth-Century Russian Literature* (Princeton, N.J.: Princeton University Press, 1990).

6. St. Augustine, *Confessions of St. Augustine* (New York: Modern Library, 1999); Terry Sherwood, *The Self in Early Modern Literature: For the Common Good* (Pittsburgh, Pa.: Duquesne University Press, 2007); Loïc Thommeret, *La mémoire créatrice: Essai sur l'écriture de soi au XVIIIe siècle* (Paris: L'Harmattan, 2006); Philippe Lejeune, *Signes de vie: Le pacte autobiographique, 2* (Paris: Seuil, 2005).

7. John Witte, Jr., and Frank S. Alexander, eds., *The Teachings of Modern Orthodox Christianity on Law, Politics, and Human Nature* (New York: Columbia University Press, 2007); John Panteleimon Manoussakis, *God after Metaphysics: A Theological Aesthetic* (Bloomington:

Indiana University Press, 2007); Edmund J. Rybarczyk, *Beyond Salvation: Eastern Ortho-doxy and Classical Pentecostalism on Becoming Like Christ* (Carlisle, UK, Waynesboro, Ga.: Paternoster Press, 2004); Alexei Nesteruk, *Logos i kosmos: Bogoslovie, nauka i pravoslavnoe predanie* (Moscow: Bibleisko-Bogoslovskii In-t, 2006); Constantine Cavarnos, *The Future Life According to Orthodox Teaching* (Etna, Calif.: Center for Traditionalist Orthodox Studies, 1985).

8. Fussell, *Great War,* and Lejeune, *Signes de vie.*

9. For instance, Camil Petrescu makes direct reference to Proust in his writings from the interwar period. Cecilia Cuțescu-Storck, an artist who straddled the pre- and postwar periods and lived in Bucharest and Paris, offers a great deal of evidence about her travels in Parisian and various German circles, and also the extent of the Romanian participation overall in the Parisian art life after World War I; see Cecilia Cuțescu-Storck, *Fresca unei vieți* (Bucharest: Vremea, 2006). The most famous examples of this were, of course, Tristan Tzara, Victor Brauner, and Constantin Brâncuși.

10. Averescu's memoirs were first published as a feuilleton in the daily *Îndreptarea* in 1920. After assuming the leadership of the government (which he held briefly, between 30 March 1926 and 4 June 1927) and being reprimanded by a political opponent for some of his remarks in the feuilleton, Averescu ceased the publication of his war notes. They subsequently came out as a volume in 1935, more fully and carefully edited by the author with an eye on his image in history. See Mareșal Alexandru Averescu, *Notițe zilnice din război (1916–1918)* (Bucharest: Editura Cultura Națională, n.d. [1935]).

11. Marghiloman's political notes were republished in 1993; they had been first withdrawn from the market in 1927 after their publication and subsequently put into the "secret files" catalogue during the Communist years. The 1993 edition contains an excellent introductory story about the scandal surrounding the 1927 publication by Stelian Neagoe, the editor of the 1993 edition. One should also mention that the notes span the years from 1912 to 1924, but the bulk of the most controversial and detailed diary entries pertain to the wartime years. Though not exclusively, Marghiloman's political notes were in fact overwhelmingly a wartime journal. See Alexandru Marghiloman, *Note politice*, vols. 1–4 (Bucharest: Editura Scripta, 1993–1996).

12. Averescu, *Notițe,* 8–10.

13. Ibid., 106.

14. Ibid., 142. For a description of this decoration, see chapter 1.

15. For discussions of gendered forms of articulating the self, see Tess Cosslett, *Feminism and Autobiography: Texts, Theories, Methods* (London, New York: Routledge, 2000); Kristi Siegel, *Women's Autobiographies, Culture, Feminism* (New York: Peter Lang, 2001); Pauline Polkey, *Women's Lives into Print: The Theory, Practice and Writing of Feminist Auto/biography* (New York: St. Martin's Press, 1999); Leslie Bloom, *Under the Sign of Hope: Feminist Methodology and Narrative Interpretation* (Albany: State University of New York Press, 1998); Sidonie Smith, *Subjectivity, Identity, and the Body: Women's Autobiographical Practices in the Twentieth Century* (Bloomington: Indiana University Press, 1993); Sidonie Smith, *De/colonizing the Subject: The Politics of Gender in Women's Autobiography* (Minneapolis: University of Minnesota Press, 1992); Selma Leyedesdorff, Luisa Passerini, and Paul Thompson, eds., *Gender and Memory* (Oxford, New York: Oxford University Press, 1996); Janet Holmes, *The Handbook of Language and Gender* (Malden, Mass.: Blackwell, 2005).

16. Averescu, *Notițe,* 134 and 135.

17. Cancicov, *Impresiuni.*

18. Ionescu, "Iubite prieten," vi.

19. See the introduction to Kirițescu, *Istoria războiului.*

20. See Cancicov, *Impresiuni,* vol. 2, 735, author's marked-up copy.

21. Ibid., vol. 1, 235.

22. Constantin Bacalbașa, *Capitala sub ocupația dușmanului, 1916–1918* (Brăila, [1921]), 41.

23. Sabina Cantacuzino, *Războiul 1914–1919* (Bucharest: Editura Universul, 1937), 184.

24. Kirițescu, *Istoria războiului,* vol. 1, 554–555.

25. In an interview in 1937, Kirițescu described his aims in writing this book as follows: "I aimed, first to have precise information, following the truth, and stepping only on real ground." See Valer Donea, "De vorbă cu Constantin Kirițescu," *Adevărul literar și artistic* 18, no. 854 (18 April 1937): 9 and 15.

26. Already in the interwar period Kirițescu had become a "living classic." His history of World War I sold over 50,000 copies between 1921 and 1937 alone and went through four editions. Ibid.

27. Cancicov, *Impresiuni,* vol. 1, 345.

28. Ibid., 606.

29. Ibid., iii.

30. How these masculinist frameworks for remembering were in fact important for post-war generations in creating their own post-memory of World War II is a focus of my analysis in the last chapter. Unfortunately, the paucity of relevant sources for the post–World War I generation makes it difficult to even speculate on this theme for the interwar period.

31. These books included *Spionul, Prizonier în țara ta, 19 luni în Bulgaria, Însemnări roșii,* and *Ultimul erou. Spionul* had appeared at the beginning of Romania's engagement in the war, in 1917, and had sold out, making Russu Ardeleanu a popular and sought after author even before the end of the war. See Russu Ardeleanu, *Prizonier,* 2.

32. Ibid., 20. Hospital 118 is the Cantacuzino hospital, located in the heart of Bucharest, which was turned into a POW hospital by the occupying German troops. It was staffed by Romanians but closely supervised by the German authorities, because it was in fact a prison for Romanian combatants.

33. For a more thorough critical analysis of these narratives see Bucur, "Women's Stories."

34. The frustration of these veterans spilled beyond cultural life into the socioeconomic realm as well, as they were denied benefits such as pensions and reduced railway prices, which veterans fighting for the Romanian state in World War I enjoyed. My own great-grandfather, an ethnic Romanian fighting in the Habsburg army on the Italian front, never received any veteran benefits from the Romanian state after 1919.

35. Ion Chinezu tried not only to remain knowledgeable about Hungarian language publications, but also, through the Transylvanian cultural journal *Societatea de Mâine,* tried to familiarize Romanian language readers with important developments in Hungarian literature and culture. For an analysis of this work, see Nicolae Balotă, *Scriitori maghiari din România: Eseuri* (Bucharest: Kriterion, 1981), 442–454.

36. The most prominent among them are Pia Alimănișteanu, *Însemnări din timpul ocupației germane, 1916–1918* (Bucharest, 1929); Cantacuzino, *Războiu 1914–1919;* Nelli Cornea,

Însemnări din vremea războiului (Bucharest: Ed. librăriei H. Steinberg și fiu [1921]); Alexandrina Fălcoianu, *Din zile grele* (Bucharest, 1937); Raicoveanu, *Jurnalul;* Severa Sihleanu,
Note și desminițiri asupra amintirilor D-nei Sabina Cantacuzino (Bucharest, 1938); Marie
of Romania, *Ordeal: The Story of My Life* (New York: C. Scribner's Sons, 1935). There are
undoubtedly others who never published their memoirs, though they wrote long literary
journals that covered the war years alongside the pre- or postwar period. One such gem was
Martha Bibescu's journal, which appeared in print only recently. See Martha Bibescu, *Jurnal:
1915* (Bucharest: Compania, 2001). Others still await the light of the printed page, as is the
case with Maria Cantacuzino's memoir from 1918, still tucked away in the manuscript collection of the Romanian Academy. Maria Cantacuzino, "Memoirs de 1918," LRA, Manuscript
Collection, A 935.

37. Literary critics focusing on the history of Romanian literature in the twentieth century
have unfailingly ignored this phenomenon. This male-exclusivist canon was strongly established by George Călinescu in his encyclopedic *Istoria literaturii române de la origini până
în prezent,* 2nd ed. (Bucharest: Editura Minerva, 1982), and has been reinforced staunchly, or
at times carelessly, by all other scholars in this field, even those who critiqued Călinescu for
his many failings, blind spots, or outright xenophobia. Some of the other prominent titles in
this by now large scholarship include Eugen Lovinescu, "Istoria literaturii române contemporarne, 1900–1936," in Eugen Lovinescu, *Scrieri,* vol. 6 (Bucharest: Editura Minerva, 1975);
Tudor Vianu, "Arta prozatorilor români," in Tudor Vianu, *Opere,* vol. 5 (Bucharest: Editura
Minerva, 1975); Ovidiu S. Crohmălniceanu, *Literatura română între cele două războaie mon-
diale,* vol. 1 (Bucharest: Editura pentru literatură, 1967); Nicolae Manolescu, *Arca lui Noe:
Eseu despre romanul românesc,* 3 vols. (Bucharest: Editura Minerva, 1980–1983); Ioan Paler,
Romanul românesc interbelic (Bucharest: Editura paralela 45, 1998). A welcomed critique
of this masculinist view of Romanian writing is Voichița Năchescu, "The Visible Woman:
Interwar Romanian Women's Writing, Modernity, and the Gendered Public/Private Divide,"
Aspasia 2 (2008): 70–90.

38. Georgeta Nazarska, "The Bulgarian Association of University Women, 1924–1950,"
Aspasia 1 (2007): 153–175; and Irina Gigova, "The Club of Bulgarian Women Writers and the
Feminisation of Bulgarian Literature," *Aspasia* 2 (2008): 91–119.

39. See the reissue of the memoirs in Sabina Cantacuzino, *Din viața Familiei Ion C.
Brătianu,* vol. 2 (Bucharest: Editura Albatros, 1996); quote on 174.

40. Alexandrina Fălcoianu, *Un examen de conștiință și un răspuns* (Bucharest: Tipografia
Isvor, 1937), 3 and 4.

41. Fodoreanu, *Femeia-Soldat,* 9.

42. Bucur, "Between the Mother of the Wounded."

43. Fodoreanu, *Femeia-Soldat,* 74.

44. Cornea, *Insemnări.*

45. Ibid., 6; entry dated 17 August 1916.

46. Ibid., 6 and 11.

47. This attempt at claiming to be a full-blooded nationalist while retaining her pacifist
views has likely to do with Cornea's activism in the Romanian feminist movement before
and after the war. Cornea was, as her journal shows, an outspoken feminist. She had been
an active member of several feminist organizations and continued to fight for women's right

to vote after the war. But the feminist movement was quite divided before, during, and after the war along questions of patriotism. Most feminists, like Alexandrina Cantacuzino, were also aggressive, even jingoistic nationalists, while a smaller group, Cornea included, wanted to position feminists as patriots who did not favor violent solutions for political problems. On nationalism and feminism in Romania before World War I, see Bucur, "Between Liberalism and Nationalism"; on the postwar conflicts within the feminist movement see Cosma, *Femeile și politica*.

48. Cornea, *Insemnări*, 48–50; quote on 48.

49. Cantacuzino, *Războiul*, 34, 152.

50. Cornea, *Insemnări*, 65.

51. Ibid., 115.

52. Ibid., 94 and 95.

53. Ibid., 137.

54. Ibid., 138.

55. Ibid., 139.

56. See especially Institutul Social Român, comp., *Constituția din 1923 în dezbaterea contemporanilor* (Bucharest: Humanitas, 1990).

57. Cantacuzino, *Războiul*, 30.

58. Călinescu, *Istoria literaturii române*. A similar view of the war can be found in Ion Bogdan Lefter, *Scurtă istorie a romanului românesc (cu 25 de aplicații)* (Bucharest: Editura paralela 45, 2001): "After the First World War ends and peace resumes, Romanian literature . . . explodes!" 18.

59. Ibid.; Călinescu, *Istoria literaturii române*; Paler, *Romanul românesc interbelic*; Carmen Mușat, *Romanul românesc interbelic: Antologie, prefață, analize critice, note, dicționar, cronologie și bibliografie* (Bucharest: Humanitas, 1998).

60. Liviu Rebreanu, *Ion* (Timișoara: Editura Facla, 1988).

61. Lovinescu, *Istoria*, vol. 2, 264.

62. Mușat, *Romanul*, 227.

63. Călinescu, *Istoria literaturii române*, 743.

64. Camil Petrescu, *Ultima noapte de dragoste, întîia noapte de război* (Bucharest: Editura Eminescu, 1971), 118 and 120.

65. G. Șt. Cazacu, *Calea sângelui*, 5th ed. (Bucharest: Editura cronicarul, 1940), 26–27. I was unable to identify the original date of publication, but all poems are dated as having been written on the front, by date and location. For instance, the poem quoted above was penned in Costești-Argeș, on 14 November 1916, thus at the beginning of Romanian's entry in the war. The book's popularity and prominence is attested by the number of printings it saw, and by the fact that it won the prize for poetry of the Romanian Academy. In the Romanian original: "Plouă iar și gem răniții, de-ți înăbușe auzul;//. . . . plânge cerul și pământul; curg șiraguri de convoaie. . . . //un rănit rămas în urmă, sub salcîm, să-și lege rana;/un obuz crapă tulpina și-i făcu la cap o cruce." Vasile Voiculescu, an even better known poet of that period, whose work has remained more prominently recognized as original by literary critics such as George Călinescu, also published a number of poetry collections focusing on his wartime experiences, such as *Din Țara Zimbrului și alte poezii* and *Pîrga*. See Călinescu, *Istoria literaturii române*, 881–882.

66. Călinescu, *Istoria literaturii române,* 726.

67. I. Hangiu, *Dicționar al presei literare românești* (Bucharest: Editura științifică și enciclopedică, 1987) and Lucian Predescu, *Enciclopedia "Cugetarea"* (Bucharest: Editura Saeculum, I.O., and Editura Vestala, [1940] 1999).

68. The organization behind it and providing the funds for it, Heroes Cult, played a major role in constructing a bridge between official commemorative discourses, examined in detail in the next chapter, and individual voices like those that are the subject of this chapter.

69. "Dela frații de peste Ocean," *Cultul eroilor noștri* 2, no. 1 (1921): 15–16; and "Mișcătoarea manifestațiune Franco-Română dela Dieuze," *Cultul eroilor noștri* 2, no. 1 (1921): 17–20.

70. See, for instance, Ion Dragoslav, "Alba Iulia de azi și în trecut," *Cultul eroilor noștri* 3, no. 7 (October 1922): 9–15; Artur Gorovei, "Din vremea războiului nostru 1877–78," *Cultul eroilor noștri* 3, no. 10–11 (January–February 1922): 5; Maria Popp, "Omagiul premergătorilor," *Cultul eroilor noștri* 2, no. 1 (January 1921): 1.

71. Șt. Corod, "Hora recruților," *Cultul eroilor noștri* 3, no. 7 (October 1922): 16. In the Romanian original: "Războiul nu-i de un veac, de trei,/El e datină străbună/În noi nu-i suflet de femei. . . . /Tropăi hora'n voie bună!//. . . . În fine ne păli și rândul,/Și știm că avem mult de luptat/Dar nu ne speriem cu gândul:/Războiu-I doar din moși lăsat." The *hora* mentioned here is a traditional Balkan circular dance, present both among Orthodox Christians and Jews.

72. Frederic Aderca, *1916* (Bucharest: Hasefer, 1997).

73. Călinescu, *Istoria literaturii române,* 791 and 792.

74. Aladár Kuncz, *Black Monastery* (New York: Harcourt, Brace and Co., [1934]). See Balotă, *Scriitori,* 31–57; László Lörinczi, *Utazás a fekete kolostorhoz* (Bucharest: Kriterion, 1975); László Bóke, "Introductory Study," in Aladár Kuncz, *Fekete kolostor* (Bucharest: Kriterion, 1965).

75. Bóke, "Introductory Study," and Béla Pomogáts, *Kuncz Aladár* (Budapest: Akadémiai Kiadó, Irodalomtörténeti füzetek, 1968).

76. Gábor Gaál, "Kuncz Aladár," *Korunk,* no. 7–8 (1931): 583–585; and Dezsö Kosztolányi, "Fekete kolostor," *Nyugat* (1931): 819–823.

77. Aladár Kuncz, *Mănăstirea neagră* (Bucharest: Kriterion, 1971).

4. The Politics of Commemoration in Interwar Romania, 1919–1940

1. HCA, dos. 3/1919, 15.

2. NSA, Bucharest, MEA, AD, dos. 125/1938, 37.

3. NSA, Bucharest, fond NORWS, dos. 340. This includes clippings from the press on that occasion, from newspapers such as *Universul* and *Lumea Românească.*

4. "Cuvântarea Doamnei Alexandrina Gr. Cantacuzino, Președinta Generală a Societății Ortodoxe Naționale a Femeilor Române la Sfințirea Mausoleului Neamului dela Mărășești, 18 Septembrie, 1938," NSA, Bucharest, fond NORWS, dos. 339, 1.

5. "Activitatea Societății Mormintele Eroilor," *Universul* 38, no. 19 (4 December 1919): 1.

6. Law 1693, 23 August 1920.

7. "Decret regal no. 4105, 12 septembrie 1919," HCA, dos. 2/1919.

8. Ibid.

9. Prost, *Les anciens combattants;* Robert Whalen, *Bitter Wounds: German Victims of the*

Great War, 1914–1939 (Ithaca, N.Y.: Cornell University Press, 1984); Peter Fritzsche, *Germans into Nazis* (Cambridge, Mass.: Harvard University Press, 1998).

10. HCA, dos. 3/1919.

11. See, for instance, HCA, dos. 12 and 15. Both are summaries of the activities and expenditures of the organization for the years 1926 and 1927, respectively.

12. In Orthodox tradition, Easter is the most important day of the religious calendar, celebrated with great pomp and traditionally lasting for the whole week following Easter Sunday. Usually Orthodox believers do not work during that week, especially those engaged in agricultural or private enterprise. The fact that the second day of Easter would always fall on a Monday seemed not to pose a great problem in terms of the attention and attendance it would elicit.

13. HCA, dos. 3/1919, 51.

14. Bălescu, *Soldatul.*

15. HCA, dos. 3/1919, 53.

16. Ibid., 15.

17. An attempt was made in the interwar period to put up a plaque for the women who had served on the front as volunteers and died during the war, but, after an initial approval of the proposal, albeit conditional on women's having "died during and because of the war," there was no followup, and to my knowledge none has been erected since. The phrase used in the approval, "during and because of the war," is in fact a rather broad category compared to our contemporary concept of total war, but even after two years of intense total war for civilians, it appears that in this context, the National Military Museum, where the plaque was to be placed, wanted to equate the war with the fighting front. See NMMA, dos. 5.

18. The Greek-Catholic/Uniate Church followed the same religious calendar as the Orthodox. So virtually all ethnic Romanians, with the exception of Old Believers, Catholics, Protestants, or atheists, were in fact aware of and likely followed the Orthodox religious calendar.

19. Bucur, "Between the Mother of the Wounded"; Marie of Romania, *Însemnări zilnice* (Bucharest: Editura Albatros, 1996).

20. "Cinstirea eroilor," *Universul* 38, no. 124 (20 May 1920): 3.

21. Ibid.

22. Among large cities, Iași had the largest percentage of Jews among its inhabitants. More Jews lived in Iași, in total numbers, than in any other city in Romania.

23. "Requiem pentru soldații evrei morți în războiul României," *Curierul israelit* 11, no. 38 (29 May 1919): 4.

24. This local inflection continued throughout the interwar period and until 1941.

25. It should be noted that here, as with most other official appropriations of religious traditions, government officials and the press did not identify who was to prepare the *parastas.* But, based on our knowledge of traditional practices, it is safe to assume that the Patriarchate and other religious authorities called upon a reliable community of faithful women to be in charge of preparing these meals. Where there is more information available about such grandiose public feasts, as in the case of Mărășești (detailed further on in this chapter), it is explicitly stated that women were in fact the ones who took care of these rituals.

26. The Regat refers here to the territories encompassed by the Romanian kingdom between 1881 and 1918. The term is still used in common parlance to refer to this area.

27. Alas, we do not have evidence of exactly how many children did in fact participate in these commemorations throughout the interwar period. However, newspapers commented on the large size and variety of constituencies present in these commemorations, and on the presence of children. See "Programul comemorării," *Curentul* 5, no. 1565 (9 June 1932): 4; "Programul comemorării eroilor din capitală," *Curentul* 10, no. 3359–3360 (9–10 June 1937): 5; "Ziua Eroilor," *Universul* 49, no. 157 (9 June 1932): 1.

28. The creation of the *străjeri*, a personal initiative of Charles II, was in line with the direction taken by many governments in Europe in the 1930s, to copy the Italian Fascist and later Nazi paramilitary youth groups. These organizations had a Fascist look to them, and some of their actions appeared similarly prone to violence and reflecting the Führerprinzip that defined the structure of the Nazi youth groups. However, they were not as radical in their aims as the Fascist and Nazi groups. In Romania, the *străjeri* were actually Charles's counterpoint to the growing popularity of the radical fascist group, the Iron Guard. See Paul Quinlan, *The Playboy King: Carol II of Romania* (Westport, Conn.: Greenwood Press, 1995) and Maria Bucur, "Carol II of Romania," in Berndt Fischer, ed., *Balkan Dictators in the Twentieth Century* (London: Hurst, 2006), 87–118. See references to the *străjeri* in the newspaper articles cited in note 27 above.

29. "Meet me at the horse's tail," meaning the tail of horse on which Michael the Brave sat, was already a common reference point.

30. On nationalism in Romanian education, and especially the mythologization of Michael the Brave, see Murgescu, *Între*.

31. *Universul* 38, no. 124 (20 May 1920): 3; for later descriptions of similar commemorations, see note 27 above.

32. The "Romania as island of Latinity in a sea of Slavdom" image. See Murgescu, *Între*.

33. *Universul* 38, no. 124 (20 May 1920): 4; see also "Ziua eroilor în Iași," *Evenimentul* (Iași) 31, no. 629 (16 May 1923): 2.

34. *Universul* 38, no. 124 (20 May 1920): 4.

35. "Comemorarea Eroilor Neamului: Programul de sate." NSA, Iași County, fond MOA Iași, dos. 11/1920, 30. For subsequent years see also NMMA, dos. 1, 20–23 [1925] and HCA, dos. 17, 5 [1929]. This file also contains evidence of an attempt by the National Society of Romanian Orthodox Women to alter the Bucharest commemorations to include a nod to women's sacrifice in the war (Mothers Day fell on the same date as Heroes Day that year) and the government's rejection of such a suggestion (ibid., 7).

36. See, for instance, NSA, Iași County, fond MOA Iași, dos. 11/1920, 30–35; and fond RPA, Iași, dos. 55/1939, 15–16.

37. "Comemorarea Eroilor Neamului: Programul de sate."

38. HCA, dos. 17, 5 [1929].

39. NSA, Bucharest, MEA, dos. 362/1931, 111. This circular was in fact a rectification of a previous directive sent out that year by the Ministry, which was itself a new development. The fact that the ministry retracted it so quickly (the very next day after it went out) suggests that it was quite unwilling to entertain any kind of changes to the established ritual.

40. "Comemorarea Eroilor Neamului: Programul de sate."

41. Connerton, *How Societies Remember*.

42. Bokovoy, "Scattered Graves."

43. Mick, "The Dead and the Living."

44. See, for instance, NSA, RPA, Iaşi, dos. 154/1940, 40.

45. On 10 May all schools, government offices, and even any public businesses were closed. Banks, for instance, were not in operation. Of course, for people in the countryside, the vast majority of inhabitants of the country, this meant very little, as they wouldn't take the day off from working in the fields.

46. The Tomb of the Unknown Soldier was inaugurated in 1923, but on Heroes Day, which that year came after 10 May. The first occasion to use the Tomb on 10 May was the next year. More on the Tomb of the Unknown Soldier in the following section.

47. Somebody from the court was always present, watching the ceremonies and taking notes for the king and queen.

48. Transylvania had been ceded to Romania in the Treaty of Trianon (1920), and thus was considered legally part of that country, according to the international community, including defeated Hungary.

49. Maria Bucur, "Birth of a Nation: Commemorations of December 1st, 1918 and the Construction of National Identity in Communist Romania," in Bucur and Wingfield, eds., *Staging the Past,* 286–325.

50. Horia Carp, "Evreii şi încoronarea," *Curierul israelit* 15, no. 5 (15 October 1922): 1.

51. During the war Charles II fled his post at the front and his responsibilities as an officer in the army to marry an older woman, a divorcee below princely status, in Odessa. It was a major embarrassment for his parents and almost paralyzed Ferdinand, who was unable to act effectively as leader of the fighting forces for a short period of time. His mother orchestrated his return, sending emissaries to goad Charles into divorcing his new wife and returning to Iaşi. Charles did, and spent most of the rest of the war confined to a monastery in Moldavia, basically in jail. See Quinlan, *Playboy King.*

52. Bucur, "Carol II"; Quinlan, *Playboy King;* Matthieu Boisdron, *La Roumanie des années trente: De l'avènement de Carol II au démembrement du royaume (1930–1940)* (Parçay-sur-Vienne, France: Editions Anovi, 2007); Radu Florian Bruja, *Carol al II-lea şi partidul unic: Frontul Renaşterii Naţionale* (Iaşi: Junimea, 2006).

53. This date was also a school holiday in the country as a whole, and in Transylvania it was also a government and public business holiday.

54. Though promised full political rights at the 1 December 1918 meeting, women gained only limited enfranchisement in 1929, on the basis of age and education, and only in municipal and local elections. Universal male suffrage had been established right after the war. See Bucur, "Calypso Botez"; Câncea, *Mişcarea;* Cosma, *Femeile şi politica.*

55. Bucur, "Birth of a Nation."

56. Others include Mărăşti, Oituz, and Turtucaia. But 6 August seems to have caught on very early on as a major news item to be featured in all the press, who did not mark any commemorations at the site of these other battles with the same attention to detail. By "official date" I mean the date on which the battle is said to have been won or lost. In the case of Mărăşeşti, it was a victory. The battle itself, of course, lasted for months, as was the case with many other battles of World War I, such as Verdun or the Marne.

57. The fact that this date coincided with an important holiday in the Orthodox calendar, the Transfiguration, was not lost on the organizers. Yet they never played up the religious

significance beyond the historic reference during the interwar period. More recently, however, observers in post-Communist Romania have actually made more of this connection in their marking of the Mărăşeşti battle anniversary.

58. HCA, dos. 3/1919, 15 (verso).

59. The participation of veterans and representatives of the military establishment was also a part of these ceremonies from the start, though they were included as participants, rather than organizers. The role of the military at the beginning was marginal in terms of spectacle and logistics.

60. "Pelerinaj la Mărăşeşti," *Universul* (8 July 1937). A group of 150 students might not appear to be much, but given the lack of government support and the small number of girls' schools in Bucharest, it was nonetheless an impressive feat.

61. "Pelerinajul şcoalei centrale de fete din Capitală, la Mărăşeşti: Un exemplu ce va trebui urmat," *Curentul* (10 October 1938).

62. NSA, Bucharest, fond NORWS, dos. 339, 7.

63. Bălescu, *Soldatul,* 73.

64. It is important to underscore that in this case, with the state fully in charge of the process, non-governmental organizations, such as the prominent National Orthodox Romanian Women's Society, were excluded from these discussions. For the sake of expediency, or in the hope of better controlling the outcome, the government decided to forgo a wider legitimizing dialogue with the citizens of Romania. The only non-governmental voice heard in the discussion (though not counting as having a direct role in decision making) was the press, which commented repeatedly on the building of the monument.

65. Bălescu, *Soldatul,* 74.

66. Ibid., 74–75; "Unde trebuie pus soldatul necunoscut: Se impune alegerea unui loc potrivit," *Universul* no. 118 (9 May 1923): 1.

67. Bălescu, *Soldatul,* 88–91.

68. The other nine were reburied at Mărăşeşti alongside their comrades in arms. This ceremony reinforced the growing centrality of Mărăşeşti in the collective memory of the war. Ibid., 95.

69. There is no evidence of protests during this staged reburial on the part of ethnic and religious minorities. But given the fact that the route of the train was through an area predominantly ethnically Romanian and Orthodox, this is not surprising. There is also no evidence that there was an exclusionary intention on the part of the planners. Rather, it seems that the coincidence of the location of Mărăşeşti worked to the advantage of such an Orthodox Romanian presence at the expense of all others. One possible exception were members of the Jewish communities who lived in the towns and villages where the trained passed. Though the most widely read Jewish newspaper in Romania, *Curierul Israelit,* does not report anything about such activities, it did publish a moving article on the "Unknown Hero" on 20 May 1923, which spoke to the self-identification of the Jewish community with this symbol: "All of us alive here, on this beautiful land blessed by God and as sons of this country, all of us have somewhere, in a corner of the country, a son, brother, or dear comrade who died for the unification of the country." "Eroul necunoscut," *Curierul Israelit* 16, no. 19 (20 May 1923): 1.

70. See, for instance, Cezar Petrescu "Criptele dela Mărăşeşti," *România* (6 August 1938); "Sfinţirea 'Bisericii Neamului,'" *Lupta* no. 836 (24 September 1924); S.P., "Solemnitatea dela

Mărăşeşti," *Universul* no. 218 (28 September 1924); Dinu Dumbravă, "Cripta dela Mărăşeşti," *Dimineaţa* no. 6396 (24 August 1924). See also NSA, Bucharest, fond NORWS, dos. 318, 18–20.

71. See for instance NSA, Bucharest, MEA, dos. 739/1924, 154; also fond NORWS, dos. 307.

72. Valeria Bălescu, *Mausoleul de la Mărăşeşti* (Bucharest: Editura militară, 1993), 11.

73. Ibid., 11.

74. Ibid., 93.

75. Ibid., 16.

76. In Romanian, "Întru slava eroilor neamului."

77. Both had fought in the war and had great credentials with the military because of that.

78. The long inscription, in gold letters, includes in the third paragraph the phrase: "The pious building was built at the initiative, through the work and great efforts [*strădaniile*] of the National Orthodox Romanian Women's Society, with Princess Alexandrina Gr. Cantacuzino as its General President, Mrs. Elena M. Seulescu as its General Vice-president, Mrs. Col. Zefira Voiculescu as its General Secretary, Mrs. Maria El. Georgescu as its General Treasurer, and with the full support of the Royal Councilor Gh. Tătărăscu, Gen. Ilasivici, Gen. Tone Sinegreanu, and Col. Fotescu." Bălescu, *Mausoleul*, 85.

79. Ibid., 68.

80. To underscore the unusual nature of such a marker, one should contrast it with the absence of any other such marker, despite requests to that effect. Gen. Constantin Christescu made a similar request to have his body placed at Mărăşeşti after his death. Initially both Christescu and Grigorescu were to have sarcophagi in the Mausoleum, something that the National Orthodox Society of Romanian Women supported. But Christescu's family's requests (from 1923 and until the Communist period) were rejected, initially by Charles II and subsequently by Ion Antonescu and the Central Committee of the Romanian Communist Party. The force behind these rejections, at least in the first two attempts, was the family of Gen. Eremia Grigorescu, who strongly disapproved of Christescu being added. Camaraderie and love of the fellow soldiers did not preclude a great deal of competitiveness and animosity, even in death. Gen. Christescu's body remains buried in the Bellu cemetery in Bucharest, where it was originally placed. Ibid., 3–4.

81. On the mythologizing of Ecaterina Teodoroiu's and Queen Marie's roles in the war, see Bucur, "Between the Mother of the Wounded."

82. Bălescu, *Maulsoleul*, 70–71.

83. Bucur, "Between the Mother of the Wounded."

84. See Armin Heinen, *Legiunea "Arhanghelul Mihail": Mişcare socială şi organizaţie politică; O contribuţie la problema Fascismului internaţional* (Bucharest: Humanitas, 1999).

85. A short story published in 1931, "The Heroes Monument," offers a biting satire of these local contests, in this case with a strong anti-Semitic flavor. Ion Dongorozi, *Monumentul Eroilor: Nuvele şi schiţe* (Bucharest: Editura Naţională S. Ciornei, 1931), 127–187.

86. NSA, Bucharest, MEA, AD, dos. 790/1922, 37.

87. HCA, dos. 3, 1919, 49–50.

88. HCA, dos. 8, 51.

89. NSA, Bucharest, MEA, AD, dos. 125/1938, 37.

90. In most documents from the 1930s there are a president, a secretary (both bureaucrats of the Ministry), and three artist members, two sculptors and a painter (sometimes there were

a sculptor, a painter, and an architect). The Ministry of Education changed its name several times over the interwar period.

91. NSA, Bucharest, MEA, AD, dos. 125/1938, 32. Emphasis in the original.

92. Ibid., dos. 57/1936, 44.

93. Ibid., dos. 57/1936, 1.

94. Ibid., dos. 91/1938; dos. 5/1936; dos. 98/1937; dos. 97/1938; dos. 86/1934; dos. 56/1936; dos. 89/1937; dos. 85/1937.

95. Ibid., dos. 127/1938, 9.

96. Ibid., dos. 60/1935, 3.

97. Ibid., dos. 60/1935, 4.

98. Livezeanu, *Cultural Politics.*

99. NSA, Bucharest, MEA, AD, dos. 60/1935, 50–52.

100. Ibid., dos. 60/1935, 52. The handwritten comments stated: "Our opinion is to raise the monument, with the exception of the warring sword in the claws of the eagle."

101. Ibid., emphasis in the original.

102. I have found similar monuments in Hungarian and Jewish communities. They are inside churches or synagogues, and in prominent places inside graveyards of these communities, which would have buried their dead separately from the Romanian ethnic communities (generally by virtue of religious differences), and thus somewhat invisible from the scrutiny of ethnic Romanian authorities.

103. The status of the Orthodox Church was different, as it was the official "national" religion of Romania, and the clergy and other staff of the Orthodox Church received direct financial support from the state.

104. See, for instance, ibid., dos. 60/1935, 42; and dos. 82/1934, 62, 64–65.

105. Ibid., dos. 61/1935, 63.

106. Ibid., dos. 61/1935, 64.

107. Quinlan, *Playboy King;* Bucur, "Carol II"; on Charles's interest in the spectacle of commemorations, see Col. Gabriel Marinescu et al., eds., *Carol al II-lea, regele Românilor: Cinci ani de domnie (8 iunie 1930–8 iunie 1935)* (Bucharest: Institutul de arte grafice "Eminescu," 1935).

108. Bucur, "Carol II"; Marinescu et al., eds., *Carol al II-lea.*

109. NSA, Bucharest, MEA, AD, dos. 97/1938, 33–36. The new regulations regarding punishments are under art. 35, on 36 (verso).

110. Ibid., dos. 97/1938, 33.

111. HCA, dos. 424, 43.

112. NSA, Bucharest, MEA, AD, dos. 81/1938, esp. 3, 28–29, 35–39, 77; and dos. 57/1939, 15.

5. War Commemorations and State Propaganda under Dictatorship

1. NSA, Bucharest, MEA, AD, dos. 101/1941, 224.

2. From the propaganda film produced by the Ministry of Defense on the occasion of the fiftieth anniversary of the battle of Mărășești; "The Semi-centenary of Mărășești and Oituz," MND, dos. 11295/1968, inventory number 1449.

3. "Rules for applying the law on the regime of wartime funerary and commemorative works during military campaigns," HCA, dos. 31/1941.

4. Decree signed by Charles II on 12 December 1938 and registered on 16 December 1938, titled "Regulations for Public Monuments," NSA, Bucharest, MEA, AD, dos. 97/1938, 33–35.

5. "Rules for applying."

6. Transnistria was occupied for part of the war and administered by the Romanian State. It was, however, not fully incorporated into the Romanian State, but rather ruled by a civilian governor and a military regime. Olivian Verenca and Șerban Alexianu, *Administrația civilă română în Transnistria 1941–1944*, 2nd ed. (Bucharest: Editura Vremea, 2000).

7. I am using the term "culturnik" as a specific type of "apparatchik." The Romanian Communist state, as Katherine Verdery has shown with great clarity, made the production of nationalist cultural discourses one of the pillars of its centralized system of controlling resources. The pervasiveness of this operation came to grow so much as to make it virtually impossible for any other producers of culture to have any real autonomy (in terms of material security and the possibility of bringing one's cultural production before an audience, in print, on stage, on film, in sound, etc.). However, many of these people preserved their self-image (successfully projected before their audiences) of representing authentic talent, intellectual brilliance, and scholarly erudition. It seems more proper to identify these employees of the great cultural production apparatus as culturniks rather than either artists or apparatchiks. The term has been used widely in Romania since 1989 as either "culturnic" or "culturnik" but doesn't actually appear in Katherine Verdery, *National Ideology under Socialism: Identity and Cultural Politics in Ceaușescu's Romania* (Berkeley: University of California Press, 1991).

8. Ibid.

9. Verdery, *Political Lives of Dead Bodies.*

10. Bucur, "Carol II"; Quinlan, *Playboy King.*

11. Hitchins, *Rumania;* Vlad Georgescu, *Istoria românilor de la origini pîna în zilele noastre,* 4th ed. (Bucharest: Humanitas, 1995); Kurt W. Treptow, ed., *Romania and World War II* (Iași: Centrul de studii românești, 1996); Cornel Grad, *Al doilea arbitraj de la Viena* (Iași: Institutul European, 1998); Aurel Marinescu, *Înainte și după Dictatul de la Viena* (Bucharest: Editura Vremea, 2000); A. Simion, *Dictatul de la Viena,* 2nd rev. ed. (Bucharest: Editura Albatros, 1996); Platon Chirnoagă, *Istoria politică și militară a războiului României contra Rusiei sovietice, 22 iunie 1941–23 august 1944,* 4th ed. (Iași: Fides, 1998); Dinu Giurescu, *România în al doilea război mondial: 1939–1945* (Bucharest: All educațional, 1999); Florin Constantiniu, *De la războiul fierbinte la războiul rece* (Bucharest: Corint, 1998).

12. Ildikó Lipcsey, *Romania and Transylvania in the Twentieth Century* (Buffalo, Toronto: Corvinus, 2006); on the Hungarian perspective, see Balázs Balogh, "History, Memory, and the Other: Narratives of Ethnic Tensions between Hungarians and Romanians in the Light of the Conflicts of 1940–1944," paper presented at György Ránki Hungarian Chair Symposium "Strategies of Identity Construction: Ethnic Politics, Minorities, and European Integration in Transylvania," Bloomington, Ind., April 2007; for Romanian-centric perspectives, see Ioan-Aurel Pop et al., eds., *The History of Transylvania* (Cluj-Napoca: Romanian Cultural Institute, 2005); Gheorghe Bodea, Vasile T. Suciu, and Ilie I. Pușcaș, *Administrația militară*

Horthystă în Nord-Vestul României, septembrie–noiembrie 1940 (Cluj-Napoca: Editura Dacia, 1988); Giurescu, *România*.

13. International Commission on the Holocaust in Romania, *Final Report* (Iași: Polirom, 2005).

14. During World War II women were allowed to enlist as medical volunteers, serving with regular units on the front. See Andrei Șiperco, *Crucea Roșie Internațională și România în perioada celui de-al Doilea Război mondial: 1 septembrie 1939–23 august 1944; Prizonierii de război anglo-americani și sovietici; deportații evrei din Transnistria și emigrarea evreilor în Palestina în atenția Crucii Roșii Internaționale* (Bucharest: Editura enciclopedică, 1997).

15. The exact figures are still contested, but recent estimates put them at 11.38 percent in Latvia; 13.71 percent in Lithuania; 18.51 percent in Poland; 13.44 percent in the Soviet Union; and 6.7 percent in Yugoslavia. See G. F. Krivosheev, ed., *Soviet Casualties and Combat Losses in the Twentieth Century* (London: Greenhill Books, 1997); Biuro Odszkodowan Wojennych, *Statement on War Losses and Damages of Poland in 1939–1945* (Warsaw: n.p., 1947); Parker Maudlin, *The Population of Poland* (Washington, D.C.: U.S. Government Printing Office, 1954); R. B. Evdokimov, ed., *Liudskie poteri SSSR v period vtoroi mirovoi voiny: sbornik statei* (St. Petersburg: In-t rossiiskoi istorii RAN, 1995).

16. NSA, Bucharest, MEA, AD, dos. 1732/1941, 59–61. Two of these authors, Eminescu and Sadoveanu, remained in the literary canon in the 1950s, while the rest were purged. In the 1960s, however, all of these names slowly made their way back into public discussion. Gusti and Goga, in particular, saw a fullblown revival, with their work republished.

17. NSA, RPA, Iași, dos. 11/1941, 33.

18. Radu Ioanid, *The Holocaust in Romania: The Destruction of Jews and Gypsies under the Antonescu Regime, 1940–1944* (Chicago: Ivan R. Dee, 2000); Jean Ancel, *Preludiu la asasinat: Pogromul de la Iași, 29 iunie 1941* (Iași: Polirom, 2005).

19. NSA, RPA, Iași, dos. 11/1941, 45–47.

20. "Rules for applying," 3–4.

21. "Rules for applying," annexes 4–11 offer blueprints for such funerary markers.

22. Maria Bucur, *Eugenics and Modernization in Interwar Romania* (Pittsburgh, Pa.: Pittsburgh University Press, 2002); Bucur, "Between the Mother of the Wounded."

23. HCA, dos. 118, esp. 73, 144, 145, 146, 166, 171, 172, 195, 243, 246, 259.

24. Ibid., dos. 118, 7–9.

25. Law no. 537, *Monitorul Oficial* part 1, no. 170 (1942): 5149 (decree passed on 23 July 1942).

26. NSA, Bucharest, MEA, AD, dos. 99/1943, 60–61.

27. Ibid., 77.

28. Ibid., dos. 94/1943, 107.

29. Ibid., dos. 42/1944, 86 and dos. 246/1944, 131.

30. The Sântimbru monography.

31. NSA, Bucharest, MEA, AD, dos. 42/1944, 128.

32. Jan-Werner Müller, ed., *Memory and Power in Post-War Europe: Studies in the Presence of the Past* (Cambridge: Cambridge University Press, 2002); Höepken, "War, Memory and Education"; Heike Karge, "From 'Frozen Memory' to the Encounter of Remembrance: Memorials to the Second World War in Tito's Yugoslavia," *Memoria e Ricerca* no. 21 (2006): 81–100, available at http://www.fondazionecasadioriani.it/modules.php?name=MR&op=body&id=367

(accessed 11 January 2009); Nikolai Voukov, "Death and the Desecrated: Monuments of the Socialist Past in Post-1989 Bulgaria," *Anthropology of East Europe Review: Central Europe, Eastern Europe and Eurasia* 21, no. 2 (Autumn 2003), available at http://condor.depaul.edu/%7Errotenbe/aeer/v21n2/Voukov.pdf (accessed 11 January 2009).

33. Müller, ed., *Memory and Power;* Winter and Sivan, eds., *War and Remembrance;* Kansteiner, and Lebow, eds., *Politics of Memory.*

34. Marcel-Dumitru Ciucă, *Procesul Mareşalului Antonescu,* vol. 2 (Bucharest: Editura Saeculum I.O., 1998), 55.

35. Gheorghe Buzatu, *Mareşalul Antonescu în faţa istoriei,* 3 vols. (Iaşi: B.A.I., 1990); Rotaru Jipa, *Mareşalul Antonescu la Odessa: Grandoarea şi amărăciunea unei victorii* (Bucharest: Editura Paideia, 1999); Teodor Mavrodin, *Mareşalul Antonescu întemniţat la Moscova* (Piteşti: Editura Carminis, 1998); Gheorghe Buzatu, *Din istoria secretă a celui de-al doilea război mondial* (Bucharest: Editura enciclopedică, 1995); Gheorghe Buzatu, *Românii în arhivele Kremlinului* (Bucharest: Editura univers enciclopedic, 1996); Ioan Coja, *Marele manipulator şi asasinarea lui Culianu, Ceauşescu, Iorga* (Bucharest: Editura miracol, 1999).

36. International Commission on the Holocaust in Romania, *Final report,* available at http://www1.yadvashem.org/about_yad/what_new/data_whats_new/pdf/english/1.12_Trials_of_War_Criminals.pdf, esp. 3–4 (accessed 11 January 2009).

37. Cristina Păuşan, "Justiţia populară şi criminalii de război," *Arhivele totalitarismului* 7, no. 1–2 (1999): 150–165. Her total figure is slightly lower than subsequent estimates. See International Commission on the Holocaust in Romania, *Final report.*

38. Gross, *Neighbors.*

39. The Romanian authorities used the argument that ethnic Germans in Transylvania had acted as pawns of Nazi Germany to deport massive numbers from this community to the Soviet Union. Subsequently, the Romanian authorities carried out their own internal deportations to the Bărăgan region. See Georg Weber et al., *Die Deportation von Siebenbürger Sachsen in die Sowjetunion 1945–1949,* 3 vols. (Cologne: Böhlau, 1997); and Michael Kroner, "Deportation vor 60 Jahren war völkerrechtliches Kriegsverbrechen," *Siebenbürger Sachsen* (12 January 2005), available at http://www.siebenbuerger.de/zeitung/artikel/alteartikel/3860-deportation-vor-60-jahren-war.html (accessed 11 January 2009).

40. USHMM, SRI, RG 25.004M, Roll 16, fond Anchetă.

41. "Comemorarea victimelor masacrului dela Iaşi," *Universul* 65, no. 148 (1 July 1948): 5.

42. "Zece ani de la masacrele dela Iaşi," *Universul* 68, no. 151 (30 June 1951): 2.

43. MND, SDEP, 1945–1948; fond microfilm 3570, dos. 81, 4–2464.

44. For some reports on the "positive" and "negative" responses of individual officers and soldiers, see ibid., dos. 2775, 4-2742/2743.

45. Ibid., dos. 16, 4-2457-3570, 168.

46. Alessandru Duţu, *Sub povara armistiţiului: Armata româna în perioada 1944–1947* (Bucharest: Editura Tritonic, 2003); Florica Dobre, *Distrugerea elitei militare sub regimul ocupaţiei sovietice în România* (Bucharest: Institutul Naţional pentru Studiul Totalitarismului, 2000–2001).

47. HCA, dos. 37, 121, emphasis in the original.

48. MND, SDEP, dos. 356, 4-2502, 92 (verso).

49. Tismăneanu, *Stalinism.*

50. MND, SDEP, dos. 6878, 4-5818, 89–90.

51. Voukov, "Death and the Desecrated"; Maria Todorova, "Contemporary Issues in Historical Perspective: The Mausoleum of Georgi Dimitrov as Lieu de Memoire," *Journal of Modern History* 78 (June 2006): 377–411.

52. MND, SDEP, fond microfilm 3570, dos. 6405, 4-5736.

53. Robert Levy, *Ana Pauker: The Rise and Fall of a Jewish Communist* (Berkeley: University of California Press, 2001).

54. The terminology used to identify 25 October as an important national day came close to the kind of nationalist narratives constructed after 1918 to define World War I as one of defense. The text on the Tomb of the Unknown Soldier sounded similar to this, in terms of the links it established between the sacrifices of the army and the goal of liberating legitimate Romanian territory, even while both wars were fought largely beyond Romania's boundaries and were thus by definition wars of aggression: "Here sleeps happily under God the unknown soldier, who sacrificed his life for the unity of the Romanian people; on his bones rests the soil of unified Romania: 1916–1919."

55. One could select other sites for propaganda in education and public spaces, but my analysis aims at being suggestive of wider phenomena, rather than a faithful reflection of all the forms taken by this propaganda.

56. Though not all people in these professions were Communist Party members, most cultural producers in the realm of the social sciences, education (especially in social science disciplines), as well as cultural propaganda, were in fact Party members, especially in the higher, decision making echelons.

57. *Lecții în ajutorul celor care studiază istoria P.M.R.* (Bucharest: Editura politică, [1960]), 424.

58. Ibid., 428.

59. Ibid., 507.

60. Ibid., 428 and 463.

61. To be sure, the role of King Michael in connection to the Holocaust has continued to be a contentious issue, as the king never made a public apology about his symbolic role as head of the state during the period of the harshest anti-Semitic policies of the Romanian state. While his mother did act on behalf of the Romanian Jews, intervening with the Antonescu dictatorship, the same cannot be said for the young king, who remained passive in the matter.

62. Marin Mihalache, *Muzeele din București* (Bucharest: Editura meridiane, 1963); and Victor Adrian, Ion Burțea, and Petre Lupan, *România: Monumente istorice și de artă* (Bucharest: Editura meridiane, 1972).

63. See cover of *Time,* 20 September 1948, available at http://www.time.com/time/covers/0,16641,19480920,00.html (accessed 11 January 2009).

64. Over the fifty years of Communist rule most people came to view books as a vital part of their lives. The Party made great efforts to make books accessible by keeping prices extremely low, bringing book salespersons into factories (they would come on payday, and people could even pay in installments), and helping construct a network of neighborhood libraries, especially in working-class neighborhoods. Films were also accessible to any income, as ticket prices remained extremely low (2–5 lei, where the average monthly salary was around 2000 lei). See Maria Bucur, "Book Collecting and Reading in Brașov, Romania

under Communism," *NCEEER Working Paper* (1 March 2003), available at http://www.ucis
.pitt.edu/nceeer/2003–817–19n-Bucur.pdf (accessed 11 January 2009).

65. Marius Mîrcu, *Pogromurile din Bucovina și Dorohoi* (Bucharest: Glob, 1945), *Pogromurile de la Iași* (Bucharest: Glob, 1944), and *Pogromurile din Basarabia și din Transnistria* (Bucharest: Glob, 1947); Matatias Carp, *Cartea Neagră: Suferințele evreilor din România 1940–1944*, 3 vols. (Bucharest: Socec, 1946–1948); Sergiu Lezea, *Ninge peste Ucraina*
(Bucharest: Scânteia, 1946).

66. Romanian literary critics have been feuding over this question starting from diverging ideological, aesthetic, or personal loyalties, some of them also of a generational nature.
The main problem with these debates is that authors start from different definitions of what
constitutes "quality" and "compromise" in literature, and thus in effect either speak past
each other about the qualities and defects of particular authors, or are unable (or unwilling)
to relate their own definitions to others, remaining thus un-self-reflexive about their own
subjectivities—ideological, aesthetic, or personal. These debates never really rise above the
level of a provincial struggle for resources (intellectual, moral, or maybe even material).
See Alex Ştefănescu, "O nouă lectură: Titus Popovici, Elogiul nebuniei," *România literară*
35, no. 25 (26 June 2002): 10–11; Alexandra Olivotto, "Cele mai nocive cărți din literatura
românească," *Cotidianul* (18 October 2005), available at http://www.9am.ro/stiri-revista-
presei/Social/20915/Cele-mai-nocive-carti-din-cultura-romaneasca.html (accessed 8 February 2009); László Alexandru, "Frînarul," available at http://193.226.7.140/~laszlo/Frinarul
.htm (accessed 11 January 2009); Lucian Bâgiu, "Alex Ştefănescu și istoria literaturii române
contemporane," *agonia.net,* posted 23 May 2007, available at http://www.poezie.ro/index.php/
article/247413/index.html (accessed 11 January 2009). For an analysis of socialist realism more
broadly, see Thomas Lahusen and Evgeny Dobrenko, eds., *Socialist Realism without Shores*
(Durham, N.C.: Duke University Press, 1997).

67. The term "obsessive decade" pertains broadly to the period of socialist realism in
Romanian literature and film. The actual periodization of this decade varies, with the most
inclusive definition being that of Ion Istrate in his study, *Romanul "obsedantului deceniu"*
(1945–1964) (Cluj-Napoca: Diamondia, 1995).

68. On the literature of this period see Monica Spiridon, Ion Bogdan Lefter, and Gheorghe
Crăciun, *Experiment in Post-War Romanian Literature,* trans. Della Marcus, Ruxandra-Ioana
Patrichi, and David Hill (Pitești: Editura paralela 45, 1999); Henri Zalis, *O istorie condensată*
a literaturii române: 1880–2000 (Tîrgoviște: Editura Bibliotheca, 2005–2006); Ion Bogdan
Lefter, *Recapitularea modernității: Pentru o nouă istorie a literaturii române* (Pitești: Editura
paralela 45, 2000).

69. Laurențiu Fulga, *Eroica, I: Oameni fără glorie* (Bucharest: Editura tineretului, 1956).

70. Dumitru Micu, *Literatura română în secolul al XX-lea* (Bucharest: Editura Fundației
Culturale Române, 2000), 284–285.

71. The title of the book suggests a parallel with Albert Camus' famous *L'Etranger* (1942).
While the main character of Popovici's novel is a young man, Andrei Sabin, in search for the
meaning of life in the midst of war, violence, and profound social instability, the conclusion of
the Romanian novel is in line with the materialist determinism of Communist ideology, aban-
doning the existential angst that dominates Camus' novel and philosophy. There are echoes of
the despair and unfruitful search for meaning that can be traced in Popovici's novel as well.

72. Villages in northern Transylvania that were part of the territory retroceded to Hungary in August 1940, where massacres, largely against the Romanian population, took place right after the Hungarian authorities took over. See Petre Țurlea, *Ip și Trăznea, atrocități maghiare și acțiune diplomatică* (Bucharest: Editura enciclopedică, 1996); for a balanced view, see Maria Bucur, "Treznea: Trauma, Nationalism and the Memory of World War II in Romania," *Rethinking History* 6, no. 1 (2002): 35–55.

73. These guards existed in real life. Some of them went by the name *Sumanele negre* (the Black Coats), which is one of the informal ways in which they are described in the book as well. The actions of these paramilitary groups became a taboo subject again later on, since they claimed great prestige among the counter-memories of especially rural populations living in the Southern Carpathian region (especially in Făgăraș County). They have become subject of a great deal of research, media attention, and many oral history projects since the mid-1990s. See Cicerone Ionițoiu, *Victimele terorii comuniste: Arestați, torturați, întemnițați, uciși* (Bucharest: Editura mașina de scris, 2000–2006).

74. See E. D. Tappe, *Rumanian Prose and Verse* (London: Athlone, 1956); J. Steinberg, ed., *Introduction to Rumanian Literature* (New York: Twayne, 1966); "Romanian Literature," *The Columbia Encyclopedia*, 6th ed. (New York: Columbia University Press, 2007), available at http://www.encyclopedia.com/doc/1E1-Romnilit.html (accessed 2 February 2009).

75. Călin Căliman, *Istoria filmului românesc: 1897–2000* (Bucharest: Editura Fundației Culturale Române, 2000).

76. Among them are Ștefan Iordache and Șerban Cantacuzino, who had their film debut here, along with Irina Petrescu, already a veteran at twenty-two, but getting her first top billing here.

77. Dina Iordanova, *Cinema of the Other Europe: The Industry and Artistry of East Central European Film* (London, New York: Wallflower, 2003).

78. For instance, in *National Ideology* Verdery identifies Ceaușescu's coming to power as a new course.

79. MND, SDEP, dos. 11295, 5-1449.

80. This was even more the case after the refusal of the Romanian regime to send troops into Czechoslovakia in August 1968, after the crackdown against the Prague Spring.

81. MND, SDEP, dos. 11295, 5-1449, 100–101.

82. Ibid., dos. 11295, 5-1449.

83. On veterans' pensions during the Communist years, see Dan Cernovodeanu, "Dramatica situație a membrilor armatei regale române în anii comunismului," *Revista Memoria*, available at http://revista.memoria.ro/?location=view_article&id=292 (accessed 5 December 2007).

84. A pioneer was a member of a Party-sponsored youth organization similar to scouting.

85. Bucur, "Birth of a Nation."

86. A perusal of the 23 August issues of the main newspapers in Romania (e.g, *Evenimentul Zilei, Ziua, România Liberă, Adevărul, Gândul, Jurnalul Național*) in the last fifteen years shows this ambivalent attitude.

87. Personal communication with the director of the County Office of National Patrimony, Sibiu, 2000.

88. Béla Köpeczi, ed., *Erdély története* (Budapest: Akadémiai Kiadó, 1986).

89. In addition, Sibiu was also under the local party leadership of Nicu Ceauşescu, the son of the dreaded dictator, who was himself an unabashed nationalist and dictatorial personality.

90. Horváth, "Divided War Memory."

91. Bodea, Suciu, and Puşcaş, *Administraţia militară Horthystă.*

92. Of course, the definition of northern Transylvania as Romanian territory in World War II was incorrect and presumptuous, resting on the assumption that the retrocession of that territory was illegitimate, and could thus be incorporated in the discussion of the Holocaust in Romania.

93. Petru Popescu, interview by *Conexiuni* no. 15 (2006), available at http://conexiuni.net/autori/Petru%20Popescu/pornire_Petru%20Popescu.htm (accessed 11 January 2009). In this interview, Petru Popescu identifies Romanian writers of that period as "emasculated," in the sense of being forced into self-censorship of the most humiliating kind from the point of view of writing as an expression of one's sincere inner creative impulses. In his view, such direct writing had become impossible in Romania, despite the appearance of liberalization, as seen in his novel from 1970, *Sweet as the Honey is the Fatherland's Bullet* [*Dulce ca mierea e glonţul patriei*] (Bucharest: Editura Cartea Românească, 1972).

94. Popescu, *Dulce ca mierea,* 403–404.

95. P. Popescu, interview in *Conexiuni.*

96. For admiring views, see Constantin Coroiu, "Marin Preda şi cel mai greu roman al său," *Evenimentul* (14 May 2005), available at http://www.evenimentul.ro/articol/marin-preda-si-cel.html (accessed 11 January 2009); a more critical view appears in S. Damian, "Favorizarea eroului naţional," *Revista 22* 14, no. 790 (26 April–2 May 2005), available at http://www.revista22.ro/html/index.php?nr=2005-04-28&art=1691 (accessed 11 January 2009); Emil Berdeli, "Marin Preda în delirul denigrărilor," *Gardianul* (18 August 2007), available at http://www.gardianul.ro/2007/08/18/actualitate-c24/marin_preda_n_delirul_denigr_rilor-s99697.html (accessed 11 January 2009); Victor Eskenasy, "The Holocaust in Romanian Historiography: Communist and Neo-Communist Revisionism," in Randolph L. Braham, ed., *The Tragedy of Romanian Jewry* (New York: Rosenthal Institute for Holocaust Studies, Graduate Center/The City University of New York, 1994).

97. Marin Preda, *Delirul,* 2nd rev. ed. (Bucharest: Editura Cartea Românească, 1975), 156.

98. I was able to observe this in my interviews in Braşov conducted as part of the larger oral history project, "Reading under Communism"; see Bucur, "Book Collecting and Reading."

6. Everyone a Victim

1. Leo Schaddach, *Orăşelul pierdut* (Bucharest: Kriterion, 1996), 162. The book was written in the 1980s.

2. Alice Voinescu, *Jurnal* (Bucharest: Editura Albatros, 1997), 414. The journal was penned throughout the interwar, during the war, and into the Communist period.

3. See, for instance, Emil Dorian, *The Quality of Witness: A Romanian Diary, 1937–1944* (Philadelphia: Jewish Publication Society of America, 1982); Elie Wiesel, *Night* (New York: Bantam, 1982); Siegfried Jagendorf, *Jagendorf's Foundry: A Memoir of the Romanian Holocaust* (New York: Harper Collins, 1991); Anna Wittmann, *Balkan Nightmare: A Transylvanian Saxon in World War II* (New York: Columbia University Press, 2000); Ştefan Palaghiţă, *Garda*

de Fier spre reînvierea României (Buenos Aires: Editura autorului, 1951); Károly Kapronczay, *Refugees in Hungary: Shelter from Storm during World War II* (Budapest: Corvinus Library, 1999).

4. On the difficulties of doing oral history research, see Paul Thompson, *The Voice of the Past: Oral History* (New York: Oxford University Press, 2000); Donald Ritchie, *Doing Oral History* (New York: Oxford University Press, 2003); Ronald J. Grele et al., *Envelopes of Sound: The Art of Oral History* (Westport, Conn.: Praeger, 1991). On the difficulty of working on oral history with subjects from Communist regimes, see David Ransel, *Village Mothers: Three Generations of Change in Russia and Tataria* (Bloomington: Indiana University Press, 2001); *Oral History Yearbook* (the totalitarianism issue); and Rubie Watson, ed., *Memory, History, and Opposition under State Socialism* (Santa Fe, N.M.: School of American Research, 1994).

5. Remus Cucoș, interview by Stejărel Olaru, 6 July 2001, Brașov.

6. Ibid.

7. Randolph Braham, *The Politics of Genocide: The Holocaust in Hungary* (New York: East European Monographs, 1994).

8. On anti-Semitic legislation in 1938 and later see, Lya Benjamin, ed., *Evreii din România între anii 1940–1944: Legislația antievreiască*, vol. 1 (Bucharest: Editura Hasefer, 1993); International Commission on the Holocaust in Romania, *Final Report;* Victor Eskenasy, *Izvoare și mărturii referitoare la evreii din România*, 2nd rev. ed. (Bucharest: Editura Hasefer, 1995).

9. Jean Ancel, *Contribuții la istoria României: Problema evreiască* (Bucharest: Editura Hasefer, 2001).

10. Ibid.; Ioanid, *The Holocaust in Romania.*

11. Mihail Sebastian, *Jurnal, 1935–1945* (Bucharest: Editura Humanitas, 1996), 288, 295, and 298.

12. Voinescu, *Jurnal,* 218, 23 January 1941 entry.

13. Ibid., 238, 22 June 1941 entry.

14. My point in this paragraph is not to construct a "better" way of remembering the Iași pogrom, but rather to underscore the wider social significance of the ways in which the event was remembered and forgotten by various categories of people in Romania. The justification for focusing on this moment of violence is, however, quantitative. The number of victims of this one single act of violence surpassed any other such violent incidents that took place between 1939 and 1941. In other words, this was not an isolated event that could have easily been painted over without hundreds or even thousands of bystanders being able to observe it.

15. Sebastian, *Jurnal,* 353.

16. Ibid., 446, 6 March 1942 entry. I interpret his reference to "an amazing people" to mean the Jewish people, rather than ethnic Romanians. At this point in his journal, Sebastian is still vacillating between his Romanianness and his Jewishness, believing he can be both, but he is leaning more and more to identifying with the Jewish community rather than with his Romanian friends. This inclination stems partly from his feeling of abandonment at the hands of his friends, Mircea Eliade, Camil Petrescu, and others, who are growing increasingly anti-Semitic. Partly it is due simply to his empathy and growing sense that he can find relief and a true sense of acceptance among his family and other Jews.

17. Voinescu, *Jurnal,* 356, 25 July 1941 entry.

18. Ibid., 280, 20 September 1941 entry.

19. Florentina Scârneci and Ştefan Ungurean, eds., *Vieţi paralele în secolul XX: Istorie orală şi memorie recentă în Ţara Bârsei* (Braşov: Editura Phoenix, 2002); Vultur, *Germanii din Banat*, and *Istorie trăită—istorie povestită: Deportarea în Bărăgan, 1951–1956* (Timişoara: Editura Amarcord, 1997).

20. Aurora Liiceanu, *Rănile memoriei: Nucşoara şi rezistenţa din munţi* (Iaşi: Polirom, 2003); Cicerone Ioniţoiu, *Rezistenţa anticomunistă din munţii României, 1946–1958*, 2nd rev. ed. (Bucharest: Gîndirea Românească, 1993); Ioana Raluca Arnăuţoiu and Voicu Arnăuţoiu, eds., *Luptătorii din munţi: Toma Arnăuţoiu şi grupul de la Nucşoara; Documente ale anchetei, procesului, detenţiei* (Bucharest: Editura Vremea, 1997); Doru Radosav et al., eds., *Rezistenţa anticomunistă din Apuseni, Grupurile "Teodor Şuşman," "Capota-Dejeu," "Cruce şi Spadă": Studii de istorie orală* (Cluj-Napoca: Argonaut, 2003).

21. Jan Gross, "Themes for a Social History of War Experience and Collaboration," in Gross, Judt, and Deák, eds., *Politics of Retribution*, 15–38; Kenez, *Hungary*; Case, "Suspending the Axe"; Judt, *Postwar*.

22. From the vast literature on the subject, see Karen Till, *The New Berlin: Memory, Politics, Place* (Minneapolis: University of Minnesota Press, 2005); Dagmar Barnouw, *The War in the Empty Air: Victims, Perpetrators, and Postwar Germans* (Bloomington: Indiana University Press, 2005); Laurel Cohen-Pfister, *Victims and Perpetrators, 1933–1945: (Re)presenting the Past in Post-Unification Culture* (Berlin: W. de Gruyter, 2006); Sue Weissmark, *Justice Matters: Legacies of the Holocaust and World War II* (New York: Oxford University Press, 2003); Bejamin Valentino, *Final Solutions: Mass Killing and Genocide in the Twentieth Century* (Ithaca, N.Y.: Cornell University Press, 2004); Leonard Newman, *Understanding Genocide: The Social Psychology of the Holocaust* (Oxford: Oxford University Press, 2002); István Deák, *Essays on Hitler's Europe* (Lincoln: University of Nebraska Press, 2001); Alan Berger, *Second Generation Voices: Reflections by Children of Holocaust Survivors and Perpetrators* (Syracuse, N.Y.: Syracuse University Press, 2001); Donald Niewyk, *The Columbia Guide to the Holocaust* (New York: Columbia University Press, 2000); Gabriele Rosenthal, *The Holocaust in Three Generations: Families of Victims and Perpetrators of the Nazi Regime* (London: Cassell, 1998); Michael Burleigh, *Confronting the Nazi Past: New Debates on Modern German History* (New York: St. Martin's Press, 1996); Raul Hilberg, *Perpetrators, Victims, Bystanders: The Jewish Catastrophe, 1933–1945* (New York: Harper Perennial, 1993); Daniel Goldhagen, *Hitler's Willing Executioners: Ordinary Germans and the Holocaust* (New York: Vintage Books, 1997).

23. Stefan Korbonski, *Jews and the Poles in World War II* (New York: Hippocrene Books, 1989); Jan Gross, *Fear: Anti-Semitism in Poland after Auschwitz; An Essay in Historical Interpretation* (New York: Random House, 2006); Gross, *Neighbors*; Stephanie Kowitz, *Jedwabne: Kollektives Gedächtnis und tabuisierte Vergangenheit* (Berlin: Bebra Wissenschaft, 2004); Polonsky and Michlick, eds., *The Neighbors Respond*; Polonsky, "My Brother's Keeper."

24. In describing his wife on the eve of his second tour of service on the eastern front, Bălaj writes: "She takes part equally with me in all the events our Nation has gone in the last years. . . . She feels proud that I am leaving for the front a second time, while others are finding ways out of serving . . . She has my full admiration." Mihai Bălaj, *Jurnal de front (1942–1943)* (Baia Mare: Editura Gutinul, 1999), 14 and 15.

25. Ibid., 46.

26. Ibid., 41.

27. Ibid., 49. The quote is not attributed to anyone in particular, so it might have been uttered by someone other than the author, but by not distinguishing this voice as another's, the author seems to accept it as possibly his. In general, he is precise in his notations in attributing specific actions and words to individual people identified by name.

28. Ibid., 59.

29. Ibid.

30. Ibid., 115.

31. Ibid., 113–114.

32. Scârneci and Ungurean, eds., *Vieţi paralele.*

33. Stanciu Stroia, with Dan Duşleag, *My Second University: Memories from Romanian Communist Prisons* (New York: iUniverse, 2005).

34. Ibid., 63.

35. Bucur, *Eugenics and Modernization*, 214–216; Ioanid, *The Holocaust in Romania*; Jean Ancel, *Transnistria*, 3 vols. (Bucharest: DU Style, 1998).

36. The Oceacov camp was not strictly a death camp, unlike places like Bogdanovka, where Jews were deported with the purpose of being killed.

37. Goldhagen, *Hitler's Willing Executioners*; Gross, *Neighbors.*

38. Stroia, *My Second University*, 107.

39. Alexandru Teodorescu-Schei, *Învins şi învingător, 1941–1949: Campania din est şi prizonieratul* (Bucharest: Editura All, 1998), 27–28. I include this post-1989 publication here for reasons similar to others discussed above. The memoir was written in 1959 and is overtly identified as such. It is possible the author made some changes in the intervening years, but we are not privy to such insights and must take this information as given.

40. Ibid., 55.

41. Ibid., 15.

42. Ibid., 22 and 23.

43. Ibid., 60.

44. Ibid., 57.

45. Ibid., 56–57.

46. The better documented case of the Soviet soldiers' behavior toward German women shows similarities: Elizabeth Heineman, "Gender, Sexuality, and Coming to Terms with the Past in Germany," *Central European History* 38, no. 1 (2005): 41–74, and "The Hour of Woman." For experiences of other civilian women in Eastern Europe, see Jolluck, *Exile and Identity* and "The Nation's Pain"; Wedy Jo Gertjajanssen, "Victims, Heroes, Survivors: Sexual Violence on the Eastern Front during World War II" (PhD diss., University of Minnesota, 2004).

47. ONP, Satu Mare, dos. 37/1986. There are many other similar examples in both Satu Mare and Sibiu (see ONP, Sibiu): Crucişor in 1947, with local funds; Viile, Satu Mare, 1942; Botiz, Satu Mare, 1942; Sinniclaus, Satu Mare, 1946; Lipău, Satu Mare, 1945; Arpaşu de Jos, Sibiu, 1944; Orlat, Sibiu, 1947; Presaca, Sibiu, 1974; Chirpar, Sibiu, 1971 (monument identified as raised by the Romanian diaspora from the United States); Scorei, Sibiu, 1978; Şeica Mică, Sibiu, 1977; Tilişca, Sibiu, 1947; Vard, Sibiu, 1983; Veştem, Sibiu, after 1944; Galeş, Sibiu, built in 1930 and repaired in 1981 (names for 1941–1944 added after 1944).

48. ONP, Satu Mare, dos. 38/1985. Similar monuments, built during either World War II or the Communist period to commemorate the war dead of these ethnic minorities and which

remained standing throughout the Communist period, include Urziceni, Satu Mare, after 1948; Irina, Satu Mare, 1945; Miercurea, Sibiu, 1970; Şeica Mică, Sibiu 1984; Şura Mare, Sibiu 1974; Cristian, Sibiu, 1982; Caşolt, Sibiu, 1966; Axente Sever, Sibiu, 1970.

49. "European Road" is still the designation for preferred routes recommended on all road maps in Europe. They tend to be paved and well-maintained, the closest thing to a highway in a country that still has less than five hundred kilometers of high-speed divided highways.

50. Vladimir Wertsman, *The Romanians in America and Canada: A Guide to Information Sources* (Detroit: Gale Research, 1980) and *The Romanians in America, 1748–1974: A Chronology and Factbook* (Dobbs Ferry, N.Y.: Oceana Publications, 1975).

51. Horváth, "Divided War Memory"; Balázs Balogh and Ágnes Fülemile, *Társadalom, tájszerkezet, identitás Kalotaszegen: Fejezetek a regionális csoportképzés történeti folyamatairól* (Budapest: Akadémiai Kiadó, 2005).

52. ONP, Satu Mare, dos. 69/1984.

53. One soldier writes about his memories of the two fronts and being taken prisoner by the Soviets: "On 23 January 1943 we all fell prisoner. . . . The space here doesn't allow me to give details about the difficult and humiliating life I endured there—as a Romanian prisoner of war—in Soviet Russia, far away from my country, at the crossroads of my life. But we had a bit of luck and made it back home safe, after many other interesting episodes of battle, this time on the western front. But that is for another time." *Lupte şi jertfe: Memorii şi evocări din război, 1940–1945* (Baia Mare: Ed. Gutinul, S.R.L., 1993), 133.

54. These elements are characteristic of soldiers' diaries produced on both the eastern and the western front in Europe. The Romanian case is typical, rather than extraordinary, in this sense.

55. In his comparative study on the memory of World War II in Poland and the Czech Republic, Padraic Kenney establishes a persuasive contrast between the two countries on the basis of political cultures in the Communist and post-Communist periods, as well as longer cultural traditions. The particularities he introduces in that study are useful for considering the regional great variances of the commemorative discourses about the war. They reinforce the point I make here about the significance of facts as well as the wider cultural discourse in how remembrance takes shape and meaning. Along those lines, the Romanian participation in the war alongside the Nazis, in numbers much greater than the Bulgarians and Hungarians and certainly unparalleled in any way in Czechoslovakia, Poland, and Yugoslavia, makes the Romanian case quite different from these others. See Padraic Kenney, "Martyrs and Neighbors: Sources of Reconciliation in Central Europe," *Common Knowledge* 13, no. 1 (Winter 2007): 149–169.

56. Ioan Hudiţă, *Jurnal politic: 1 ianuarie–24 august 1944* (Bucharest: Editura Roza Vânturilor, 1997), 49.

57. Voinescu, *Jurnal*, 407 and 411–412.

58. Scârneci and Ungurean, eds., *Vieţi paralele.*

59. Voinescu, *Jurnal*, 201.

60. Gheorghe Ionescu, oral history interview by Ioana Manoliu, 7 July 2001, Braşov.

61. Palaghiţă, *Garda*; Nicolae Petraşcu, *Din viaţa legionară*, 3rd ed. (Bucharest: Editura Majadahonda, 1995); http://www.fgmanu.net/istorie/horia_sima1.htm (accessed 13 January 2009).

62. Aurel Socol, *Furtună deasupra Ardealului* (Cluj: Bilbioteca Tribuna, 1991); see also Scârneci and Ungurean, eds., *Vieți paralele.*

63. Scârneci and Ungurean, eds., *Vieți paralele.*

64. Interviews conducted by the author in Treznea in April 2000.

65. Anița Nandriș-Cudla, *Amintiri din viață: 20 de ani în Siberia* (Bucharest: Humanitas, 2006); Vasile Ilica, *Fântâna Albă: O mărturie de sânge; Istorie, amintiri, mărturii* (Oradea: Editura imprimeriei de vest, 1999); Johann Urwich-Ferry, *Fără pașaport prin URSS: Amintiri* (Bucharest: Editura Eminescu, 1999).

66. Vultur, *Istorie trăită;* Viorel Marineasa, *Rusalii '51: Fragmente din deportarea în Bărăgan* (Timișoara: Editura Marineasa, 1994).

67. Pavel Polian, *Against Their Will: The History and Geography of Forced Migrations in the USSR* (Budapest: Central European University Press, 2004); Jill Massino, "Gender as Survival: German Women's Stories of Deportation from Romania to the Soviet Union," *Nationalities Papers* 36, no. 1 (March 2008): 55–83, available at http://www.informaworld.com/smpp/title~content=t713439073~db=all~tab=issueslist~branches=36—v36 (accessed 13 January 2009; search author's name).

68. Jolluck, *Exile and Identity;* Polian, *Against Their Will;* Visvaldis Mangulis, *Latvia in the Wars of the Twentieth Century* (Princeton Junction, N.J.: Cognition Books, 1983); Valdis Lumans, *Latvia in World War II* (New York: Fordham University Press, 2006); *Unpunished Crimes: Latvia under Three Occupations* (Stockholm: Memento, 2003); Tsvetan Todorov, ed., *Voices from the Gulag: Life and Death in Communist Bulgaria* (University Park: Pennsylvania State University Press, 1999).

69. On the various constituencies of the resistance, see Cicerone Ionițoiu, *Album al martirilor genocidului comunist* (Sibiu: Editura Casa de Presă și Tribuna SRL, 1999); Ionițoiu, *Victimele terorii comuniste;* Radosav et al., *Rezistența anticomunistă;* Liiceanu, *Rănile memoriei.*

70. Liiceanu, *Rănile memoriei;* Cosmin Budeancă, "Aspecte privind implicarea femeilor în rezistența anticomunistă din munții României: Cazul Lucreției Jurj (Grupul Șușman)," in Ghizela Cosma and Virgiliu Țârău, eds., *Condiția femeii în România în secolul XX: Studii de caz* (Cluj-Napoca: Presa Universitară Clujeană, 2003), 161–177.

71. Remus Cucoș, interview by Stejărel Olaru, Brașov, July 2001. The subject was extremely detailed about every subject he described, except for this one. It is clear from his imprecise references that he neither met any of these partisans, nor had any evidence of their activities, other than stories he had heard told in the Făgăraș rural area where he lived at that time.

72. See the site of the Polish Resistance Home Army (AK) Museum, http://biega.com/museumAK/AKMuseum.html (accessed 29 November 2007). For English-language sympathetic treatments of the Home Army, see Stefan Korbonski, *The Polish Underground State 1939–1945* (New York: Columbia University Press, 1978); Norman Davies, *Rising '44: The Battle for Warsaw* (New York: Viking Penguin, 2004); Tadeusz Piotrowski, *Poland's Holocaust* (New York: McFarland, 1997); Richard Lukasz, *Forgotten Holocaust: The Poles under German Occupation 1939–1944* (New York: Hippocrene Books, 2001); for a critical view of the heroic memory of the Home Army, see Michael C. Steinlauf, *Bondage to the Dead: Poland and the Memory of the Holocaust* (Ithaca, N.Y.: Syracuse University Press, 1997) and Snyder, *The Reconstruction of Nations.*

73. Voinescu, *Jurnal*, 262, 7 August 1941 entry.

74. Voinescu, *Jurnal*, 364, 13 August 1941 entry.

75. Oral history interviews, April 2000, Treznea.

76. Five of the people who were killed at the beginning of the war in the 9 September 1940 massacre were Jews. Their remains are buried in a common grave together with the Romanian victims in the Orthodox cemetery, and their faces are represented in a mural on the back wall of the Orthodox church. Though aware of their different religious identity and customs, the population has never marked them as different than the rest of the victims, in a way that might be construed as solidarity, but which, in the context of the unwillingness to acknowledge the significant Jewish presence in the village in general, would be best described as a willful forgetting and lack of solidarity.

77. See Jolluck, *Exile and Identity* and "The Nation's Pain"; Gertjajanssen, *Victims, Heroes, Survivors*; Barbara Jancar-Webster, *Women and Revolution in Yugoslavia, 1941–1945* (Denver: Arden Press, 1990).

78. Richard Landwehr, "The European Volunteer Movement in World War II," *The Journal of Historical Review* 2, no. 1 (Spring 1981): 59, available at http://www.ihr.org/jhr/v02/v02p-59_Landwehr.html (accessed 18 January 2009).

79. Massino, "Gender as Survival."

80. Vultur, *Germanii din Banat*; Scârneci and Ungurean, eds., *Vieți.*

81. Ștefan Ionescu, "În umbra morții: Memoria supraviețuitorilor Holocaustului din România," http://www.ceeol.com/aspx/getdocument.aspx?logid=5&id=d7dca8a2-4587-46ad-8208-4edd7195b9e1 (accessed 13 January 2009); Braham, ed., *The Tragedy of Romanian Jewry*; Annette Wieviorka, "From Survivor to Witness: Voices from the Shoah," in Winter and Sivan, eds., *War and Remembrance*, 125–141.

82. Schaddach, *Orășelul pierdut*, 162.

83. Mîrcu, *Pogromurile din Bucovina*; *Pogromulrile de la Iași*; *Pogromurile din Basarabia*; Carp, *Cartea Neagră*; Lezea, *Ninge peste Ucraina.*

84. Dorian, *The Quality of Witness*; Arthur Raymond Davies, *Odyssey through Hell* (New York: L. B. Fischer, 1946); Alexandru Șafran, *Resisting the Storm, Romania, 1940–1947: Memoirs*, ed. Jean Ancel (Jerusalem: Yad Vashem, 1987).

85. Braham, *Politics of Genocide.*

86. The scandal surrounding the publication of Günter Grass's memoirs occasioned a revisiting of this ever-widening array of publicly accepted narratives that coexist as part of the larger field of remembrance discourses about the war.

7. The Dilemmas of Post-Memory in Post-Communist Romania

1. Stroia, *My Second University*, 16.

2. "Marian," message posted on the Ziare.com forum, 18 April 2007, available at http://www.ziare.com/_Steaua_Romaniei__pentru_profesorul_Librescu-82364.html (accessed 14 January 2009).

3. Florin Abraham, *România de la comunism la capitalism, 1989–2004: Sistemul politic* (Bucharest: Tritonic, 2006); Steven Roper, *Romania: The Unfinished Revolution* (Amsterdam:

Harwood Academic, 2000); Andrei Pleşu, *Comédii la porţile Orientului* (Bucharest: Humanitas, 2005); Tom Gallagher, *Theft of a Nation: Romania since Communism* (London: Hurst, 2005); Vladimir Tismăneanu, with Mircea Mihăieş, *Scheletele în dulap* (Iaşi: Polirom, 2004).

4. Adam Michnik, "Gray is Beautiful," in *Letters from Freedom: Post-Cold War Realities and Perspectives* (Berkeley: University of California Press, 1998).

5. Stelian Neagoe, *Istorie politică încarcerată* (Bucharest: Editura Institutului de Ştiinţe Politice şi Relaţii Internaţionale, 2006); Corneliu Coposu, *Dialoguri cu Vartan Arachelian* (Bucharest: Editura Anastasia, [1992]); Corneliu Coposu, *Semnele timpului: Articole politice, meditaţii, atitudini,* ed. and comp. Mircea Popa (Timişoara: Editura de Vest, 1997).

6. Olaf Leisse and Utta-Kristin Leisse, *Barometru de aderare: România; Problemele fundamentale ale ţării şi atitudinile tinerilor români cu privire la integrarea în Uniunea Europeană,* trans. Ioana and Irina Cristescu (Bucharest: Dominor, 2005).

7. Kevin McDermott and Matthew Stibbe, eds., *Revolution and Resistance in Eastern Europe: Challenges to Communist Rule* (Oxford: Berg, 2006); Dennis Deletant, *Ceauşescu and the Securitate: Coercion and Dissent in Romania, 1965–1989* (Armonk, N.Y.: M.E. Sharpe, 1995); Mariana Şipoş, *Destinul unui disident: Paul Goma* (Bucharest: Editura Dalsi, 2005); Mihaela Azoiţei, *Totalitarism şi rezistenţă în România comunistă: Cazul Goma* (Bucharest: Paideia, 2002).

8. Deletant, *Ceauşescu and the Securitate.*

9. Katherine Verdery, *What Was Socialism, and What Comes Next?* (Princeton, N.J.: Princeton University Press, 1996); Andrei Pleşu, *Jurnalul de la Tescani* (Bucharest: Humanitas, 1993); Gabriel Liiceanu, *The Păltiniş Diary: A Paideic Model in Humanist Culture* (Budapest: Central European University Press, 2000); Livius Ciocârlie, *De la Sancho Panza la Cavalerul Tristei Figuri: Jurnal* (Iaşi: Polirom, Colecţia Ego, 2001).

10. Roper, *Romania.*

11. In her Pulitzer winning book, *The Haunted Land: Facing Europe's Ghosts after Communism* (New York: Random House, 1995), Tina Rosenberg pays a great deal of attention to the impact on the Communist past in altering the ability of people in eastern Europe to view political solutions in nuanced ways, akin to Michnik's call for embracing "the gray" in politics. Her analysis leans toward a normative view that tolerance is necessary, and that remaining tied to the past as a way to judge the present is not a productive means to construct a peaceful, democratic polity. In all, she seems to misjudge the level of connection between the past and people's self-identification as victims. Remembering and forgetting are not entirely political acts, but rather processes that take place in an inchoate, dispersed fashion.

12. See, for instance, Stephen Holmes, "Introducing the Center: A Project to Promote Clear Thinking about the Design of Liberal-Democratic Institutions," *East European Constitutional Review* 1, no. 1 (Spring 1992); Bruce Ackerman, *The Future of Liberal Revolution* (New Haven, Conn.: Yale University Press, 1992). Jeff Isaac offers a good overview of the different interpretations of the liberal potentialities of eastern Europe after Communism in "The Meanings of 1989—Central and Eastern Europe: Gains and Losses in the Transition to Democracy," *Social Research* 63, no. 2 (Summer 1996): 291–344.

13. Law no. 10, 31 July 1990, in *Monitorul Oficial* no. 95 (1 August 1990).

14. There is evidence of this at virtually every anniversary since 1990. See, for instance, the links constructed between Romania's democratic future in the EU and direct references to

Trianon and 1 December in the Parliamentary Debates (the Senate) from 30 November 2004, published in *Monitorul Oficial* part 2, no. 164 (8 December 2004), also available at http://www .cdep.ro/pls/steno/steno.stenograma?ids=5782&idm=3,02&idl=1, as well as http://diasan .vsat.ro/pls/steno/steno.stenograma?ids=6005&idm=1,04&idl=1 (accessed 14 January 2009).

15. See Rodica Costea, "Semnificația zilei de 1 Decembrie pentru minoritatea maghiară," *Adevărul de Cluj* no. 767 (1 December 1992), 3; Mircea Iorgulescu, "Provocarea," *Dilema* (29 October–4 November 1999), 4; Levente Szabó, "Touchy Issues: Historical Myths and Their Pragmatics in Post-Socialist Romania," ed. Enikő Magyari-Vincze, *European Anthropology: Theoretical Perspectives and Case-Studies* (Cluj-Kolozsvár, 2004), available at http:// szabol.adatbank.transindex.ro/belso.php?k=8&p=1157 (accessed 14 January 2009). For more recent commentaries, see the blog "Phoenix Transilvania" at http://phoenixtrans.blogspot .com/2007/12/1-de-ce-mbrie.html (accessed 14 January 2009).

16. "1 Decembrie, ziua naționala a tuturor românilor," at *HotNews.ro,* available at http:// www.hotnews.ro/stiri-arhiva-1139048-1-decembrie-ziua-nationala-tuturor-romanilor.htm (accessed 15 January 2009).

17. Interviews by the author in December 1998, Bucharest.

18. See, for instance, photo file of the Embassy from the 2006 celebration, at http://bucharest .usembassy.gov/4th_of_July/Photos.html (accessed 15 January 2009). I attended two of these parties myself, in 1999 and 2000, and both were extremely large, well-attended affairs, where both the political elite and average Bucureșteni got a chance to sample various types of traditional dishes and beverages served on 4 July in the U.S., as well as stupendous fireworks at night.

19. See the text of Law no. 48 (30 May 1995), *Monitorul Oficial* no. 107 (31 May 1995), available at http://www.legestart.ro/Lege-no-48-din-1995-(MjExNTg-).htm (accessed 7 February 2009).

20. Bălescu, *Soldatul.*

21. See, for instance, the photo album for the 2007 official Bucharest commemoration at *Jurnalul Național* 15, no. 4581 (2 December 2007): 1–11.

22. Lajos Kristof, "În memoria eroilor neamului românesc," *Ziarul de Mureș* (21 May 2007), available at http://www.ziaruldemures.ro/fullnews.php?ID=7432 (accessed 18 January 2009).

23. Verdery, *Political Lives of Dead Bodies.*

24. Interviews by author and ethnographic observations, 1999.

25. I had been there myself during the day, in the late morning, when the ceremony took place, and was able to see the setting without being constrained by the angles of the camera or editing in the studio, as the ceremony was presented later on in the evening.

26. For a brief video of such a broadcast see http://www.youtube.com/watch?v=_ bC9pYlPPNk (accessed 23 September 2008), starting at minute 3:37 in the clip.

27. Author's ethnographic observations from 1999, 2000, 2002, 2005, and 2008.

28. I have seen these posters at the university on several occasions when I happened to be traveling through Bucharest around the date of the commemoration.

29. In addition to considering films in the context of their production and release in movie theatres, I view the impact of movies even more prominently in terms of their broadcasting on television and release on DVD/VHS, both pre- and post-1989 productions. Cinema viewership in movie theatres has become secondary to these two other important avenues.

30. Căliman, *Istoria filmului românesc.*

31. On the successes and failures of Romanian post-Communist cinema from the perspective of movie critics, see "Special Issue: Contemporary Romanian Cinema," *MovEast* no. 8 (2008); Andrei Gorzo, "Cum se prezintă filmul românesc?" *Dilema* no. 507 (2002): 15, available at www.ceeol.com/aspx/getdocument.aspx?logid=5&id=F83B63AF-1FC4-4023-BF7F-A2DE67250A3C (accessed 15 January 2009).

32. Căliman, *Istoria filmului românesc.* All of these movies have been re-released on DVD and have seen a growing fan base among younger generations of viewers.

33. He was a Social Democrat senator (Iliescu's neo-Communist Party) who, at one time, called for burning the alternative history textbooks that deviated from the standard nationalist discourse established during the late Communist period. For the debates around the alternative textbooks, which also aimed to introduce Antonescu's responsibility in World War II and the Holocaust more fully, see Boris Singer, "În aprilie-mai 1999, Ministerul Educației Naționale . . . ," *Observatorul Cultural* no. 99 (16 January 2002), available at http://www.observatorcultural.ro/In-aprilie-mai-1999-Ministerul-Educatiei-Nationale . . . *articleID_403-articles_details.html (accessed on 7 February 2009), as well as the Parliamentary Debates (Chamber of Deputies) from 15 October 1999, available at http://www.cdep.ro/comisii/invatamant/pdf/1999/pv1013.pdf (accessed 18 January 2009).

34. Căliman, *Istoria filmului românesc,* 421.

35. Ibid., 422; capitalization in the original.

36. Commenting on the popularity of Nicolaescu's movies, film critic Marian Țuțui writes that "he enjoyed enormous box office success with his historical movies . . . entering public consciousness as an American-type movie maker." See Marian Țuțui, "Istoria filmului românesc in 7000 de cuvinte," available at http://www.cncinema.abt.ro/Files/Documents/fls-258.doc (accessed 28 September 2008; this link downloads a Microsoft Word document), 12–13.

37. See, for instance, comments at the bottom of http://www.trilulilu.ro/BulleT/58dobeoa17eodc (clip of the final scene from the movie), which include: "GREAT MOVIE! GREAT DIRECTOR!" (accessed 15 January 2009; emphasis in the original).

38. Maria Bucur, "The Death Triangle [Feature Film]," *American Historical Review* 104 no. 4 (October 1999): 1427–1428.

39. In its reporting on the December 1989 Revolution in Romania, the *New York Times* misidentified Ana Ipătescu as a "Communist heroine," likely on the basis of anecdotal evidence from people interviewed by the journalist in Bucharest. This suggests to some extent how the past came to be re-signified by many people in connection to the hated Communist propaganda behind such renaming efforts, rather than any real historical realities about the people whose names were being used. See John Kifner, "Upheaval in the East; Army Executes Ceaucescu [sic] and Wife for 'Genocide' Role, Bucharest Says," *New York Times* (26 December 1989), available at http://query.nytimes.com/gst/fullpage.html?res=950DE3DF153EF935A15751C1A96F948260&sec=&spon=&pagewanted=all (accessed 15 January 2009).

40. In fact, there are still many streets and institutions in Romania today named for Ipătescu, which suggests that the negative connotations associated with her name were linked only with the particular action of renaming a downtown landmark during a period that people simply wanted to forget by way of returning the pre-Communist street name to that space.

41. My observations here come from ethnographic notes taken in 1999, 2000, 2002, and 2005, from many informal conversations I had with people who lived on streets that were renamed, sometimes several times, after 1990. Alas, there wasn't a general practice of keeping minutes for neighborhood meetings where these topics were discussed.

42. The first relevant law, "The Law for the privatization of commercial enterprises," was published in 1991 as Law no. 58 (14 August 1991) and subsequently modified multiple times, until article forty-four of the 2003 Constitution finally settled the various legal inconsistencies of the first decade and half after the fall of Communism.

43. Andrei Oişteanu, "De la Bucureşti la Auschwitz şi retur," *Revista 22* 14, no. 777 (28 January–4 February 2005), available at http://www.revista22.ro/html/index.php?art=1464&nr=2005-01-28 (accessed 14 January 2009); about the resistance of the local authorities against changing the name, see William Totok, "Mistificări şi falsificări: Contrareacţii la Ordonanţă," *Observator cultural* no. 156 (21–27 January 2003), available at http://www.observatorcultural. ro/Mistificari-si-falsificari*articleID_7373-articles_details.html (accessed 13 March 2009).

44. Oişteanu, "De la Bucureşti"; International Commission on the Holocaust in Romania, *Final Report*.

45. International Commission on the Holocaust in Romania, *Final Report*.

46. Andrei Pippidi, *Despre statui şi morminte: Pentru o teorie a istoriei simbolice* (Iaşi: Polirom, 2000).

47. Oişteanu, "De la Bucureşti."

48. See *Lupte şi jertfe,* for a press with a small circulation, and Titus Popescu, ed., *Veteranii pe drumul onoarei şi jertfei (1941–1945): De la Nistru la Marea de Azov* (Bucharest: Editura Vasile Cârlova, 1997) for a publisher with wider circulation (though it is by no means a household name, as are Polirom and Humanitas).

49. Oral history interview by Ioana Ceapă, 31 July 2001, Braşov. See other examples in *Lupte şi jertfe; Veteranii pe drumul;* Asociaţia Naţională a Veteranilor de Război, Victor Atanasiu, coord., *Veteranii pe drumul onoarei şi jertfei 1940–1945: Ultime mărturii 1940–1945* (Bucharest: Editura Academiei de Înalte Studii Militare, 2002).

50. Wittman, *Balkan Nightmare;* Kapronczay, *Refugees in Hungary;* Károly Kapronczay, *Magyarok és lengyelek, 1939–1945: Menekültügy* (Budapest: Gondolat, 1991); Krisztián Ungváry, *Battle for Budapest: 100 Days in World War II,* trans. Ladislaus Löb (London: I. B. Tauris, 2003); Krisztián Ungváry, *A Második világháború* (Budapest: Osiris, 2005).

51. On the mythical status of these radical–right wing intellectuals in the eyes of the Romanian intelligentsia of the 1980s, see Verdery, *National Ideology,* especially chapter 7.

52. Gabriel Liiceanu, "Sebastian, mon frère," in Iordan Chimet, ed., *Dosar Mihail Sebastian* (Bucharest: Editura Universal Dalsi, 2001 [1997]), 3–10.

53. See note 22 in chapter 6.

54. The "Altfel" ("Otherwise" or "Another Way") talk show is co-hosted by Liiceanu and Andrei Pleşu on the Realitatea TV Channel.

55. An "emergency executive order" was passed in 2000 to deal with this. See *Monitorul Oficial* no. 797 (1 September 2005), available at http://www.legestart.ro/AfisareAct.aspx?id_act=156839 (accessed 9 February 2009); it subsequently has been modified, most recently in 2006. And see Law no. 465, *Monitorul Oficial* no. 1019 (12 December 2006), available at http://www.legestart.ro/lege-no-465-din-2006-(MjlxMzA1).htm (accessed 9 February 2009).

56. Centrul de Resurse pentru Diversitate Etnoculturală, "Cu jumătate de masură: Procesul retrocedării proprietăților care au aparținut cultelor religioase în România," available at http://www.edrc.ro/docs/docs/provocdivers/010-032.pdf (accessed 15 January 2009); Rodica Culcer, "Manipulatori în civil și-n sutană," *Formula AS* no. 726 (2006), available at http://www.formula-as.ro/2006/726/intrebarile-saptamanii-23/manipulatori-in-civil-si-n-sutana-7153 (accessed 15 January 2009); "Restituirea proprietăților bisericești," *BBC Bucharest* (14 July 2006), available at http://www.9am.ro/stiri-revista-presei/Social/38282/Restituirea-proprietatilor-bisericesti (accessed 15 January 2009).

57. "Justiția a confirmat legalitatea restituirii Domeniului Peleș," *Gardianul* (7 December 2007), available at http://www.gardianul.ro/2007/12/07/media_cultura-c20/justitia_a_confirmat_legalitatea_restituirii_domeniului_peles-s96887.html (accessed 15 January 2009); and "Regele Mihai—din nou proprietar la Peleș," *BBC Romania,* available at http://www.bbc.co.uk/romanian/news/story/2007/03/070301_peles.shtml (accessed 15 January 2009).

58. Sânziana Demian, "Despre retrocedările clădirilor vechi din Cluj," *Formula AS* no. 748 (2006), available at http://www.formula-as.ro/2006/748/spectator-38/despre-retrocedarile-cladirilor-vechi-din-cluj-7584 (accessed 15 January 2009).

59. Dennis Deletant, "Romania, 1945–89: Resistance, Protest and Dissent," in McDermott and Stibbe, eds., *Revolution and Resistance,* 81–100.

60. It eventually became an ally of a political party, the Civic Alliance Party, which counted among its prominent representatives in the parliament the literary critic Nicolae Manolescu, one of the people who intervened vocally in the Liiceanu-Sebastian scandal to defend his colleague. See Nicolae Manolescu, "Răspuns la răspuns," *România literară* nos. 23–24 (17–23 June 1998), "Ce înseamnă să fii rasist," *România literară* no. 19 (20–26 May 1998), and "Holocaustul și Gulagul," *România literară* no. 9 (11–17 March 1998).

61. There are many testimonials of participants at all the summer schools held there since the 1990s. See for instance, Alexadru Zub, "Memorialul Sighet," available at http://destinatii.liternet.ro/articol/164//Alexandru-Zub/Memorial-Sighet.html (accessed 10 December 2007); Dan Nicu, "Sighet: O școală a neuitării," *Contrafort* 8, no. 154 (August 2007), available at http://www.contrafort.md/2007/154/1263.html (accessed 15 January 2009).

62. Good examples of this obliviousness can be seen in the presentation of the museum ("Scurt istoric al Muzeului Memorial," on the official site of the Museum, at http://www.memorialsighet.ro/ro/istoric_muzeu_memorial.asp (accessed 15 January 2009); and Nicu, "Sighet." The history of violence inside the Sighet Prison, now turned Memorial/Museum, and around it before 1945, when it was turned into a site of imprisonment for enemies of the Communist Party, is absent from the self-contextualization of the founders of the Civic Academy. One example of an attempt to account for the complexity of Sighet's narratives of victimization over the 1944 divide is Robert Fürtos, "Sighet, preambul al Holocaustului, punct central al Gulagului," *Caietele Echinox* no. 13 (2007): 226–241, available at www.ceeol.com/aspx/getdocument.aspx?logid=5&id=72121964-2bf7-4a26-a3e4-58dc94fdb8c5 (accessed 15 January 2009).

63. *Exerciții de memorie.*

64. Oblia, "Excelsior," blog posted on 24 January 2008 at http://oblia.wordpress.com/2008/01/24/cool%E2%80%A6/ (accessed 15 January 2009).

65. Article 12, Chapter IV (Public administration officials' duties), from Emergency Order no. 31/2002, published in *Monitorul Oficial* no. 214, 28 March 2002, and available at http://www.clr.ro/rep_htm/OUG31_2002.htm (accessed 15 January 2009).

66. As an illustration, see Carmen Epuran, "A fost Holocaust," *Ziua* no. 3170 (12 November 2004), available at http://www.ziua.ro/display.php?data=2004-11-12&id=162290&kword=comisia+wiesel (accessed 15 January 2009). Most revealing here are the 842 comments posted in connection to this article, available at http://www.ziua.ro/f.php?data=2004-11-12&thread=162290 (accessed 15 January 2009). An excellent lucid analysis of these responses is William Totok, "Receptarea publicistică a raportului final al Comisiei Wiesel în presa românească şi germană," *Studia Hebraica* no. 5 (2005): 186–195, available at www.ceeol.com/aspx/getdocument.aspx?logid=5&id=de624a2d-8f93-4325-b1d0-9a58eed9aab9 (accessed 15 January 2009).

67. International Commission on the Holocaust in Romania, *Final Report.*

68. Viorel Ilişoi, "Istoria Holocaustului, greu de predat într-un loc cu trecut legionar," *Cotidianul* (23 October 2007), available at http://www.cotidianul.ro/index.php?id=15029&art=37650&cHash=cb0c1c176e (accessed 15 January 2009).

69. On the controversy about the continued presence of this plaque, see Robert Bălan, "Bustul lui 'Ion Antonescu' n-a 'rezistat' decât şase ani," *Gândul* (30 July 2007), available at http://www.gandul.info/arte/bustul-ion-antonescu-n-rezistat-sase-ani.html?3940;866960 (accessed 15 January 2009).

70. Bălan, "Bustul," Internet forum, posting by "e404rror" on 30 July 2007.

71. William Totok, "Febra răsăriteană a reabilitarilor: Cazul Albert Wass," *Observator Cultural* no. 184 (2 September 2003), available at http://www.observatorcultural.ro/Febra-rasariteana-a-reabilitarilor*articleID_9031-articles_details.html (accessed 16 January 2009).

72. "Marian," message posted on Ziare.com; for the discussion in the forum follow the links under "Adaugă opinia ta"—in Romanian, "Add your opinion"; for similar strands of discussion, see the internet forum connected to the article by Adina Şuteu and Alina Anghel, "Profesorul Librescu a murit salvându-şi studenţii," *Adevărul OnLine* no. 5215 (18 April 2007), available at http://www.adevarul.ro/articole/2007/profesorul-librescu-a-murit-salvandu-si-studentii.html (accessed 21 April 2007); one of the postings states: "Honorables, Librescu is not a Jew, he is a Romanian from every point of view, a Jew doesn't endanger his life for goys. . . . This man died defending the future of humanity, he was an old man with a youthful heart, he knew what he was doing. The education he received in Romania had a hand in this. May he rest in peace."

73. See the two internet forums mentioned in the previous note at Ziare.com and *Adevărul OnLine.*

74. Hirsch, *Family Frames;* Shelley Hornstein, *Image and Remembrance: Representation and the Holocaust* (Bloomington: Indiana University Press, 2003); T. G. Ashplant, Graham Dawson, and Michael Roper, eds., *The Politics of War Memory and Commemoration* (London: Routledge, 2000); Eva Hoffman, *After Such Knowledge: Memory, History, and the Legacy of the Holocaust* (New York: Public Affairs, 2004); Alison Landsberg, *Prosthetic Memory: The Transformation of American Remembrance in the Age of Mass Culture* (New York: Columbia University Press, 2004).

75. Skultans, *Testimony of Lives;* Rudolf Krueger, *The Krueger Memoir: Life after Death in the Soviet Union,* trans. J. Gregory Oswald (Huntington, W.Va.: Aegina Press, 1993); Ann Lehtmets, *Sentence Siberia: A Story of Survival* (Adelaide: Wakefield Press, 1994).

76. Mariana Spătari, "Deportări, represalii, foamete," in *Exerciții de memorie,* 145–148 (quote on 146).

77. Dan Dușleag, "Introduction," in Stroia, *My Second University,* 16.

78. Ibid.

79. Ibid., 18.

80. Till, *New Berlin;* Jürgen Habermas, *Time of Transitions,* ed. and trans. Ciaran Cronin and Max Pensky (Cambridge: Polity, 2006); Müller, ed., *Memory and Power.*

81. Leggewie, "Equally Criminal?" and related articles at http://www.eurozine.com/comp/ focalpoints/eurohistories.html (accessed 16 January 2009).

82. See "Declaration of 9 May 1950," available at http://europa.eu/abc/symbols/9-may/ decl_en.htm.

Selected Bibliography

Primary Sources

Archives

Archival sources are referenced in the text and footnotes as indicated in italics in parentheses below:

National State Archives (*NSA*), Bucharest, Sibiu, Cluj, Satu Mare, Zalău, Brașov, and Iași
Specific collections:

> Ministry of Education/Instruction and Arts (*MEA*), Arts Direction (*AD*)
> Mayoral Office Archives (*MOA*), Iași, Sibiu, Zalău
> Regional Prefecture Archives (*RPA*), Iași, Sibiu, Satu Mare, Zalău
> National Orthodox Romanian Women's Society (*NORWS*), Bucharest
> Romanian Communist Party (*RCP*), Central Committee (*CC*)
> Romanian Communist Party (*RCP*), Regional Offices (*RO*), Cluj
> Ministry of National Defense (*MND*), Superior Direction for Education and
>   Propaganda (*SDEP*), post-1945 period

National Film Archives (*NFA*), Bucharest
The Office of National Patrimony (*ONP*), County Archives, Sibiu, Satu Mare, Baia Mare, Tîrgu Mureș
National Military Museum Archive (*NMMA*), Bucharest
Heroes Cult Archive (*HCA*), Bucharest
Library of the Romanian Academy (*LRA*), Manuscript Collection
United States Holocaust Memorial Museum (*USHMM*)

Museum Exhibits (permanent collections)

Brașov History Museum
Brukhental Museum, Sibiu
Ethnographic Museum, Baia Mare
Ethnographic Museum, Sighet
Jewish History Museum (community-based exhibit in the active Synagogue), Sighet
Jewish History Museum, Bucharest
Mărășești Mausoleum Museum, Mărășești

National History Museum, Cluj
National History Museum, Iaşi
National History Museum, Satu Mare
National History Museum, Zalău
National Museum of History, Bucharest
National Museum of Military History, Bucharest
National Peasant Museum, Bucharest
Sighet Memorial Museum, Sighet
Transylvania History Museum, Cluj
United States Holocaust Memorial Museum, Washington, D.C.
Village Museum, Bucharest

Oral History Interviews and Ethnographic Fieldwork

Baia Mare, 1999
Braşov, 2000, 2002
Bucharest, 1998, 1999, 2000, 2002
Cluj, 1999, 2000
Focşani, 1999
Iaşi, 1999
Ineu, 1999
Satu Mare, 1999
Sibiu, 1999, 2000
Sighet, 1999
Tîrgu Mureş, 1999
Treznea, 2000
Zalău, 2000

Periodicals

Adevărul literar şi artistic, 1920–1939
Adevărul, 1918–1938, 1991–2007
Alba Iulia, 1921–1945
Amicul poporului, 1919, 1921–1941
Arhitectura, 1920–1944, 1950–1994
Aurora, 1923–1928
Buletinul Muzeului Militar Naţional, 1937–1942
Buletinul veteranilor de război, Sibiu, 1993–1996
Calendarul Astra, 1918, 1919, 1921–1935
Calendarul Ligiei Culturale, 1920–1934
Căminul, Focşani, 1927–1934
Convorbiri literare, 1919–1942
Cotidianul, 1992–present
Cultul eroilor noştri, 1921–1938
Curentul, 1928–1944
Curierul israelit, 1918–1940, 1944–1945

Cuvîntul, 1924–1941

Dilema/Dilema veche, 1990–2008

Dimineața, 1914–1937

Dreptatea, 1944

Egalitatea, 1919–1940

Eroii neamului (România), 1916–1920, 1921

Eroii patriei, 1920–1922, 1944–1946

Evenimentul zilei, 1994–present

Evenimentul de Iași, Iași, 1921–1942

Expresul, Brăila, 1920–1940

Familia, 1926–1929, 1934–1944

Frontul Mărășești, 1936–1939

Gândirea, 1921–1937

Gazeta luptătorilor, 1944–1945

Jurnalul național, 1993–present

Luceafărul, 1958–1989

Magazin istoric, 1968–present

Magyar Szó, 1990–2000

Neamul românesc, 1914–1940

Observator Cultural, 2000–present

Opinia, Iași, 1921–1951

Parliamentary Debates, Senate and Chamber of Deputies, Romania, 1990–2007

Patria, 1919–1938

Revista 22, 1990–present

Revista cultului mozaic, 1956–1981, 1983–1999

Revista de istorie militară, 1990–2002

Revista fundațiilor regale, 1934–1947

Revista Memoria, 1991–present

Revista virtutea militară de razboi, 1930–1934

Romania eroică

Romania liberă, 1948–present

Romania literară, 1968–present

Romania Mare, 1990–2004

Romania militară, 1921–1940

Săptămîna, 1963–1989

Scînteia, 1947–1989

Szabadság, 1990–2000

Teatrul, Iași, 1917–1938

Timpul, 1937–1947

Tribuna, 1953–1989

Universul, 1918–1953

Vatra, Craiova, 1929–1947

Veteranul de război, Bacău, 1993–1999

Veteranul, 1935–1938

Viața mlitară, 1959–2006

Ziua, 1998–present

Internet Forum at *Adevarul OnLine,* 2004–2007

Internet Forum at *Ziare.com,* 2004–2007

Films (Documentary, Shorts, Features, Television Series)

Note: In the following list, D connotes documentary films, TV connotes television series, and the year in parenthesis is the date of the premiere of the movie or initial airing of the TV series.

Actorul și sălbaticii (1975)

Alarmă în munți (1955)

Am fost șaisprezece (1980)

Asediul (1971)

Capcana mercenarilor (1981)

Cătușe roșii (1942)

Cei care plătescu cu viața (1989)

Cu mîinile curate (1972)

Datorie și sacrificiu (1925)

Destinul Mareșalului, D (1994)

Detașameanul "Concordia" (1981)

Ecaterina Teodoroiu (Eroina de la Jiu) (1931)

Filmul încoronării, D (1922)

Începutul adevărului—Oglinda (1993)

Între oglinzi paralele (1979)

Liniștea din adîncuri (1982)

Lumini și umbre, TV (1982)

Memorialul durerii, TV (1991)

Nepoții gornistului (1953)

Noi, cei din linia întîi (1986)

Pădurea spînzuraților (1964)

Pe aici nu se trece (1975)

Pe malul stîng al Dunării albastre (1983)

Pistruiatul, TV (1973)

Pistruiatul (Evadatul) (1986)

Pentru patrie (1977)

Porțile albastre ale orașului (1973)

Procesul alb (1966)

Răsuna valea (1949)

Războiul nostru sfânt, D (1942?)

Ringul (1984)

România în lupta contra bolșevismului, D (1941)

România la a 70-a aniversare a Marii Uniri, D (1988)

Roșcovanul (1976)

Semnul șarpelui (1982)

Serata (1971)

Serbările Unirii, D (1929)

Setea (1961)

Stejar, extremă urgență (1974)

Străinul (1964)

Triunghiul morții (1999)

Ultima frontieră a morții (1979)

Ultima noapte de dragoste, întîia noapte de război (1980)

Ultimul cartuş (1973)

Un august în flăcări, TV

Un comisar acuză (1974)

Valurile Dunării (1960)

Viața nu iartă (1959)

Ziua "Z" (1985)

Memoirs, Journals, Novels, and Documents

Aderca, Felix. 1916. Bucharest: Editura Hasefer, 1997.

Alecsandri, Vasile. Poezii populare ale românilor. Bucharest, 1866.

Alimănişteanu, Pia. Însemnări din timpul ocupației germane, 1916–1918. Bucharest, 1929.

Arnăuțoiu, Ioana Raluca, and Voicu Arnăuțoiu, eds. Luptătorii din munți: Toma Arnăuțoiu şi grupul de la Nucşoara; Documente ale anchetei, procesului, detenției. Bucharest: Editura Vremea, 1997.

Asociația Națională a Veteranilor de Război, Victor Atanasiu, coord. Veteranii pe drumul onoarei şi jertfei 1940–1945: Ultime mărturii 1940–1945. Bucharest: Editura Academiei de Înalte Studii Militare, 2002.

Averescu, Mareşal Alexandru. Notițe zilnice din războiu (1916–1918). Bucharest: Editura Cultura Națională, n.d. [1935].

Bacalbaşa, Constantin. Capitala sub ocupația duşmanului, 1916–1918. Brăila, [1921].

Bălaj, Mihai. Jurnal de front (1942–1943). Baia Mare: Editura Gutinul, 1999.

Benjamin, Lya, ed. Evreii din România între anii 1940–1944: Legislația antievreiască. Vol. 1. Bucharest: Editura Hasefer, 1993.

Bibescu, Martha. Jurnal: 1915. Bucharest: Compania, 2001.

Cancicov, Vasile Th. Impresiuni şi păreri personale din timpul războiului României: Jurnal zilnic, 13 august 1916–31 decembrie 1918. 2 vols. Bucharest: Atelierele societății Universul, 1921.

Cantacuzino, Maria. "Memoirs de 1918." LRA, Manuscript Collection, A 935.

Cantacuzino, Sabina. Din viața Familiei Ion C. Brătianu. Vol. 2. Bucharest: Editura Albatros, 1996.

———. Războiul 1914–1919. Bucharest: Editura Universul, 1937.

Carp, Matatias. Cartea Neagră: Suferințele evreilor din România 1940–1944. 3 vols. Bucharest: Socec, 1946–1948.

Cazacu, G. Şt. Calea sângelui. 5th ed. Bucharest: Editura cronicarul, 1940.

Centrul de Resurse pentru Diversitate Etnoculturală. "Cu jumătate de masură: Procesul retrocedării proprietăților care au aparținut cultelor religioase în România." Available at http://www.edrc.ro/docs/docs/provocdivers/010-032.pdf (accessed 18 January 2009).

Ciocârlie, Livius. *De la Sancho Panza la Cavalerul Tristei Figuri: Jurnal*. Iaşi: Polirom, Colecţia Ego, 2001.

Cornea, Nelli. *Însemnări din vremea războiului*. Bucharest: Ed. librăriei H. Steinberg şi fiu, [1921].

Cuţescu-Storck, Cecilia. *Fresca unei vieţi*. Bucharest: Vremea, 2006.

Davies, Arthur Raymond. *Odyssey through Hell*. New York: L. B. Fischer, 1946.

Dongorozi, Ion. *Monumentul Eroilor: Nuvele şi schiţe*. Bucharest: Editura Naţională S. Ciornei, 1931, 127–187.

Dorian, Emil. *The Quality of Witness: A Romanian Diary, 1937–1944*. Philadelphia: Jewish Publication Society of America, 1982.

Durham, Edith. *The Burden of the Balkans*. London: E. Arnold, 1905.

Elisabeth, Queen of Romania. *From Memory's Shrine: The Reminiscences of Carmen Sylva*. Trans. Edith Hopkirk. Philadelphia: J. B. Lippincott, 1911.

Eskenasy, Victor. *Izvoare şi mărturii referitoare la evreii din România*. 2nd rev. ed. Bucharest: Editura Hasefer, 1995.

Exerciţii de memorie: Biblioteca Sighet. Bucharest: Academia Civică, 1999.

Fălcoianu, Alexandrina. *Din zile grele*. Bucharest, 1937.

———. *Un examen de conştiinţă şi un răspuns*. Bucharest: Tipografia Isvor, 1937.

Fodoreanu, Jeana Col. *Femeia-Soldat*. Bucharest, 1928.

Fulga, Laurenţiu. *Eroica, I: Oameni fără glorie*. Bucharest: Editura tineretului, 1956.

Halevy, M. A. *Comunităţile evreieşti din Iaşi şi Bucureşti pînă la 1821*. N.p.: Institutul de istorie evreo-română, 1931.

Hudiţă, Ioan. *Jurnal politic: 1 ianuarie–24 august 1944*. Bucharest: Editura Roza Vânturilor, 1997.

Ilica, Vasile. *Fântâna Albă: O mărturie de sânge; Istorie, amintiri, mărturii*. Oradea: Editura imprimeriei de vest, 1999.

Institutul Social Roman, comp. *Constituţia din 1923 în dezbaterea contemporanilor*. Bucharest: Humanitas, 1990.

Instrucţiunile asupra aplicării legei cinstirei memoriei Eroilor căzuţi şi a statutului societătii "Mormintele Eroilor căzuţi în războiu." Bucharest: Editura Răsăritul, 1921.

Ionescu, Take. "Iubite prieten." In Cancicov, *Impresiuni*. Vol. 1.

Ioniţoiu, Cicerone. *Album al martirilor genocidului comunist*. Sibiu: Editura Casa de Presă şi Tribuna SRL, 1999.

———. *Rezistenţa anticomunistă din munţii României, 1946–1958*. 2nd rev. ed. Bucharest: Gîndirea Românească, 1993.

———. *Victimele terorii comuniste: Arestaţi, torturaţi, întemniţaţi, ucişi*. Bucharest: Editura maşina de scris, 2000–2006.

Jagendorf, Siegfried. *Jagendorf's Foundry: A Memoir of the Romanian Holocaust 1941–1944*. New York: Harper Collins, 1991.

Kapronczay, Károly. *Magyarok és lengyelek, 1939–1945: Menekültügy*. Budapest: Gondolat, 1991.

———. *Refugees in Hungary: Shelter from Storm during World War II*. Budapest: Corvinus Library, 1999.

Karadžić, Vuk. *Narodne srpske poslovice i druge različne, kao i one u običaj uzete riječi.* Cetinje: U Narodnoj štampariji, 1836.

———. *Songs of the Serbian People: From the Collections of Vuk Karadzic.* Pittsburgh, Pa.: University of Pittsburgh Press, 1997.

Kara-Schwartz, I. *Mărturii din veacuri: Din istoria evreilor în România.* Bacău, 1947.

Krueger, Rudolf M. *The Krueger Memoir: Life after Death in the Soviet Union.* Trans. J. Gregory Oswald. Huntington, W.Va.: Aegina Press, 1993.

Kuncz, Aladár. *Black Monastery.* New York: Harcourt, Brace, [1934]. Trans. into Romanian as *Mănăstirea neagră.* Bucharest: Kriterion, 1971.

Lecții în ajutorul celor care studiază istoria P.M.R. Bucharest: Editura politică, [1960].

Lehtmets, Ann. *Sentence Siberia: A Story of Survival.* Adelaide: Wakefield Press, 1994.

Lezea, Sergiu. *Ninge peste Ucraina.* Bucharest: Scânteia, 1946.

Liiceanu, Gabriel. *The Păltiniș Diary: A Paideic Model in Humanist Culture.* Budapest: Central European University Press, 2000.

Lupte și jertfe: Memorii și evocări din război, 1940–1945. Baia Mare: Ed. Gutinul, S.R.L., 1993.

Marghiloman, Alexandru. *Note politice.* Vols. 1–4. Bucharest: Editura Scripta, 1993–1996.

Marie of Romania. *Însemnări zilnice.* Bucharest: Editura Albatros, 1996.

———. *Ordeal: The Story of My Life.* New York: C. Scribner's Sons, 1935.

Marineasa, Viorel. *Rusalii '51: Fragmente din deportarea în Bărăgan.* Timișoara: Editura Marineasa, 1994.

Marinescu, Col. Gabriel, et al., eds. *Carol al II-lea, regele Românilor: Cinci ani de domnie (8 iunie 1930–8 iunie 1935.* Bucharest: Institutul de arte grafice Eminescu, 1935.

Ministerul de Război. *Statutul Societății "Mormintele eroilor căzuți în războiu."* Bucharest: Editura Răsăritul, 1921.

Mîrcu, Marius. *Pogromurile de la Iași.* Bucharest: Glob, 1944.

———. *Pogromurile din Basarabia și din Transnistria.* Bucharest: Glob, 1947.

———. *Pogromurile din Bucovina și Dorohoi.* Bucharest: Glob, 1945.

Miroiu, Mihaela, and Mircea Miclea. *R'estul si vestul.* Iași: Polirom, 2002.

Mózes, Téreza. *Evreii din Oradea.* Bucharest: Hasefer, 1997.

Nandriș-Cudla, Anița. *Amintiri din viață: 20 de ani în Siberia.* Bucharest: Humanitas, 2006.

The Other Balkan Wars: A 1913 Carnegie Endowment Inquiry in Retrospect. Washington, D.C.: Carnegie Endowment for International Peace, distributed by Brookings Institution Publications, 1993.

Palaghiță, Ștefan. *Garda de Fier spre reînvierea României.* Buenos Aires: Editura autorului, 1951.

Petrașcu, Nicolae. *Din viața legionară.* 3rd ed. Bucharest: Editura Majadahonda, 1995.

Petrescu, Camil. *Ultima noapte de dragoste, întîia noapte de război.* Bucharest: Editura Eminescu, 1971.

Pleșu, Andrei. *Jurnalul de la Tescani.* Bucharest: Humanitas, 1993.

Popescu, Petru. *Dulce ca mierea e glonțul patriei.* Bucharest: Editura Cartea Românească, 1972.

Popescu, Titus, ed. *Veteranii pe drumul onoarei și jertfei (1941–1945): De la Nistru la Marea de Azov.* Bucharest: Editura Vasile Cârlova, 1997.

Popovici, Titus. *Străinul.* Bucharest: Editura Eminescu, 1979.

Preda, Marin. *Delirul.* 2nd rev. ed. Bucharest: Editura Cartea Românească, 1975.

Raicoveanu (Fulmen), Ecaterina. *Jurnalul unei surori de caritate, 1916–1918.* Brăila, 1920.

Rebreanu, Liviu. *Ion.* Timişoara: Editura Facla, 1988.

Russu Ardeleanu, Nicolae. *Prizonier în ţara ta.* Botoşani, 1918.

Şafran, Alexandru. *Resisting the Storm, Romania, 1940–1947: Memoirs,* ed. Jean Ancel. Jerusalem: Yad Vashem, 1987.

Schaddach, Leo. *Orăşelul pierdut.* Bucharest: Kriterion, 1996.

Sebastian, Mihail. *Jurnal, 1935–1945.* Bucharest: Editura Humanitas, 1996.

Sevastos, El. *Călătorii prin Ţara Românească.* Iaşi, 1888.

Sihleanu, Severa. *Note şi desminiţiri asupra amintirilor D-nei Sabina Cantacuzino.* Bucharest, 1938.

Socol, Aurel. *Furtună deasupra Ardealului.* Cluj: Bilbioteca Tribuna, 1991.

Stroia, Stanciu, with Dan Duşleag. *My Second University: Memories from Romanian Communist Prisons.* New York: iUniverse, 2005.

Teodorescu-Schei, Alexandru. *Învins şi învingător, 1941–1949: Campania din est şi prizonieratul.* Bucharest: Editura All, 1998.

Ungváry, Krisztián. *A Második világháború.* Budapest: Osiris, 2005.

———. *Battle for Budapest: 100 Days in World War II,* trans. Ladislaus Löb. London: I. B. Tauris, 2003.

Urwich-Ferry, Johann. *Fără paşaport prin URSS: Amintiri.* Bucharest: Editura Eminescu, 1999.

Voinescu, Alice. *Jurnal.* Bucharest: Editura Albatros, 1997.

West, Rebecca. *Black Lamb and Grey Falcon: A Journey through Yugoslavia.* New York: Penguin, 1994.

Wiesel, Elie. *Night.* New York: Bantam, 1982.

Wittmann, Anna. *Balkan Nightmare: A Transylvanian Saxon in World War II.* New York: Columbia University Press, 2000.

Secondary Sources

Abraham, Florin. *România de la comunism la capitalism, 1989–2004: Sistemul politic.* Bucharest: Tritonic, 2006.

Ackerman, Bruce. *The Future of Liberal Revolution.* New Haven, Conn.: Yale University Press, 1992.

Adrian, Victor, Ion Burţea, and Petre Lupan. *România: Monumente istorice şi de artă.* Bucharest: Editura meridiane, 1972.

Ancel, Jean. *Contribuţii la istoria României: Problema evreiască.* Bucharest: Hasefer, 2001.

———. *Preludiu la asasinat: Pogromul de la Iaşi, 29 iunie 1941.* Iaşi: Polirom, 2005.

———. *Transnistria.* 3 vols. Bucharest: DU Style, 1998.

Anderson, Benedict. *Imagined Communities: Reflections on the Origin and Spread of Nationalism.* London: Verso, 1983.

Anderson, Leona, and Pamela Dickey Young, eds. *Women and Religious Traditions.* New York: Oxford University Press, 2004.

Antohi, Sorin, Balázs Trencsényi, and Péter Apor, eds. *Narratives Unbound: Historical Studies in Post-Communist Eastern Europe.* New York and Budapest: Central European University Press, 2007.

Ariès, Philippe. *Western Attitudes toward Death: From the Middle Ages to the Present.* Trans. Patricia M. Ranum. Baltimore, Md.: Johns Hopkins University Press, 1975.

Ashplant, T. G., Graham Dawson, and Michael Roper, eds. *The Politics of War Memory and Commemoration.* London: Routledge, 2000.

Azoiței, Mihaela. *Totalitarism și rezistență în România comunistă: Cazul Goma.* Bucharest: Paideia, 2002.

Bălescu, Valeria. *Mausoleul de la Mărășești.* Bucharest: Editura militară, 1993.

———. *Soldatul Necunoscut.* Bucharest: Editura militară, 2005.

Balogh, Balázs. "History, Memory, and the Other: Narratives of Ethnic Tensions between Hungarians and Romanians in the Light of the Conflicts of 1940–1944." Paper presented at György Ránki Hungarian Chair Symposium "Strategies of Identity Construction: Ethnic Politics, Minorities, and European Integration in Transylvania," Bloomington, Ind., April 2007.

Balogh, Balázs, and Ágnes Fülemile. *Társadalom, tájszerkezet, identitás Kalotaszegen: Fejezetek a regionális csoportképzés történeti folyamatairól.* Budapest: Akadémiai Kiadó, 2005.

Balotă, Nicolae. *Scriitori maghiari din România: Eseuri.* Bucharest: Kriterion, 1981, 442–454.

Barasch, Iulius. "Evreii din Moldova și Valachia: Studiu istorico-social." In Lya Benjamin, ed., *Evreii din România în texte istoriografice: Antologie.* Bucharest: Hasefer, 2002.

Barkey, Karen, and Mark von Hagen, eds. *After Empire: Multiethnic Societies and Nation-building; The Soviet Union and the Russian, Ottoman, and Habsburg Empires.* Boulder, Colo.: Westview Press, 1997.

Barnouw, Dagmar. *The War in the Empty Air: Victims, Perpetrators, and Postwar Germans.* Bloomington: Indiana University Press, 2005.

Bartal, Yisra'el. *The Jews of Eastern Europe, 1772–1881.* Philadelphia: University of Pennsylvania Press, 2005.

Basilescu, Nicolae. *La Roumanie dans la guerre et dans la paix.* Paris: F. Alcan, 1919.

Baskin, Judith R., ed. *Jewish Women in Historical Perspective.* 2nd ed. Detroit, Mich.: Wayne State University Press, 1998.

Bastea, Eleni. *The Creation of Modern Athens: Planning the Myth.* New York: Cambridge University Press, 1999.

Baucom, Ian. *Out of Place: Englishness, Empire, and the Locations of Identity.* Princeton, N.J.: Princeton University Press, 1999.

Beldiceanu, Nicoară. *Le monde ottoman des Balkans (1402–1566): Institutions, société, économie.* London: Variorum Reprints, 1976.

Beller, Steven. "Kraus's Firework: State Consciousness Raising in the 1908 Jubilee Parade in Vienna and the Problem of Austrian Identity." In Bucur and Wingfield, eds., *Staging the Past,* 46–71.

Berger, Alan. *Second Generation Voices: Reflections by Children of Holocaust Survivors and Perpetrators.* Syracuse, N.Y.: Syracuse University Press, 2001.

Bet-El, Ilana. "Unimagined Communities: The Power of Memory and the Conflict in the Former Yugoslavia." In Müller, ed., *Memory and Power,* 206–222.

Biuro Odszkodowan Wojennych. *Statement on War Losses and Damages of Poland in 1939–1945*. Warsaw, 1947.

Bloom, Leslie. *Under the Sign of Hope: Feminist Methodology and Narrative Interpretation*. Albany: State University of New York Press, 1998.

Bocșan, Nicolae, Ion Lumperdean, and Ioan-Aurel Pop, eds. *Etnie și confesiune în Transilvania (sec. XIII–XIX)*. Oradea: Fundația "Cele Trei Crișuri," 1994.

Bodea, Gheorghe, Vasile T. Suciu, and Ilie I. Pușcaș. *Administrația militară horthystă în Nord-Vestul României, septembrie–noiembrie 1940*. Cluj-Napoca: Editura Dacia, 1988.

Bodnar, John. *Remaking America: Public Memory, Commemoration, and Patriotism in the Twentieth Century*. Princeton, N.J.: Princeton University Press, 1992.

Boisdron, Matthieu. *La Roumanie des années trente: De l'avènement de Carol II au démembrement du royaume (1930–1940)*. Parçay-sur-Vienne, France: Editions Anovi, 2007.

Bóke, László. "Introductory Study." In Aladár Kuncz, *Fekete kolostor*. Bucharest: Kriterion, 1965.

Bokovoy, Melissa. "Kosovo Maiden(s): Serbian Women Commemorate the Wars of National Liberation, 1912–1918." In Wingfield and Bucur, eds., *Gender and War*, 157–171.

———. "Scattered Graves, Ordered Cemeteries: Commemorating Serbia's Wars of National Liberation, 1912–1918." In Bucur and Wingfield, eds., *Staging the Past*, 236–254.

Braham, Randolph. *The Politics of Genocide: The Holocaust in Hungary*. New York: East European Monographs, distributed by Columbia University Press, 1994.

Braham, Randolph, ed. *The Tragedy of the Romanian Jewry*. New York: Rosenthal Institute for Holocaust Studies of the City University of New York, distributed by Columbia University Press, 1994.

Bremner, J. Douglas, and Charles R. Marmar, eds. *Trauma, Memory and Dissociation*. Washington, D.C.: APA Press, 1998.

Brown, L. Carl, ed. *Imperial Legacy: The Ottoman Imprint on the Balkans and the Middle East*. New York: Columbia University Press, 1996.

Brubaker, Rogers. *Ethnicity without Groups*. Cambridge, Mass.: Harvard University Press, 2004.

Brubaker, Rogers, and Frederick Cooper. "Beyond 'Identity.'" *Theory and Society* 29, no. 1 (2000): 1–47.

Brubaker, Rogers, et al. *Nationalist Politics and Everyday Ethnicity in a Transylvanian Town*. Princeton, N.J.: Princeton University Press, 2006.

Bruja, Radu Florian. *Carol al II-lea și partidul unic: Frontul Renașterii Naționale*. Iași: Junimea, 2006.

Bucholtz, Mary, A. C. Liang, and Laurel A. Sutton, eds. *Reinventing Identities: The Gendered Self in Discourse*. New York: Oxford University Press, 1999.

Bucsay, Mihály. *A protestantizmus története Magyarországon, 1521–1945*. Budapest: Gondolat, 1985.

Bucur, Maria. "An Archipelago of Stories: Gender History in Eastern Europe." *American Historical Review* 113, no. 5 (December 2008): 1375–1389.

———. "Between Liberal and Republican Citizenship: Romanian Feminists and Nationalism, 1880–1918." *Aspasia* 1 (2007): 84–102.

———. "Between the Mother of the Wounded and the Virgin from Jiu: Romanian Women and the Gender of Heroism during the Great War." *Journal of Women's History* 12, no. 2 (Summer 2000): 30–56.

———. "Birth of a Nation: Commemorations of December 1st, 1918 and the Construction of National Identity in Communist Romania." In Bucur and Wingfield, eds., *Staging the Past*, 286–325.

———. "Book Collecting and Reading in Braşov, Romania under Communism." *NCEEER Working Paper* (1 March 2003), available at http://www.ucis.pitt.edu/nceeer/2003-817-19n-Bucur.pdf (accessed 11 January 2009).

———. "Calypso Botez: Gender Difference and the Limits of Pluralism in Interwar Romania." *Jahrbücher für Geschichte und Kultur Südosteuropas* 3 (2001): 63–78.

———. "Carol II of Romania." In Berndt Fischer, ed., *Balkan Dictators in the Twentieth Century*. London: Hurst and Co., 2006, 87–118.

———. "The Death Triangle [Feature Film]." *American Historical Review* 104, no. 4 (October 1999): 1427–1428.

———. *Eugenics and Modernization in Interwar Romania*. Pittsburgh, Pa.: Pittsburgh University Press, 2002.

———. "Fallen Women and Necessary Evils: Eugenicist Cultural Representations of and Legal Battles over Prostitution in Interwar Romania." In Marius Turda and Paul Weindling, eds., *"Blood and Homeland": Eugenics and Racial Nationalism in Central and Southeast Europe, 1900–1940*. Budapest, New York: Central European University Press, 2006, 335–352.

———. "Romania: War, Occupation, Liberation." In Aviel Roshwald and Richard Stites, eds., *European Culture in the Great War: The Arts, Entertainment, and Propaganda*. Cambridge: Cambridge University Press, 1999, 243–266.

———. "Treznea: Trauma, Nationalism and the Memory of World War II in Romania." *Rethinking History* 6, no. 1 (2002): 35–55.

———. "Women's Stories as Sites of Memory: Remembering Romania's World Wars." In Wingfield and Bucur, eds., *Gender and War*, 171–192.

Bucur, Maria, and Nancy Wingfield, eds. *Staging the Past: The Politics of Commemoration in Habsburg Central Europe, 1848 to the Present*. West Lafayette, Ind.: Purdue University Press, 2001.

Budeancă, Cosmin. "Aspecte privind implicarea femeilor în rezistenţa anticomunistă din munţii României: Cazul Lucreţiei Jurj (Grupul Şuşman)." In Ghizela Cosma and Virgiliu Ţârău, eds., *Condiţia femeii în România în secolul XX: Studii de caz*. Cluj-Napoca: Presa Universitară Clujeană, 2003, 161–177.

Burada, T. T. *Datinele poporului român la înmormântări*. Iaşi, 1882.

Burleigh, Michael. *Confronting the Nazi Past: New Debates on Modern German History*. New York: St. Martin's Press, 1996.

Buzatu, Gheorghe. *Din istoria secretă a celui de-al doilea război mondial*. Bucharest: Editura enciclopedică, 1995.

———. *Mareşalul Antonescu în faţa istoriei*. 3 vols. Iaşi: B.A.I., 1990.

———. *Românii în arhivele Kremlinului*. Bucharest: Editura univers enciclopedic, 1996.

Căliman, Călin. *Istoria filmului românesc: 1897–2000*. Bucharest: Editura Fundaţiei Culturale Române, 2000.

Călinescu, George. *Istoria literaturii române de la origini până în present.* 2nd ed. Bucharest: Editura Minerva, 1982.

Caloianu, Ana-Maria. *Istoria comunității evreiești din Alba Iulia.* Bucharest: Hasefer, 2006.

Cameron, Deborah. *The Myth of Mars and Venus.* Oxford: Oxford University Press, 2007.

Cameron, Deborah, and Don Kulick, eds. *The Language and Sexuality Reader.* London: Routledge, 2006.

Câncea, Paraschiva. *Mișcarea pentru emanciparea femeii în România.* Bucharest: Editura politică, 1976.

Cannadine, David. "The Context, Performance and Meaning of Ritual: The British Monarchy and the 'Invention of Tradition,' c. 1820–1977." In Eric Hobsbawm and Terence Ranger, eds., *The Invention of Tradition,* 101–164.

Caraveli-Chaves, Anna. "Bridge between Worlds: The Greek Women's Lament as Communicative Event." *Journal of American Folklore* 93 (1980): 129–157.

Carmilly-Weinberger, Moshe. *Istoria evreilor din Transilvania.* Bucharest: Editura enciclopedică, 1994.

Cavarnos, Constantine. *The Future Life According to Orthodox Teaching.* Etna, Calif.: Center for Traditionalist Orthodox Studies, 1985.

Chirnoagă, Platon. *Istoria politică și militară a războiului României contra Rusiei sovietice, 22 iunie 1941–23 august 1944.* 4th ed. Iași: Fides, 1998.

Ciocâlteau, Michel. *Les Régimes matrimoniaux dans le projet de code civil roumain.* Paris: Rousseau et Cie, 1936.

Ciucă, Marcel-Dumitru. *Procesul Mareșalului Antonescu.* 2 vols. Bucharest: Editura Saeculum I.O., 1998.

Clogg, Richard. *A Concise History of Greece.* 2nd ed. Cambridge: Cambridge University Press, 2002.

Coch, Donna, Kurt W. Fischer, and Geraldine Dawson, eds. *Human Behavior, Learning, and the Developing Brain: Typical Development.* New York: Guilford Press, 2007.

Cohen, Daniel J., and Roy Rosenzweig. "Web of Lies? Historical Knowledge on the Internet." *First Monday* 10, no. 12 (December 2005), available at http://firstmonday.org/issues/issue10_12/cohen/index.html (accessed 2 January 2009).

Cohen-Pfister, Laurel. *Victims and Perpetrators, 1933–1945: (Re)presenting the Past in Post-Unification Culture.* Berlin: W. de Gruyter, 2006.

Cohn, Bernard. "Representing Authority in Victorian India." In Hobsbawm and Ranger, eds., *Invention of Tradition,* 165–210.

Coja, Ioan. *Marele manipulator și asasinarea lui Culianu, Ceaușescu, Iorga.* Bucharest: Editura Miracol, 1999.

Cole, Lawrence. "Patriotic Celebrations in Late-Nineteenth- and Early-Twentieth-Century Tirol." In Bucur and Wingfield, eds., *Staging the Past,* 75–111.

Connerton, Paul. *How Societies Remember.* Cambridge: Cambridge University Press, 1989.

Constantiniu, Florin. *De la războiul fierbinte la războiul rece.* Bucharest: Corint, 1998.

Coposu, Corneliu. *Dialoguri cu Vartan Arachelian.* Bucharest: Editura Anastasia, [1992].

———. *Semnele timpului: Articole politice, meditații, atitudini.* Ed. and comp. Mircea Popa. Timișoara: Editura de Vest, 1997.

Corbea-Hoisie, Andrei. *La Bucovine: Éléments d'histoire politique et culturelle.* Paris: Institut d'études slaves, 2004.

Corbu, Constantin. *Răscoala ţăranilor de la 1888.* Bucharest: Editura ştiinţifică şi enciclopedică, 1978.

Cosma, Ghizela. *Femeile şi politica în România: Evoluţia dreptului de vot în perioada interbelică.* Cluj-Napoca: Presa universitară clujeană, 2002.

Cosslett, Tess. *Feminism and Autobiography: Texts, Theories, Methods.* London, New York: Routledge, 2000.

Costea, Rodica. "Semnificaţia zilei de 1 decembrie pentru minoritatea maghiară." *Adevărul de Cluj* no. 767 (1 December 1992).

Crohmălniceanu, Ovidiu S. *Literatura română între cele două războaie mondiale.* Vol. 1. Bucharest: Editura pentru literatură, 1967.

Crowley, David, and Susan E. Reid. "Style and Socialism: Modernity and Material Culture in Post-War Eastern Europe." In Susan E. Reid and David Crowley, eds., *Style and Socialism: Modernity and Material Culture in Post-War Eastern Europe.* Oxford: Berg, 2000, 1–24.

Dabrowski, Patrice. *Commemorations and the Shaping of Modern Poland.* Bloomington: Indiana University Press, 2004.

Danforth, Loring M. *The Death Rituals of Rural Greece.* Princeton, N.J.: Princeton University Press, 1982.

Davies, Norman. *Rising '44: The Battle for Warsaw.* New York: Viking Penguin, 2004.

de Vries, Brian, ed. *End of Life Issues: Interdisciplinary and Multidimensional Perspectives.* New York: Springer, 1999.

Deák, István. *Beyond Nationalism: A Social and Political History of the Habsburg Officer Corps, 1848–1918.* New York: Columbia University Press, 1990.

———. *Essays on Hitler's Europe.* Lincoln: University of Nebraska Press, 2001.

Deletant, Dennis. *Ceauşescu and the Securitate: Coercion and Dissent in Romania, 1965–1989.* Armonk, N.Y.: M.E. Sharpe, 1995.

———. "Romania, 1945–89: Resistance, Protest and Dissent." In McDermott and Stibbe, eds., *Revolution and Resistance,* 81–100.

Denich, Bette. "Sex and Power in the Balkans." In M. Rosaldo and L. Lamphere, eds., *Woman, Culture, and Society.* Stanford, Calif.: Stanford University Press, 1974, 243–262.

Dezsö, Kosztolányi. "Fekete kolostor." *Nyugat* (1931): 819–823.

Diamant, Anita. *Saying Kaddish: How to Comfort the Dying, Bury the Dead, and Mourn as a Jew.* New York: Schocken Books, 1998.

Dimitrova, Snezhana. "'The Experienced War' and Bulgarian Modernization in the Inter-War Years." *Rethinking History* 6, no. 1 (April 2002): 15–34.

Dobre, Florica. *Distrugerea elitei militare sub regimul ocupaţiei sovietice în România.* Bucharest: Institutul Naţional pentru Studiul Totalitarismului, 2000–2001.

Dobrincu, Dorin, ed. *Ţărănimea şi puterea: Procesul de colectivizare a agriculturii în România (1949–1962).* Iaşi: Polirom, 2005.

Dorondel, Ştefan. *Moartea şi apa: Ritualuri funerare, simbolism acvatic şi structura lumii de dincolo în imaginarul ţărănesc.* Bucharest: Paideia, 2004.

Duţu, Alessandru. *Sub povara armistiţiului: Armata română în perioada 1944–1947.* Bucharest: Editura Tritonic, 2003.

Eidelberg, Philip G. *The Great Rumanian Peasant Revolt of 1907.* Leiden: Brill, 1974.

Eley, Geoff. "Finding the People's War: Film, British Collective Memory, and World War II." *The American Historical Review* 106, no. 3 (June 2001), available at http://www.history cooperative.org/journals/ahr/106.3/ah000818.html (accessed 19 January 2009).

Eliade, Mircea. *De la Zalmoxis la Genghis-Han: Studii comparative despre religiile și folclorul Daciei și Europei Orientale.* Trans. Maria and Cezar Ivănescu. Bucharest: Humanitas, 1995.

Emilien, Gérard, et al. *Memory: Neuropsychological, Imaging, and Psychopharmacological Perspectives.* Hove, UK: Psychology Press, 2004.

Engel, Barbara Alpern. *Women in Russia, 1700–2000.* Cambridge, New York: Cambridge University Press, 2004.

Eskenasy, Victor. "The Holocaust in Romanian Historiography: Communist and Neo-Communist Revisionism." In Braham, ed., *Tragedy of Romanian Jewry.*

Evdokimov, R. B., ed. *Liudskie poteri SSSR v period vtoroi mirovoi voiny: sbornik statei.* St. Petersburg: In-t rossiiskoi istorii RAN, 1995.

Falvey, Kevin. "Memory and Knowledge of Content." In Susana Nuccetelli, ed., *New Essays on Semantic Externalism and Self-Knowledge.* Cambridge, Mass.: MIT Press, 2003, 219–240.

Farrington, Karen. *Historical Atlas of Religions.* New York: Checkmark Books, 2002.

Fentress, James, and Chris Wickham. *Social Memory.* Oxford: Blackwell, 1992.

Fisli, Eva. "Hungarian Remembrance of the Great War in Mohács." Paper presented at the conference "Sacrifice and Regeneration," Southampton, September 2007.

Foster, Gaines M. *Ghosts of the Confederacy: Defeat, the Lost Cause, and the Emergence of the New South, 1865 to 1913.* New York: Oxford University Press, 1987.

Freifeld, Alice. "The Cult of March 15: Sustaining the Hungarian Myth of Revolution, 1849–1999." In Bucur and Wingfield, eds., *Staging the Past,* 255–285.

Fritzsche, Peter. *Germans into Nazis.* Cambridge, Mass.: Harvard University Press, 1998.

Fuhrmann, Malte. *Der Traum vom deutschen Orient: Zwei deutsche Kolonien im Osmanischen Reich 1851–1918.* Frankfurt am Main: Campus, 2006.

Fürtos, Robert. "Sighet, preambul al Holocaustului, punct central al Gulagului." *Caietele Echinox* no. 13 (2007): 226–241, available at www.ceeol.com/aspx/getdocument.aspx?logid= 5&id=72121964-2bf7-4a26-a3e4-58dc94fdb8c5 (accessed 19 January 2009).

Fussell, Paul. *The Great War and Modern Memory.* 25th anniversary ed. New York: Oxford University Press, 2000.

Gaál, Gábor. "Kuncz Aladár." *Korunk* no. 7–8 (1931).

Gallagher, Tom. *Theft of a Nation: Romania since Communism.* London: Hurst, 2005.

Gardner, Martin. "The False Memory Syndrome." *Skeptical Inquirer* (Summer 1993): 370–375.

Gedi, Noa, and Yigal Elam. "Collective Memory: What Is It?" *History and Memory* 8, no. 1 (1996): 30–50.

Gellner, Ernest. *Encounters with Nationalism.* Oxford: Blackwell, 1994.

Georgescu, Vlad. *Istoria românilor de la origini pîna în zilele noastre.* 4th ed. Bucharest: Humanitas, 1995.

———. *Political Ideas and the Enlightenment in the Romanian Principalities, 1750–1831.* Boulder, Colo.: East European Quarterly, distributed by Columbia University Press, New York, 1971.

Geraci, Robert P., and Michael Khodarkovsky, eds. *Of Religion and Empire: Missions, Conversion, and Tolerance in Tsarist Russia.* Ithaca, N.Y.: Cornell University Press, 2001.

Gertjajanssen, Wedy Jo. "Victims, Heroes, Survivors: Sexual Violence on the Eastern Front during World War II." PhD diss., University of Minnesota, 2004.

Gigova, Irina. "The Club of Bulgarian Women Writers and the Feminisation of Bulgarian Literature." *Aspasia* 2 (2008): 91–119.

Gillis, John, ed. *Commemorations: The Politics of National Identity.* Princeton, N.J.: Princeton University Press, 1996.

Giurescu, Dinu. *România în al doilea război mondial: 1939–1945.* Bucharest: All educaţional, 1999.

Goldhagen, Daniel. *Hitler's Willing Executioners: Ordinary Germans and the Holocaust.* New York: Vintage Books, 1997.

Grad, Cornel. *Al doilea arbitraj de la Viena.* Iaşi: Institutul European, 1998.

Grayzel, Susan. *Women and the First World War.* London, New York: Longman, 2002.

———. *Women's Identities at War: Gender, Motherhood, and Politics in Britain and France during the First World War.* Chapel Hill: University of North Carolina Press, 1999.

Grele, Ronald J., et al. *Envelopes of Sound: The Art of Oral History.* Westport, Conn.: Praeger, 1991.

Gross, Jan. *Fear: Anti-Semitism in Poland after Auschwitz: An Essay in Historical Interpretation.* New York: Random House, 2006.

———. *Neighbors: The Destruction of the Jewish Community in Jedwabne, Poland.* New York: Penguin, 2002.

———. "Themes for a Social History of War Experience and Collaboration." In Gross, Judt, and Deák, eds., *Politics of Retribution,* 15–38.

Gross, Jan, Tony Judt, and Istvan Deák, eds. *The Politics of Retribution in Europe: World War II and Its Aftermath.* Princeton, N.J.: Princeton University Press, 2000.

Gudkov, Lev. "The Fetters of Victory: How the War Provides Russia with Its Identity." Posted on *Eurozine* on 3 May 2005, available at http://www.eurozine.com/articles/2005-05-03-gudkov-en.html (accessed 2 January 2009).

Gullace, Nicoletta F. *The Blood of Our Sons: Men, Women, and the Renegotiation of British Citizenship during the Great War.* New York: Palgrave Macmillian, 2002.

Gürsan-Salzmann, Ayşe, and Laurence Salzmann. *The Last Jews of Rădăuţi.* New York: Dial Press, 1983.

Gyáni, Gábor. "Uses and Misuses of Public Space in Budapest, 1873–1914." In Thomas Bender and Carl Schorske, eds., *Budapest and New York: Studies in Metropolitan Transformation, 1870–1930.* New York: Russell Sage Foundation, 1994.

Habermas, Jürgen. *Time of Transitions.* Ed. and trans. Ciaran Cronin and Max Pensky. Cambridge: Polity, 2006.

Haker, Hille, Susan Ross, and Marie-Therese Wacker, eds. *Women's Voices in World Religions.* London: SCM Press, 2006.

Halbwachs, Maurice. *On Collective Memory.* Chicago: University of Chicago Press, 1992 [1952].

Hanák, Peter. *The Garden and the Workshop.* New ed. Princeton, N.J.: Princeton University Press, 1999.

Hanák, Peter, Peter F. Sugar, and Tibor Frank, eds. *A History of Hungary.* Bloomington: Indiana University Press, 1994.

Hangiu, I. *Dicționar al presei literare românești.* Bucharest: Editura științifică și enciclopedică, 1987.

Haret, Mihai. *Castelul Peleș: Monografie istorică, geografică, turistică, pitorească, descriptivă a Castelelor Regale din Sinaia cu împrejurimile lor.* Bucharest: Cartea Românească, 1924.

Hargreaves, Alec G., ed. *Memory, Empire, and Postcolonialism: Legacies of French Colonialism.* Lanham, Md.: Lexington, 2005.

Harris, Jane Gary. *Autobiographical Statements in Twentieth-Century Russian Literature.* Princeton, N.J.: Princeton University Press, 1990.

Haumann, Heiko. *A History of East European Jews.* Budapest: Central European University Press, 2002.

Hautaniemi, Petri, Helena Jerman, and Sharon MacDonald, eds. *Anthropological Perspectives on Social Memory.* Münster: Lit; London, distributed by Global, 2006.

Healy, Maureen. *Vienna and the Fall of the Habsburg Empire: Total War and Everyday Life in World War I.* New York, Cambridge: Cambridge University Press, 2004.

Heilman, Samuel C. *When a Jew Dies: The Ethnography of a Bereaved Son.* Berkeley: University of California Press, 2001.

Hein, Laura, and Mark Selden, eds. *Censoring History: Citizenship and Memory in Japan, Germany, and the United States, Asia and the Pacific.* New York: M. E. Sharpe, 2000.

Heineman, Elizabeth. "Gender, Sexuality, and Coming to Terms with the Past in Germany." *Central European History* 38, no. 1 (2005): 41–74.

———. "The Hour of Woman: Memories of Germany's 'Crisis Years' and West German National Identity." *American Historical Review* 101, no. 2 (1996): 354–395.

Heinen, Armin. *Legiunea "Arhanghelul Mihail": Mișcare socială și organizație politică; O contribuție la problema fascismului internațional.* Bucharest: Humanitas, 1999.

Hilberg, Raul. *Perpetrators, Victims, Bystanders: The Jewish Catastrophe, 1933–1945.* New York: Harper Perennial, 1993.

Hirsch, Marianne. *Family Frames: Photography, Narrative, and Postmemory.* Cambridge, Mass.: Harvard University Press, 1997.

History of the Protestant Church in Hungary, from the Beginning of the Reformation to 1850; with Special Reference to Transylvania. Trans. Rev. J. Craig. London: J. Nisbet and Co., 1854.

Hitchins, Keith. *Rumania, 1866–1947.* Oxford: Clarendon, 1994.

———. *The Rumanians, 1774–1866.* Oxford: Clarendon, 1996.

Hobsbawm, Eric, and Terence Ranger, eds. *The Invention of Tradition.* Cambridge: Cambridge University Press, 1992.

Höepken, Wolfgang. "War, Memory and Education in a Fragmented Society: The Case of Yugoslavia." *East European Politics and Societies* 13, no. 1 (1999): 190–227.

Hoffman, Eva. *After such Knowledge: Memory, History, and the Legacy of the Holocaust.* New York: Public Affairs, 2004.

Holmes, Janet. *The Handbook of Language and Gender.* Malden, Mass.: Blackwell, 2005.

Holmes, Stephen. "Introducing the Center: A Project to Promote Clear Thinking about the Design of Liberal-Democratic Institutions." *East European Constitutional Review* 1, no. 1 (Spring 1992).

Hornstein, Shelley. *Image and Remembrance: Representation and the Holocaust.* Bloomington: Indiana University Press, 2003.

Horváth, Franz. "The Divided War Memory of the Transylvanian Hungarians." Paper presented at the conference "Sacrifice and Regeneration," Southampton, September 2007.

Howarth, Glennys, and Peter C. Jupp, eds. *The Changing Face of Death: Historical Accounts of Death and Disposal.* New York: St. Martin's Press, 1997.

Hryniuk, Stella. *Peasants with Promise: Ukrainians in Southeastern Galicia 1880–1900.* Edmonton: University of Alberta, 1991.

Hunt, R. Reed, and James B. Worthen, eds. *Distinctiveness and Memory.* Oxford: Oxford University Press, 2006.

Hutton, Marceline. *Russian and West European Women, 1860–1939: Dreams, Struggles, and Nightmares.* Lanham, Md.: Rowman & Littlefield, 2001.

Iancu, Carol. *Jews in Romania, 1866–1919: From Exclusion to Emancipation.* Boulder, Colo.: East European Monographs; distributed by Columbia University Press, New York, 1996.

International Commission on the Holocaust in Romania. *Final Report.* Iași: Polirom, 2005.

Ioanid, Radu. *The Holocaust in Romania: The Destruction of Jews and Gypsies under the Antonescu Regime, 1940–1944.* Chicago: Ivan R. Dee, 2000.

Ionescu, Grigore. *Istoria Arhitecturii în România.* Vols. 1–2. Bucharest: Editura Academiei R.S.R., 1963–1964.

Ionescu, Ștefan. "În umbra morții: Memoria supraviețuitorilor Holocaustului din România." http://www.ceeol.com/aspx/getdocument.aspx?logid=5&id=d7dca8a2-4587-46ad-8208-4edd7195b9e1 (accessed 13 January 2009).

Iordachi, Constantin. "From the 'Right of the Natives' to 'Constitutional Nationalism': The Making of Romanian Citizenship, 1817–1919." PhD diss., Central European University, 2003.

Iordanova, Dina. *Cinema of the Other Europe: The Industry and Artistry of East Central European Film.* London, New York: Wallflower, 2003.

Iorgulescu, Mircea. "Provocarea." *Dilema* (29 October–4 November 1999).

Isaac, Jeff. "The Meanings of 1989—Central and Eastern Europe: Gains and Losses in the Transition to Democracy." *Social Research* 63, no. 2 (Summer 1996): 291–344.

Isenberg, Nancy, and Andrew Burstein, eds. *Mortal Remains: Death in Early America.* Philadelphia: University of Pennsylvania Press, 2003.

Istoria învățământului din Romania, Vol. 2 (1821–1918). Bucharest: Editura didactică și pedagogică, 1993.

Istrate, Ion. *Romanul "obsedantului deceniu" (1945–1964).* Cluj-Napoca: Diamondia, 1995.

Iuga, Anamaria. "Rolul femeilor în constituirea identității maramureșene." In Ghizela Cosma, Enikő Magyari-Vincze, Ovidiu Pecican, eds., *Prezențe feminine: Studii despre femei în România.* Cluj-Napoca: Editura Fundației DESIRE, 2002, 347–374.

Ivaș, Angela Doina. "Cultul strămoșilor la români." PhD diss., Babeș-Bolyai University, Cluj, 1993.

Jancar-Webster, Barbara. *Women and Revolution in Yugoslavia, 1941–1945.* Denver, Colo.: Arden Press, 1990.

Jansen, Stef. "The Violence of Memories: Local Narratives of the Past after Ethnic Cleansing in Croatia." *Rethinking History* 6, no. 1 (April 2002): 77–93.

Jeffreys, David, ed. *Views of Ancient Egypt since Napoleon Bonaparte: Imperialism, Colonialism and Modern Appropriations*. Oxford: Berg, 2006.

Jelavich, Barbara. *Russia's Balkan Entanglements, 1806–1914*. Cambridge: Cambridge University Press, 1991.

Jelavich, Charles. *South-Slav Nationalism: Textbooks and Yugoslav Union before 1914*. Columbus: Ohio University Press, 1994.

Jensen, Eric. *Teaching with the Brain in Mind*. 2nd rev. ed. Alexandria, Va.: Association for Supervision and Curriculum Development, 2005.

Jersild, Austin. *Orientalism and Empire: North Caucasus Mountain Peoples and the Georgian Frontier, 1845–1917*. Montreal, Ithaca, N.Y.: McGill-Queen's University Press, 2002.

Jipa, Rotaru. *Mareşalul Antonescu la Odessa: Grandoarea şi amărăciunea unei victorii*. Bucharest: Editura Paideia, 1999.

Johnson, Graham. *Social Democratic Politics in Britain, 1881–1911*. Lewiston, N.Y.: E. Mellen, 2002.

Jolluck, Katherine R. *Exile and Identity: Polish Women in the Soviet Union during World War II*. Pittsburgh, Pa.: University of Pittsburgh Press, 2002.

———. "The Nation's Pain and Women's Shame: Polish Women and Wartime Violence." In Wingfield and Bucur, eds., *Gender and War*, 193–219.

Judt, Tony. *Postwar: A History of Europe since 1945*. New York: Penguin, 2005.

Kaindl, R. H., and Al. Manstyrski. *Die Rutenen in der Bukowina*. Vol. 2. Cernowitz: Theil, 1890.

Kalish, Richard A., ed. *Death and Dying: Views from Many Cultures*. Farmingdale, N.Y.: Baywood, 1980.

Kallestrup, Shona. *Art and Design in Romania 1866–1927: Local and International Aspects of the Search for National Expression*. Boulder, Colo.: Eastern European Monographs; distributed by Columbia University Press, New York, 2006.

Kann, Robert. *The Multinational Empire: Nationalism and National Reform in the Habsburg Monarchy, 1848–1918*. 2 vols. New York: Columbia University Press, 1950.

Kansteiner, Wulf. "Finding Meaning in Memory: A Methodological Critique of Collective Memory Studies." *History and Theory* 41 (May 2002): 179–197.

Karge, Heike. "From 'Frozen Memory' to the Encounter of Remembrance: Memorials to the Second World War in Tito's Yugoslavia." *Memoria e Ricerca* no. 21 (2006): 81–100, available at http://www.fondazionecasadioriani.it/modules.php?name=MR&op=body&id=367 (accessed 11 January 2009).

Karnoouh, Claude. *Rituri şi discursuri versificate la ţăranii maramureşeni: A trăi şi a supravieţui în România comunistă*. Cluj: Editura Dacia, 1998.

Kassabova-Dincheva, Anelia. *Migration und Familie: Familienforschung und Politik (Am Beispiel Bulgariens)*. Sofia: Variant 2000, 2002.

Kellogg, Frederick. *The Road to Romanian Independence*. West Lafayette, Ind.: Purdue University Press, 1995.

Kenez, Peter. *Hungary from the Nazis to the Soviets: The Establishment of the Communist Regime in Hungary, 1944–1948*. Cambridge: Cambridge University Press, 2006.

Kenney, Padraic. "Martyrs and Neighbors: Sources of Reconciliation in Central Europe." *Common Knowledge* 13, no. 1 (Winter 2007): 149–169.

Kerr, D. A., ed. *Religion, State and Ethnic Groups*. New York: New York University Press, 1992.

Kesner, Raymond P., and Joe L. Martinez, Jr., eds. *Neurobiology of Learning and Memory.* 2nd ed. Amsterdam: Academic Press, 2007.

Kideckel, David. *The Solitude of Collectivism: Romanian Villagers to the Revolution and Beyond.* Ithaca, N.Y.: Cornell University Press, 1993.

Kieval, Hillel. *The Making of Czech Jewry: National Conflict and Jewish Society in Bohemia, 1870–1918.* New York: Oxford University Press, 1988.

Kifner, John. "Upheaval in the East; Army Executes Ceaucescu [sic] and Wife for 'Genocide' Role, Bucharest Says." *New York Times* (26 December 1989). Available at http://query .nytimes.com/gst/fullpage.html?res=950DE3DF153EF935A15751C1A96F948260&sec= &spon=&pagewanted=all (accessed 15 January 2009).

Kihlstrom, John F. "The Trauma-Memory Argument." *Consciousness and Cognition* 4, no. 1 (March 1995): 63–67.

King, Jeremy. *Budweisers into Czechs and Germans: A Local History of Bohemian Politics, 1848–1948.* Princeton, N.J.: Princeton University Press, 2002.

———. "The Nationalization of East Central Europe: Ethnicism, Ethnicity, and Beyond." In Bucur and Wingfield, eds., *Staging the Past*, 112–152.

Kiriţescu, Constantin. *Istoria războiului pentru întregirea României, 1916–1919.* 2 vols. 3rd rev. ed. Bucharest: Editura ştiinţifică şi enciclopedică, 1989.

Kirschenbaum, Lisa A. "'The Alienated Body': Gender Identity and the Memory of the Siege of Leningrad." In Wingfield and Bucur, eds., *Gender and War,* 220–234.

Kivelson, Valerie. *Cartographies of Tsardom. The Land and Its Meanings in Seventeenth-Century Russia.* Ithaca, N.Y.: Cornell University Press, 2006.

Kivelson, Valerie A., and Robert H. Greene, eds. *Orthodox Russia: Belief and Practice under the Tsars.* University Park: Pennsylvania State University Press, 2003.

Kligman, Gail. *The Wedding of the Dead: Ritual, Poetics, and Popular Culture in Transylvania.* Berkeley: University of California Press, 1988.

Knižević, Jovana. "War, Occupation, and Liberation: Women's Sacrifice and the First World War in Yugoslavia." Paper presented at the conference "Sacrifice and Regeneration," Southampton, September 2007.

Kodo, Matsunami. *International Handbook of Funeral Customs.* Westport, Conn.: Greenwood Press, 1998.

Köpeczi, Béla, ed. *Erdély története.* Budapest: Akadémiai Kiadó, 1986.

Korbonski, Stefan. *Jews and the Poles in World War II.* New York: Hippocrene Books, 1989.

———. *The Polish Underground State 1939–1945.* New York: Columbia University Press, 1978.

Kornis, Gyula. *Education in Hungary.* New York: Teachers College, Columbia University, 1932.

Kovács, Mária. *Liberal Professions and Illiberal Politics: Hungary from the Habsburgs to the Holocaust.* Washington, D.C.: Wilson Center Press; Oxford: Oxford University Press, 1994.

Kowitz, Stephanie. *Jedwabne: Kollektives Gedächtnis und tabuisierte Vergangenheit.* Berlin: Bebra Wissenschaft, 2004.

Kristof, Lajos. "În memoria eroilor neamului românesc." *Ziarul de Mureş* (21 May 2007). Available at http://www.ziaruldemures.ro/fullnews.php?ID=7432 (accessed 18 January 2009).

Krivosheev, G. F., ed. *Soviet Casualties and Combat Losses in the Twentieth Century.* London: Greenhill Books; Pennsylvania: Stackpole Books, 1997.

Kroner, Michael. "Deportation vor 60 Jahren war völkerrechtliches Kriegsverbrechen." *Siebenbürger Sachsen* (12 January 2005), available at http://www.siebenbuerger.de/zeitung/artikel/alteartikel/3860-deportation-vor-60-jahren-war.html (accessed 11 January 2009).

Krzeminski, Adam. "As Many Wars as Nations." Published initially in *Polytika* and referenced in the *Eurozine* exchange, available in English at http://www.signandsight.com/features/96.html (accessed 2 January 2009).

Kyle, Donald. *Spectacles of Death in Ancient Rome.* New York: Routledge, 1998.

Lahusen, Thomas, and Evgeny Dobrenko, eds. *Socialist Realism without Shores.* Durham, N.C.: Duke University Press, 1997.

Lambrior, A. "Obiceiuri și credințe la români: Înmormântările." *Convorbiri literare* 9 (1875).

Lamm, Maurice. *The Jewish Way in Death and Mourning.* New York: Jonathan David, 2000.

Lampe, John R., and Mark Mazower, eds. *Ideologies and National Identities: The Case of Twentieth-Century Southeastern Europe.* Budapest: Central European University Press, 2004.

Landsberg, Alison. *Prosthetic Memory: The Transformation of American Remembrance in the Age of Mass Culture.* New York: Columbia University Press, 2004.

Landwehr, Richard. "The European Volunteer Movement in World War II." *Journal of Historical Review* 2, no. 1 (Spring 1981), available at http://www.ihr.org/jhr/v02/v02p-59_Landwehr.html (accessed 19 January 2009).

Laqueur, Thomas. "Memory and Naming in the Great War." In Gillis, ed., *Commemorations,* 150–167.

Lebow, Richard Ned. "The Memory of Politics in Postwar Europe." In Lebow, Kansteiner, and Fogu, eds., *Politics of Memory,* 1–39.

Lebow, Richard Ned, Wulf Kansteiner, and Claudio Fogu. *The Politics of Memory in Postwar Europe.* Durham, N.C.: Duke University Press, 2006.

Lefter, Ion Bogdan. *Recapitularea modernității: Pentru o nouă istorie a literaturii române.* Pitești: Editura paralela 45, 2000.

———. *Scurtă istorie a romanului românesc (cu 25 de aplicații).* Bucharest: Editura paralela 45, 2001.

Leggewie, Claus. "Equally Criminal? Totalitarian Experience and European Memory." First published in *Transit: Europäische Revue,* submitted to *Eurozine* on 1 June 2006, available at http://www.eurozine.com/articles/2006-06-01-leggewie-en.html (accessed 16 January 2009).

Leisse, Olaf, and Utta-Kristin Leisse. *Barometru de aderare: România; Problemele fundamentale ale țării și atitudinile tinerilor români cu privire la integrarea în Uniunea Europeană,* trans. Ioana and Irina Cristescu. Bucharest: Dominor, 2005.

Lejeune, Philippe. *Signes de vie: Le pacte autobiographique, 2.* Paris: Seuil, 2005.

Lemny, Ștefan. *Sensibilitate și istorie în secolul XVIII românesc.* Bucharest: Editura Meridiane, 1990.

Levin, Eve. *Sex and Society in the World of the Orthodox Slavs, 900–1700.* Ithaca, N.Y.: Cornell University Press, 1989.

Levy, Robert. *Ana Pauker: The Rise and Fall of a Jewish Communist.* Berkeley: University of California Press, 2001.

Leyedesdorff, Selma, Luisa Passerini, and Paul Thompson, eds. *Gender and Memory.* Oxford, New York: Oxford University Press, 1996.

Liiceanu, Aurora. *Nici alb, nici negru: Radiografia unui sat românesc, 1948–1998.* Bucharest: Nemira, 2000.

———. *Rănile memorie: Nucşoara şi rezistenţa din munţi.* Iaşi: Polirom, 2003.

———. *Valurile, smintelile, păcatele: Psihologiile românilor de azi.* Bucharest: Nemira, 1998.

Liiceanu, Gabriel. "Sebastian, mon frère." In Iordan Chimet, ed., *Dosar Mihail Sebastian.* Bucharest: Editura Universal Dalsi, 2001 [1997], 3–10.

Lincoln, Bruce. *Death, War, and Sacrifice: Studies in Ideology and Practice.* Chicago: University of Chicago Press, 1991.

Lipcsey, Ildikó. *Romania and Transylvania in the Twentieth Century.* Buffalo, Toronto: Corvinus, 2006.

Livezeanu, Irina. *Cultural Politics in Greater Romania: Regionalism, Nation Building, and Ethnic Struggle, 1918–1930.* Ithaca, N.Y.: Cornell University Press, 1995.

Livia, Anna. *Queerly Phrased: Language, Gender, and Sexuality.* New York: Oxford University Press, 1997.

Loftus, Elizabeth. "The Reality of Repressed Memories." *American Psychologist* 48 (May 1993): 518–537.

Lörinczi, László. *Utazás a fekete kolostorhoz* (Journey to the Black Monastery). Bucharest: Kriterion, 1975.

Losurdo, Domenico. "Towards a Critique of the Category of Totalitarianism." *Historical Materialism* 12, no. 2 (2004): 25–55.

Lovinescu, Eugen. "Istoria literaturii române contemporarne, 1900–1936." In Eugen Lovinescu, *Scrieri.* Vol. 6. Bucharest: Editura Minerva, 1975.

Lukács, John. *Budapest 1900: A Historical Portrait of a City and Its Culture.* New York: Grove, 1994.

Lukasz, Richard. *Forgotten Holocaust: The Poles under German Occupation 1939–1944.* New York: Hippocrene Books, 2001.

Lumans, Valdis. *Latvia in World War II.* New York: Fordham University Press, 2006.

Magocsi, Paul Robert. *The Roots of Ukrainian Nationalism: Galicia as Ukraine's Piedmont.* Toronto: University of Toronto Press, 2002.

Maior, Liviu. "Contribuţii la istoria raportului biserică-putere în Transilvania (1867–1918)." In Nicolae Bocşan, Nicolae Edroiu, and Vasile Vesa, eds., *Convergenţe europene: Istorie şi societate în epoca modernă.* Cluj-Napoca: Editura Dacia, 1993, 174–182.

Mamina, Ion. *Regalitatea în România: 1866–1947: Instituţia monarhică, Familia regală, domniile, contribuţii la dezvoltarea instituţiilor culturale, monumentele de for public, cronologie.* Bucharest: Compania, 2004.

Mangulis, Visvaldis. *Latvia in the Wars of the Twentieth Century.* Princeton Junction, N.J.: Cognition Books, 1983.

Mani, Lata. *Contentious Traditions: The Debate on Sati in Colonial India.* San Francisco: University of California Press, 1998.

Manolescu, Nicolae. *Arca lui Noe: Eseu despre romanul românesc.* 3 vols. Bucharest: Editura Minerva, 1980–1983.

Manoussakis, John Panteleimon. *God after Metaphysics: A Theological Aesthetic.* Bloomington: Indiana University Press, 2007.

Marian, Simion Florea. *Înmormântarea la români: Studiu etnografic*. Bucharest: Editura Grai și Suflet, Cultura Națională, 1995.

——. *[Trilogia vieții,] I: Nunta la români* (Bucharest: Tipografia Carol Göbl, 1890); *II: Nașterea la români* (Bucharest: Tipografia Carol Göbl, 1892); *III: Înmormântarea la români* (Bucharest: Tipografia Carol Göbl, 1892).

Marinescu, Aurel. *Înainte și după Dictatul de la Viena*. Bucharest: Editura Vremea, 2000.

Marinescu, Valentina. *Muncile casnice în satul românesc actual: Studii de caz*. Iași: Polirom, 2002.

Massino, Jill. "Gender as Survival: German Women's Stories of Deportation from Romania to the Soviet Union." *Nationalities Papers* 36, no. 1 (March 2008): 55–83.

Maudlin, Parker. *The Population of Poland*. Washington, D.C.: U.S. Government Printing Office, 1954.

Mavrodin, Teodor. *Mareșalul Antonescu întemnițat la Moscova*. Pitești: Editura Carminis, 1998.

McClintock, Anne. *Imperial Leather: Race, Gender, and Sexuality in the Colonial Contest*. New York: Routledge, 1995.

McDermott, Kevin, and Matthew Stibbe, eds. *Revolution and Resistance in Eastern Europe: Challenges to Communist Rule*. Oxford: Berg, 2006.

Mendelsohn, Ezra. *The Jews o f East Central Europe between the World Wars*. Bloomington: Indiana University Press, 1983.

Merridale, Catherine. *Night of Stone: Death and Memory in Twentieth Century Russia*. New York: Viking, 2001.

Michnik, Adam. "Gray is Beautiful." In Adam Michnik, *Letters from Freedom: Post-Cold War Realities and Perspectives*. Ed. Irena Grudzínska Gross. Berkeley: University of California Press, 1998.

Mick, Christoph. "The Dead and the Living: War Veterans and Memorial Culture in East Galicia." Paper presented at the conference "Sacrifice and Regeneration: The Legacy of the Great War in Interwar Eastern Europe," Southampton, September 2007.

Micu, Dumitru. *Literatura română în secolul al XX-lea*. Bucharest: Editura Fundației Culturale Române, 2000.

Midgley, Magdalena. *The Monumental Cemeteries of Prehistoric Europe*. Stroud: Tempus, 2005.

Mihăilescu, Ștefania. *Emanciparea femeii române: Studiu și antologie de texte. Vol. II (1919–1948)*. Bucharest: Editura ecumenică, 2005.

Mihalache, Marin. *Muzeele din București*. Bucharest: Editura meridiane, 1963.

Millen, Rochelle L. *Women, Birth, and Death in Jewish Law and Practice*. Hanover: Brandeis University Press, published by University Press of New England, 2004.

Mitrache, Georgică. *Tradiție și modernism în arhitectura românească*. Bucharest: Editura universitară Ion Mincu, 2002.

Mitrany, David. *The Land and the Peasant in Rumania: The War and Agrarian Reform, 1917–21*. New York: Greenwood Press [1968].

Moeller, Robert. *War Stories: The Search for a Usable Past in the Federal Republic of Germany*. London: University of California Press, 2003.

Moisescu, Cristian. *Arhitectura epocii lui Matei Basarab*. Bucharest: Editura meridiane, 2002.

Müller, Jan-Werner, ed. *Memory and Power in Post-War Europe: Studies in the Presence of the Past*. Cambridge: Cambridge University Press, 2002.

Murdock, Graeme. *Calvinism on the Frontier, 1600–1660: International Calvinism and the Reformed Church in Hungary and Transylvania*. Oxford: Clarendon, 2000.

Murgescu, Luminița. *Între "bunul creștin" și "bravul român." Rolul școlii primare în construirea identității naționale românești (1831–1878)*. Iași: Editura A '92, 1999.

Mușat, Carmen. *Romanul românesc interbelic: Antologie, prefață, analize critice, note, dicționar, cronologie și bibliografie*. Bucharest: Humanitas, 1998.

Năchescu, Voichița. "The Visible Woman: Interwar Romanian Women's Writing, Modernity, and the Gendered Public/Private Divide." *Aspasia* 2 (2008): 70–90.

Nazarska, Georgeta. "The Bulgarian Association of University Women, 1924–1950." *Aspasia* 1 (2007): 153–175.

Neagoe, Stelian. *Istorie politică încarcerată*. Bucharest: Editura Institutului de Științe Politice și Relații Internaționale, 2006.

Nesteruk, Alexei. *Logos i kosmos: Bogoslovie, nauka i pravoslavnoe predanie*. Moscow: Bibleisko-Bogoslovskii In-t, 2006.

Neuman, Victor. *Istoria evreilor din Romania*. Timișoara: Editura Amarcord, 1996.

Newman, Leonard. *Understanding Genocide: The Social Psychology of the Holocaust*. Oxford: Oxford University Press, 2002.

Nicoară, Toader. *Transilvania la începuturlie timpurilor moderne (1680–1800: Societate rurală și mentalități collective*. Cluj: Presa universitară clujeană, 1997.

Nicolaescu-Plopșor, Dardu, and Wanda Wolski. *Elemente de demografie și ritual funerar la populațiile vechi din România*. Bucharest: Editura Academiei Republicii Socialiste România, 1975.

Nicolescu, Corina. *Moștenirea artei bizantine în România*. Bucharest: Editura meridiane, 1971.

Niewyk, Donald. *The Columbia Guide to the Holocaust*. New York: Columbia University Press, 2000.

Nistor, Ion. *Românii și rutenii din Bucovina*. Iași: Do-MinoR, 2001 [1915].

Nora, Pierre, gen. ed. *Realms of Memory: Rethinking the French Past*. New York: Columbia University Press, 1996.

Ogășanu, Dumitru. *Legitimitatea Marii Uniri: 1 Decembrie 1918*. Oradea: Editura Universității din Oradea, 2002.

Oldson, William. *A Providential Anti-Semitism: Nationalism and Policy in Nineteenth Century Romania*. Philadelphia: American Philosophical Society, 1991.

Olick, Jeffrey K. *The Politics of Regret: On Collective Memory and Historical Responsibility*. New York: Routledge, 2007.

Opitz, Claudia. "Von Frauen im Krieg zum Krieg gegen Frauen: Krieg, Gewalt und Geschlechterbeziehungen aus historischer Sicht." *L'homme: Europäische Zeitschrift für feministische Geschichts-wissenschaft* 3 (1992): 31–44.

Orla-Bukowska, Anamaria. "New Threads on an Old Loom: National Memory and Social Identity in Postwar and Post-Communist Poland." In Lebow, Kansteiner, and Fogu, eds., *Politics of Memory*, 177–209.

Osaka, Naoyuki, Robert H. Logie, and Mark D'Esposito, eds. *The Cognitive Neuroscience of Working Memory*. Oxford: Oxford University Press, 2007.

Paler, Ioan. *Romanul românesc interbelic*. Bucharest: Editura paralela 45, 1998.

Pametnitsi na bălgaro-ruskata i bălgaro-săvetskata druzhba v Plovdivski okrăg. Plovdiv, 1980.

Passerini, Luisa, special ed. *Memory and Totalitarianism: International Yearbook of Oral History and Life Stories*. Vol. 1. Oxford: Oxford University Press, 1992.

Păușan, Cristina. "Justiția populară și criminalii de război." *Arhivele totalitarismului* 7, no. 1–2 (1999): 150–165.

Petrescu-Comnene, Nicolae. *The Great War and the Romanians: Notes and Documents on World War 1*. Iași: Centre for Romanian Studies, 2000.

Phillips, Adam. "The Forgetting Museum." First published in *Index on Censorship* 34, no. 2 (2005), available at http://www.eurozine.com/articles/2005-06-24-phillips-en.html?filename=article/2005-06-24-phillips-en (accessed 2 January 2009).

Piotrowski, Tadeusz. *Poland's Holocaust*. New York: McFarland, 1997.

Pippidi, Andrei. *Despre statui și morminte: Pentru o teorie a istoriei simbolice*. Iași: Polirom, 2000.

Pleșu, Andrei. *Comédii la porțile Orientului*. Bucharest: Humanitas, 2005.

Polian, Pavel. *Against Their Will: The History and Geography of Forced Migrations in the USSR*. Budapest: Central European University Press, 2004.

Polkey, Pauline. W*omen's Lives into Print: The Theory, Practice and Writing of Feminist Auto/biography*. New York: St. Martin's Press, 1999.

Polonsky, Antony, ed. *"My Brother's Keeper": Recent Polish Debates on the Holocaust*. London: Routledge, for the Institute for Polish-Jewish Studies, 1989.

Polonsky, Antony, and Joanna Michlick, eds. *The Neighbors Respond: The Controversy over the Jedwabne Massacre in Poland*. Princeton, N.J.: Princeton University Press, 2004.

Pomogáts, Béla. *Kuncz Aladár*. Budapest: Akadémiai Kiadó, Irodalomtörténeti füzetek, 1968.

Pop, Ioan-Aurel, Mihai Barbulescu, and Thomas Nagler. *The History of Transylvania*. Cluj-Napoca: Romanian Cultural Institute, 2005.

Popescu, Carmen. *Le style national roumain: Construire une nation à travers l'architecture, 1881–1945*. Rennes: Presses universitaires de Rennes; Bucharest: Simetria, 2004.

Popescu, Florentin. *Ctitorii brâncovenești*. 2nd rev. ed. Târgoviște: Editura Bibliotheca, 2004.

Popovici, Ileana. *Evreii din România în secolul XX, 1900–1920: Fast și nefast într-un răstimp istoric; Documente și mărturii*. Bucharest: Hasefer, 2003.

Porter, Brian. *When Nationalism Began to Hate: Imagining Modern Politics in Nineteenth-Century Poland*. New York: Oxford University Press, 2000.

Porterfield, Todd B. *The Allure of Empire: Art in the Service of French Imperialism, 1798–1836*. Princeton, N.J.: Princeton University Press, 1998.

Predescu, Lucian. *Enciclopedia Cugetarea*. Bucharest: Editura Saeculum, I.O., and Editura Vestala, [1940] 1999.

Prost, Antoine. *Les anciens combattants et la société française: 1914–1939*. [Paris]: Presses de la Fondation nationale des sciences politiques, 1977.

Puckle, Bertram S. *Funeral Customs: Their Origin and Development*. London: T. Werner Laurie, 1926.

Pushkareva, Natalia. *Women in Russian History: From the Tenth to the Twentieth Century*. Stroud: Sutton, 1999.

Quinlan, Paul. *The Playboy King: Carol II of Romania.* Westport, Conn.: Greenwood Press, 1995.

Rachamimov, Alon. *POWs and the Great War: Captivity on the Eastern Front.* Oxford, New York: Berg, 2002.

Radosav, Doru, et al., eds. *Rezistenţa anticomunistă din Apuseni, Grupurile "Teodor Şuşman," "Capota-Dejeu," "Cruce şi Spadă": Studii de istorie orală.* Cluj-Napoca: Argonaut, 2003.

Rădulescu-Zoner, Constantin, and Beatrice Marinescu. *Bucureştii în anii primului război mondial, 1914–1918.* Bucharest: Editura Albatros, 1993.

Raichev, M. *Muzei, starini i pametnitsi v Bulgaria.* Sofia: Nauka i izkustvo, 1981.

Ramet, Sabrina P., ed. *Gender Politics in the Western Balkans: Women and Society in Yugoslavia and the Yugoslav Successor States.* University Park: Pennsylvania State University Press, 1999.

Ranger, Terence. "The Invention of Tradition in Colonial Africa." In Hobsbawm and Ranger, eds., *Invention of Tradition,* 211–262.

Ransel, David. *Village Mothers: Three Generations of Change in Russia and Tataria.* Bloomington: Indiana University Press, 2001.

Ransel, David, and Bozena Shallcross, eds. *Polish Encounters, Russian Identity.* Bloomington: Indiana University Press, 2005.

Rhode, Gotthold. *Juden in Ostmitteleuropa von der Emanzipation bis zum Ersten Weltkrieg.* Marburg/Lahn: J.G. Herder-Institut, 1989.

Riff, Michael. *The Face of Survival: Jewish Life in Eastern Europe Past and Present.* London: V. Mitchell, 1992.

Ritchie, Donald. *Doing Oral History.* New York: Oxford University Press, 2003.

Robben, Antonius C. G. M., ed. *Death, Mourning and Burial: A Cross-Cultural Reader.* Malden, Mass.: Blackwell, 2004.

Roberts, Henry. *Rumania: Political Problems of an Agrarian State.* New Haven, Conn.: Yale University Press, 1951.

"Romanian Literature." *The Columbia Encyclopedia.* 6th ed. New York: Columbia University Press, 2007. Available also at http://www.encyclopedia.com/doc/1E1-Romnilit.html (accessed 3 April 2008).

Roper, Steven. *Romania: The Unfinished Revolution.* Amsterdam: Harwood Academic; Abingdon, UK: Marston, 2000.

Rosenberg, Tina. *The Haunted Land: Facing Europe's Ghosts after Communism.* New York: Random House, 1995.

Rosenthal, Gabriele. *The Holocaust in Three Generations: Families of Victims and Perpetrators of the Nazi Regime.* London: Cassell, 1998.

Roshwald, Aviel. *Ethnic Nationalism and the Fall of Empires: Central Europe, Russia, and the Middle East, 1914–1923.* London, New York: Routledge, 2001.

Rybarczyk, Edmund J. *Beyond Salvation: Eastern Orthodoxy and Classical Pentecostalism on Becoming Like Christ.* Carlisle, U.K., Waynesboro, Ga.: Paternoster Press, 2004.

Safta, Ion, Rotaru Jipa, Tiberiu Velter, and Floricel Marinescu. *Decoraţii româneşti de război, 1860–1947.* Bucharest: Editura Universitaria, 1993.

Sasarman, Gheorghe, ed. *Gîndirea estetică în arhitectura românească: a doua jumătate a secolului XIX, şi prima jumătate a secolului XX.* Bucharest: Editura meridiane, 1983.

Scârneci, Florentina, and Ştefan Ungurean, eds. *Vieţi paralele în secolul XX. Istorie orală şi memorie recentă în Ţara Bârsei.* Braşov: Editura Phoenix, 2002.

Scott, James C. *Seeing Like a State: How Certain Schemes to Improve the Human Condition Have Failed.* New Haven, Conn.: Yale University Press, 1998.

Scott, Joan. "The Evidence of Experience." *Critical Inquiry* 17 (Summer 1991): 773–797.

———. *Parité! Sexual Equality and the Crisis of French Universalism.* Chicago: University of Chicago Press, 2005.

Seremetakis, Nadia. *The Last Word: Women, Death, and Divination in Inner Mani.* Chicago: University of Chicago Press, 1991.

Sheringham, Michael. *French Autobiography: Devices and Desires; Rousseau to Perec.* Oxford, New York: Oxford University Press, 1993.

Sherman, Daniel. "Bodies and Names: The Emergence of Commemoration in Interwar France." *American Historical Review* 103, no. 2 (April 1998): 443–466.

Sherwood, Terry. *The Self in Early Modern Literature: For the Common Good.* Pittsburgh, Pa.: Duquesne University Press, 2007.

Siegel, Kristi. *Women's Autobiographies, Culture, Feminism.* New York: Peter Lang, 2001.

Silbey, David. *The British Working Class and Enthusiasm for War, 1914–1916.* London, New York: Frank Cass, 2005.

Simion, A. *Dictatul de la Viena.* 2nd rev. ed. Bucharest: Editura Albatros, 1996.

Şiperco, Andrei. *Crucea Roşie Internaţională şi România în perioada celui de-al Doilea Război mondial: 1 septembrie 1939–23 august 1944: Prizonierii de război anglo-americani şi sovietici; deportaţii evrei din Transnistria şi emigrarea evreilor în Palestina în atenţia Crucii Roşii Internaţionale.* Bucharest: Editura enciclopedică, 1997.

Şipoş, Mariana. *Destinul unui disident: Paul Goma.* Bucharest: Editura Dalsi, 2005.

Skultans, Vieda. *The Testimony of Lives: Narrative and Memory in Post-Soviet Latvia.* London: Routledge, 1998.

Smith, Anthony D. *Myths and Memories of the Nation.* Oxford: Oxford University Press, 1999.

Smith, Sidonie. *De/colonizing the Subject: The Politics of Gender in Women's Autobiography.* Minneapolis: University of Minnesota Press, 1992.

———. *Subjectivity, Identity, and the Body: Women's Autobiographical Practices in the Twentieth Century.* Bloomington: Indiana University Press, 1993.

Snyder, Timothy. "Balancing the Books." *Index on Censorship* 34, no. 2 (2005), also in *Eurozine,* available at http://www.eurozine.com/articles/2005-05-03-snyder-en.html (accessed 2 January 2009).

———. *The Reconstruction of Nations: Poland, Ukraine, Lithuania, Belarus, 1569–1999.* New Haven, Conn.: Yale University Press, 2003.

"Special Issue: Contemporary Romanian Cinema." *MovEast* no. 8 (2008).

Spiridon, Monica, Ion Bogdan Lefter, and Gheorghe Crăciun. *Experiment in Post-War Romanian Literature,* trans. Della Marcus, Ruxandra-Ioana Patrichi, and David Hill. Piteşti: Editura paralela 45, 1999.

St. Augustine. *Confessions of St. Augustine.* New York: Modern Library, 1999.

Stănescu, D. "Obiceiuri religioase." *Biserica ortodoxă română* 9 (1885): 330.

Stanislawski, Michael. *Murder in Lemberg: Politics, Religion, and Violence in Modern Jewish History.* Princeton, N.J.: Princeton University Press, 2007.

"Statutele Confreriei Sacre (Hevra Kadisa) din Arad, 1835, februarie 9–1838, februarie, Arad." In Ladislau Gyémánt and Lya Benjamin, eds. *Izvoare și mărturii referitoare la evreii din Romania.* Vol. 3, part 2. Bucharest: Hasefer, 1999, 82.

Stauter-Halstead, Keely. "Rural Myth and the Modern Nation: Peasant Commemorations of Polish National Holidays, 1879–1910." In Bucur and Wingfield, eds., *Staging the Past,* 153–177.

Ştefănescu, I. D. *Arta feudală în Ţările Române: Pictura murală și icoanele de la origini pînă in secolul al XIX-lea.* Timișoara: Editura Mitropoliei Banatului, 1981.

——. *Iconografia artei bizantine și a picturii feudale românești.* Bucharest: Editura meridiane, 1973.

Steinberg, J., ed. *Introduction to Rumanian Literature.* New York: Twayne, 1966.

Steinlauf, Michael C. *Bondage to the Dead: Poland and the Memory of the Holocaust.* Ithaca, N.Y.: Syracuse University Press, 1997.

Stites, Richard. *The Women's Liberation Movement in Russia: Feminism, Nihilism, and Bolshevism, 1860–1930.* New rev. ed. Princeton, N.J.: Princeton University Press, 1991.

Strachan, Hew. *The First World War.* Oxford: Oxford University Press, 2001.

Sugar, Peter. *Southeastern Europe under Ottoman Rule, 1354–1804.* Seattle: University of Washington Press, 1977.

Szabó, Levente. "Touchy Issues: Historical Myths and Their Pragmatics in Post-Socialist Romania," ed. Enikő Magyari-Vincze, *European Anthropology: Theoretical Perspectives and Case-Studies* (Cluj-Kolozsvár, 2004), available at http://szabol.adatbank.transindex .ro/belso.php?k=8&p=1157 (accessed 14 January 2009).

Tănăsoiu, Carmen. *Iconografia regelui Carol I.* Timișoara: Editura Amarcord, 1999.

Tannen, Deborah. *Gender and Discourse.* New York: Oxford University Press, 1994.

Tappe, E. D. *Rumanian Prose and Verse.* London: Athlone, 1956.

Tarlow, Sarah. *Bereavement and Commemoration: An Archaeology of Mortality.* Oxford: Blackwell, 1999.

Terrace, Herbert S., and Janet Metcalfe, eds. *The Missing Link in Cognition: Origins of Self-Reflective Consciousness.* Oxford, New York: Oxford University Press, 2005.

Teter, Magda. *Jews and Heretics in Catholic Poland: A Beleaguered Church in the Post-Reformation Era.* Cambridge: Cambridge University Press, 2006.

Thomas, Louis-Vincent. "La mort: un objet anthropologique." In M. Mafessoli and C. Rivière, eds., *Une anthropologie des turbulences: Hommage à Georges Balandier.* Paris: Berg International Editeurs, 1985.

Thommeret, Loïc. *La mémoire créatrice: Essai sur l'écriture de soi au XVIIIe siècle.* Paris: L'Harmattan, 2006.

Thompson, Paul. *The Voice of the Past: Oral History.* New York: Oxford University Press, 2000.

Till, Karen. *The New Berlin: Memory, Politics, Place.* Minneapolis: University of Minnesota Press, 2005.

Tismăneanu, Vladimir. *Stalinism for All Seasons: A Political History of Romanian Communism.* Berkeley: University of California Press, 2003.

Tismăneanu, Vladimir, with Mircea Mihăieș. *Scheletele în dulap.* Iași: Polirom, 2004.

Todorov, Tsvetan, ed. *Voices from the Gulag: Life and Death in Communist Bulgaria.* University Park: Pennsylvania State University Press, 1999.

Todorova, Maria. "The Mausoleum of Georgi Dimitrov as Lieu de Mémoire." *Journal of Modern History* 78, no. 2 (June 2005): 374–411.

———. "Creating a National Hero: Vasil Levski in Bulgarian Public Memory." In Sabrina P. Ramet, James R. Felak, and Herbert J. Ellison, eds., *Nations and Nationalisms in East-Central Europe, 1806–1948: A Festschrift for Peter Sugar*. Bloomington, Ind.: Slavica, 2002, 159–181.

———. "Contemporary Issues in Historical Perspective: The Mausoleum of Georgi Dimitrov as Lieu de Memoire." *Journal of Modern History* 78 (June 2006): 377–411.

———, ed. *Balkan Identities: Nation and Memory*. New York: New York University Press, 2004.

Tooley, Hunt. *The Western Front: Battleground and Home Front in the First World War*. New York: Palgrave, 2003.

Totok, William. "Receptarea publicistică a raportului final al Comisiei Wiesel în presa românească şi germană." *Studia Hebraica* no. 5 (2005): 186–195, available at www.ceeol.com/aspx/getdocument.aspx?logid=5&id=de624a2d-8f93-4325-b1d0-9a58eed9aab9 (accessed 28 September 2008).

Treptow, Kurt W., ed. *Romania and World War II*. Iaşi: Centrul de studii româneşti, 1996.

Tucă, Col. Dr. Florian, and Mircea Cociu. *Monumente ale anilor de luptă şi jertfă*. Bucharest: Editura militară, 1983.

Tumarkin, Nina. *The Living and the Dead: The Rise and Fall of the Cult of World War II in Russia*. New York: Basic Books, 1994.

Turc, Corina. "Nation et confession dans l'opinion des représentants de l'Église orthodoxe et gréco-catholique en Transylvanie (dans la seconde moitié du XIXe siècle)." In Maria Crăciun and Ovidiu Ghitta, eds., *Ethnicity and Religion in Central and Eastern Europe*. Cluj: Cluj University Press, 1995, 292–301.

Ţurlea, Petre. *Ip şi Trăznea, atrocităţi maghiare şi acţiune diplomatică*. Bucharest: Editura enciclopedică, 1996.

Ţuţui, Marian. "Istoria filmului românesc in 7000 de cuvinte." Available at http://www.cncinema.abt.ro/Files/Documents/fls-258.doc (accessed 28 September 2008).

Unowsky, Daniel. "Reasserting Empire: Habsburg Imperial Celebrations after the Revolutions of 1848–1849." In Bucur and Wingfield, eds., *Staging the Past*, 13–45.

———. *The Pomp and Politics of Patriotism: Imperial Celebrations in Habsburg Austria, 1848–1916*. West Lafayette, Ind.: Purdue University Press, 2005.

Unpunished Crimes: Latvia under Three Occupations. Stockholm: Memento; Toronto: Latvian Relief Society Daugavas Vanagi, 2003.

Văduva, Ofelia. *Steps towards the Sacred*. Bucharest: Editura Fundaţiei Culturale Române, 1999.

Valentino, Bejamin. *Final Solutions: Mass Killing and Genocide in the Twentieth Century*. Ithaca, N.Y.: Cornell University Press, 2004.

van der Kolk, Bessel A., Alexander C. McFarlane, and Lars Weisaeth, eds. *Traumatic Stress: The Effects of Overwhelming Experience on Mind, Body and Society*. New York: Guilford Press, 1996.

Verdery, Katherine. *National Ideology under Socialism: Identity and Cultural Politics in Ceauşescu's Romania*. Berkeley & Los Angeles & Oxford: University of California Press, 1991.

——. *The Political Lives of Dead Bodies: Reburial and Postsocialist Change.* New York: Columbia University Press, 1999.

——. *Transylvanian Villagers: Three Centuries of Political, Economic, and Ethnic Change.* Berkeley: University of California Press, 1983.

——. *What Was Socialism, and What Comes Next?* Princeton, N.J.: Princeton University Press, 1996.

Verenca, Olivian, and Şerban Alexianu. *Administraţia civilă română în Transnistria 1941–1944.* 2nd ed. Bucharest: Editura Vremea, 2000.

Vianu, Tudor. "Arta prozatorilor români." In Tudor Vianu, *Opere*, vol. 5. Bucharest: Editura Minerva, 1975.

Volovici, Leon. *Ideologia naţionalistă şi "problema evreiască" în România anilor '30.* Bucharest: Humanitas, 1995.

von Hagen, Mark, Jane Burbank, and Anatolyi Remnev, eds. *Russian Empire: Space, People, Power, 1700–1930.* Bloomington: Indiana University Press, 2007.

Voukov, Nikolai. "Death and the Desecrated: Monuments of the Socialist Past in Post-1989 Bulgaria." *Anthropology of East Europe Review: Central Europe, Eastern Europe and Eurasia* 21, no. 2 (Autumn 2003), available at http://condor.depaul.edu/%7Errotenbe/aeer/v21n2/Voukov.pdf (accessed 11 January 2009).

Vultur, Smaranda. *Germanii din Banat prin povestirile lor.* Bucharest: Paideia, 2000.

——. *Istorie trăită—istorie povestită: Deportarea în Bărăgan, 1951–1956.* Timişoara: Editura Amarcord, 1997.

——, ed. *Memoria salvată: Evreii din Banat, ieri şi azi.* Iaşi: Polirom, 2002.

Walicki, Andrzej. *Philosophy and Romantic Nationalism: The Case of Poland.* Oxford: Clarendon Press, 1982.

Watson, Rubie, ed. *Memory, History, and Opposition under State Socialism.* Santa Fe, N.M.: School of American Research Press; distributed by University of Washington Press, Seattle, 1994.

Weber, Georg, et al. *Die Deportation von Siebenbürger Sachsen in die Sowjetunion 1945–1949.* 3 vols. Cologne: Böhlau, 1997.

Weissmark, Sue. *Justice Matters: Legacies of the Holocaust and World War II.* New York: Oxford University Press, 2003.

Wertsman, Vladimir. *The Romanians in America and Canada: A Guide to Information Sources.* Detroit, Mich.: Gale Research, 1980.

——. *The Romanians in America, 1748–1974: A Chronology and Factbook.* Dobbs Ferry, N.Y.: Oceana, 1975.

Whalen, Robert. *Bitter Wounds: German Victims of the Great War, 1914–1939.* Ithaca, N.Y.: Cornell University Press, 1984.

Wieviorka, Annette. "From Survivor to Witness: Voices from the Shoah." In Winter and Sivan, eds., *War and Remembrance,* 125–141.

Willmott, H. P. *World War I.* London: Dorling Kindersley, 2003.

Wingfield, Nancy M. "Statues of Emperor Joseph II as Sites of German Identity." In Bucur and Wingfield, eds., *Staging the Past,* 178–208.

——. *Flag Wars and Stone Saints: How the Bohemian Lands Became Czech.* Cambridge, Mass.: Harvard University Press, 2007.

Wingfield, Nancy M., and Maria Bucur, eds. *Gender and War in Twentieth-Century Eastern Europe*. Bloomington: Indiana University Press, 2006.

Winter, Jay. *Remembering War: The Great War and Historical Memory in the Twentieth Century*. New Haven, Conn.: Yale University Press, 2006.

———. *Sites of Memory, Sites of Mourning: The Great War in European Cultural History*. Cambridge: Cambridge University Press, 1995.

———. *The Experience of World War I*. New York: Oxford University Press, 1995.

Winter, Jay, and Antoine Prost. *The Great War in History: Debates and Controversies, 1914 to the Present*. New York: Cambridge University Press, 2005.

Winter, Jay, and Emmanuel Sivan. "Setting the Framework." In Winter and Sivan, eds., *War and Remembrance*, 6–39.

Winter, Jay, and Emmanuel Sivan, eds. *War and Remembrance in the Twentieth Century*. Cambridge: Cambridge University Press, 1999.

Witte, John, Jr., and Frank S. Alexander, eds. *The Teachings of Modern Orthodox Christianity on Law, Politics, and Human Nature*. New York: Columbia University Press, 2007.

Wolfe, Thomas C. "Past as Present, Myth, or History? Discourses of Time and the Great Fatherland War." In Lebow, Kansteiner, and Fogu, eds., *Politics of Memory*, 249–283.

Wolff, Larry. "Dynastic Conservatism and Poetic Violence in Fin-de-Siècle Cracow: The Habsburg Matrix of Polish Modernism." *American Historical Review* 106, no. 3 (June 2001): 735–764.

———. *The Enlightenment and the Orthodox World*. Athens: Institute for Neohellenic Research, National Hellenic Research Foundation, 2001.

Wood, Nathan. "Becoming Metropolitan: Cracow's Popular Press and the Representation of Modern Urban Life, 1900–1915." PhD diss., Indiana University, 2004.

Young, James. *At Memory's Edge: After-Images of the Holocaust in Contemporary Art and Architecture*. New Haven, Conn.: Yale University Press, 2000.

Zach, Krista. "Toleranța religioasă și construirea stereotipurilor într-o regiune multiculturală: 'Biserici populare' în Transilvania." In Asociația de Studii Transilvane Heidelberg, eds., *Transilvania și sașii ardeleni în istoriografie*. Sibiu: Editura hora și Arbeitskreis für Siebenbürgische Landeskunde e. V. Heidelberg, 2001, 83.

Zalis, Henri. *O istorie condensată a literaturii române: 1880–2000*. Tîrgoviște: Editura Bibliotheca, 2005–2006.

Zentai, Tunde. "The Sign-Language of Hungarian Graveyards." *Folklore* 90, no. 2 (1979): 131–140.

Žižek, Slavoj. *Did Somebody Say Totalitarianism?* London: Verso, 2001.

Zull, James. *The Art of Changing the Brain: Enriching Teaching by Exploring the Biology of Learning*. Sterling, Va.: Stylus, 2002.

Index

Maria Bucur is John W. Hill Chair in East European History, Associate Professor of History, and Director of the Russian and East European Institute at Indiana University Bloomington. She is author of *Eugenics and Modernization in Interwar Romania* and co-editor of *Gender and War in Twentieth-Century Eastern Europe* (Indiana University Press, 2006).